THE NONSENSE CLUB

THE NONSENSE CLUB

Literature and Popular Culture,
1749–1764

LANCE BERTELSEN

CLARENDON PRESS OXFORD

1986

Oxford University Press, Walton Street, Oxford OX2 6DP
Oxford New York Toronto
Delhi Bombay Calcutta Madras Karachi
Kuala Lumpur Singapore Hong Kong Tokyo
Nairobi Dar es Salaam Cape Town
Melbourne Auckland
and associated companies in
Beirut Berlin Ibadan Nicosia

Oxford is a trade mark of Oxford University Press

Published in the United States
by Oxford University Press, New York

British Library Cataloguing in Publication Data
Bertelsen, Lance
The Nonsense Club: literature and popular
culture, 1749-1764.
1. English literature—18th century—History
and criticism
I. Title
820.9'006   PR441
ISBN 0-19-812859-2

Library of Congress Cataloging-in-Publication Data
Bertelsen, Lance.
The Nonsense Club.
Bibliography: p.
Includes index.
1. English literature—18th century—History and
criticism.   2. Nonsense Club (Group of writers)
3. England—Popular culture—History—18th century.
4. London (England)—Intellectual life—18th century.
5. Authors, English—18th century—Biography.   I. Title.
PR448.N66B47   1986   820'.9'006   85-32104
ISBN 0-19-812859-2

Set by Downdell Ltd.,
Printed in Great Britain
at the University Printing House, Oxford
by David Stanford
Printer to the University

To my parents,
Niels and Vey Bertelsen,
and to the memory of my Bestemor,
Ellen

Acknowledgements

I would like to thank those friends and colleagues who were interested enough in the Nonsense Club to read and write on its behalf. Thomas Lockwood supervised the dissertation and provided unfailing support for the larger project. Otto Reinert and Ronald Paulson were consistently helpful. At the University of Texas, Larry Carver and James Garrison gave generously of their time and good advice. Among those who in less direct ways contributed to the book, William Goodfellow, Vincent Carretta, and Robert Halsband deserve special mention.

I owe a material debt to the institutions which provided support and assistance over a number of years: the University of Washington, the American Council of Learned Societies, the National Humanities Center, the Yale Center for British Art, and the University of Texas at Austin. My research was facilitated enormously by the staffs of the following research centres: the British Museum, the British Library, the Huntington Library, the Beinecke Rare Book and Manuscript Library, the Humanities Research Center at the University of Texas, the Lewis Walpole Library, the Houghton Library, the National Humanities Center, and the Yale Center for British Art.

Parts of the study have appeared in a different form in *The Huntington Library Quarterly, Eighteenth-Century Life*, and *Philological Quarterly*. My thanks to the editors of those journals for their permission to reprint that material here.

All quotations from *Boswell's London Journal* and other Boswell material are reproduced by the kind permission of the McGraw-Hill Book company.

Finally, I wish to express my gratitude to my family: to Matt and Elin for putting up with all this *Nonsense*, and to my wife, Mitzi, for the roses.

Austin   L.B.

Contents

List of Illustrations

But why, when present times my care engage,
Must I go back to the *Augustan* age?

Charles Churchill, *Independence.*

A historio-social moment is never homogeneous; it is, on the contrary, rich in contradictions. It acquires a distinctive character; it is a moment of unfolding due to the fact that a certain fundamental activity of life predominates there over others; it represents an historical point: but this presupposes a hierarchy, a contrast, a struggle.

Antonio Gramsci, *Quaderni.*

Idleness is only a coarse name for [an] infinite capacity for living in the present.

Cyril Connolly, Journal.

Introduction

On 24 May 1763 James Boswell visited Bonnell Thornton for the first time. A 'well-bred, agreeable man', Boswell found him, 'lively and odd. He had about £15,000 left him by his father, was bred to physic, but was fond of writing. So he employs himself in that way.' Boswell lingered for a time. 'In a little, Mr. Wilkes came in, to whom I was introduced, as I also was to Mr. Churchill. Wilkes is a lively, facetious man, Churchill a rough, blunt fellow, very clever. Lloyd too was there, so that I was just got into the middle of the London Geniuses. They were high-spirited and boisterous, but were very civil to me, and Wilkes said he would be glad to see me in George Street.'[1]

The 'London Geniuses' were at the moment of Boswell's visit engaged in a fight for John Wilkes's political life. From Wilkes's house in Great George Street, Westminster, and Thornton's in Bow Street, Covent Garden, the four carried on a paper war against an administration that had already imprisoned Wilkes and narrowly missed capturing Churchill, and which since Wilkes's release from the Tower had been reeling under the concerted propaganda campaign mounted by the 'Geniuses'. Charles Churchill, besides being a Wilkes ally and editor of the opposition paper, *The North Briton*, was the most feared satiric poet of his time. A bluff, iconoclastic clergyman-turned-libertine, his attacks on the stage, on Smollett, Johnson, and the Bute administration—not to mention the sensational details of his personal life—had been the talk of the town for over two years. Boswell's host, Bonnell Thornton, was an experienced journalist and one of the more eccentric and original of London wits. As a major shareholder of the tri-weekly *St. James's Chronicle* and chief adviser to Henry Sampson Woodfall's *Public Advertiser*, Thornton enjoyed an access to and influence over the press that was of central importance to Wilkes's defensive strategy. A master of burlesque, he had joined with William Hogarth the year before to put together the controversial Sign Painters' Exhibition, and within a month of Boswell's visit Thornton's burlesque *Ode on Saint*

Cæcilia's Day would delight the town on its performance at Ranelagh House. The fourth of the 'Geniuses', Robert Lloyd, was the editor of the monthly *St James's Magazine*, a poet of some note, and a veteran of the literary and political battles that had swirled around Churchill's *Rosciad* (1761) and *The North Briton*.

For Thornton, Churchill, and Lloyd, the Wilkes cause was only the latest, though certainly the most profound, in a series of literary, theatrical, and political skirmishes that had engaged them as a group for the last three years. Along with George Colman, a well-known young playwright and Garrick's lieutenant at Drury Lane, and William Cowper, in later life a renowned poet, but at this time an unenthusiastic lawyer with a fondness for literature, the 'London Geniuses' formed the core of the Nonsense Club.

The 'Nonsense Club' refers, historically, to a group of Old Westminsters and London wits who met regularly every Thursday evening during the late 1750s and early 1760s. While the exact membership of the club is somewhat unclear, the title itself (as used by George Sherburn and others) has come to denote the literary core of this group: Bonnell Thornton, George Colman, Robert Lloyd, and William Cowper.[2] Charles Churchill's membership in the club is disputed (mainly because he did not return to London until 1758), but it is clear that his literary and political activities were intimately connected with those of the above writers—who were also his closest friends. In this study, I use 'Nonsense Club' as a convenient title for the literary association of Thornton, Colman, Lloyd, Churchill, and Cowper.

During the years 1749 to 1764 these five friends, singly and in varying combinations, conducted one of the more popular essay series of the century, edited several literary magazines and journals, produced two of the finest examples of mid-century 'laughing comedy', fought a virulent paper war over contemporary drama and acting, burlesqued subjects ranging from Gray's odes to the Society of Arts Exhibition, produced a large and fitfully brilliant body of satiric poetry, and joined with John Wilkes in fomenting the most important domestic political debate of their time.

One of the members of the group, William Cowper, has been treated extensively by literary historians, though they have tended to focus primarily on his later life. Only Charles Ryskamp in his *William Cowper of the Inner Temple, Esq.* has attempted a detailed picture of the poet's early years, and he confines his comments on the Nonsense Club to a single chapter.[3] Charles Churchill has had a less than definitive biography, Douglas Grant's excellent edition of the poetry, two recent books of criticism, and numerous critical articles. Of the three other members, Colman has had a helpful biography by Eugene Page and mention in various books on the drama, Lloyd a lucid essay by Austin Dobson, and Thornton practically nothing. The Nonsense Club as a whole has not been studied, nor has the relationship between the works of these writers been examined. Yet the closest possible connections exist: for example, Lloyd's poetic epistle, *The Actor*, is addressed to Thornton; Churchill's *Rosciad* is, to some extent, a continuation of *The Actor*, and his later poem, *Night*, is addressed to Lloyd; the *Two Odes* burlesquing Mason and Gray were jointly written by Colman and Lloyd (supposedly at a Nonsense Club meeting); and *The Connoisseur* essay series was co-written by Thornton and Colman, with contributions from Lloyd and Cowper (among others).

In this study, I have attempted to trace the careers of five writers who shared not only a common background but a lasting friendship, and to emphasize in their lives and work the collective attitudes that characterized the group as a whole. In following their various paths, I have necessarily omitted much biographical information, concentrating primarily on that which illuminates their literature, their friendship, and the motivations underlying both. A history of the group's literary and personal interrelationships thus forms the core of the study and determines its chronological organization. My method has been both synthetic and interpretive. I have tried to bring together for the first time material on the individual members which, although well known, has been until now isolated from the informing context provided by the group; and I have sought to develop new historical and critical points of view from which to examine the most important aspects of the Nonsense Club's endeavour.

My first object has been to describe and assess the Nonsense Club's literature—a literature that falls athwart the so-called 'late Augustanism' of Samuel Johnson and the 'pre-Romanticism' of the poets of Sensibility—and through this body of work to explore and define certain features of the literary and aesthetic climate of mid-eighteenth-century England. Because of the range of concerns and activities represented by the Nonsense Club, their literature opens a fresh window on the London of the 1750s and 1760s: a window disclosing the town as seen by writers obsessively interested in the topical issues of the day. One question that has occupied me throughout the course of the study is, put very simply, what did the London 'wit' of the period think about? What symbols, metaphors, and images did he employ? In other words, what kind of contemporary cultural furniture did he carry about in his head? The Nonsense Club's strong inter-disciplinary interests have allowed a range of responses to this question wider than would have been possible in any single-figure study, while at the same time drawing a fundamental unity from the shared aesthetic and ethical assumptions of the group.

My second object has been more ambitious. Drawing on recent developments in political history, social history, and interdisciplinary cultural studies, I have attempted to track in the Nonsense Club's work a pattern of response to the institutions and symbols of both sophisticated and popular English culture—a pattern indicative not only of the group's particular preoccupations, but more generally representative of the confluence of cultural phenomena at the level of 'middling' culture. In the eighteenth century, the term 'middling' usually denoted that protean segment of society above the poor and below the gentry and nobility; in my usage, it simultaneously connotes the centripetal processes of assimilation, mimicry, mystification, and education by which the myriad elements constituting 'hegemony'—the stabilizing rules, values, and symbols of the social order—were continually renegotiated.[4] Not so much a social class as a frame of reference, and less a frame of reference than a continuing dialectic, middling culture was the psychological and material arena in which the elections of what has been called the 'politics of signification' were contested.[5]

At mid-century the nexus of this exchange was the press, and at the heart of the periodical and newspaper trade was the Nonsense Club. Early Wilkite activity pivoted on the issue of the press and its liberties; the burgeoning consumer culture was recorded and materially advanced by the daily advertisers; the men who ran the newspapers and print shops were themselves middling men. This massive creation—or mediation—of culture was at bottom a commercial enterprise; but its effects were educative and ideological. The press was both an instrument of hegemony and a continuous critique and redefinition of it. Michel Foucault has written that the 'exercise of power is not simply a relationship between partners, individual or collective; it is a way in which certain actions modify others.'[6] These modifying relations—the processes of 'mimesis' linking subordinate and dominant groups, the commercial ties binding literary and political activity, the definition and redefinition of the symbols and values which constitute hegemony—I have attempted to concretize in the practice of the Nonsense Club.

This study is not an effort to rehabilitate the Nonsense Club. Much of the group's work is third-rate and deserves attention only to the extent that it exposes or reflects larger cultural issues. Nevertheless, the reader will discern in my handling of Churchill's poetry a conviction that his work should be reintroduced into basic eighteenth-century studies, and that a poem such as *The Prophecy of Famine* stands well against the precious obscurities of, for instance, Collins's *Ode on the Popular Superstitions of the Highlands in Scotland*—a poem that has replaced it in many anthologies of the post-Frye era. My hope is that the study will provide a more complex description than has been heretofore available of the cultural situation from which Churchill's poetry grew and in which Cowper spent the years before his madness. A good deal of the information is new, and all of it has been re-evaluated in light of the overall pattern of concerns, attitudes, and behaviour that has emerged during the course of my investigation.

1 *Students of the Town*

It was at Westminster School, in the shadow of the Abbey, that
Bonnell Thornton, George Colman, Robert Lloyd, Charles
Churchill, and William Cowper first became friends. In
various ways, their school days at Westminster were to haunt
them for the rest of their lives. In 1760, as a rising town wit,
Thornton signed his *City Latin*, 'the Rev. Busby Birch'; in
1784, as a religious melancholic, Cowper wrote *Tirocinium: A
Review of Schools*. Lloyd, after taking his degree at Cambridge,
returned to Westminster as an usher, became bored and frus-
trated, launched himself on the literary tides, and slowly, but
steadily, sank to his death; and Colman, as manager of Covent
Garden Theatre, so obviously welcomed his son's Westminster
schoolmates to the playhouse that he 'set a fashion in breaking
bounds at night'.[1] A particular Westminster ethos—an ethos I
will shortly attempt to define—steeped the lives of these writers
and provided a basis for much of their literary and extra-literary
activity. On the shared experience of Westminster School they
founded their continuing strong friendship, numerous joint
literary ventures, and the high-spirited association of the
Nonsense Club.

The Westminster School to which they came in the early 1740s
was close to the heart of the English nation. The main school
building stood just below the south transept of Westminster
Abbey, a quarter mile from Parliament, and only a slightly
longer walk across St James's Park from St James's Palace. London's West End, of which Westminster School marked roughly
the southern boundary, was punctuated with the great mansions
of the Whig oligarchy: Devonshire House and Burlington House
lay not quite a mile to the north-west of the school; Marlborough
House and Buckingham House were even closer, on the edges of
St James's Park. Westminster Hall, only a few hundred yards
from the school, housed the Courts of King's Bench, Common
Pleas, and Chancery, as well as serving as the southern nexus of
the print, pamphlet, and bookselling trades. Here, in the 1730s
and 1740s, Westminster students could experience first hand the

workings of the English system while simultaneously perusing the witty and scurrilous prints and pamphlets about it. Colman, during the formative years between ten and fourteen, would have seen his uncle, William Pulteney, hailed as a 'patriot' while in opposition to Walpole and damned as a hypocrite for accepting a peerage after Walpole's fall.[2]

At the very centre, geographically and ideologically, of the British establishment, Westminster School was an institution specifically designed to reproduce patrician values: classical languages and hierarchical thinking, deference to one's betters and superciliousness to one's inferiors. Yet the school reproduced much more than this. Surrounded by neighbourhoods ranging from town houses to tenements, open to a massive literary stimulus in the form of the daily, weekly, and monthly productions of the London press, Westminster School represented a kind of crucible for the complex negotiations of eighteenth-century English society. A heterogeneous mixture of boys ranging from the sons of lords to the sons of apothecaries, Westminster students experienced with unique immediacy the rituals of power and the counter-rituals of irreverence, the paradoxes of birth and rank within the dominant ideology of liberty, and, particularly for boys of the middling sort, the confusing pressures of social aspiration and traditional deference in a society whose people were becoming more sophisticated as the circle of real power became more exclusive.

Since 1733, the Headmaster of Westminster School had been John Nicoll. A man of taste and honour, he seems also to have possessed qualities rare in a headmaster: sympathy and leniency. 'Was it possible not to love a character like this? Nichols certainly was a complete fine gentleman in his office, and intitled to the respect and affection of his scholars, who in his person found a master not only of the dead languages, but also of the living manners.'[3] So wrote Richard Cumberland, who entered Westminster as an upperclassman in 1744 while Colman, Lloyd, Churchill, and Cowper were still in the lower forms, and whose *Memoirs* give an intimate picture of Nicoll's unorthodox pedagogical and disciplinary methods.

According to Cumberland, Nicoll had instituted at Westminster an unofficial but highly effective 'court of honour' among the students, 'to whose unwritten laws every member of our community was amenable, and which to transgress by any act of meaness, that exposed the offender to public contempt, was a degree of punishment, compared to which being sentenced to the rod would have been considered as an acquittal or reprieve.'[4] Cumberland described a case in which a boy from the fifth form 'was summoned before the seniors in the seventh, and convicted of an offence, which in the high spirit of that school argued an abasement of principle and honour: Doctor Nichols having stated the case, demanded their opinion of the crime and what degree of punishment they conceived it to deserve; their answer was unanimously—"The severest that could be inflicted"—"I can inflict none more severe than you have given him," said the master, and dismissed him without any other chastisement.'[5] The institution of such a 'court of honour' among equals, and the resulting fear of public exposure for 'any act of meaness', were central ingredients of a system based on individual pride and peer pressure. But in stressing self-regulation and peer-responsibility, Nicoll also fostered an atmosphere of ribald anarchy and petty tyranny that could produce psychological and physical trauma far exceeding anything engendered by the master's rod.[6]

Despite Nicoll's enlightened intentions, life at Westminster was often coarse and brutal. For boys of smaller stature and greater sensitivity, like Cowper, the rough-housing and 'frolics' of the school could lead to lingering fear and insecurity —and to attacks on the public schools like *Tirocinium*. For boys of larger stature and more courage, like Churchill, the school could be a place to assert leadership and independence early in life, to sample the vices of the town, and to develop a great respect for both self-sufficiency and loyalty. One passage from *Tirocinium* captures vividly the temptations, recklessness, and emulation of life at the school, and seems to contain Cowper's portrait of the young Churchill as Captain of the King's Scholars:

> Would your son should be a sot or dunce,
> Lascivious, headstrong; or all of these at once . . .
> Train him in public with a mob of boys,
> Childish in mischief only and in noise,
> In infidelity and lewdness men.
> There shall he learn, ere sixteen winters old,

That authors are most useful pawn'd or sold;
That pedantry is all that schools impart,
But taverns teach the knowledge of the heart;
There waiter Dick, with Bacchanalian lays,
Shall win his heart, and have his drunken praise,
His counsellor and bosom-friend shall prove,
And some street-pacing harlot his first love. . . .
The stout tall captain, whose superior size
The minor heroes view with envious eyes,
Becomes their pattern, upon whom they fix
Their whole attention, and ape all his tricks.
His pride, that scorns t' obey or to submit,
With them is courage; his effront'ry wit.
His wild excursions, window-breaking feats,
Robb'ry of gardens, quarrels in the streets,
His hair-breadth 'scapes, and all his daring schemes,
Transport them, and are made their fav'rite themes.[7]

(202–3, 207–17, 222–31)

Despite the virulence of the opening attack, there is a secret fascination lurking in this passage—a fascination that becomes overt as the deeds of the 'stout tall captain' multiply, enlarge, and finally become the stuff of schoolboy epic: 'His hair-breadth 'scapes, and all his daring schemes, / Transport them, and are made their fav'rite themes.' Cowper succumbs to the same reckless charm as the 'minor heroes'—and his captain becomes an epic hero in miniature. Southey has written that 'so far were the years which passed at Westminster from being years of misery, that they were probably the happiest of [Cowper's] life.'[8] This, however, is not to say that they were the happiest of years—the radical wretchedness of Cowper's later life offers little comparison. The truth, as his letters make clear, is that Cowper retained both good and bad memories of Westminster; it was only in his lurid melancholic reveries that the bad was accentuated and *Tirocinium* produced. Yet, despite Cowper's intention, the excitement and intensity of life at Westminster crackles from its lines.

Like all public schools, Westminster offered as its staple fare the classical languages, but during Nicoll's tenure these were administered only in moderate doses. The ushers of Westminster's upper forms, particularly Pierson Lloyd (father of

Robert Lloyd) and Vincent Bourne, were notoriously lax in
their duties. Cowper remembered that Bourne was 'so good
natur'd and so indolent, that I lost more than I got by him, for
he made me as idle as himself'; and Lloyd was 'kind, and gentle, hating strife'.[9] But if formal learning languished, informal
literary endeavour flourished. Many of the boys—including
Colman, Lloyd, and Churchill—wrote poetry. Cowper studied
Homer with his friend Richard Sutton, and Cumberland translated portions of Virgil's *Georgics*. Bourne, the ineffectual fifth
form usher, was a particularly important literary influence in
the school. His elegant Latin poems were greatly admired by
the scholars, and Cowper, in later life, was fond of comparing
them to the work of Ovid and Tibullus.

The composition of Latin poetry was encouraged not only by
example, but by active competition for public praise and
private gain. Cowper, many years later, recalled this atmosphere of poetic endeavour and reward:

> At Westminster, where little poets strive
> To set a distich upon six and five,
> Where discipline helps op'ning buds of sense,
> And makes his pupils proud with silver-pence,
> I was a poet too.[10]

(506–10)

And, in a waking dream, he once imagined himself 'a schoolboy in high favour with the Master', who 'received a silver
groat for my exercise, and had had the pleasure of seeing it sent
from form to form for the admiration of all who were able to
understand it.'[11] For Cowper, as for Cumberland, Nicoll's
Westminster seems to have been a place 'where to attempt was
to succeed'.[12] It was certainly a place where independent (and
joint) literary effort was encouraged—and, perhaps, necessi-
tated—by the lenient policy of Nicoll and the genial idleness of
Lloyd and Bourne. Young authors could gather what they
needed in relative freedom, and practise their skills (at least, in
Latin) in a competitive arena. They could not, however,
depend on inspiring (or even regular) formal instruction. The
paradox of Nicoll's academic method is perhaps best summed
up by the Westminster historian John Sargeaunt when he says
that there were no periods in the history of the school 'when

less knowledge was imparted, and few when more was acquired'.[13]

A special feature of Westminster life that acted as a bridge between the Latin of the schoolroom and the literary exhibitionism of the town was the annual production of Terentian comedy. These performances drew many Londoners and were considered a major event of the winter 'season'. On 1 December 1762 Boswell reported: 'I . . . went to a play of Terence's (*The Eunuch*) performed by the King's Scholars of Westminster School. There was a very numerous audience, not one of whom I knew, except Churchill, and him only by sight. Although I seldom understood them, yet I was entertained to see the boys play and hear them speak Latin.'[14] And in December of 1765 Thornton sent two tickets to Caleb Whitefoord with this admonition: 'One Thing I must recommend to you for the honour of the School—Pray ye, look as much like Gentlemen as your Sunday cloaths will let you . . . the Westm^n Lads are so knowing, they can tell how much knowledge of Latin you have upon your Coat, and place you accordingly.'[15] The 'Westm^n Lads' not only ushered, produced, and acted the Latin plays; each year they composed an original epilogue satirizing current political and social events. These performances must have been stimulating experiences for fledgling literary men. The large crowds, the applause, the glory of public recognition surely conspired to turn many a scholar toward a literary career. Certainly they had their effect on Colman, who as a schoolboy acted parts in two plays: Geta in the 1749 production of *Phormio* and Davus in *The Adelphi* of 1750.

The 350 Westminster boys grew up with future peers in their midst, with Parliament a stone's throw away (they had special permission to attend debates), and with the burial place of English monarchs as their chapel. One would assume that such close contact with the power and traditions of the state would have inspired reverence and loyalty. But in the boys it seems mostly to have inspired horseplay. Lawrence Tanner reports that in the eighteenth century, 'the Abbey Carpenter was kept busy in devising means to prevent the boys from climbing over the roof of the School and Abbey.' And in 1766 a Westminster boy 'put his hand into an unrepaired hole in the tomb of Richard II and drew out the jawbone of the King'.[16]

This act of unpremeditated sacrilege seems a kind of metaphor for the irreverence produced by having national monuments as one's playground. If, on first view, the massive hammer-beam ceiling of the School and the sacred memorials of the Abbey might inspire awe, a repeated familiarity could breed, if not contempt, at least objectivity. Churchill's earliest poem, in fact, is a satire 'On the Monuments of Westminster-Abbey'. He facetiously pictures the Abbey as a prospective learning aid for the Westminster scholars, who, 'Being thus greatly edyfy'd, / May throw their books of Heathen Gods aside; / And, shortly, there (I fear) see rise / In statuary, *The whole Pantheon*' (17–21).[17] Similarly, the Westminster boys' constant 'intercourse with peers, and sons of peers' must have contributed, at least in part, to our five subjects' habitual lack of awe in the presence of a title. This irreverent streak—this tendency to view the great, the powerful, the sacred, with a knowing eye—was the natural outgrowth of a continued, first-hand exposure to government, to the nobility, to the landmarks of the state.

Less accessible than the Abbey and Parliament, but infinitely more exciting, were the pleasures of the 'town'. In *Tirocinium* it is the 'waiter Dick, with Bacchanalian lays' who wins the scholar's heart, and a 'street-pacing harlot' who supplies his first love. Exaggerated as Cowper's account may be (and it is probably not at all), the 'town' certainly held a great attraction for the older Westminster students, who viewed it as an inexhaustible source of pleasure and amusement. Lichtenberg leaves us a vivid recreation of the sights and, especially, the sounds of eighteenth-century London: the incessant rumbling of vehicles over cobblestones and dirt, the ubiquitous street instruments and street criers, the shouting and the laughter of a heterogeneous, energetic, and sometimes violent urban population. It seems an adolescent's garden of earthly delights:

In the middle of the street roll chaises, carriages, and drays in an unending stream. Above this din and the hum and clatter of thousands of tongues and feet one hears the chimes from the church towers, the bells of the postmen, the organs, fiddles, hurdy-gurdies, and tamborines of English mountebanks, and the cries of those who sell hot and cold viands in the open at the street corners. Then you will see a bonfire of shavings flaring up as high as the upper floors of the houses in a circle of merrily shouting beggar boys, sailors, and rogues. Suddenly a man whose handerchief has been stolen will cry: 'Stop thief', and every one will begin running and pushing and shoving. . . . Before you know where you are, a pretty, nicely dressed miss will take you by the hand: 'Come, my Lord, come along, let us drink a glass together.' . . . then there is an accident forty paces from you; 'God bless me,' cries one, 'Poor creature,' another . . . but all of a sudden they are laughing again, because some one has lain down by mistake in the gutter; 'Look there, damn me,' says a third, and then the procession moves on.[18]

In time, of course, certain features of town life would cease to fascinate and become the subject of attack. But London's kaleidoscopic excitement—like the ever-shifting scenes of an enormous undirected play—would never cease to charm and seduce the members of the Nonsense Club.

Cowper, the only one of the Nonsense Club writers to express a lasting revulsion for London, was also the only one raised in the country. He was born in 1731 to gentry in rural Berkhamsted, Hertfordshire. The other members of the group were all city boys of one sort or another. Churchill and Lloyd (born respectively in 1732 and 1733) were both natives of Westminster. Lloyd's father was Pierson Lloyd, the Westminster usher; Churchill was the son of the curate of a local church, St John the Evangelist. Colman was born to the British envoy at Florence in 1732 but was carried to England as an infant, and grew up in his mother's house in St James's Park. Thornton, the oldest of the group, was born in 1725 to a Maiden Lane apothecary. The date of his birth has been somewhat confused: the *Dictionary of National Biography* lists 1724; *Alumni Westmonasterienses*, 1726. The date of his christening, 28 September 1725, is recorded in the register of St Paul, Covent Garden.[19] All of the boys, including Cowper, seem to have thrived at Westminster. All, except Cowper, were King's Scholars, the élite group of students who won their title and privileges by competitive examination, and who lived in the new Palladian dormitory designed by Lord Burlington.[20] The Westminster ethos I have been describing was strongest within the ranks of the King's Scholars. It was they who felt most acutely the contradictory alignment of forces playing upon all Westminster boys. First, there was the validation of English patrician culture implied by a classical curriculum and privileged educational access. Then there was the irreverence and independence produced by lax discipline, coupled with loyalty to, and dependence upon, one's schoolmates in a system based on honour and principle (but sometimes lapsing into tyranny). And, finally, there was the 'gentlemanly' presence of Nicoll, embodying social grace and self-regulation in an atmosphere otherwise characterized by boyish coarseness and experimental vice. It was a complex curriculum, teaching complex lessons.

II

We know that Colman, Cowper, Lloyd, and Churchill were companions (to a greater or lesser degree) during their Westminster days. Bonnell Thornton, however, left the school for Christ Church, Oxford, in 1743—while this group was still in the Under School—and was probably known to the younger boys only as a respected and witty upperclassman; a departing hero, one might say. Once at Christ Church, Thornton applied himself with graceful assiduity; he received three degrees at regular intervals, including his Master of Arts in 1750 and his Bachelor of Physic (supposedly at the wish of his father) in 1754.

During his time at the University, Thornton seems to have studied contemporary literature, especially journalism, with equal attention and success. By the year of his final degree, he had worked on several periodicals with Christopher Smart, fought a paper war against Henry Fielding, and set a standard of journalistic success for his younger school friends to emulate. As a student of commercial journalism and contemporary life, he acquired sources of knowledge which he in turn passed on to the others, and, when their time came, his connections in the press smoothed a path for them to follow. In this respect Thornton's formative literary experience, though outside the realm of the Nonsense Club proper, is of considerable importance. The London journalistic world into which he was initiated was to become the world of the Nonsense Club; and the themes and preoccupations of his early writing were to influence indelibly the later work of his Westminster friends.

BONNELL THORNTON ESQ.ʳ

1. Bonnell Thornton. Anonymous engraving

Thornton's first publication appeared in April 1749. An *Ode on Saint Cæcilia's Day, Adapted to the Ancient British Musick* was the first version of the burlesque musical ode that was later performed at Ranelagh Gardens on 10 June 1763. Although detailed analysis of the ode will be deferred until my discussion of that period (Chapter 5, Section III), one point must be mentioned now. Because of the second part of the title—*As it was performed on the Twenty-second of November*—it has often been thought that the 1749 version was actually presented publicly. But, as A. D. McKillop has pointed out, November 22 *is* St Cecilia's Day and, as such, 'the date appears here . . . as part of a typical St. Caecilia's title, not as a record of actual performance'.[21] This conclusion would seem to be borne out by a notice in *The Public Advertiser* of 26 May 1763 (probably penned by Thornton himself) which states that after the ode was written at Oxford, 'no able Master . . . thought of giving it the further Help of harmonious sounds'.

Had the 'harmonious sounds' been added in 1749, they would have been provided by the ubiquitous instruments of the British vulgar: the hurdy-gurdy, Jew's harp, salt-box, and marrow bone and cleaver. These instruments were to be found in the hands of hundreds of street musicians in London, as well as doing yeoman's duty (in the case of the cleavers) in the butchers' shambles of Clare Market. They are alluded to in many earlier works—including Shakespeare's *A Midsummer Night's Dream*—and are usually called 'rustick' instruments, or 'old fashioned' instruments, or something of that sort.[22]

Thornton's use of such 'British Musick' as the major element in his burlesque poem was a notable innovation, and it seems to have highlighted the satiric possibilities of these instruments for at least one of the ode's readers, the madcap Cambridge scholar, Christopher Smart. (Thornton, in fact, alludes to Smart's serious St Cecilia's Day ode of 1746 when, in his preface, he lists 'little *Kit Smart*' along with '*Johnny Dryden, Jemmy Addison, Sawney Pope*', and others as purveyors of this kind of entertainment.[23]) Smart may have found in Thornton's ode not only a congenial burlesque vehicle, but the hint of a money-making scheme, for on 30 December 1751 he opened, in the first of its many manifestations, his 'Old Woman's Oratory'—a burlesque of John 'Orator' Henley of

Clare Market and of Italian music—which included a ragged band playing the native British instruments. A contemporary puff found 'more *real casuistry* in the Jew's Harp, and more *Sterling Sense* in the Salt Box, than ever came from the Tub, at the Slaughter House of Sense, Wit, and Reason, near Clare Market'.[24] Thornton, by 1751, had become a close friend of Smart's, and he took an almost proprietary interest in these burlesque entertainments (which continued under names like Mrs Midnight's Oratory, Mrs Midnight's Grand Concert, The Old Woman's Concert, The British Roratory, etc., throughout the 1750s), alluding to them—and to the instruments—often and favourably in *The Drury-Lane Journal*, *The Adventurer*, and *The Connoisseur*.

Thornton's first close contact with Smart probably dates from the time of *The Student, or The Oxford and Cambridge Monthly Miscellany*—a periodical medley of prose and verse supplied in greater part by University men—which appeared from 31 January 1750 to approximately July 1751. Smart's contributions to this periodical have been well documented: he did not become fully involved until the sixth number (30 June 1750) when 'Cambridge' was added to the title; and after the sixth number he was a major contributor and perhaps the editor (his father-in-law-to-be, John Newbery, was the publisher).[25] Thornton's role is less clear. He has always been acknowledged as one of the earliest contributors (Alexander Chalmers assigns him the poems signed 'B. T.' in the first number), but considerable evidence points to his having been the magazine's first editor.[26] George Colman in a satire written for the Oxford Encaenia of 1763 called Thornton 'that Rattle the STUDENT' —an allusion clearly implying some sort of editorial responsibility.[27] And the only essay in the first six numbers to be signed by 'The Student' anticipates to a remarkable degree not only the subject matter, but the phrasing of some of Thornton's later work.[28]

Thornton's editorial association with *The Student* may have prompted contributions from some of his Westminster friends. Lloyd, Churchill, Cowper, and Colman have all been connected with *The Student*. A poem entitled 'On the prefixing the Names of *The* MUSES *to the* STUDENT' was identified (presumably by Thornton) as being by '*the ingenious author of* . . .

the PROGRESS OF ENVY', a work which Lloyd had written in early 1751, and which would have been known to few people outside his school friends.[29] The poem which appears im-mediately below Lloyd's piece, 'RURAL HAPPINESS: An ODE to R—— L——, Esq; *By a country Clergyman*', has been assigned to Churchill by W. C. Brown on the evidence of Churchill's being a country clergyman and the initials standing for Robert Lloyd.[30] Although the poem is utterly unlike Churchill's later work in either form or content, its appearance below Lloyd's piece adds strength to Brown's attribution. Charles Ryskamp has suggested that the poem 'A REFLEC-TION *on the Year* 1720' by 'W.C.' may be Cowper's.[31] And James Boswell went as far as to call Colman a 'major contribu-tor'.[32] Although only Lloyd's poem can be assigned on the basis of hard evidence, it is certainly possible that Thornton's editorial relationship with *The Student* provided a number of his Westminster friends with their first chance to appear in print.

During the time of *The Student*, Thornton may also have helped with Smart's *The Midwife, or The Old Woman's Magazine*. This magazine—one of the most original and frenetic of the eighteenth century—first appeared on 16 October 1750, a little over a year before Smart's 'Old Woman's Oratory'. Smart, in the person of 'Mary Midnight' (the nominal proprietor, as well, of The Old Woman's Oratory, Mrs Midnight's concert, *et al.*), was the editor and by far the most frequent contributor. But that Thornton, at least tangentially, was involved with *The Midwife* would seem assured by the elaborate effort his persona, 'Madam Roxana Termagant', feels compelled to make in the first number of *The Drury-Lane Journal* to dispel the rumour that 'from the similitude of our manner, I am the very, identical, one and the same person with the famous, the celebrated, the remarkable, the notified Mrs. Mary Midnight'.[33]

Have At You All: or, The Drury-Lane Journal is the first periodi-cal thought to have been written wholly by Bonnell Thornton. The journal commenced publication on 16 January 1752 and, as its title implies, was devoted mainly to satiric and burlesque attacks on a large number of London's periodical writers. Johnson, Smollett, Hill—none escaped Thornton's laughter and strictures. But the inspiration for the journal, and the main subject of ridicule, was the literary activity of one 'Sir Alexander Drawcansir': Henry Fielding.

In undertaking *The Drury-Lane Journal*, Thornton launched himself into a literary marketplace with strong connections to the world of business. Dr John Hill's 'Inspector' essays were intended primarily to enliven the commerce-oriented *London Daily Advertiser*. Fielding's *Covent-Garden Journal* specifically puffed the Universal Register Office operated by himself and his brother, Sir John Fielding. And Smart, at this stage, was using *The Midwife* primarily as a vehicle for advertising his Old Woman's Oratory, even to the extent of reprinting in it much of the material used in his performances. Thornton's *Drury-Lane Journal* followed this pattern, originating as an advertising instrument for the Public Register Office in King Street, Covent Garden.

The Public Register Office, founded in 1751 by a Belgian named Dullwin, was an employment office ('Servants in any upper station'), brokerage house (land, commissions, annuities), and general business agency. Thornton's job was to promote the Public Register Office and to ridicule Fielding's Universal Register Office (where Dullwin had learned the trade).[34] The by-play in the *London Daily Advertiser* of January 1752 offers some insights into the nexus of commercial and literary influences affecting *The Drury-Lane Journal*. Besides Hill's lucubrations, the newspaper regularly carried competing advertisements for the Universal and Public Register offices: on 9 January, for example, the Public's advertisement accused the Universal's clerks of being 'master of all the secrets of every family in the Kingdom'—a claim Fielding himself had made in the recently published *Amelia,* and one which Thornton would use against him a week later in the first number of *The Drury-Lane Journal*. Intermittently, advertisements appeared for Smart's Old Woman's Oratory, then performing at the Castle Tavern, Paternoster Row. This extraordinary undertaking had as its major target the religio-educational institution of Henley's Oratory, itself something of a travesty of the religious and educational institutions of the establishment. Henley's rambling, disjunctive orations and advertisements commented on current events, politics, and history, serving as a model for Smart's clever parodies and raucous humour.[35] It is this double influence—on the commercial side, the duel of the Register Offices; on the literary side, Smart's (and behind them, Henley's) irreverent parodies—that provided the initial inspiration for Thornton's efforts in *The Drury-Lane Journal*.

G. E. Jensen, in his preface to *The Covent-Garden Journal*, has charted the progress and outcome of the paper war that sustained *The Drury-Lane Journal*.[36] The major antagonists were Fielding ('Sir Alexander Drawcansir'), Hill ('The Inspector'), and Thornton ('Madam Roxana Termagant'). The war, at least in its non-commercial context, was over nothing more serious than the enemy writers' alleged dullness; a contest of wit, one might say. Thus, in the first number of *The Drury-Lane Journal*, Thornton adheres very closely to the material in the previous issues of *The Covent-Garden Journal*, providing what amounts to a running commentary on Fielding's sentiments and style. When, for example, in his second number Fielding translates, with loving attention to detail, Tacitus' account of Nero's orgies, Thornton condemns his sensationalism and accuses him of adding the lewdness of the Ancients to his already notorious taste for the 'low':

Go on, thou curious Translator: rake together the most dirty, filthy, nasty, lewd transactions of the most profligate creatures. Not only rifle TACITUS for them; ransack PETRONIUS ARBITER, modernise the PRIAPEIA and let MEURSIUS appear before us *in puris naturalibus*, in naked English. . . . Let every luscious hint receive a higher relish from your seasoning stile; that every modest virgin, every experienc'd matron, every diffident youth, and every sly old lecher may be thoroughly instructed in the antient as well as modern arts of lasciviousness.[37]

Most of the first number of *The Drury-Lane Journal* is in this anti-Fielding mode, though Thornton does stop now and then to burlesque other contemporary writers:

'To vivify the dormant faculties of Rationality, and to dissipate the nebulous obscurity expanded over the Intellect by Insensibility, while the officiousness of Complaisance obtrudes upon the flexibility of Good-Nature, and Mendacity closes the portal against the ingress of Veracity';—This, I say, must be only the arduous task of that incomprehensible Highflyer, whose meaning is absorb'd in metaphor, and sense swallow'd up in similitude.[38]

It seems superfluous to say that this is Thornton's version of, and comment on, Johnson's *Rambler*. This alternation of satiric commentary and burlesque demonstration typifies the early format of *The Drury-Lane Journal*. The paper made no pretence of being a 'real' periodical—even the advertisements were fakes. Thornton's mission, purely and simply, was to ridicule and absurdly imitate the works of others.

Throughout its run, *The Drury-Lane Journal* kept to a regular formula with slight variations. Each paper, which appeared every Thursday—except 2 April—to 9 April 1752, included a series of comic and burlesque articles, most of which were directed at Fielding.[39] Many of these burlesques are merely amusing, but some function as rather acute criticism. Particularly noteworthy in this respect is 'A New Chapter in Amelia' in the issue of 13 February 1752. To my mind, it is one of the best and certainly one of the most entertaining pieces of criticism on *Amelia* ever written.

Contemporary criticism of *Amelia* focused on two related failings. First, like all of Fielding's fiction, *Amelia* was considered 'low'. But worse than this, and unlike his other novels, it was thought not only 'low' but 'dull'. If Fielding's critics had been more than happy to deplore the low humour of his two previous novels, they took even greater delight in dismissing condescendingly the low seriousness of his latest. How this catch-22 style of criticism worked can be seen in some remarks by contemporary letter writers:

We are reading Mr. Fielding's Amelia. . . . I don't like it at all; D.D. won't listen to it. It has more a moral design than either appears in Joseph Andrews or Tom Jones, but has not so much humour; it neither makes one laugh or cry, though there are some very dismal scenes described.

As for poor Amelia, she is so great a fool we pity her, but cannot be humble enough to desire to imitate her. But pray, Sir, you that desire women should be learned, what do you say to Mrs. Atkinson? Must we suppose that if a woman knows a little Greek and Latin she must be a drunkard, and a virago? . . . Poor Fielding, I believe, designed to be good, but did not know how, and in the attempt lost his genius, low humour.[40]

More particular faults are also mentioned—chief among them being Booth's profligacy, Amelia's milksoppishness (and lack of nose), Mrs Atkinson's tippling, and the 'children'—but these are generally subsumed under the headings of lowness and tediousness. The problem of lowness, of course, has long been erased from Fielding's debit sheet, but over his favourite child *Amelia* the inexorable creditor Dullness continues to hover.

As an allegedly low, dull work, *Amelia* made a perfect model for burlesque, and Thornton seems to have recognized all its possibilities. If, as Richmond Bond has said, good burlesque is an act of both criticism and creation, then Thornton's chapter is a model of the form.[41] His method of attack is double-edged. First, he makes *Amelia* very 'low' indeed by employing sponging-house language and slapstick comedy; and, in so doing, he makes it very funny. In effect, he comments on *Amelia*'s lowness by exaggerating it, and he critiques its dullness by creating in its place uproarious farce. Thornton's heading to the chapter reads, 'More witty than the rest, if the Reader has but sense enough to find out the Humour'. To this general method, Thornton adds his own fascination with the particulars of vulgar life in such a way that for a moment we seem to have a preview of the intimate but slightly distorted Shandean perspective of eight years hence:

Amelia, finding her husband did not come home, sat herself down contented to her supper, which consisted of no other variety than a Welch rabbit, and of which I have told my reader she was particularly fond. Her little family were squatted upon the hearth close by her knees, and knawing each of them an huge luncheon of bread and butter, with windows cut upon it, and strew'd with brown sugar. Poor Mrs. Atkinson, who had taken too large a sip of the Cherry Brandy bottle that evening, had loll'd herself back against her chair by the fireside, and sat snoring.

The disconsolate turtle was lamenting the long absence of her mate, when the old decrepit magistrate of the night went his rounds, and with an hearty bounce at the door proclaim'd it—past twelve o'clock, and a frosty morning. Booth was not yet return'd; and Amelia, who was sitting all the while upon tenter-hooks, had enough to do to quiet her babes, who incessantly worried her with, Mammy!—where's Pappy?—Mammy!—where's Pappy?—Mammy!—Where's Pappy?[42]

The slangy detail of the opening vignette adds realism as well as humour to the scene. Rarely in earlier eighteenth-century literature do we find the kind of textured close-ups Thornton deals with here. A more obvious burlesque device is Thornton's juxtaposition of stilted literary language (usually Latinate) and rollicking, realistic street jargon (usually Anglo-Saxon). The word 'bounce' activates the second paragraph; it verbally jars us, as it must have jarred Amelia, out of the tired Latinate reverie of the opening phrase. The same kind of humorous realism ends the passage, where, in place of Fielding's rather maudlin, artificial mother and child conversations, we find children importuning with the single-minded persistence of real children.

Having set the domestic stage, Thornton is ready for Booth to return home, which he does with much riot. This uproar gives Thornton a chance to highlight Amelia's delicacy and tendency to take weak drink as a tranquillizer: 'Amelia's gentle spirits were so much agitated, that if she had not gulp'd down some small oats, which she had warm'd in a tin cup at supper, she must infallibly have fainted away.' He also indulges in some slapstick as Mrs Atkinson falls off her chair, and introduces a slice of verbal low life as 'Little Betty' comes in drawling like a street urchin: '"La Mistress," says she, "here's Master com'd home, as drunk as a piper; to be sure, he's in a woundy sad pickle, that sartain: he's all over of a gore of blood, and as nasty!—I wouldn't touch him with a pair of tongs."' Eventually 'the staggering Booth' is brought in; and Thornton, in a happy stroke, provides him with an injury that highlights Amelia's facial problem: 'She then clap'd him down upon a chair, and was going to wipe his mouth with her muckender: but what was her consternation, when she found his high-arch'd Roman Nose, that heretofore resembled the bridge of a fiddle, had been beat all to pieces! As herself had before lost the handle to her face, she now truly sympathis'd with him in their mutual want of snout.' No matter how much one may admire Amelia, it is hard not to smile at Thornton's phrasing.

The first thing we need to understand about the above 'chapter'—and about Thornton's burlesques of *The Convent-Garden Journal*—is how much Thornton learned from Fielding. To deal in burlesque is necessarily to learn the conventions of the form burlesqued; and Thornton's mock-Drawcansirian essays and 'New Chapter' clearly indicate his close study of

Fielding's manner. In the case of the 'New Chapter', Thornton particularly focused on the new conventions Fielding had tried and failed to handle in *Amelia*. Thornton's humorous domestic circumstantiality simply would not have been possible had not Fielding himself been experimenting with similar effects. Michael Irwin has noted that in *Amelia*'s domestic passages, 'consisting of small particulars irrelevant to the main story, Fielding suggests the daily routine surrounding the central events he has chosen to describe. Unlike Tom Jones or Joseph Andrews, the Booths have a way of life'.[43] But Fielding did not take his new approach far enough in the psychological direction of Richardsonian realism to make it effective, and—as our letter writers noted—he simultaneously retrenched the humour and ironic playfulness that so vivified *Tom Jones*. In the 'New Chapter', Thornton does in excess what he thought Fielding should have done in moderation: he combines new found domestic particularity with the old lively wit and irreverent humour. Like the opening scene of Dryden's *Essay on Dramatic Poetry*, Thornton's burlesque chapter is intriguing because it makes us wonder what the author might have been capable of achieving had he chosen to cultivate the field of prose fiction. In this case, however, I feel it is safe to say that without a model—and faced with a long haul—Thornton would simply have lost interest, and his prose its freshness.

At least one contemporary writer seems to have recognized the literary attraction underlying Thornton's attacks on Fielding. William Kenrick in *Fun*—'a parodi-tragi-comical satire' aimed mainly at the war between Fielding, Hill, and Thornton—includes a scene in which Roxana Termagant (ostensibly Drawcansir's enemy) admits to a secret passion for the knight in terms that seem to allude to a literary as well as emotional relationship:

> Drawcansir trembles at the Name of me,
> My Ranks in *King-Street* shine—but oh my Heart!
> I'm sick of Love, and for my mortal Foe;
> *Drawcansir's* Charms have pierc'd my tender Breast.[44]

After this soliloquy, 'Mountain' (Hill) enters and is scorned by Roxana who confesses her love for Drawcansir again, causing much jealousy. In terms of the relative space and treatment allotted to Fielding and Hill in *The Drury-Lane Journal*, this little allegory could not be truer. Hill is given much less attention and care. In effect, he is contemptuously dismissed. Fielding, on the other hand, is continually attacked, burlesqued, and parodied with close attention to detail. Although his mode of study was burlesque, Thornton was a close student of the literature of Henry Fielding.

III

But Thornton was also a student of the culture, and his work in *The Drury-Lane Journal* was not limited simply to literary burlesque. Perhaps its most distinctive element is its supposed authoress, Madam Roxana Termagant. In Roxana, Thornton developed not only a humorous spokeswoman for the battle against Fielding, but a figure offering a complex insight into the situation of a certain class of woman in eighteenth-century urban society. In this respect, both Thornton's Roxana and Smart's Mary Midnight are significant creations. Both, in a phenomenological sense, are disreputable women deeply involved in the literary industry of London. They are not mere contributors, but editors and primary writers of papers with often aggressively satirical and lower-class content, although this content is usually mediated by the conventional 'humour' assumed to accompany their fictional circumstances.[45] Thornton's Roxana Termagant, as her surname implies, is no stranger to the London street life. Tough, knowing, self-sufficient, she projects the persistence and belligerence typical of the common prostitute of the period—an identification made implicitly by Thornton in the title of his journal.[46] Mary Midnight, of course, is a midwife: a folk figure known for gossiping, tippling, and disposing of—as well as delivering—newborn babies. Their existence is a wretched one—a point made explicitly in *The Drury-Lane Journal* when Mary Midnight visits Roxana at her chambers above a 'rotting Chandler's shop' in Drury Lane:

Upon enquiring for the Authoress we were conducted up a pair of rotten worm-eaten stairs . . . into a little room, which you could scarce stand upright in, because of the raftors that hung just as if they were going to drop upon your head. 'Tis impossible to describe the wretchedness of the place: in one corner of it there was a window, but the greatest part of the casement being broke, the vacant quarrels were supplied with proof-sheets of the *Drury-Lane Journal*: over the chimney hung a VINCENT WING's Almanack for the year 1737, and the bare walls were set off with five wooden pictures, half torn, of the *Harlot's Progress*. By the fireplace stood a jointstool with several bits of paper scatter'd upon it; and over it dangled a pint bottle of ink, hanging down by a piece of an old lace that was fasten'd to the cieling.[47]

This fiction of a lone urban woman, living in poverty and drudging for the press, describes material reality for an unknown number of female 'hack' writers who eked out a living in London's garrets. One of them, Charlotte Forman, wrote of her lodgings and life in 1769: 'I have now lived, or rather I have been buried alive two years and a half between bare walls, where a wholesome breeze never makes its way; where I am never cool in summer, nor never warm in winter; where I am obliged to stop the chasms of the old casements with rags to keep out the wind; where I lie without coverlid or curtain or sheet to my bed; where, in short, everything wears the aspect of wretchedness.'[48] Charlotte Forman herself was a writer of political letters to the press and a staunch Wilkite, but Roxana and Mary Midnight's fictional roles seem more closely related to the 'unruly' woman of the popular culture: the female (or disguised male) who challenges conventional authority, treats men rudely, and puts 'women on top'.[49]

Usually Roxana's cavilling is presented in a somewhat snippish, affected version of genteel language, for as she explains in her autobiographical sketch, she *is* the daughter of a clergyman (although she is also a hack writer and, Thornton implies, a whore).[50] But sometimes the brutal dialect of lower-class London breaks through the pseudo-genteel camouflage, exposing the layers of authorial (and, by implication, reader-supplied) repression necessary to keep 'down' the irreverent and potentially rebellious energy of the exploited:

If *Welch*, *Irish*, *Scotch*, or the gibberish of *Hottentots* will not serve, I'll have at you with the lingo and cant terms of prisons and spunging houses, tho' I should be forced to attend the Thief-catcher's Office in *Covent-Garden*, or ransack *Amelia* for them. Nor shall I gather less emolument than your Knightship from the place of my habitation;

whence, as you have entitled your Journal, so have I mine. And tho'
Drury-Lane cannot furnish me with the witty and humorous depositions
of blundering servant-girls, yet it will supply me with the equally in-
structive and polite conversation of the hundreds—To give you a
specimen in your own stile and manner.

Drury-lane, Jan. 16

Sunday last MOLL DRAGGLETAIL, alias FOUL-MOUTH, alias
FIRE-SHIP, alias STRIP ME NAKED, alias BUNG YOUR EYE,
was seiz'd by old ROGER MOUTHWATER the watchman, and
carried before Justice SCRIBBLE; being charg'd with an intent to
commit fornication, by street-walking in the *Strand*. As she was dragging along, they discoursed litterally as followeth. '*D-mme, you old rotten
son of a b-tch, you lives by us poor girls mesfortins, G-d blast ye*'— '*Come along,
wool ye, I'll carry ye*'— '*Carry me to number hell, you dog; you shan't haul me so,
by G-d.*'— '*If you won't come civilly, I'll call my partner,*'— '*Call and be
d-mn'd to ye, I'll have attendance, d-mme, I'll have attendance.*'— '*Watch,
watch! here lay hould on her, do.*'— '*Come along, mistress.*'— '*G-d d-mn your
eyes, your hearts, your liver, your lungs, your lights, your odd joints, your
members, &c. &c. &c.*'[51]

There is tension between the genteel introduction (with its
hit at Fielding) and the following conversation that resists easy
interpretation. Depending on one's ideological preoccupations,
it is possible to discern in the passage a conventional separation
of superior author from inferior and ludicrous object of ridicule
(in this case, both Moll and Fielding); a verbal example,
despite the contradictory ideological stance of the introduction,
of the coarse popular language asserting itself against the
homogenizing 'metalanguage' of the bourgeoisie; or even an
allegory of the oppression of lower-class women at the hands of
male hirelings under the control of authority.[52] But the more
immediate context is Fielding's practice of including the latest
cases from the Bow Street Magistrates Office in *The Covent-
Garden Journal*: cases involving prostitution, adultery, and theft
among the lower and middling people. The language of
authority in Fielding's journal becomes in Thornton's parodic
version the language of the streets: coarse, irreverent, defiant.
This is not to say that Thornton and Smart, two university
men of the professional class, were crypto-feminists or radical
reformers, but that their irreverent, carnivalesque journals and
the 'women' who supposedly conduct them speak to larger

issues than perhaps they were themselves aware. Yet, having
made this disclaimer, let me suggest that there is evidence that
they were quite aware of the dynamics of exploitation; and that
they dealt with it in their own oblique fashion.

Thornton's choice of persona in *The Drury-Lane Journal* is
informed not only by satiric intention and literary emulation
but by the real commercial practices of the Public Register
Office. As part of 'the most safe, easy, and gainful branches of
agency, factorage, brokerage, negotiation, and insurances'
that proliferated in the eighteenth century, the Public Register
Office represented an important link between the town and the
country.[53] As a brokerage, it increased the control of rural
landowners in London over their landed capital; but more importantly, as an employment office, it served as a way-station
for country people (primarily women) coming to London to
seek places as domestic servants.[54] The Public Register Office
specialized in a particular kind of servant: those 'in any upper
station . . . House-keeper, Waiting-women, Chamber-maids'.[55]
Reasonably well-bred, healthy, often young and sometimes
pretty, the women filling the Public Register Office were part
of a general influx of country people to London. But theirs was
a special case, for places in an 'upper station' were in extremely
short supply. Sir John Fielding in 1753 spoke of the 'amazing
number' of female servants out of place: 'The body of servants
. . . that are chiefly unemployed . . . are those of a higher
nature such as chambermaids, etc., whose number far exceeds
the places they stand candidates for, and as the chief of these
come from the country, they are obliged when out of place to
go into lodgings and there subsist on their little savings, til they
get places agreeable to their inclinations . . . and this is one of
the grand sources which furnish this town with PROSTI-
TUTES.'[56] In large capitals, Fielding spells out the mystified
connection between the Public Register Office and Roxana's
world. It is an addition of meaning that allows us to retranslate
their printer's 'ironic' suggestion that 'instead of the Drury-
Lane Journal, suppose you was to call yours *The Bawd*'s, or
The Kept Mistress's MAGAZINE'.[57]

There can be little doubt that among the women with whom
Thornton rubbed shoulders at the Public Register Office were
a substantial number of potential and actual prostitutes. More

than that, there was in such an office an atmosphere of ingrained innuendo and (at worst) physical coercion that Rowlandson's drawing of 1803 catches so vividly: servants stand about like so many disposable goods; old men inspect young women they may hire as 'chambermaids'.[58] The encoded message of Roxana Termagant's ribaldry and wretchedness, then, is as complex as the relations that inform, create, and deflect it. The message is that there are girls in the town being sexually exploited, that the Public Register Office is a good place to find one, and that we can all laugh because everyone does it. But it is also that these women have a voice—sardonic, aggressive, crude, or genteel—and that they will make themselves heard. The excruciating tension between the two lessons—the moral anaesthesia administered by respectability in the service of exploitation; and the power of irreverence and sardonic anger to expose it—is given an extraordinary articulation in Mary Midnight's description of fallen maidservants sleeping in the London streets:

Boy, snuff the Candle, and see who these are that lodge themselves on the Bulks, and lay naked at the Shop Doors. Oh! I see myself now, they are poor Orphans, young helpless Girls, that have been debauch'd and ruin'd by the Sons, and 'Prentices of the honest Citizens, and after that turn'd out by their generous and compassionate Masters. Or perchance, they are brought to this wretched State, by some of the righteous Lads of the *Temple* and Inns of Court. However that may be, it need not affect us Boy. Lay still my Heart! Women are not of the Human Species, so down with them, down with them. Boy, if ever thou livest to be a Man (as in all probability thou wilt, if the Halter don't catch thee soon) do thou, whenever any poor Creatures tumble down, kick them about, 'tis the way of the World Boy, and all must conform to Custom.[59]

It is a powerful performance by Smart, as complex in tone as the psychological negotiations faced by every woman in the eighteenth century.

With the demise of *The Drury-Lane Journal* on 9 April 1752, Thornton's literary activity, as far as we know, ceased until November, when he began two new projects. One, *The Spring-Garden Journal*, commenced on 16 November and amounted to a revival of *The Drury-Lane Journal*.[60] The second, beginning on 14 November, was a series of essays for John Hawkesworth's new *Adventurer*.[61] Thornton's contributions to *The Adventurer* have long been disputed. In several older editions they are listed as being by Richard Bathurst, Samuel Johnson's friend. Recently, however, Victor Lams has presented strong internal evidence that seems to cement the claims of such notables as Arthur Murphy and Alexander Chalmers that Thornton wrote the eight essays signed 'A' and was, in fact, a key man in Hawkesworth's early editorial scheme.[62]

Thornton's connection with *The Adventurer* lasted until 3 April 1753. Half a year later (15 September 1753), a very young writer, perhaps encouraged by Thornton's friendship and literary success, saw his first published essay appear in *The Adventurer*. The twenty-one-year-old George Colman's single contribution, 'Literary Offerings in the Temple of Fame: A Vision', marks the beginning of his literary career. Colman had come to Christ Church, Oxford, in the autumn of 1751. This was also Thornton's college, and the two, knowing each other from the Westminster days, became fast friends. Colman's steady wit and excellent connections (his uncle was the Earl of Bath) would have favourably impressed Thornton. And Thornton's literary friends and accomplishments must have had a compelling effect on Colman, who was always an ambitious writer.

The remainder of the Westminster friends were widely scattered, but each, in his own way, was engaged in a literary self-education. Robert Lloyd, who entered Trinity College, Cambridge, in 1751, completed that same year an ambitious and interminable Spenserian imitation called *The Progress of Envy*. The poem has little to recommend it; but in light of his later satire on imitators of Spenser, one at least has to admit that Lloyd learned from the experience.[63]

Charles Churchill in 1748 enrolled for a brief unhappy career at St John's College, Cambridge—which he left the same year under mysterious circumstances. By 1751 he was married to one Martha Scott and living in Sunderland in the north of England, ostensibly preparing to take holy orders. However, his nineteenth-century editor, William Tooke, says that during the Sunderland period, Churchill 'devoted almost the whole of his time to his favourite poetical amusements'.[64]

William Cowper, the only member of the group not to attend
(however fleetingly) one of the universities, remained in London
as a law clerk in the house of a Mr Chapman, solicitor. In
November of 1753, he moved to the Inner Temple. Much of
Cowper's poetry from this period survives, the earliest piece
being a parody of Milton, 'Verses Written at Bath on Finding
the Heel of a Shoe' (1748). Certainly the most interesting of his
early poems is 'An Epistle to Robert Lloyd, Esqr.' (1754), in
which Cowper describes Lloyd as the 'sole heir, and single, / Of
dear Mat Prior's easy jingle', and metaphorically recounts his
own affliction by 'fierce banditti':

> (Sworn foes to every thing that's witty!)
> That, with a black, infernal train,
> Make cruel inroads in my brain,
> And daily threaten to drive thence
> My little garrison of sense:
> The fierce banditti, which I mean,
> Are gloomy thoughts, led on by spleen.
>
> (14–20)[65]

Although the style of the poem—its tetrameter couplets and
jingly rhymes—is very like the happy-go-lucky verse that Lloyd
would submit to *The Connoisseur*, its sentiment reveals for the
first time the seemingly objectless despair that was increasingly
to undermine the lightheartedness that Cowper and his friends
aspired to.

In early 1755, Colman joined Cowper as a law student at the
Inns of Court, though at Lincoln's Inn, not the Inner Temple.
Lloyd returned to town regularly while taking his two degrees
(BA 1755, MA 1758) at Cambridge. And Churchill was slowly
working his way back to London as a clergyman. But by the
time of his arrival in 1758, the first joint literary effort of the
Nonsense Club—the ironically and appropriately named *Con-
noisseur*—was already an accomplished fact.

2 *Taste and* The Connoisseur

I

On Thursday, 31 January 1754 the first issue of *The Connoisseur* appeared, sheet and a half folio, two pence a paper. It was written by the witty 'Mr Town'—descendant of a long line of Towns and Townleys who had inhabited the periodicals and stage since early in the century. Mr Town, however, was the first of this family to get his own essay series; and once an essayist he became the first to appropriate for himself the ambiguous and somewhat tainted title of connoisseur. In 1754, both terms—'town' and 'connoisseur'—were rich in serious and satiric connotations. In choosing their persona and his title, the editors and chief writers of the essay series—Bonnell Thornton and George Colman—at once imbued the paper with topical panache and provided themselves with a flexible vehicle for the development of authorial tone and point of view.

The 'Town', of course, signified London. But it was the London of coffee-houses, gaming houses, stylish 'bagnios', and theatres, the more affluent London, not the world of out-of-work servants, female hacks, and broken prostitutes that formed the implicit backdrop for *The Drury-Lane Journal* and *The Midwife*. The headquarters of the 'Town' was Covent Garden—'the acknowledg'd region of gallantry, wit, and criticism' (4)—with its theatres and surrounding resorts of pleasure and conversation: the Bedford Coffee House, George's, the Rose, and innumerable others. This is not to say that the two worlds did not overlap. They were in fact superimposed upon each other: prostitutes worked the taverns and theatres, thugs worked over their patrons and passers-by. It was a matter of selective point of view. In the first essay of *The Connoisseur*, for example, Mr Town, after giving us what he calls a 'cursory survey of what is usually called The Town', feels it necessary to apologize for having 'confined myself principally to Coffee-houses' (5).[1]

The phrase 'the Town', however, also carried a narrowed connotation in the literary and theatrical worlds, where it was

often used ironically to signify a body of self-important and unforgiving critics. On *The Connoisseur*'s title-page, Mr Town is
designated 'critic and censor-general', and in the essay series
itself 'the Town' is used in the theatrical sense: 'The Pit is the
grand Court of Criticism, and in the centre of it is collected that
awful body, distinguished by the title of *the Town*. Hence are
issued the irrevocable decrees, and here final sentence is pronounced on plays and players' (No. 43; 256). These theatrical
and literary denotations are merged in a later description of
'the several tribes of play-house and coffee-house Critics, and
that collective body of them, called the TOWN' (No. 48; 345).
As 'Mr Town', then, Colman and Thornton project a certain
urbanity but also a fatuousness that years of ironic use had
attached to the name. In short, the persona is not meant to
inspire moral or critical confidence. Instead it alludes to a
certain insider's knowledge of London (which, as Old
Westminsters, Thornton and Colman unquestionably possessed) and to an enjoyment of the follies of the metropolis
not strictly consistent with Mr Town's role as 'censor general'.

But if because of his very name Mr Town cannot sustain the
morally and critically upright character implied by the 'Spectator', he nevertheless articulates his own, more ambiguous,
approach to the periodical essay. He promises to avoid 'the
worn out practice of retailing scraps of morality, and affecting
to dogmatize on the common duties of life'—a practice in
which *The Spectator* is called 'inimitable'. Instead, Mr Town has
chosen 'to undermine our fashionable excesses by secret sap-
ping' and 'to laugh people into a better behaviour'. 'I am convinced', he writes, 'that the sting of reproof is not less sharp for
being concealed: and advice never comes with a better face,
than when it comes with a laughing one' (No. 71; 423).
Evidently Mr Town's 'laughter' is meant to balance delicately
between the old tradition of satiric ridicule and the gradually
predominating idea of 'amiable humour'.[2] His concern with
reform is clearly never a serious crusade. As one of the final
essays makes clear, Mr Town accepts his failure with
equanimity and, in fact, a kind of impish pride. 'Village', Mr
Town's country cousin, writes that 'whatever reformation you
may have worked in town, give me leave to tell you, that you

have sometimes done us harm in the country, by the bare mention of the vices and follies now in vogue':

From your intelligence some of our most polite ladies have learned,
that it is highly genteel to have a rout; and some have copied the
fashion so exactly, as to play at cards on *Sundays.* Your papers upon
dress set all our belles at work in following the mode: you no sooner
took notice of cocked hats, but every hat in the parish was turned up
behind and before; and when you told us, that the town-beauties went
naked, our rural damsels immediately began to throw off their
clothes.

(No. 139; 837–8)

It is this ambiguous approach that Oliver Goldsmith rather
effusively praised in *The Monthly Review* when he wrote of Mr
Town: 'He is the first writer since Bickerstaff, who has been
perfectly satirical, yet perfectly good-natured; and who never,
for the sake of declamation, represents simple folly as absolutely
criminal. He has the solidity to please the grave, and the
humour and wit to allure the gay.'[3]

In 1754 the word 'connoisseur' was in a semantic crisis. The
term had come into the language (at least, in printed form)
only forty years earlier, in two works that provided an extended
and influential treatise on its meaning. Jonathan Richardson's
*The Connoisseur: An Essay on the Whole Art of Criticism as it relates to
Painting* and the subsequent *Discourse of the Dignity, Certainty,
Pleasure, and Advantage of the Science of a Connoisseur* (1719) had
helped enormously to popularize an aesthetic current since the
late seventeenth century and destined to become a dominant
force as the century progressed. This aesthetic, sometimes called
the 'Georgian Rule of Taste', held up the ideal of 'a
Gentleman of Taste', a 'man of breeding', a connoisseur who
knew the 'right models' for art because of a thorough ground-
ing in the art, architecture, and literature of classical antiquity.
In its most characteristic form, the Rule of Taste represented,
in Joseph Burke's words, 'a tripartite canon of antiquity, the
Renaissance, and seventeenth century classicism . . . grounded
by the moralizing "good sense" of the Augustans.'[4] Generally,
classical sculpture, continental history painting in the grand
manner, and the architecture of Vitruvius, Palladio, and Inigo
Jones were considered the 'right models'. The refinement of

the arts and the refinement of morality were equated, and the qualities of order, harmony, and proportion were held in high esteem. This idea of a connoisseur had a great influence on the English aristocracy, and particularly on the circle that formed around the third Earl of Burlington and his executor in matters of taste, William Kent. Indeed, Alexander Pope's *Epistle to Burlington* (1731) used this aesthetic as the implicit yardstick against which the excesses and perversions of pseudo-connoisseurs were measured. But Pope's complaint also indicates the extent to which the idea (and terminology) had been vulgarized in the few years since Richardson's publication.

Originally, the term 'connoisseur' was brought into the English language to replace the tainted 'virtuoso' of the seventeenth century. The latter word had been so degraded in numerous plays and satires that it could hardly have been used without drawing a snicker (that the word survives today only in a sense completely different from its original meaning attests to the thoroughness of its satiric destruction).[5] In addition, its inclusiveness of reference was not compatible with the new aesthetic. For the 'virtuoso' was, in effect, a Renaissance man gone to seed: a person interested in *everything* (so long, the satirists would add, as it is useless). Butterflies, flowers, stuffed birds, mechanical 'wonders', waxworks, old coins, gimcracks, monsters, prodigies of the Royal Society—all found their way into the minds (and often the 'cabinets') of these curious men.[6] A connoisseur, on the other hand, was to be a collector of the highest order: an expert on art, architecture, and literature, but always with reference to their moral and practical significance (what Pope would have called their 'use'). However, as soon as the word gained general currency—and its speedy proliferation was certainly helped by the fact that Addison and Steele had just fed a culture-hungry middle class a solid diet of manners, art, and morality—it began to take on many of the unseemly connotations of the old 'virtuoso'. This confusion of meaning is exemplified by Fielding in *Tom Jones*, when he contrasts Augustan 'Men of Wit and Pleasure' with modern 'Men of Wisdom and *Vertu* (take heed you do not read Virtue)', the kind of man who for his amusements has 'the vast Circle of Connoisseurship, Painting, Music, Statuary, and natural Philosophy, or rather *unnatural*, which deals in the Wonderful,

and knows nothing of Nature, except her Monsters and Imper-
fections'.[7]

Hogarth, too, attacked the connoisseurs—but on different
grounds. Although Richardson had originally hoped to foster
the development of an English school of painting as well as to
see the English aristocracy develop into connoisseurs, the aristocrats chose to ignore the first part of his formula, and concentrating their efforts (and money) on the second, simply
purchased 'Old Masters' from the continent with greater enthusiasm.[8] These collectors were the objects of Hogarth's
scorn: pretenders to culture who, instead of patronizing native
British artists, chased around Europe buying up 'dark pictures'
and classical artifacts. Such 'connoisseurship' was also picked
up by the affluent middle classes who, under the influence of
The Spectator, were resolutely aping the preoccupations of their
betters. Indeed, by midcentury, Robert Lloyd could characterize the time as a 'Blest age! when all men may procure / The
title of a Connoisseur; / When noble and ignoble herd / Are
govern'd by a single word'—an era when, according to Goldsmith, 'every man who now called himself a connoisseur,
became such to all intents and purposes'.[9] It was at this
moment in history that the ironically entitled *Connoisseur* appeared.

Besides being a topical title, and one that fitted well with
Thornton's pro-Hogarthian leanings, the name of the essay
series also served as an allusion to the contemporary work on
which *The Connoisseur* was modelled: Edward Moore's *The
World*. That Colman and Thornton were seeking both to
emulate and to rival this paper (which had run weekly since
4 February 1753) becomes evident early in *The Connoisseur*. In
essay No. 1 Mr Town declares, 'Wherever the WORLD is, I
am' (5), and a little later he writes tauntingly of 'Mr. Fitz-
Adam' (Town's counterpart on *The World*): 'When he gave his
paper the title *The* WORLD, I suppose he meant to intimate
his design of describing that part of it, who are known to
account all other persons No Body, and therefore emphatically
call'd *The* WORLD. If this was to be pictured out in the head-
piece, a lady at her toilette, a party at whist, or the jovial
members of the *Dilettanti* tapping the world for champagne, had
been the most natural and obvious hieroglyphics' (No. 8; 44).

The snobbery and dilettantism ascribed to *The World* in this light satire had a basis in fact. Part of the original appeal of the paper had been the rank and position of some of its contributors. Horace Walpole, Chesterfield, and William Pulteney (the Earl of Bath)—all lent a hand. The first, of course, was a noted collector, at this time in the early stages of his lifelong quest of *objets d'art*; the latter two had been intimates in the circle of wits, tastemakers, and politicians—including Pope and Swift—that in early days had waged such brilliant literary and political warfare against Horace Walpole's father. All were conspicuous and tasteful peers, and their interests certainly rubbed off on the editor, Edward Moore. In its first forty essays (i.e. those written up to the time *The Connoisseur* commenced publication), *The World* devoted unprecedented space to the topics of art, architecture, furniture, gardening, and Taste—the by-word of the connoisseur.

As both an allusion to and an attack on *The World*, the title of *The Connoisseur* was a natural choice. But Colman and Thornton's decision to challenge *The World* may have sprung in part from even more personal motives. The Earl of Bath was George Colman's guardian, and between them there was constant friction. We catch the tone of their relationship in a letter from Bath to Colman of 20 January 1755 concerning arrangements for Colman's removal from Oxford to Lincoln's Inn:

You must not think of trifling away any of your time in vain and idle amusements, such as those can afford who are born to estates. Your subsistence must be got by toil and drudgery in the profession you have chosen; but then, let me tell you, you will enjoy every shilling so got with much greater satisfaction. . . . I tell you before hand, that I will have you closely watched, and be constantly informed how you employ your time. I must have no running to play-houses, or other places of public diversion, but your whole time must be given up to attend the courts of Westminster-hall during their sittings in a morning; and your evenings must be employed at home at your own chambers in assiduous application and study, till you have fitted yourself to make a figure at the bar.[10]

One can imagine the response of the witty and knowing Mr Town—who had just completed his first year as a popular essayist—to such injunctions as these. They are not atypical; in a

2. George Colman. Engraving after a portrait by Thomas Gainsborough, *c*.1770

letter written in December 1753, Bath had planned Colman's Christmas holiday: 'You shall stay with me in my house, for about three weeks, but not to be at your mamma's, where you have opportunities of strolling idly about the town, wherever your inclination may lead you; not that you shall be unreasonably confined at home, but have liberty now and then to visit your favourite play-houses, as well as your friends and acquaintances.'[11] Given these circumstances, it is hardly surprising that Colman developed a rebellious attitude toward Bath. For Colman *The Connoisseur* may have been a way of rivalling an overbearing father figure who wrote for *The World*.

Despite their rivalry, *The Connoisseur* and *The World* are very similar in tone and subject matter. Both deal in a bantering style with the exterior features and foibles of society—not with deep moral questions nor, for that matter, with deep questions of any kind. The great value of this kind of essay series has always been its ability to capture the historical moment: the current jargon, the topical symbols, the passing fads. *The World* and *The Connoisseur* both perform this task admirably. But their profundity —and value as 'literature'—is another question. Samuel Johnson said that both 'wanted matter'. But we must remember Boswell's qualification: 'no doubt it [*The Connoisseur*] has not the deep thinking of Johnson's writings. But surely it has just views on the surface of life, and a very sprightly manner.'[12]

II

This is not the place to undertake a complete descriptive and analytical account of *The Connoisseur*. Many of its essays, however, provide a valuable context for understanding the Nonsense Club's future literary, dramatic, and political activities. I have attempted under the following headings to distil some of its 'sprightly manner' and to summarize those subjects and techniques that anticipate the Nonsense Club's later work.

Taste and Society

As Mr Town is quick to explain in essay No. 2, *The Connoisseur* does not live up to the promise of its title:

I have already received letters from several *Virtuosi*, expressing their astonishment and concern at my disappointing the warm hopes they had conceived of my undertaking from the title of my paper. They tell me, that by deserting the paths of *Virtu* I at once neglect the public interest and my own; that by supporting the character of a CON-NOISSEUR in its usual sense, I might have obtained considerable salaries from the principal Auction-rooms, Toy-shops, and Repositories, and might besides very plausibly have recommended myself as the properest person in the world to be keeper of Sir *Hans Sloane's Museum*. (7)

The 'usual sense' Mr Town refers to is, of course, the tainted one, incorporating all the unfortunate connotations of 'vir-tuoso'. In his first essay, he discards this sense in favour of a broader definition (rather loosely translated from Horace):

> Who better knows to build, and who to dance,
> Or this from Italy, or that from France,
> Our Connoisseur will ne'er pretend to scan,
> But point the follies of mankind to man. (6)

But despite this disclaimer, Mr Town is careful to reassure the connoisseurs in his audience that he 'cannot be insensible of the importance of this capital business of TASTE', and to in-clude, as his own, a long list of interests typical of the virtuoso. He praises the 'discovery of a new *Zoophyte*, or species of the *Polype*'; he assures us that he has 'climb'd Mount *Vesuvio* in the midst of its eruptions, and dug some time underground in the ruins of *Herculaneum*'; he expresses his desire to be elected to the Royal Society and the Society of Antiquarians. But along with this fooling, Mr Town also alludes to two recent events in the English art world that would immediately have alerted the contemporary reader to the authors' true aesthetic prejudices. Mr Town, as a connoisseur, is supposedly saying these things seriously, but the fatuous overstatement of his prose clearly reveals Colman and Thornton's anti-connoisseur position:

Of what consequence would it be to point out the distinctions of Originals from Copies so precisely, that the paultry scratchings of a Modern may never hereafter be palmed on a *Connoisseur* for the labours of a *Rembrandt*! I should command applause from adorers of Antiquity, were I to demonstrate, that Merit never existed but in the Schools of the Old Painters, never flourished but in the warm climate of *Italy*; and how should I rise in the esteem of my countrymen, by chastising the arrogance of an *Englishman* in presuming to determine the *Analysis of Beauty*! (8)

The first of these events—the passing off of a spurious 'Rembrandt' print—alludes to a victory for the anti-connoisseur forces that occurred in the spring of 1751. The painter and amateur scientist Benjamin Wilson, in collusion with Hogarth, had executed a 'Rembrandt' etching and succeeded in foisting it upon Thomas Hudson, a former student of Jonathan Richardson's and a well-known painter and connoisseur. Hudson's outspoken pride in his connoisseurship made the prank doubly effective; and when he failed to own his mistake, Wilson went public, advertising the print for general sale.[13] For the anti-connoisseurs this event represented proof positive that English artists could equal, or even surpass, the Old Masters; and, at the same time, it offered a stinging rebuttal to the supposed 'science' of a connoisseur. The second allusion is to an even more recent event, the publication of Hogarth's *Analysis of Beauty* (1753). Hogarth was the acknowledged leader of the anti-connoisseur forces; and the comments on Italy immediately preceding the allusion to the *Analysis* summarize, in only slightly exaggerated form, his view of the connoisseurs' doctrines. In both cases, Colman and Thornton come down strongly on the side of the anti-connoisseurs, while Mr Town continues blithely down the 'paths of *Virtu*'.

With a beginning such as this, one might imagine that the rest of Mr Town's pronouncements on connoisseurship would run in a similarly mock-sympathetic vein. But this is not the case. Part of the attractiveness of the Town persona is his ability to work both sides of a question—sometimes serving as a satiric target, sometimes as a serious spokesman.[14] In essay No. 18, for instance, Mr Town (writing 'as a Connoisseur') reflects 'on the known dishonesty of my learned brethren'. Using the neat conceit of a connoisseur who is charged with coining only to be acquitted because 'there was no law which made it high-treason to counterfeit the image of a *Tiberius*', Mr Town points out the intrinsic worthlessness of the objects coveted by the connoisseurs and then uses this idea to begin a discussion of the dishonesty engendered by a constant dealing in objects and materials devoid of usefulness or moral value. To exemplify the lack of virtue that characterizes the connoisseurs, Mr Town lists a long series of 'crimes' perpetrated by collectors, ranging from purposely 'losing' borrowed books and then offering to buy the spoiled set to switching religions in order to pilfer from monasteries. He conjectures that 'many of the maimed statues at Rome perhaps owe their present ruinous condition to the depredations made on them by *Virtuosos*' and that 'the head of *Henry* the Fifth, in *Westminster Abbey* was in all probability stolen by a *Connoisseur*' (106–7). 'While I was at *Rome*', he writes, 'a young physician of our party, who was eaten up with Virtu, made a serious proposal to us of breaking into St. *Peter's* by night, and taking away the famous painting over the altarpiece. As I had not quite taste enough to come into his scheme, I could not help objecting to him that it was a robbery' (108).

This notion of 'Taste' as both a spur to and an ideological camouflage for material acquisitiveness is not merely a burlesque exaggeration, but an indication of the diverse and contradictory connotations that by mid-century had grown up around the word. As Raymond Williams has noted, in the late seventeenth and early eighteenth centuries, the original physical denotation of 'taste' had become increasingly complicated by its expansion (signified by capitalization) to include such concepts as discrimination, manners, and aesthetic convention: 'the strong and active sense of *taste* had been replaced by the weak because habitual attributes of *Taste*'.[15] But 'replaced' is the wrong word. For at mid-century, active/physical taste and aesthetic/moral Taste were part of a continuing debate; one that forms a central preoccupation of *The Connoisseur*.

As a critical concept, Taste had first gained general currency through the efforts of Shaftesbury, Richardson, Hutcheson, and others to improve spontaneous susceptibility to the arts.[16] J. G. Cooper, writing in 1755, provided a typical definition: 'The effect of a *good* TASTE is that instantaneous Glow of Pleasure which thrills thro' our whole Frame, and seizes upon the Applause of the Heart, before the intellectual Power, Reason, can descend from the Throne of the mind to ratify its Approbation.'[17] However, most theorists admitted that training was necessary to the development of Taste; and thus what began as an advocacy of a more spontaneous response to aesthetic and moral stimuli almost immediately began to be transformed into an incipient code of cultural snobbery: one had to cultivate one's Taste in order to qualify as a connoisseur, a critic, or even a respectable member of society. At the same time, as the critical concept of Taste was defined and redefined, at a less sophisticated level the term and its ideological baggage underwent a process of popular dissemination not unlike the bastardization of Freudian terminology in our own day. This development had the effect of spawning a popular critical sub-vocabulary linking art with food, and both with the notion of material consumption. At the popular level, 'Taste' met 'taste' in its vulgar material form—a form typified by the elaborate food fetishes of the poor, the symbolic associations of various kinds of food, and, at mid-century, by the literal refinement (towards whiteness in bread for example) of foodstuffs and other consumer items. Louise Lippincott remarks that Richardson felt the promulgation of the notion of Taste 'a necessary precondition for raising English manufactures to competitive levels with continental luxury goods'.[18] In other words, Taste was not, as some critics assume, a purely aesthetic or moral proposition. It was an ideology of nascent consumerism evolving out of the conjunction of aesthetic theory and material desire.

By mid-century a network of allusions had developed around Taste which, in popular usage, linked aesthetic, culinary, and even political ideas. Both as song and as food (one thinks of Hogarth's famous painting), 'The Roast Beef of Old England' served as a rallying symbol against not only foreign food, but foreign fashions, foreign soldiers, foreign governments, and foreign manners. Similarly, exotic dishes were equated with exotic architecture, dress, and, by extension, un-English behaviour.[19] The number of publications dealing with aesthetic Taste (in both serious and satiric form) greatly increased. In 1753, John Armstrong published *Taste: An Epistle to a Young Critic*; in 1755, J. G. Cooper wrote his *Letters Concerning Taste*. In 1752 Samuel Foote satirized the burgeoning art market in an afterpiece entitled (what else?) *Taste*, and Fielding's famous comparison of *Tom Jones* and a public ordinary dates from 1749. I have neglected Burke, Hume, and many others, but my point I hope is clear: at mid-century, Taste was a concept of impressive diversity and power.

In *The Connoisseur*, the various manifestations of Taste receive the full satiric treatment. In a manner of speaking, the entire *Connoisseur* essay series acts as a kind of pun upon the word Taste:

> TASTE is at present the darling idol of the polite world, and the world of letters; and, indeed, seems to be considered as the quintessence of almost all the arts and sciences. The fine ladies and gentlemen dress with Taste; the architects, whether *Gothic* or *Chinese*, build with Taste; the painters paint with Taste; the poets write with Taste; the critics read with Taste; and, in short, fiddlers, players, singers, dancers, and mechanics themselves, are all sons and daughters of Taste.
>
> (No. 12; 721)

Of particular interest here is the purported extension of Taste to the underclasses—to the 'mechanics themselves'. As Neil McKendrick has recently demonstrated, the ubiquitous eighteenth-century complaint that fashion and Taste had descended 'among the lowest ranks of society' was not merely indignant exaggeration.[20] The 1750s and 1760s saw a substantial quickening of the English economy and population growth after a period of slowing down, if not stagnation, during the Walpole era: consumer demand, available goods, disposable income—all were up.[21] The previous era of expansion, which had ended in the late 1710s, had spawned the prototypical social essay series *The Tatler* and *The Spectator*. It is certainly possible that the much-remarked-upon resurgence of the essay series in the 1750s (*The Rambler, Adventurer, World, Connoisseur, Bee, Idler*, etc.) had its stimulus in the resurgence of prosperity and population during this period.

It was during this era, as J. H. Plumb remarks, that realizing 'there was a market for culture, men of business began quite deliberately to exploit it, expand it, and to pursue innovation and sophistication in order to reap the profits that were there'.[22] Luxuries became more available and consumer goods more attractively packaged. This 'birth of a consumer soceity', as it has been called, was manifested in increasingly sophisticated advertising techniques, in the creation of artificial desires, in the elaborate window displays so often noted by foreigners (an invitation to 'impulse buying'); in short, in the embryonic formation of many of those techniques we associate with the manipulation of desire in modern capitalist society.[23]

As McKendrick writes, 'social emulation made men pursue "luxuries" where they had previously bought "decencies", and "decencies" where they had previously bought only "necessities".'[24] And, as Plumb adds, 'Every aspect of leisure . . . [was] aided in its development by print'.[25] It was in this atmosphere of burgeoning consumption that Taste became the vogue: a code word for knowing how and what to consume, and for judging how and what one's neighbour consumed.

But what to the progressive might seem 'leisure' or 'abundance' was to many conservative moralists the ancient vice of 'luxury' in a new and particularly threatening form. By the mid-1750s, the spread of 'luxury', coupled with a series of military and political débâcles, had led to what many critics saw as a slackening of English sinew, and to the dreaded possibility that, to use a metaphor current at the time, the Roast Beef of Old England would soon be replaced forever by sickly French ragouts. John Sekora has written that 'from about 1750 to 1763 . . . previous arguments against luxury flowed together and raised the tide of condemnation to its highest crest in English history'.[26] Dozens of works deploring luxury (particularly in the middling and lower classes) appeared in the 1750s, the most renowned perhaps being John Brown's searing *Estimate of the Manners and Principles of the Times* (1757). If abundance and discrimination formed the positive pole of Taste, luxury and conspicuous consumption—spurred on by advertisement and fostering social insubordination—represented to many writers its darker potential.[27]

The cornucopia of material goods and cultural sophistication and the threatening growth of luxury and insubordination form the antitheses between which Mr Town moves in a continual state of attraction and repulsion. Thornton and Colman's patrician education would naturally have predisposed them to disapprove of the pretensions of the vulgar and to fear the social instability it implied. But as men making their way 'by toil and drudgery' (the words are Bath's to Colman) in their professions and deeply implicated in the commercial press, theirs was a practical fascination and, indeed, self-interest in the transformation of English culture. These pressures are not easily reconcilable, and in *The Connoisseur* no reconciliation is attempted. Instead we find an essay series that lightly satirizes luxury while describing its manifestations in particular, vivid terms. The taste in Kevanhuller hats, royal washballs, pompous middle-class funerals, proliferating pleasure gardens, newspaper advertisements, and various other manifestations of middling culture form the predominant subject matter of *The Connoisseur*. With its great attention to detail and its focus on social levels ranging from quality to lower tradesman, *The Connoisseur* goes to the heart of the paradoxes inherent in an 'improving' society.

In *The Connoisseur*'s treatment of the individual arts—particularly architecture and gardening—we get our clearest picture of the effects of the cultural ferment at mid-century. In the field of architecture, the spread of the Chinese and neo-Gothic styles (recently made accessible by the publication in 1752 of William and John Halfpenny's *Chinese and Gothic Architecture Properly Ornamented*) is predictably, though indulgently, satirized. Lloyd's 'The Cit's Country Box', for example, chronicles the efforts of a wealthy tradesman to fit up his 'box' according to the latest mode. The poem contains a vivid catalogue of the workers and alterations involved in such a project—a pastiche that reflects as much on the tastemakers and their agents as on the cit who is influenced by them:

> Now bricklayers, carpenters, and joiners,
> With *Chinese* artists and designers,
> Produce their schemes of alteration,
> To work this wondrous reformation.
> The useful dome, which secret stood
> Embosom'd in the yew-tree's wood,
> The trav'ler with amazement sees
> Chang'd to a Temple *tout Chinese*,
> With many a bell and tawdry rag on,
> And crested with a sprawling dragon.
> A wooden arch is bent astride
> A ditch of water four foot wide,
> With angles, curves, and zigzag lines,
> From *Halfpenny's* exact designs.
> In front a level lawn is seen,
> Without a shrub upon the green;
> Where Taste would want its first great law,
> But for the sculking sly *Ha-Ha*;
> By whose miraculous assistance
> You gain a prospect two fields distance.

(No. 135; 815–16)

Lloyd's emphasis on fashion and conspicuous consumption is echoed in *Connoisseur* No. 33, the Earl of Cork's hypothetical summary of the 'plebian's' aspirations in housing:

We read . . . of country seats, belonging to *Pliny, Hortensius Lucullus,* and other *Romans.* They were patricians of great rank and fortune: there can therefore be no doubt of the excellence of their *Villas.* But who has ever read of a *Chinese*-bridge belonging to a *roman* pastry-cook? or could any of their shoemakers or taylors boast a *Villa* with his tin cascades, paper statues, and *Gothic* root-houses! Upon the above principles we may expect, that posterity will perhaps see a cheese-monger's *Apiarium* at *Brentford,* a poulterer's *Theriotrophium* at *Chiswick,* and a *Ornithon* in a fishmonger's garden at *Putney.*

(No. 33; 197–8)

Nor were the clergy immune to Taste. Cowper writes of a country vicar 'indulging his genius for improvements, by inclosing his gooseberry bushes with a *Chinese* rail, and converting half an acre of his glebe-land into a bowling green' (No. 134; 806). And strict followers of Burlington are slightingly referred to as 'the Connoisseurs in Architecture, who build ruins after *Vitruvius,* and necessaries according to *Palladio*' (No. 120; 725). References similar to this one crop up throughout the essay series and, of course, are nothing new: Pope had satirized the indiscriminate imitation of Burlingtonian models twenty years earlier. But the possibility of such architectural pretensions descending to the underclasses *is* new, and marks not only the spread of commercialized culture at mid-century but its implications for the future. For however critical in intention (and, as I have suggested, Colman and Thornton are characteristically ambiguous), the fictions of *The Connoisseur's* satire posit a society in which the subordinate classes participate fully in the ethos of mass consumption, joining the aristocrats and *haute bourgeoisie* in the race for goods and services.

In the history of Taste, then, *The Connoisseur,* while breaking no new theoretical ground, does give a panoramic view of the day-to-day significance and popular usage of the term in the era of its greatest vogue. Robert Lloyd summarized the catchwords of the day as 'Genius, Fancy, Judgement, Gout, / Whim, Caprice, Je-ne-scai quoi, Virtu: / Which appellations all describe / TASTE, and the modern *tasteful* tribe' (No. 135; 815).

But jostling alongside this newly-popularized abstraction was the original notion of taste as material bodily experience: one enacted daily in the prodigious and patriotic consumption of roast beef (by those who could afford it) and in the symbolic equation of styles of eating and styles of life (e.g. *The Connoisseur* No. 87). At the Sublime Society of Beefsteaks (to which Thornton, Colman, and Churchill would all eventually belong), the metaphor of political 'taste' was acted out every Saturday, when the members assembled would 'never suffer any dish except beef-steaks to appear'. And one 'T. Savoury' wrote to *The Connoisseur* No. 19, 'When I would form a just opinion of any man's temper and inclination, I always enquire, where does he dine?' These more traditional forms of food symbolism —what might be called the 'semiotics of eating'—were particularly salient in mid-century political disputes, and could function in primitive, ritualistic, and sometimes violent ways.

Perhaps the most detailed exploration of food as a political sign system occurs in *The Connoisseur* No. 13, an essay in which 'Village' (Colman) gives an account of the famous Oxford election of April 1754. Besides the conventional hurly-burly, the Oxford election was given a special violence by the lingering suspicions generated by the fight over the Jewish Naturalization Act of 1753.[28] This relatively innocuous piece of legislation had been painted by groups in opposition—city merchants, country Tories, and anti-Pelhamite Whigs—as the ultimate subversion of English citizenship and English blood. Various subcultural practices—circumcision and usury, for example—had been employed as propaganda weapons against the English Jews, but a central element in the attacks, and one which lingered into the Oxford contest, was the contrast between Jewish and English eating habits:

The town I have been speaking of, is divided into two parties, who are distinguish'd by the appellation of *Christians* and *Jews*. The Jews, it seems, are those, who are in the interest of a nobleman who gave his vote for passing the *Jew-bill*, and are held in abomination by the *Christians*. . . . This truly *Christian* spirit is nowhere more manifest than at their public feasts. I was at one of their dinners, where I found a great variety of pig-meat was provided. The table was covered from one end to the other with hams, legs of pork, spare-ribs, griskins, haslets, feet and ears, brawn, and the like: in the middle there smoaked a large barbicued hog, which was soon devour'd to the bone; so desirous was everyone to prove his *Christianity* by the quantity he could swallow of that Anti-judaic food.

(74–7)

None of these particulars is exaggerated. Feasts of pork were held by anti-Jew bill politicians, 'The Roast Beef of Old England' was satirically altered to 'The Roast Pork of Old England', and Whigs supporting the bill were branded 'Jews'.[29]

In his rendition of the 'Jew Bill' election, Village offers a cogent insight into the semiotics of the popular culture. At Oxford, the willingness to eat pork identifies the consumer not only as a 'Christian' (a religious distinction) but as 'anti-Jew Bill' (a political distinction) and, by implication, 'anti-Semitic' (a racial distinction). A social ritual is employed to exclude symbolically from 'naturalization' (both in a political and social sense) a racial group whose cultural taboos prohibit the eating of a certain kind of food. The consumption of pork becomes a kind of test meant to isolate a segment of the population whose enfranchisement (even in the most minimal sense) is thought to threaten the stability and purity of the English system. This notion of ostracism through food-association was neither new nor confined to Jews. Catholics (Christ's flesh), Frenchmen (ragouts and soup maigre), even, as we shall see, Scots (oats and thistle)—all felt the power of popular prejudice at this lowest level of taste.

Literature and the Stage

Robert Lloyd supplied *The Connoisseur* with its most serious, and paradoxical, attempt at literary criticism in a verse epistle 'To a Friend' inserted into the second edition of No. 125 to replace his earlier 'Ode on Friendship'. Anticipating the central tenet of the Nonsense Club's literary aesthetic, the preface to this poem contains a strong statement on the pernicious effect of modern 'correctness' on the poetic imagination:

We are now become such exact critics, that there are scarce any tolerable poets. . . . We get an early knowledge of what chaste writing is, and even school-boys are checked in the luxuriancy of their genius, and not suffered to run riot in their imaginations. I must own I cannot help looking on it as a bad omen in poetry, that there is now-a-days scarce any such thing to be met with as fustian and bombast: for our authors, dreading the vice of incorrectness above all others, grow ridiculously precise and affected. In short, however paradoxical it may seem, we have now, in my opinion, too correct a taste. It is to no purpose for such prudent sober wooers, as our modern bards, to knock at the door of the Muses. They, as well as mortal ladies, love to be attacked briskly.[30]

Clearly, untutored genius—not formal perfection—is for Lloyd the soul of true poetry. Lloyd goes on to associate such rude genius with Chaucer and Spenser, and finds the 'material difference' between the past and present age of poetry to be 'that the writers in the first thought poetically; and in the last they only express themselves so'.

In the poem itself, Lloyd expands his attack against 'modern rules' and places 'genius' above all literary norms ('Rise what exalted flights it will, / True genius will be genius still'). Shakespeare (just then rising to the status of national literary deity under the enterprising guidance of David Garrick) is held up as the ideal of such undisciplined genius:

> Had Shakespeare crept by modern rules
> We'd lost his witches, fairies, fools.
> Instead of all that wild creation,
> He'd formed a regular plantation,
> Or garden trim and all inclosed,
> In nicest symmetry disposed,
> The hedges cut in proper order,
> Nor e'en a branch beyond its border.
> Now like a forest he appears,
> The growth of twice three hundred years;
> Where many a tree aspiring shrouds
> Its very summit in the clouds,
> While round its root still loves to twine
> The ivy and wild eglantine.[31]

Lloyd's garden versus wild metaphor denigrates the trim symmetry and 'proper order' that give the formal garden, the 'correct' couplet, and the classical drama their strength, because to him these formal restrictions threaten spontaneity and genius.

In his admiration for Chaucer, Spenser, and Shakespeare, Lloyd follows the rising fashion of the period; a period in which a new emphasis on imagination, with its attendants, untutored genius and inspired spontaneity, was giving birth to Young's *Conjectures on Original Composition*, Collins's odes, and Macpherson's treks through the Highlands in search of Ossian. Yet Lloyd himself writes in bland jogtrot couplets, with rather less than Shakespearian luxuriancy. In effect, he is caught between his style and his sentiment; a position not unusual for himself or his friends in the Nonsense Club.

Correctness and imitation also form the major targets of Mr Town's infrequent pronouncements on the state of English poetry. In perhaps his most important statement on the matter, Mr Town reiterates Lloyd's views on the necessity of *thinking* poetically, rather than merely writing in a 'poetical' manner: 'Poetry should seem at least to flow from the imagination, and not be squeezed from the droppings of the brain. If we endeavour to acquire a full idea of what we mean to describe, we should then of course express ourselves with force, elegance, and perspecuity; and this native strength of expression would have more true energy than elaborate phrases, and a quaint and studied combination of words and letters' (No. 83; 502). The poetic process Mr Town describes is the process of 'genius': unimpeded by elaborate formal artifice, the 'native strength' of the genius's language—taking its force from his fully realized conception of his subject—generates more 'true energy' than is possible in any acquired poetic idiom, where poetic force is dissipated by too great a concern with 'a quaint and studied combination of words and letters'. If this statement is not as serious as Wordsworth's on the 'real language of men', it nevertheless lays the critical foundation for much of the Nonsense Club's poetry. Churchill's work especially is characterized by its consistently high energy, insistent spontaneity, and reckless prosody.

'Genius', like Taste, was a word with many connotations—some serious, some not. In its most exalted usage, it could mean 'creative originality' or, more rarely, 'transcendent imagination'; in its most derogatory sense, something like 'superficial facility' or 'impertinent dilettantism'.[32] The view expressed most frequently in *The Connoisseur* is that while 'true

genius' is a gift of God—and absolutely necessary for the production of anything great in literature, art, or science—its pos-
sessor must devote 'close and unwearied application to his
respective business or profession' in order to fulfil his potential
(No. 90; 542). Yet even as Thornton and Colman profess this
view, their compulsive irreverence and scepticism cause them
to trot out, as their prime examples of genius misapplied, *themselves*: 'The Inns of Court are full of these men of parts, who
cannot bear the drudgery of turning over dry Cases and Reports;
but, though they appear ever so eloquent in taverns and coffee-
houses, not the nearest relation will trust them with a Brief:
and many a sprightly physician has walked on foot all his life,
with no more knowledge of his profession than what lies in his
perriwig' (542–3). This is a virtual portrait of Colman and
Thornton in 1755: one a half-hearted law student who aspired
to literary fame, the other a bachelor of physic who did not care
to practise.[33] And Lloyd, whose downward slide was certainly
assisted by too great a reliance on superficial facility, in this
same number illustrates the misfortunes of erring genius in a
redaction of Aesop's *The Hare and the Tortoise*; a piece which,
incidentally, holds his poetry's single claim to schoolroom
recognition. The closing line—'slow and steady wins the race'
—has since become the proverbial phrasing of Aesop's moral.

In the introduction to this tale Lloyd moves uneasily from
one pole of 'genius' to the other. He begins by equating genius
with mental prowess—'Whate'er he tries with due intention, /
Rarely escapes his apprehension; / Surmounting ev'ry opposition, / You'd swear he learned by intuition'—but is forced by
the circumstances of the fable to admit that without application
'Genius vainly tries', and finally to conclude (rather lamely)
that 'Application will prevail, / When braggart parts and
Genius fail' (otherwise the tortoise would not win). Lloyd's
uneasy vacillation here exemplifies, in a facetious but nevertheless significant way, the real conflict of values experienced by
all of the Nonsense Club members. All were quick, all hated
drudgery, but all were assailed by doubts as to the real value
and sustaining power of their genius. Viewed in this context,
the two conflicting denotations of the word 'genius'—'creative
originality' and 'superficial facility'—represent important
polarities in the lives and aesthetics of the Nonsense Club

members: the former marks their sustaining virtue, the latter their dissipating vice.

One especially interesting feature of Mr Town's 'genius' as an essayist is his remarkably historiographic view of the value of the topical essay and the newspaper. In No. 45, he discusses the historical importance of such ephemeral literature: 'The common intelligence in our public papers, with the long train of advertisements annexed to it is the best account of the present domestic state of *England*, that can possibly be compiled: nor do I know anything, which would give posterity so clear an idea of the taste and morals of the present age, as a bundle of our daily papers' (268). This emphasis on the value of the fleeting, the particular, and the commercial, is extended to the essay series itself. Mr Town looks 'upon the works of Mr *Jenour* in the *Daily Advertiser* as a kind of supplement to the intelligence of Mr TOWN'; and to help the researchers of posterity he includes at the end of the essay 'a few advertisements, which if they have not all actually been inserted in our papers, are at least of the same nature with those, that daily have a place there' (269). (Though these advertisements undergo a slight satiric exaggeration, they are very close to the real thing.) This interest in historical trivia further leads Town to wish that the ancients had invented the daily press: 'With what pleasure should we have perused an *Athenian* Advertiser, or a *Roman* Gazetteer! A curious critic or antiquarian would place them on the same shelf with the Classics, and would be highly pleased at discovering what days *Tully* went to his *Tusculum*, or *Pliny* to his magnificent *Villa*; who was the capital singer at the *Grecian* Opera, and in what characters *Roscius* appeared with most success' (268). While the irony in this passage is palpable, Thornton and Colman's real opinion, I suspect, may be closer to that of the 'curious critic': a strong attraction to the particulars not only of ancient but of modern life. Such a divided attitude is apparent in a later description of antiquarians who 'can distinguish a *Tiberius* from a *Trajan*, know the *Pantheon* from the *Ampitheatre*, and can explain the difference between the *praetexta* and the *tunica*: which (only supposing the present times to have elapsed some hundred years) is just as deep knowledge as if some future antiquarian should discover the difference between a *Carolus* and an *Anna*, or *St. Paul's* church and *Drury-lane* playhouse, or a

full-trimmed suit and a French frock' (No. 113; 680). Despite
the satiric intent, one can sense Colman and Thornton's real
fascination with historical particulars, and perhaps even a hope
that someday someone might be interested enough in the trivia
of 1755 to read about them in *The Connoisseur.*

In his opinion of contemporary drama, Mr Town reflects the
conventional view of the period: 'We are indebted to the present times for a judicious reformation of the stage in point of
acting: and . . . I could wish, that the same good consequences
had been produced with respect to our poets' (No. 34; 200).
With the advent of Garrick, his natural acting style and emphasis on tight ensemble performance, the English stage in the
1750s was graced with the brightest galaxy of players in its
history. Contemporary plays, however, failed to shine. Farces
and adaptations abounded, along with many older stock
pieces, but new drama languished due mainly to the expense
and risk of mounting untried productions. Both Drury Lane
and Covent Garden limited themselves to an average of less
than two new mainpieces per year.[34] Mr Town alludes to this
situation when he notes that most new comedies are 'in reality
nothing but overgrown Farces . . . what authors are now
pleased to call a Comedy of two Acts' (No. 6; 36). Such works
could be mounted as after-pieces and thus were far more marketable than five act main-pieces—a fact that had a sufficiently
dampening effect on contemporary playwrights. In a proposal
for a 'Literary Register Office' from a supposed correspondent
('J. Witsell'), we get a satiric view of the commercially degraded
state of the drama as Colman and Thornton saw it. 'For comic
pieces', Witsell writes, 'I shall employ a poet, who had long
worked for the drolls at *Bartholomew* and *Southwark* fairs, and
has printed a comedy as it was *half* acted at Drury-lane. . . .
Any old play of *Shakespeare* or *Ben Johnson* shall be pieced with
modern ones according to the present taste, or cut out in airs
and recitative for an *English Opera.* Rhymes for Pantomimes
may be had, to be set to the clack of a mill, the thinking of a tin
cascade, or the slaps of *Harlequin's* wooden sword' (No. 96;
580).

The satiric emphasis on drolls, pantomimes, and mechanical
contrivances represents a thumbnail sketch of the other side of
the theatre. Pantomimes had been extremely popular—and

much satirized—for the last thirty years, and they were becoming more elaborate each season.[35] With their spectacular props, exotic animals, and musical accompaniment, they combined in the theatre three of London's most popular attractions. The headquarters for pantomime was John Rich's Covent-Garden Theatre, and Mr Town doesn't miss his chance to get in a satiric swipe at it. In the midst of a dream vision, we find a metamorphosing hound who first 'cast his skin and became an OSTRICH; and presently after shed his feathers, and terrified us with shaggy figure of a BEAR. Then he was a LION, then a HORSE, then again a BABOON; and after many other amazing transformations leaped out an HARLEQUIN, and before they could take hold of him, skipped away to *Covent-Garden Theatre*' (No. 12; 71).

If Covent-Garden Theatre bears the brunt of the wit expended on pantomime, Garrick's staging and acting at Drury Lane receive most of the serious theatrical criticism. Mr Town devotes all of essay No. 34 to what he calls 'the juggle of the theatre': staging, acting, costume. In general terms he attacks the players for unnatural speech ('startings, roarings, and whinings') and movement ('various strange attitudes'), though at the same time admitting that the 'stage is considerably improved' over the strutting and bombast of the preceding age (201–2). In other words, Garrick's effect had been great, but not great enough. However, even the 'Modern Roscius' himself does not escape censure. Mr Town confronts him directly on the matter of costume: 'When the *Romeo* of *Drury Lane* comes to die at *Juliet's* monument we are surprized to see him enter in a suit of black. This I suppose is intended as a stroke of the pathetic: but not to dwell on the poverty of the artifice, it is in the place a manifest violation of the poet's meaning. Romeo is supposed to come post from Mantua—'get me post-horses, I will be hence tonight'—so that if our Roscius must be so very exact in dressing the character, he should appear at the tomb in riding frock and boots' (204).[36] Nit-picking as this criticism may seem, it is doubtless an exact reproduction of the kind of wit one would have found arising from the pit on any given night at Drury-Lane Theatre. More importantly, it represents the popular model for the extremely close observation of the players that would characterize Churchill's

Rosciad. The Rosciad is clearly far more than a catalogue of witty comments from the pit, but it has its critical roots there.

Point of View

The majority of the *Connoisseur* essays deal with the conventional vices and foibles of London society. Gaming, fashion, public gardens, the effeminacy of modern beaux, the forwardness of the ladies—all are treated in Mr Town's bantering, ironic style. But there are also moments when a particular subject provokes a highly visceral reaction from Mr Town, and an unexpected savagery gets mixed up with the usual light wit. Such a moment occurs in a passage on suicide, a subject that comes up a surprising number of times in *The Connoisseur*. Mr Town is discussing ways of dissuading would-be self-murderers:

> Every man in his sober senses must wish, that the most severe laws that could possibly be contrived were enacted against Suicide. This shocking bravado never did (and I am confident never will!) prevail among the more delicate and tender sex in our own nation: tho' history informs us, that the *Roman* ladies were once so infatuated as to throw off the softness of their nature, and commit violence on themselves, till the madness was curbed by exposing their naked bodies in the public streets. This, I think, would afford a hint for fixing the like marks of ignominy on our Male suicides, and I would have every lower wretch of this sort dragged at the cart's tail, and afterwards hung in chains at his own door, or have his quarters put up *in terrorem* in the most public places, as a rebel to his Maker. But that the suicide of quality might be treated with more respect, he should be indulged in having his wounded corpse and shattered brains lay (as it were) in state for some days; of which dreadful spectacle we may conceive the horror.

> (No. 50; 298)

The reason for this outburst I can only attribute to a real prevalence of suicide at mid-century, and perhaps to its special vogue among the very class of people with whom Thornton and Colman most often consorted: men of the town, gallants, wits, coffee-house critics.[37] Of course, Cowper's later suicide attempts, his admission in the *Epistle to Lloyd* of affliction by a motiveless despair, and Lloyd and Churchill's later compulsive self-destruction by drink and dissipation, only add to our sense that beneath the Nonsense Club's cultivated flippancy there lurked a threatening darkness. Throughout *The Connoisseur* one gets the feeling that while the writers lean heavily on old truths (e.g. the necessity of subordination, the validity of orthodox religion), their actual psychological response is closer to a kind of unwelcome scepticism; a scepticism that while fashionable is also frightening. They seem, beneath their flippancy, to be searching for a set of values they really *can* believe in—and not finding them.

It is clear that Colman, Thornton, and their contributors understood the conventions of the essay journal and the audience expectations it provoked. Yet their own attitude toward the genre's moral and critical dimensions often seems irreverent to the point of cynicism. Thus we find them not only overtly under-cutting Mr Town's status as a connoisseur and critic, but also secretly contaminating even serious essays by including 'insider' references that perhaps only they and their closest friends would recognize. The usual subjects are given a speciously con-ventional treatment that is in itself implicitly ironic, and the result of a kind of 'mock essay series' rather than an essay series in earnest. For example, we have found Colman delighting in the fact that Mr Town's attempts at reformation have allowed the ladies of the country to copy the vices of the town 'exactly' (No. 139; 837–8); or Thornton and Colman secretly using themselves, in an essay on genius, as examples of genius gone astray (No, 90; 542–3); or a satire on the trivial interests of antiquarians that betrays its authors' evident in-terest in historical trivia (No. 113; 680). In those essays where we expect seriousness we often find hidden irony; in those essays where we expect satire we often sense suppressed delight. Beneath the conventional text of *The Connoisseur*, then, there exists a subtext of indifference and confusion. The incli-nation of its writers to laugh secretly at principles they publicly espouse betrays an ethical dislocation of considerable import-ance: one that looks forward to the pervasive scepticism of Churchill's later critique of self and society.

III

Thornton and Colman's literary collaboration was very close, and has ever since stymied attempts to ascribe individual essays to one or the other.[38] As the authors explain in their final paper: 'We have not only joined in the work taken together, but almost every single paper is the joint product of both: and, as we have laboured equally in erecting the fabric, we cannot pretend, that any particular part is the sole workmanship of either. A hint has perhaps been started by one of us, improved by the other, and still farther heightened by a happy coalition of sentiment in both' (No. 140; 845).

There is, however, one clue to Colman and Thornton's authorial relationship. George Colman the younger recorded a conversation that took place in 1775 between his father and the former Oxford printer of *The Connoisseur* in which one particularly trying editorial meeting was rehashed. This conversation, like many over strong liquor (they were drinking what the innkeeper hopefully called 'supernaculum'), tended toward the aspersion of character—specifically Bonnell Thornton's. With alcohol no doubt stimulating the criticism, Thornton was called 'incorrigibly lazy' and accused of throwing 'very much more than a proportionate share of drudgery upon his literary colleague . . . that is, he was delinquent, after having promised to be punctual; and at almost the very last moment, his partner was left to supply his deficiency.' At this rather catty point, the story continues:

On one of these occasions the joint authors met, in hurry and irritation, to extricate themselves from the dilemma; my father enraged or sulky, Thornton muzzy with liquor: the essay to be published on the next morning: not a word of it written, nor even a subject thought on, and the press waiting: nothing to be done but to scribble helter skelter. 'Sit down, Colman,' said Thornton, 'by 'od! we must give the blockheads something.' My industrious sire, conscious of obligations to be fulfilled, sat down immediately, writing whatever came into his head, *currente calamo*. Thornton in the mean time walked up and down, taking huge pinches of snuff, seeming to ruminate, but not suggesting one word, or contributing one thought. When my father had thrown upon paper about half a moral Essay, Thornton, who was still pacing the room, with a glass of brandy and water in his hand, stuttered out, 'Write away, Colman! by 'od! you are a bold fellow! you can tell them that virtue is a fine thing'; and implying that my father wrote nothing but mere common-place, and instructed his readers in what every body knew before.[39]

While doubtless exaggerated by the passage of twenty years—and who knows how much 'supernaculum'—this vignette seems essentially accurate, and it certainly accounts for the palpably specious tone of many of *The Connoisseur*'s 'moral' essays. Thornton's jibes at Colman are to the point: he was less original, and as his son says, he was 'industrious . . . conscious of obligations to be fulfilled'. Certainly Colman was the chief editor and prime mover of *The Connoisseur*; his industry, conscientiousness, and ambition all marked him out for the job.[40] But we must remember that Thornton was the older, more experienced writer. He was also, to use modern jargon, an 'idea man'; one whose mind was extremely fertile, but whose ideas were very often only partially or fitfully implemented. Colman, on the other hand, was something of a 'rewrite man'. Throughout his career this is apparent: in his working up of *The Jealous Wife* from various sources, in his collaboration with Garrick over a period of years to produce *The Clandestine Marriage*, and in the numerous stage adaptations of older plays that were to mark his later career. Leigh Hunt described this 'want of originality, and at the same time this art of managing originals' as the defining characteristic of Colman the playwright.[41] Given this background, it seems reasonable to assume that while Thornton contributed a good deal to the content and spirit of *The Connoisseur*, the majority of essays probably reached their final form under Colman's hand.

The Connoisseur continued to appear each Thursday through 30 September 1756, running eventually to 140 numbers.[42] It was published by Robert Baldwin at the Rose in Paternoster Row and marked Colman and Thornton's first business connection with the publishing Baldwin brothers—Robert, Richard, and Henry—with whom they would later participate in other literary projects. One significant spin-off of *The Connoisseur* was Baldwin's publication in 1755 of the two-volume compilation, *Poems by Eminent Ladies*, edited by Colman and Thornton. Including works by Aphra Behn, Lady Mary Wortley Montagu, and other female authors from hacks to heiresses, the volumes were puffed as 'perhaps the most solid compliment that can possibly be paid to the Fair Sex. They are standing proof that great abilities are not confined to the men.'[43]

Three other members of the Nonsense Club made substantial contributions to *The Connoisseur*. William Cowper is usually assigned five essays: Nos. 111, 115, 119, 134, and 138. In his correspondence, Cowper describes No. 119 as his; he is said to have pointed out to William Hayley Nos. 119, 134, and 138; and Alexander Chalmers tells us that he heard from Samuel Rose that Nos. 119, 134, and 138 were Cowper's.[44] However, in their final number, Colman and Thornton ascribed to Cowper (whom they list as 'a friend, a gentleman of the *Temple*') only Nos. 111, 115, and 119 (No. 140; 843). Although all five essays are probably Cowper's, it should be recognized that these attributions are not fact. Robert Lloyd contributed 'the Song in No. 72, and the Verses in No. 67, 90, 125, and 135' (843)—a substantial body of poetry for an essay series which Colman wanted to carry 'as little poetry as possible'.[45] And James Bensley—an Old Westminster, student of the law, and relatively non-literary member of the Nonsense Club (see below)—is credited with sketches of Nos. 75, 78, 87, and 104.

Of the other contributors by far the most important was John Boyle, Earl of Cork and Orrery, who was described as *The Connoisseur*'s 'earliest and most frequent correspondent' (842). Early in life, John Boyle had been an intimate of the aging Swift and Pope, and his memoirs of Swift have made his name generally a despised one among modern scholars.[46] This is unfortunate because Boyle is a fluid and entertaining essayist. Some of the best *Connoisseur* essays on the popular manifestations of Taste are his. Of course, his background—friend to Pope, kin to Burlington, member of the aristocracy—would have predisposed him to such topics.[47] He had written fleetingly for *The World* but clearly found himself at home in *The Connoisseur*. To him (under a pseudonym of course), Colman and Thornton found themselves 'indebted for most part of No. 14 and 17; for the letter, signed *Goliah English*, in No. 19; for a great part of No. 33 and 40; and for the letters, signed *Reginald Fitzworm, Michael Krawbridge, Moses Orthodox, T. Vainall*, in No. 102, 107, 113, and 129' (842).

In the final number of *The Connoisseur* Colman and Thornton, besides listing contributors and disclaiming individual authorship, executed a composite portrait of themselves as Mr Town:

Mr. Town is a *fair*, black, middlesized, *very short* man. He wears his own hair and a perriwig. He is about thirty years of age, and *not more than four and twenty*. He is a *Student of Law* and a Batchelor of Physic. He was bred at the University of *Oxford*; where having taken no less than three degrees, he looks down on many learned Professors, [as] his inferiors: yet having been there but little longer than to take the first degree of Batchelor of Arts, it has more than once happened, that the CENSOR GENERAL of all *England* has been reprimanded by the Censor of his College, for neglecting to furnish the usual essay, or (in the collegiate phrase) the Theme of the week.

(846; emphasis added)

The italicized characteristics in the first three sentences, and the latter summary of education, are Colman's. He was in fact *very* short, even by eighteenth-century standards—under five feet tall. Thornton's idiosyncrasy was not his height, but what was on top of his head—namely, his own hair. This rather odd couple, in the final lines of the essay series, make their exit together 'like the two Kings of *Brentford* smelling at one nosegay'. But the last word on *The Connoisseur* must be left to Robert Lloyd. On the day of the paper's demise, Lloyd wrote a poetic epistle to Colman in which he recorded his happiness as a contributor, offered some words on the difficulty of 'easy' poetry, alluded to recent military disasters and *The Connoisseur*'s going under in the same breath ('O England, how I mourn thy fate! / For sure thy losses now are great; / Two such what Briton can endure, / Minorca and the Connoisseur'), and closed with an epitaph in which we are not surprised to find that Mr Town expired in just the expected manner:

> Know, reader, that on Thursday died
> The CONNOISSEUR, a suicide!
> Yet think not that his soul is fled,
> Nor rank him 'mongst the vulgar dead.
> Howe'er defunct you set him down,
> He's only *going out* of *Town*.[48]

3   *The Theatre of Theatre*

I

About the time of *The Connoisseur*'s demise, George Colman's long association with the London stage began. Colman had been a devotee of the theatre from an early age, acting in two Latin plays while at Westminster and, along with his Nonsense Club friends, frequenting the Covent Garden district during his university days. With his move to Lincoln's Inn in 1755, his contact with the theatre became even more regular. Colman's gradual slide away from law was given a crucial push in May 1757 with the publication of his ironically entitled *Letter of Abuse to D—— G——K, Esq.* This pamphlet—a bald eulogy cloaked in the 'advice to the manager' genre—earned Colman admission to the Garrick inner circle and effectively began his career as a man of the theatre.[1]

It was during this period (1757) that Colman, as if sensing a shift in his destiny, wrote the autobiographical poem, 'The Law Student'. 'Now Christ-Church left, and fixt at Lincoln's Inn', it begins, and it traces the literary law student's progress from the Inns of Court to the theatre:

> By law let others toil to gain renown!
> Florio's a gentleman, a man o' the' town.
> He nor courts, clients, or the law regarding,
> Hurries from Nando's down to Covent garden:
> Yet he's a scholar;—mark him in the pit
> With critick catcall sound the stops of wit!
> Supreme at George's he harangues the throng,
> Censor of stile from tragedy to song:
> Him ev'ry witling views with secret awe,
> Deep in the Drama, shallow in the Law.[2]

The law student, of course, is Colman. In the ambiguous, self-satirizing style we have already seen in *The Connoisseur*, he charts his course as 'Florio'—'brisk heir to forty thousand pound'—from the paths of 'interest' to those of Covent Garden. In a particularly intimate passage (suppressed in the first edition), Colman uses his own name as he records the advice of Lord and Lady Bath:

> Well I remember oft My Lady said,
> (My Lady, whom sure maxims ever led)
> Turn Parson, Colman! That's the way to thrive;
> Your Parsons are the happiest men alive. . . .
> No, cries My Lord: I know thee better far;
> And cry stick close; close, Coley, to the Bar!
> If Genius warm thee, where can Genius call
> For nobler action than in yonder Hall?

But Colman's 'Genius', like that of the other Nonsense Club members, led him another way: he disobeyed his guardians and forsook his 'interest' for the more pleasing paths of literature:

> There are, whom Love of Poetry has smit,
> Who, blind to interest, arrant dupes to wit . . .
> Wedded to verse, embrac'd the Muse for Life,
> And ta'en, like modern bucks, their whores to wife.

The last couplet was to prove prophetic in two ways: Colman not only devoted his life to the theatre, he also married his mistress.

Colman seems quickly to have acquired some influence with Garrick, for on 23 February 1758 we find Arthur Murphy recommending his new play, *The Upholsterer*, to the 'English Roscius' by saying: 'Jack Bourke, Fitzpatrick, Colman, &c. are of the opinion it is superior to what I have done before in this way, and they assure me if Mr. Garrick cordially recommends it to the company, that they think it cannot fail.'[3] Later in the same year, Murphy—already a successful playwright—applied directly through Colman to Garrick, and Colman replied that Garrick had 'offered a meeting' to discuss Murphy's next play, *The Orphan of China*.[4] Thus, as early as 1758, Colman seems to have secured a special access to Garrick denied even experienced playwrights like Murphy. Garrick always had an eye for talent, and he seems to have grasped the importance of securing so facile a writer and adapter as Colman for an ally. By the summer of 1760 he had him at work on two dramatic pieces: a short afterpiece and a three act comedy.

The fruit of Colman's labour appeared on 5 December 1760 with the production of *Polly Honeycombe, A Dramatic Novel in One Act* at Drury-Lane Theatre. This afterpiece is a skilful amalgamation of topicality, literary criticism, and brisk characterization. The heroine is addicted to novels, and feels her life is meant to add spectacular new chapters to the genre. Colman flawlessly constructs the opening scene, in which he plays the syrupy style of Polly's reading off against her own fresh, gullible responses:

Polly, with a book in her hand.

WELL said, Sir George! Oh, the dear man! But so—'With these words the enraptur'd baronet [*reading.*] concluded his declaration of love.'—So!—'But what heart can imagine, [*reading.*] what tongue describe, or what pen delineate, the amiable confusion of Emilia?'—Well! now for it!—'Reader, if thou art a courtly reader, thou hast seen, at polite tables, iced cream crimsoned with rasberries; or, if thou art an uncourtly reader, thou hast seen the rosy-finger'd morning dawning in the golden East';—Dawning in the golden East! Very pretty.—'Thou hast seen, perhaps [*reading.*] the artificial vermilion on the cheeks of Cleora, or the vermilion of nature on those of Sylvia; thou hast seen—in a word, the lovely face of Emilia was overspread with blushes.'—This is a most beautiful passage, I protest! Well, a Novel for my money![5]

This scene introduces the central theme of the play, Polly's propensity to model her life after the heroines of her favourite novels. Thus, when she plans her elopement with 'Mr Scribble': 'It was just so with Betty Thompson, and Sally Wilkens, and Clarinda and Leonora in the History of Dick Careless, and Julia in the Adventures of Tom Ramble, and fifty others. Did they not all elope? and so will I too.' More prominent novels figure in her dismissal of her unwanted suitor, 'Mr Ledger': 'I hate you; you are as deceitful as Blifil, as rude as the Harlowes, and as ugly as Dr Slop'.[6] The plot of the play is superficial: Polly refuses her businessman suitor, vexes her father, tries to elope with Scribble, and persists in her romantic stubbornness even after it is revealed that Scribble is a lowly attorney's clerk. The play ends unresolved, with an exasperated Mr Honeycombe exclaiming: 'A man might as well turn his daughter loose in Covent-Garden, as trust the cultivation of her mind to A CIRCULATING LIBRARY!'

Although *The Connoisseur* had laughed at such comedies as being 'in reality nothing but overgrown Farces' (No. 6; 36), Colman began his theatrical career with what is essentially an overgrown farce. Such 'short comedies' formed the staple new material on the mid-century stage. More ambitious in characterization than the farce, but free from the propriety of action and coherent endings expected of the conventional mainpiece, short comedy was a theatre manager's dream: an easily-staged hybrid that while retaining the moral tone favoured by certain elements of the audience nevertheless generated some of the wit and verve of Restoration comedy.[7] (A modern analogy might be the half-hour television situation comedy.) Of this breed of play, *Polly Honeycombe* represented a typical example: it ridiculed the excesses of sentimentalism and ended without a marriage. Colman was sufficiently conscious of this latter feature of the play to comment on it in his preface. His maiden aunt, he wrote, was offended by the ending because 'Polly, having manifested her affection for him, should, to be sure, have been married to Scribble; and the parents should have been thoroughly, though suddenly, appeased by the declared reformation of both.' But in answer to this objection, he told the story of a nobleman of Madrid, who, 'being present at the Spanish Comedy, fell asleep during the first act, and never woke again till the end of the play. Then rubbing his eyes, and observing his friends laughing at the hearty nap he had taken, he cried out, How now, Gentlemen? What! Is it OVER then? Are the actors all MARRIED?'[8]

Despite its worrisome ending, *Polly Honeycombe* became a substantial success. With a new actress, Jane Pope, playing the lead, it was performed fifteen times its first season. The play appeared anonymously and for several days passed as Garrick's (until he disclaimed authorship in some lines added to the prologue on 12 December).[9] So closely kept was the secret of the author's identity that Garrick, writing to Colman about the attendance on his benefit night (31 December), spoke of him in the third person: 'I have this moment took a peep at the house for the Author of *Polly Hon*. The Pit & Galleries are cramed—the Boxes full to ye last Rows, & Every thing as You & I could Wish for our Friend—I am most happy about it & could not help communicating it to one, I so much Love & Esteem.'[10] Colman had his reasons for keeping a low profile.

The Earl of Bath would not have approved—and even at the height of his theatrical intoxication, Colman tried to keep in his Lordship's good graces. In the months following *Polly Honeycombe*'s success, however, he seems to have decided that a brazen front was the most suitable armour, because his next and best play, *The Jealous Wife*, he dedicated to his overzealous uncle, the Earl.

In his dedication to *The Jealous Wife* Colman used all the ruses and rhetoric at his command to try to placate his uncle. In perhaps the most interesting section, he alluded to the Earl's own literary past in an appeal for his indulgence in the present: 'you have passed many a social evening with Steele and Addison; you have joined in the rich humour of Arbuthnot; you have read the comedies of Congreve (my brother-student in the law) in manuscript; you have corresponded with Pope and Swift; and Gay lived and wrote in your house. . . . Filled with this idea of your character, how can I bring myself to make a formal apology for the present undertaking?'[11] If Colman's sophistry did not do the trick, the success of his play seems to have done so; Bath's letters continued friendly, and in a flirtatious note to Mrs Elizabeth Montagu, he actually seemed to take a certain disguised pride in Colman's dedication: 'There is more easy natural witt in any two of your most careless lines than there is in all Colman's play, and as for his dedication, you may be sure the Rogue meant to abuse me for pretending to chide him for his neglect of Lord Cooke.'[12]

The Jealous Wife, which opened at Drury Lane on 12 February 1761, was a typical Colman production in that it was not solely his. Garrick had a considerable part in making it ready for the stage. 'I cannot cut ye Jeal W without y^r participation,' he wrote to Colman on 31 December, 'hurry Scurry as usual.'[13] As Colman acknowledged in his advertisement, the plot evolved from a variety of sources: 'The use that has been made in this comedy of Fielding's admirable novel of Tom Jones must be obvious to the most ordinary reader. Some hints have also been taken from the account of Mr. and Mrs. Freeman, in No. 212, and No. 216, of the Spectator; and the short scene of Charles' intoxication, at the end of the third act, is partly an imitation of the behaviour of Syrus, much in the same circumstance, in the Adelphi of Terence. There are also some traces of the character of the Jealous Wife, in one of the latter papers of the Connoisseur.'[14] Besides containing a summary of Colman's literary education—Terence from his Westminster days, Fielding, *The Spectator* and *The Connoisseur* from the world of popular journalism—the advertisement defines Colman's way of working. He marshalled ideas and characters from other writers into new forms; he did not 'create'. In this practice he was not alone. The typical Georgian play, as Larry Carver remarks, 'was a highly self-conscious work, a blend of what had been successful in the past with an eye to meet the demands of the present audience'.[15] Taking the notions and sentiments of others—scenes, plots, ideas, snatches of dialogue—and refurbishing them to suit the current taste was the essence of Colman's playwriting technique.

The Jealous Wife's most memorable character is Mr Oakly, a part designed specifically for Garrick, but the cause of some misunderstanding between him and Colman. In a letter of December 1760 Garrick expressed misgivings about the part: 'I have had Burton with me to settle & go over yᵉ Part of Oakly—I have consider'd it thoroughly & I find that it will be impossible for me to get it so soon into my head as I imagin'd. . . . I must desire you to let me take a less Part, yᵉ Major, or Sʳ Harry, or Charles, I have no Objection to any of 'Em.'[16] But Garrick was to be Oakly, and after some tinkering with the character, he 'got' it. Mr Oakly is the henpecked husband *par excellence*. Furnished with a rakish brother, Major Oakly, who constantly tries to get him to assert his freedom, Mr Oakly slides between the extremes of timorous bravado and abject fear in his relations with his tyrannical wife. In a typical sequence, the Major attempts to persuade his brother to exercise his rights by going out with him for dinner:

Maj. You must overcome all difficulties. Assert your right boldly, man! give your own orders to servants, and see they observe them; read your own letters, and never let her have a sight of them; make your own appointments, and never be persuaded to break them; see what company you like; go out when you please; and don't suffer yourself to be call'd to account where you have been. In short, do but shew yourself a man of spirit, leave off whining about love and tenderness, and nonsense, and the business is done, brother!

Oak. I believe you're in the right, Major! I see you're in the right. I'll do't. I'll certainly do't. But then it hurts me to the soul, to think what uneasiness I shall give her. The first opening of my design will throw her into fits, and the pursuit of it, perhaps, may be fatal.

But Oakly soon takes heart. He closes the scene proclaiming, 'I am steel . . . Adamant'. A short episode with his nephew Charles ensues, and then Mrs Oakly enters the discussion, out-arguing the major and squelching Oakly's independent ambitions.

Mrs. Oak. [*within*] The Coach! dines out! Where is your master?
Oak. Zouns, brother, here she is!

Enter Mrs. Oakly.

Mrs. Oak. Pray, Mr. Oakly, what is the matter you cannot dine at home to-day?
Oak. Don't be uneasy, my dear! I have a little business to settle with my brother; so I am only just going to dinner with him and Charles to the tavern.
Mrs. Oak. Why cannot you settle your business here as well as at a tavern? But it is some of your *ladies'* business, I suppose, and so you must get rid of my company . . .

This argument continues for some time, ending finally with Oakly's total capitulation.

Maj. Fie, fie! go out, or you're undone.
Oak. You see it's impossible.
    [*To Mrs. Oakly.*] I'll dine at home with thee, my love.
Mrs. Oak. Ay, ay, pray do, Sir! Dine at a tavern indeed!   [*Going*]
Oak. [*Returning.*] You may depend on me another time, Major.
Maj. Steel! adamant! ah!
Mrs. Oak. [*Returning.*] Mr. Oakly!
Oak. O, my dear!   [*Exeunt.*[17]

This is not the repartee of Congreve. There are no elaborate conceits, no play of metaphorical wit. But the quick overlapping of the dialogue makes for a lively, amusing, and extremely stageable comic scene. The emphasis is not on the language, but on the acting: on the delivery and the movement the actors bring to the exchange. And Mr Oakly's phrasing—'I believe you're in the right, Major! I see you're in the right. I'll do't. I'll certainly do't'—perfectly conveys his quavering boldness.

I cannot help thinking that the character of Mrs Oakly owes something to Colman's officious uncle, the Earl of Bath. His letters to Colman often carry the same peevish yet commanding tone that marks the speech of the jealous wife: 'I tell you before hand, that I shall have you closely watched, that you do not idle away your time, in running to playhouses and such other diversions as I know you are fond of. Such amusements will not agree with your circumstances, who are by industry to get your livelihood. Revolve what I have said to you often in your mind, and resolve to do as I have directed you; you may then come to town as soon as you please.'[18] (This was written when Colman was twenty-two.) Somewhere in Mr Oakly's domestic incarceration, Colman no doubt recognized his own predicament: Mr Oakly eventually manages to break his bonds and keep his wife; Colman certainly hoped to break his bonds and keep his inheritance. Perhaps his dedication of the play to the Earl was a good deal more ironic than it first appears. Perhaps Colman did mean, as Bath himself wrote, 'to abuse me for pretending to chide him for his neglect of Lord Cooke'.

In anticipation of *The Jealous Wife*'s first night Robert Lloyd, whose prologue would introduce the play, wrote a 'Familiar Epistle' to Colman in which he described the tension of the moments immediately preceding the play's opening. The description is perhaps the most vivid rendition we have of the 'feel' of Drury-Lane Theatre just before the curtain was rung up:

> Peeping the curtain's eyelet through,
> Behold the house in dreadful view!
> Observe how close the critics sit,
> And not one bonnet in the pit.
> With horror hear the galleries ring,
> Nosy! Black Joke! God save the King!
> Sticks clatter, catcalls scream, *Encore!*
> Cocks crow, pit hisses, galleries roar:
> E'en *cha' some oranges* is found
> This night to have a dreadful sound:
> 'Till, decent sables on his back,
> (Your prologuizers all wear black)
> The prologue comes; and, if its mine,
> Its very good, and very fine.
> If not, I take a pinch of snuff

And wonder where you got such stuff.
   That done, a-gape the critics sit,
Expectant of the comic wit.
The fiddles play again pell-mell,
—But hist!—The prompter rings his bell.
—Down there! hats off!—The curtain draws!
What follows is—the just applause.[19]

In the event, Lloyd's prophecy proved accurate. *The Jealous Wife* was a great success, running twenty nights and remaining a stock piece for the next century. But Colman's skill as a dramatist was just becoming the talk of the town when an explosion called *The Rosciad* echoed his name throughout London.

II

The importance of the theatre to the social and cultural life of mid-century London is hard to overestimate. Around the play-houses stretched a complex network of literary and economic ties binding the green room, the box office, and the publishing trades to the symbolic language and material pocketbook of the play-going, play-reading Londoner. In the public mind, the typical theatre audience was divided into four symbolic classes, each with a distinct personality and point of view: aristocrats and nouveaux riches in the boxes, where they could see and be seen; professional writers, law students, coffee-house critics— in short, the 'Town'—in the pit, where with unforgiving eyes they scrutinized each player; tradesmen, citizens, and their wives in the first or 'middle' gallery, where they maintained propriety; footmen, mendicants, the 'Gentry of *Wapping* and *Rag-Fair*', in the upper gallery, where they expressed their opinions loudly and often punctuated them with spoiled fruit.[20] Underlying these symbolic divisions (which in practice were much more mixed) was an economic fact: the graduated pricing of seats, ranging from 5*s.* for the boxes to 1*s.* for the upper gallery, with the largest division between the boxes and the pit (at 3*s.*). The theatre audience, in terms of both economics and taste, represented a microcosm of London society. Indeed, Arthur Murphy wrote that the theatre 'engrossed the minds of men to such a degree, that it may now be said, that there existed in England a fourth *estate*, King's, Lords, and Commons, and

Drury-lane play-house.'[21] The theatre's offerings and intrigues provided a wealth of topical symbols and metaphors, and countless pages of copy for the press, just as the motion picture and television industry does today. Even more importantly, the theatre was the centre of a web of economic influence linking actors, managers, playwrights, publishers, critics, coffee-houses, and taverns. In effect, the playhouses formed the core of a 'theatre of operations' for aspiring authors, actors, and publishers. A successful play could lead not only to lucrative benefit nights but to play publication and other spin-offs (critiques, observations, songs, poems, etc.). A bad play or sufficiently notorious satire could spark a paper war, generating money for both authors and booksellers, but possibly jeopardizing the livelihood of actors. An effective production could bring increased trade to taverns and coffee-houses in the vicinity. The Shakespeare's Head Tavern, next to the entrance to Covent-Garden Theatre, and the Bedford Coffee House, one house beyond, were frequented by playgoers and theatre personnel. The Bedford, of course, served another purpose: it was a centre of critical discussion and something of a business office for writers and players: Quin, Foote, Garrick, and others had letters addressed there; and, according to *The Connoisseur*, it was 'every night crowded with men of parts. . . . Jokes are exchanged from box to box, every branch of literature is critically examined and the merit of every production of the press, or performance at the theatre, weighed and examined' (No. 1; 4). Churchill's famous entry into the Bedford after the publication of *The Rosciad* was in effect an assertion of territorial right: a physical metaphor for his intention to dominate the discussion of acting that season.

With dramatic literature in a fallow period and acting on the ascendant, plays as performed rather than plays as written became the literary and pictorial models in the public mind: the actors, not the drama, were of primary interest. Following Garrick's rise to fame (he first played in London in 1741), treatises on acting began to appear in unprecedented numbers. In 1746 Aaron Hill wrote *The Art of Acting*, a verse treatise, and later, in prose, *An Essay on the Art of Acting*. He was followed in 1750 by Dr John Hill (whom we met earlier as the 'Inspector' and 'Mountain') with his *The Actor: a Treatise on the Art of Playing* and a 'New Work' of the same name in 1755. These treatises were primarily generalized discussions of the theory of acting, treating such matters as movement, speech, expression, and costume. It was in this tradition that Robert Lloyd, no doubt urged on by his friend Colman's intimacy with Garrick, published in April 1760 his most successful work, *The Actor*, which he addressed 'to Bonnell Thornton, Esq.'.

In composing *The Actor* Lloyd abandoned his usual octo-syllabics for the more substantial ring of the heroic couplet, but the critical message remained the same: imitation, in acting as in writing, is restrictive and deadening; greatness can be achieved only through the realization of one's distinctive 'genius':

> ACTING, dear Thornton, its perfection draws
> From no observance of mechanic laws:
> No settled maxims of a fav'rite stage,
> No rules deliver'd down from age to age. . . .
> If, 'mongst the humble hearers of the pit,
> Some curious vet'ran critic chance to sit,
> Is he pleased more because 'twas acted so
> By Booth and Cibber thirty years ago?
> The mind recals an object held more dear,
> And hates the copy, that it comes so near.
> Why lov'd he Wilks's air, Booth's nervous tone?
> In them, 'twas natural, 'twas all their own.
> A Garrick's genius must our wonder raise,
> But gives his mimic no reflected praise.[22]

Similarly, Lloyd judges the effect of an actor by the intensity of the audience's response to his playing. He praises Garrick because his acting evokes instantaneous, unpremeditated emotion. He has the power to 'bid the bursting tear spontaneous flow', or to strike terror: 'Through ev'ry vein I feel a chilness creep, / When horrors such as thine *have murder'd sleep*'. Systems of criticism—responses that require abstract judgement—are invalidated by the unquestionable immediacy of Garrick's gift. We are not 'idly pleas'd, at judgment's dear expense, / But burst outrageous with the laugh of sense'. In a passage that harks back to Horace and seems to anticipate Stanislavsky, Lloyd summarizes his aesthetic of emotional authenticity:

The Play'r's profession (tho' I hate the phrase,
'Tis so *mechanic* in these modern days)
Lies not in trick, or attitude, or start,
Nature's true knowledge is the only art.
The strong-felt passion bolts into his face,
The mind untouch'd, what is it but grimace?
To this one standard make your just appeal,
Here lies the golden secret; learn to FEEL.
Or fool, or monarch, happy, or distrest,
No actor pleases that is not *possess'd*.

(pp. 11–12)

But Garrick and his advocates (like Lloyd and Churchill) tended to sound more modern than they were. Although their actor used emotion, he did not use it in the pursuit of personal authenticity.[23] Instead, his emotion was intended to sustain the conventions of theatrical movement, gesture, and expression; conventions perhaps most clearly manifested in the ten dramatic 'passions' mastered by every player. The excellent player, in effect, imbued the 'passions' with real passion. In the small, well-lit theatre of mid-century London, each actor was closely scrutinized to determine if his real emotions significantly informed his role's passion. Thus Aaron Hill theorized that the actor's conceiving of 'a *strong idea* of the passion' could communicate 'instantly, the same impression, to the muscles of the *body*,' which, in turn, 'by impelling or retarding the flow of animal spirits, transmit their own conceiv'd sensation, to the sound of the *voice*, and to the disposition of the *gesture*'.[24] This interaction between real feeling and acting convention formed the focal point of Lloyd and Churchill's criticism. The total integration of Garrick's acting was their expressed ideal. But a reflexive hiatus between emotional spontaneity and stage action could result in something like Churchill's portrayal of Spranger Barry's Hamlet:

Some dozen lines before the ghost is there,
Behold him for the solemn scene prepare.
See how he frames his eyes, poises each limb,
Puts the whole body into proper trim,—
From whence we learn, with no great stretch of art,
Five lines hence comes the ghost, and Ha! a start.

(907–12)

3. Robert Lloyd and Charles Churchill. Anonymous engraving, *c.*1763

Churchill's criticism in *The Rosciad* thus shares the same essential premises as Lloyd's *Actor*. In effect, Churchill personifies the theatrical faults that Lloyd addresses only in conceptual terms.

The Actor attracted considerable attention and apparently earned Garrick's favour, because 'The Tears and Triumphs of Parnassus', an ode by Lloyd on the death of George II, was performed at Drury Lane later the same year; and on 20 November Lloyd published *Shakespeare; an Epistle to Mr. Garrick*—a piece that elevates the Bard above all the ancient playwrights of Greece and Rome. Two later works by Lloyd—*Arcadia; or, the Shepherd's Wedding* (a dramatic pastoral) and *The Capricious Lovers* (a comic opera based on Favart's *Ninette à la Court*)— were also presented at Drury Lane.

The sudden flurry of Nonsense Club activity in connection with the theatre had a compelling effect on Charles Churchill, who with a wife and two children had recently come to London. During the theatrical season of 1760–1, he began attending the theatre indefatigably, where, according to Thomas Davies, 'he bestowed incessant attention on stage representation; and, by close application, laboured to understand perfectly the subject which was the choice of his muse. His observatory was generally the first row of the pit, next to the orchestra.'[25] Davies, himself an actor (among other things), was in an excellent position to note Churchill's 'observatory'; Garrick wrote to him that 'you were always *confus'd & unhappy* whenever you saw Mr Churchill before You.'[26] Davies had reason to be unhappy; he was to become the victim of *The Rosciad*'s most famous line—'He mouths a sentence, as curs mouth a bone' (l. 321)—a description that is said to have driven him from the stage.

On 14 March 1761 Churchill's long hours of observation culminated in *The Rosciad*, a satirical poem devoted to the players of the London stage. *The Rosciad* is remarkable for the extremely sharp focus of its theatrical vignettes. Churchill's keen powers of observation coupled with his razor-sharp phrasing make the poem a vivid series of theatrical snapshots: actors and actresses are captured *en role*, frozen in performance, in much the same way that theatrical conversation pieces caught them on canvas. The parallel between the rise of the theatrical conversation piece and the popularity and technique of *The*

Rosciad has never been sufficiently emphasized. Just as theatrical portraiture moved stage performances into the realm of art, so Churchill's brilliant vignettes translated contemporary acting styles into the realm of literature. Acting took its place beside life as a subject worthy of close artistic observation.

The loose structure of *The Rosciad* (made considerably looser by the addition of over 300 lines through eight editions) is provided by the fiction of disputed succession, as the players compete for the vacant chair of the great Roman actor, Roscius. Early in the poem an argument develops over who should judge the squabbling claimants; an argument that allows Churchill to link the name of one of his closest friends with two of the most famous literary figures of the time:

> For J[O]HNS[O]N some, but J[O]HNS[O]N, it was fear'd,
> Would be too grave; and ST[ER]NE too gay appear'd. . . .
> For COLMAN many, but the peevish tongue
> Or prudent Age found out that he was Young.
>
> (61–2, 65–6)

After attacks (some inserted in later editions) on Arthur Murphy, Dr John Hill, and other men-about-the-theatre, the argument is decided by yet another Nonsense Club member. From among the crowd, 'a Youth stood forth':

> Unknown his person, not unknown his worth;
> His looks bespoke applause; alone he stood,
> Alone he stemm'd the mighty critic flood. . . .
> 'May not some great extensive genius raise
> The name of Britain 'bove Athenian praise;
> And, whilst brave thirst of fame his bosom warms,
> Make England great in Letters as in Arms? . . .
> Happy in tragic and in comic pow'rs,
> Have we not SHAKESPEAR?—Is not JOHNSON ours?
> For them, your nat'ral judges, Britons, vote;
> They'll judge like Britons, who like Britons wrote.'
>   He said, and conquer'd.—Sense resum'd her sway,
> And disappointed pedants stalk'd away.
> SHAKESPEAR and JOHNSON, with deserv'd applause,
> Joint-judges were ordain'd to try to cause.
> Mean-time the stranger ev'ry voice employ'd,
> To ask or tell his name.—'Who is it?'—LLOYD.
>
> (192–4, 213–16, 223–32)

Once Lloyd has straightened out the problem of the judges the procession of competing actors advances, and Churchill begins his satiric snapshots. Havard's lifelessness, Davies's delivery, Holland's imitation of Garrick, King's overdone expressions—all are presented with great attention to detail. Particularly amusing—and incisive—is Churchill's portrait of the comedian Richard Yates:

> Lo YATES!—Without the least finesse of art
> He gets applause!—I wish he'd get his part.
> When hot impatience is in full career,
> How vilely 'Hark'e! Hark'e!' grates the ear? . . .
>   In characters of low and vulgar mould,
> Where nature's coarsest features we behold,
> Where, destitute of ev'ry decent grace,
> Unmanner'd jests are blurted in your face,
> There YATES with justice strict attention draws,
> Acts truly for himself, and gains applause.
> But when, to please himself, or charm his wife,
> He aims at something in politer life,
> When, blindly thwarting Nature's stubborn plan,
> He treads the stage, by way of gentleman,
> The fop, who no one touch of breeding knows,
> Looks like TOM ERRAND dress'd in CLINCHER's cloaths.
> Fond of his dress, fond of his person grown,
> Laugh'd at by all, and to himself unknown,
> From side to side he struts, he smiles, he prates,
> And seems to wonder what's become of YATES.

(345–8, 353–68)

Besides being a vivid portrait of the forgetful, highly entertaining, and thoroughly brazen Yates (whom the *Theatrical Review* faulted for 'being often imperfect in his parts', and for seldom knowing 'when to stop in the expression of a scene of humour . . . so as to border on buffoonery and Bartholomew-fair'),[27] Churchill's description restates the Lloydian notion that an actor must understand his own nature in order to choose his parts properly. It also contains an allusion to a scene in Colman's *Polly Honeycombe*, in which Yates played Mr Honeycombe. As an angry father, he was supposed to harangue the novel-struck Polly, beginning many of his exhortations with the phrase 'Hark ye, Miss' or 'Hark ye, Hussy'. The resourceful Yates, each time he forgot his lines, simply added more 'Hark ye's'.

After *The Rosciad* was published, Yates 'took particular care to reiterate the very words which Churchill had made the record of his satire'.[28]

At the close of *The Rosciad*, it is not surprisingly Garrick—whose talent comes from 'Nature's pure and genuine source', whose 'strokes of Acting flow with gen'rous force'—who wins Roscius's chair. The proclamation, made by Shakespeare, includes a catalogue of the histrionic virtues most prized by Churchill and Lloyd:

> 'If manly Sense; if Nature link'd with Art;
> If thorough knowledge of the Human Heart;
> If Pow'rs of acting vast and unconfin'd;
> If fewest Faults, with greatest Beauties join'd;
> If strong Expression, and strange Pow'rs, which lie
> Within the magic circle of the Eye;
> If feelings which few hearts, like his, can know,
> And which no face as well as His can show;
> Deserve the Pref'rence;—GARRICK take the Chair,
> Nor quit it—'till Thou place an Equal there.'
>
> (1081–90)

Thus the fictional competition and the poem end. But in the real theatrical world, the battle was just beginning.

III

The reaction to *The Rosciad* was as spontaneous and widespread as Churchill could ever have wished. 'The author soon found that he had no occasion to advertise his poem in the public prints; the players spread its fame all over the town; they ran about like so many stricken deer; they strove to extract the arrow from the wound by communicating the knowledge of it to their friends.'[29] The only disappointment, as far as Churchill was concerned, was that no one knew it was his. The first journal to attribute the poem incorrectly, Smollett's *Critical Review*, printed a review which nevertheless contained some useful insights. Accurately describing the criticism of *The Rosciad* as 'no more than the echo of the critics in every coffee house, put into tolerable shape' (though the sharpness and wit of the portraiture is certainly of a higher level), the *Critical* reviewer cogently discussed just the sort of contradiction that was later to become a hallmark of Churchill's style. Toward the end of the poem, Churchill had attacked Quin's inability to 'sink the Man' in his portrayal of fictional characters:

> In whate'er cast his character was laid,
> Self still, like oil, upon the surface play'd.
> Nature, in spite of all his skill, crept in:
> Horatio, Dorax, Falstaff,—still 'twas Q[UI]N.
>
> (983–6)

Of course, this directly contradicts the opinion advanced earlier in both Lloyd's *Actor* and *The Rosciad* that the 'nature' of the man, as it interacts with the role, is the key to great acting. Theoretically, I suppose, a distinction could be made between too little and too much 'nature', but the *Critical* reviewer is essentially correct when he chides the author: 'With regard to the influence which his [Quin's] *natural* turn of mind had on his *assumed* character, we shall only observe, that *nature* (as our author observes) will always *creep in*.'[30] Where the reviewer goes wrong is in using this conceit roundly to attack and tentatively to identify the author of the poem. The attack marks the opening shot of what came to be known as 'the battle of the players and poets'; and the identification represents the first public recognition of the Nonsense Club as a literary force:

It is *natural* for young authors to conceive themselves the cleverest fellows in the world, and withal, that there is not the least degree of merit subsisting but in their *own* works: it is *natural* likewise for them to imagine, that they may conceal themselves by appearing in different shapes, and that they are not to be found out by their stile; but little do these *Connoisseurs* in writing conceive, how easily they are discovered by a veteran in the service. In the title page to this performance we are told, (by way of quaint conceit) that it was written by *the author*; what if it should prove that the author and the actor are the same! certain it is, that we meet with the *same* vein of peculiar humour, the same facility of versification, the same turn of thought, the same affected contempt of the ancients, the same extravagant praise of the moderns, the same *autophilism* (there's a new word for you to bring into your next poem) which we meet with in the other. . . .

Insomuch that we are ready to make the conclusion in the author's own words:

Who is it—LLOYD

We will not pretend, however, absolutely to assert, that Mr. L—— wrote this poem; but we may venture to affirm, that it is the production, jointly or separately, of the new triumvirate of wits, who never let an opportunity slip of singing their own praises.

The 'triumvirate of wits' consisted of Lloyd, Colman, and Thornton. Throughout the paper war that followed, the term 'triumvirate' was consistently used to denote the Nonsense Club side, but once Churchill's identity became known, he generally took Thornton's place as the third, and leading, member of the alliance. The *Critical* reviewer's summary of the Nonsense Club's literary traits—peculiar humour, facility of versification, praise of the moderns, and self-love (or mutual admiration)—is extremely accurate. Unfortunately, we do not know who wrote this review.[31]

Lloyd and Colman immediately denied authorship of *The Rosciad* in the newspapers, and *The Critical Review* was forced into an apology, admitting that its remarks contained an insinuation that 'Mess. Colman and Lloyd were concerned in writing that poem . . . a hint founded on misinformation, which it is now needless to explain.'[32] But Smollett himself felt a need to explain, and on 5 April 1761 wrote to Garrick to assure him that he 'did not write one word of the article upon the Rosciad'.[33] Indeed, Smollett continued, 'I have no ill will nor envy to Mr. Colman, whom I have always respected as a man of genius.'

The victims of *The Rosciad* and their allies, however, were far from conciliatory. In the spring of 1761, a flood of satires and epigrams poured from the press, attacking the poem and its author.[34] Early on, the poets who supported the players' side took Churchill to task on the grounds that *The Rosciad* was primarily a mercenary venture: ''Twas no defect of your's, but *pocket low*, / That caus'd his putrid kennel to o'erflow'.[35] The accusation was not entirely inaccurate: certainly, Churchill did reap a great profit from *The Rosciad*. Unable to find a publisher, he had had the poem printed and distributed at his own expense, and thus shared the money from its sale with no one—a sale estimated at over £1,000. With this money he paid his debts and set himself up as a man-about-town. But Churchill's criticism of the stage was also meant to be taken seriously; and the players themselves displayed a remarkably varied array of responses to it: 'Havard was more offended than became a man so calm and dispassionate. Ross pleaded guilty, and laughed at his punishment over a glass with his friend Bonnel Thornton. Sparks was too much a man of the world to be hurt by a poetical arrow. King was displeased, but King kept his temper. Shuter, out of revenge, got very merry with the poet. Foote, who lived by degrading all characters, was outrageously offended.'[36] Foote's outrage generated perhaps the most interesting literary response of the paper war's early phase, a revised version of his 1752 afterpiece, *Taste*. This short play, satirizing crooked art dealers and their gullible patrons, had been ridiculed by Thornton in *The Drury-Lane Journal* (a 'Footy' performance, he called it), but nevertheless played intermittently throughout the 1750s. Now Foote revised it to include a short opening scene satirizing Churchill and a Colman–Lloyd–Thornton composite, and completely rewrote the second act as a comment on Churchill's theatrical criticism.

The revised play opens with 'George Townly' (Colman) reading a letter from his friend, 'Charles Manly' (Churchill). As he finishes, in walks the bearish Manly, ironically introduced as a former man-about-town now retired to domestic felicity in the country, rather than, as was Churchill's case, a man fleeing rural and domestic drudgery to become a town wit. (The reversal, one assumes, would have been recognized by the audience; the details of Churchill's private life spread with surprising speed after the publication of *The Rosciad*.) Foote pulls no punches as he has Townly allude to Churchill's unhappy domestic situation: 'And how fares it with Margery and her bawling brood? Chopping Children, I warrant, and wholesome as the breath of Morn & ruddy as the Rising Sun, ha, ha, ha!'[37] As the play proceeds, Townly and Manly visit the studio of Carmine the portrait painter (from the original *Taste*) and then the theatre operated by Project (Garrick), where they meet Fustian the poet. Edward Weatherly, in his essay on *Taste*, conjectures that Fustian is Lloyd, while W. C.

Brown contends that he more likely represents Thornton.[38]
Actually, Fustian seems merely a character introduced to facilitate the satire on Churchill's theatrical criticism: Manly and
Townly both need to be introduced to him by Project ('Mr.
Fustian . . . give me leave to introduce Mr. Manly, the ablest
critic of his time, and Mr. Townly, the most fashionable Man
of the Age, to your better Acquaintance'), and Fustian's
'tragedy'—*Love Till Death*—bears no resemblance to anything
written by either Lloyd or Thornton (in fact, Weatherly identifies Fustian's play as a parody of William Whitehead's *Fatal
Constancy*). It is Fustian's scheme for reforming acting that
forms the central conceit of the playhouse scene. Explaining
that 'it is not the Play that now draws the People together But
the Player', Fustian proposes to 'get rid of all the supernumer-
ary Personages' that cost the manager so much worry and
money:

Proj. But how can this be done?

Fust. Nothing so easy. I have here in my Pocket a peice [*sic*] that not
    only Demonstrates the Possibility but propriety of the Design. My
    title is Love till Death & my Characters are Golcondus, the Hero;
    Chrontes, the King; Lindamira, his Daughter; and Tribus, the
    Confidant. The first to be flesh & Blood, & the three last, *Paste-
    Board.*[39] (emphasis added)

This preposterous project attacks not only Churchill's satire on
the great body of secondary players, but the inflated reputation
of Garrick. In a *reductio ad absurdum* of Churchill's criticism,
Foote seems to be saying that since Churchill praises only
Garrick, perhaps Garrick alone is necessary for the successful
production of the play.

It is somewhat surprising that the revised version of *Taste*
was acted at Drury Lane, the playhouse run by Garrick and,
increasingly, Colman. Garrick's motive for presenting the play
can only be guessed at, but probably grew out of his diplomatic
desire to assuage the anger of his own supporting actors. The
new *Taste* was presented at Drury-Lane Theatre on 6 April
1761, and perhaps precipitated the attack on Garrick in
Churchill's next satirical cannonade, *The Apology Addressed to the
Critical Reviewers* (May 1761).

The Apology is notable chiefly for its statement of Churchill's
poetic ideals (see Chapter 4), and for its attacks on Garrick,

Smollett, and Arthur Murphy. Churchill's attack on Garrick
dramatizes his disdain of theatrical sycophancy—a practice
which often determined not only who was granted free passage
to the playhouse, but what plays or prologues ultimately
reached the stage. The attack is also interesting because it
represents the first manifestation of what was to become
Churchill's characteristic stance as a satirist: the bluff, independent iconoclast, defying—nay, taunting—the powers that
be:

> Let the Vain Tyrant sit amidst his guards,
> His puny GREEN-ROOM Wits and Venal Bards,
> Who meanly tremble at the Puppet's frown,
> And for a Playhouse Freedom lose their own;
> In spite of new-made Laws, and new-made Kings,
> The free-born Muse with lib'ral spirit sings,
> Bow down, ye Slaves; before these Idols fall;
> Let Genius stoop to them who've none at all;
> Ne'er will I flatter, cringe, or bend the knee
> To those who, Slaves to All, are Slaves to ME.
>
> (266–75)

Garrick, recognizing the importance of securing Churchill's
friendship, quickly responded with a long letter to Lloyd in
which he slightingly referred to himself as 'his pasteboard
majesty of Drury-lane' (a clear reference to *Taste*) and asked for
Churchill's understanding: 'In his Rosciad he raised me too
high; in his "Apology" he may have sunk me too low: he has
done as his Israelites did, made an idol of a calf, and now
—"The idol dwindles to a calf again!"' [40] Becoming more
serious, Garrick continued, 'you mentioned to me some time
ago, that Mr. Churchill was displeased with me—you must
have known whether justly or not:—if the first, you should
certainly have opened your heart to me and have heard my
apology; if the last, you should, as a common friend of both,
have vindicated me, and then I might have escaped his
"Apology": but, be it this or that, or the other, I am still his
great admirer.' This letter apparently had the desired effect,
because Churchill and Garrick were intimate thereafter—
Churchill borrowing money from Garrick on numerous
occasions.

The Apology's attack on Smollett mainly revolves around *The Critical Review*'s faulty attribution and negative assessment of *The Rosciad*. But Churchill also gets in a jab at Smollett's least successful literary work (which just happened to be a play), his ill-fated tragedy, *The Regicide*:

> Who ever read the REGICIDE but swore
> The author wrote as man ne'er wrote before?
> Others for plots and under-plots may call,
> Here's the right method—have no plot at all.
>
> (156–9)

This attack must have hurt Smollett, who was particularly touchy where *The Regicide* was concerned (Melopoyn's story in *Roderick Random* is a capsule history of the play's misfortunes); and it undoubtedly reinforced *The Critical Review*'s generally hostile view of the triumvirate.[41]

The triumvirate's chief enemy, however, was not Smollett but Arthur Murphy, whose running feud with Garrick and Colman helped exacerbate the theatrical battle begun by *The Rosciad*. Murphy, a quarrelsome and independent man, had been writing for Drury-Lane Theatre for several years under a special arrangement: instead of the usual author's benefit nights, he received a fixed amount for each play or for the year and was under contract to write for no other playhouse.[42] Garrick, however, quibbled over Murphy's plays and their relationship grew increasingly tense: Murphy, in fact, admitted to penning an anonymous pamphlet attacking Garrick as early as 1759. When Garrick 'discovered' Colman in 1760, he immediately set about finding a way to get rid of Murphy— that is, to make Murphy break his end of their bargain. Years later, Murphy summarized what he clearly felt to have been a conspiracy against him: 'Mr. Colman had entered into a league with Churchill and Bob Lloyd, and that triumvirate, he thought would be able to bear down all before them. Some certain artifices in Colman's conduct came to this author's knowledge, and, as they appeared to him in a bad light, he never listened to any terms of reconciliation; he saw evident symptoms of a bad heart, and with such a man he thought a state of war was much better than a bad peace.'[43]

And war there was. With Garrick and the Nonsense Club aligned against Murphy and Smollett's *Critical* reviewers, the battle raged through the summer and autumn of 1761. *The Churchilliad, The Murphyad, The Triumvirate,* Murphy's *Ode to the Naiads of Fleet-Ditch* and *Examiner*, Lloyd's *Epistle to C. Churchill* —these were but a few of the scores of satires and defences, in verse and prose, that grew out of the war.[44] This so-called 'battle of the players and poets' took on the typical structure of a paper war: attacks, defences, counter-attacks, replies to counter-attacks, papers urging reconciliation, and so forth. Personalities and aesthetics formed the central topics of this literature, but it is important to remember that such a controversy, by generating an interested readership, generated income for authors. Although it is clear that many of Churchill's adversaries felt a real dislike for him, his instant notoriety must also be attributed to the publishing world's recognition of his gift for provoking and sustaining marketable journalistic controversy: he was an economic asset even to his enemies. Their attacks—as much as his own poetry—made him a public figure.

Of all these attacks the most noteworthy for our purposes are Murphy's *Examiner* and the anonymous *Triumvirate*. The *Examiner*, which appeared in November of 1761, was the second of Murphy's satires against the triumvirate (the first being the unfortunate *Ode to the Naiads of Fleet-Ditch*) and is chiefly valuable for its close satiric portraits of Lloyd, Colman, and Churchill. Lloyd, who had recently resigned his position as an usher at Westminster School and whose love of alcohol already seems to have been formidable, is described as a former 'adverb-teacher' who has now set up a kind of night school at a local tavern ('Bob Derry's'). There, writes Murphy,

> . . . for instruction still
> The unfledg'd pupil shall attend his will;
> There shall he to his circle, wisely drunk!
> Now praise the *Jealous Wife*, and now a punk.[45]

Murphy's ghostly close-up of Lloyd—'His meagre cheek, 'midst his nocturnal sport / With envy pale, and his lips black with port'—seems an eerie prophecy of the poet's coming moral and physical disintegration. Colman, in keeping with

what we know of his literary practice, is denigrated as a
playhouse parasite and slavish adapter who 'sponge-like'
absorbs 'whate'er comes cross his way, / 'Till Garrick squeeze
him dry into a play'. And Churchill, 'a CALIBAN in manners
as in sense', is given a capsule biography:

> His very youth 'gainst decency rebell'd,
> From school with early infamy expell'd.
> Thence comet-like irregular he flew,
> And as he fled, still more eccentric grew.
> Still he despis'd all order, sense, and rank,
> At fairs he cudgell'd, and with porters drank. . . .
> 'Till, wond'rous to relate! his race to crown,
> He sanctify'd his scandal with a gown.

> (pp. 24–5)

What is noteworthy about this description is its early recognition of Churchill's meteoric character, his disgust with social
and literary rules, and his incipient egalitarianism. It must be
remembered that at the time of this portrait (November 1761)
Churchill had published only two poems, *The Rosciad* and *The
Apology*—his manifesto, *Night*, would appear later the same
month (see Chapter 4). There can be no better evidence of the
immediacy and strength of Churchill's impression on the public, and the quick spread of the details of his private life, than
this early attack by Arthur Murphy.

An even more interesting set of portraits appears in *The
Triumvirate*—a poem I believe to have been written by its titular
heroes. Ostensibly an attack on the Westminster threesome
plus Garrick ('See! my *TRIUMVIRATE* is *four*', writes the
poet), the poem actually contains a gradually sharpening satire
on the character of its putative author, one 'Jacky Dapper'.
Remembering that self-satire was characteristic of the Nonsense Club, it seems to me that a strong circumstantial case
can be made for *The Triumvirate*'s being a joint product of
Churchill, Colman, Lloyd, and perhaps Garrick—possibly
even a poem thrown together at a Nonsense Club meeting.

Jacky Dapper opens the poem by attacking Garrick and his
villa at Hampton, and then launches into a defence of Arthur
Murphy:

This HERO whose admir'd renown
Had fascinated all the town,

These *little* folks, but *little* known
Made *little* efforts to dethrone.
Nightly they held a consultation,
A close designing combination,
And happy in their new alliance
Bad all my friends and ME defiance.[46]

Here we catch the equivocal tone that characterizes the piece. While ostensibly an attack on the 'little folks' of the triumvirate, the poem's specious aggrandizement of Murphy (the 'HERO') and the tone of wounded pride in the final couplet reveal Dapper's personality to be both sycophantic and jealous. At the same time, the 'satire' on the triumvirate becomes an indirectly positive assessment: here are persons not nearly as powerful or well known as Murphy, making minimal ('little') efforts to 'dethrone' him. Meeting at night to form their plans (apparently a reference to tavern conclaves), they are both happy with themselves and highly disrespectful of prigs like Dapper. The portrait is no doubt very close to what the triumvirate actually thought of themselves.

The individual portraits of Churchill, Colman, and Lloyd are equally revealing. Churchill's, though certainly possessing a satiric surface, takes on a kind of heroic vitality, and in this respect is very like the self-portraits in his acknowledged poetry. We find him sitting at a play, talking 'much of SM-LL-T and REVIEWS':

In body clumsy, heavy, big,
With hat all pinch'd, and rusty wig,
In coat, which would much credit lack
Though one should swear it had been black,
With stick for beating, which would scare one
Excepting those who're us'd to bear one,
He sits secure with awkward smile,
His features lengthening half a mile.
Nor blushes He, though DOLL or ROSE,
With bubies lac'd up to her nose,
With fruit and leer upon her face,
Elbows his reverence out of place.

(p. 11)

Not only does the portrait show Churchill in his favourite environment, it paints him as just the type of lumbering but 'secure' fellow he thought himself to be: no fear of men, no

blushes for the ladies. The portrait eventually turns into a
typical 'defence through defiance', when we find that Churchill
cares not

> . . . a jot though He were seen
> At play or farce by prudish Dean;
> Who sees the same more orthodox,
> Snug in the corner of a box.

(p. 12)

Colman's portrait is likewise deprecating, but never vicious.
Predictably, his small stature ('A tiny body full of satyre')
proves an easy target—Colman himself would often laugh at
this 'shortcoming'—but the succeeding lines on his literary
opportunism suddenly transform into a revelation of Dapper's
fear of his literary powers:

> From a well acted JEALOUS WIFE
> He got a present means of life.
> For lean before, and won'drous poor,
> He starv'd upon the CONNOISSEUR:
> And who can tell but all his spite
> (For still the urchin loves to write)
> May vent its weak and saucy rage,
> By bringing *Me* upon the stage.
> Draw DAPPER running up and down,
> An errant catch-f—t of the town.

(p. 13)

And Lloyd is described as 'a *dunce*, a *knave*, a *fool*', who 'was an
USHER at a school', but now

> . . . metamorphos'd dares to drag
> An useless sword, and wear a bag.
> With solemn look and solemn stalk,
> A consequence in all his walk,
> And yet as that were not enough,
> With solemn pinch of critic snuff,
> Pronouncing vengeance on the rimes,
> And all the stuff of modern times,
> And yet so very generous grown,
> He'll give us nonsense of his own.

(pp. 16–17)

At this point the poem takes a sudden turn, and there begins
a long satiric self-portrait of Dapper: a spoiled law student,

failed writer, and critic, he now spends his time studying 'Abuse and scandal' and 'slobbering over works of learning'. The satire sharpens dramatically in the concluding lines of the poem, as Dapper exposes his own hypocrisy, and then has his true identity revealed:

> *I* Damn'd L——D's piece, tho' never seen,
> Because the man provok'd my spleen.
> Said thousand things were never said,
> Writ reams of wit were never read.
> Affecting hugely to despise,
> And lied till I believed my lies.
>   O reader here's the portrait true
> Of *what* your DAPPER is, and *who*
> From life, from observation drawn,
> Is it a likeness? Master V——n.
>
>   (p. 20)

The final identification of 'Dapper' as Thomas Vaughan, a minor wit and friend of Murphy's, is the strongest piece of extrinsic evidence linking the poem to the Nonsense Club. Vaughan had been nicknamed 'Dapper' by Colman, who also portrayed him as 'Jacky Tattle' in *The Genius* No. 6 (20 August 1761)—one of a series of essays he was writing for *The St. James's Chronicle*.[47] And Churchill added a couplet on 'VAUGHAN or DAPPER, call him which you will' to the fifth edition of *The Rosciad* (ll. 611–12). One further note may be added: in October 1761 the poem was reviewed in the *Monthly Review* by none other than Robert Lloyd, who found that 'our concealed adventurer is rather a favourer of the *new interest*' (i.e. the triumvirate). Indeed, Lloyd continued, 'we may safely venture to pronounce, that all, who are acquainted and personally unconcerned, with the present dispute, may read this performance with great satisfaction.'[48] This is hardly the response one would expect from a man who had been called in the poem 'a *dunce*, a *knave*, a *fool*'—unless, of course, he had had a hand in assigning (ironically) those descriptive terms.

Vaughan replied to *The Triumvirate* in his *Retort* (19 October), which again finds Lloyd holding forth to 'pupils' at Bob Derry's and includes the expected derogatory remarks about Colman and Churchill. But Vaughan was busy trying to

undermine the triumvirate in other ways. He figures prominently in a letter from Garrick to Colman of 17 December; a
letter that vividly exemplifies the way in which Garrick and the
Nonsense Club worked together to manipulate the press, and
incidentally summarizes the happy result of the paper war as
far as Garrick was concerned:

I have this moment seen our Friend Churchill & told him a fine
Scheme of Vaughn's in conjunction with the Gang of Pottinger—
they are going to publish a Set of Papers call'd the *Genius*, in order to
forestall Y^{rs} & deceive the Public. It is a most infamous design, & I
desir'd Churchill would Let Thornton know of it, which he will do
immediatly, & prevent their Scoundrillity by some humorous Paragraph. . . .

Pray let me see you soon with y^r Bundle of Excellencies—M^r
Murphy has at last declar'd off with us, & in a Letter to Obrien says,
that he has been so great a loser by ye Managers of Drury Lane that
he can never more have any dealings with Us—Wish Me joy my dear
Friend, but Keep this to y^{r}Self for Many Weighty reasons.[49]

Although shots would continue to be exchanged for a number
of years, this letter marks the end of the most intense phase of
the battle of the players and poets. The 'battle' had, if nothing
else, brought three of the Nonsense Club members a kind of
literary notoriety—a notoriety that would gradually increase
over the next three years. During this time, the attitudes and
subjects, the aesthetic and ethical values, that had pervaded the
group's lives at Westminster School and had achieved expression in *The Drury-Lane Journal*, *The Connoisseur*, and now in the
theatrical wars, would undergo refinement, stress, and meta-
morphosis.

4 *The Nonsense Club*

I

At some time before the battle of the players and poets, the actual 'Nonsense Club' had been formed. It consisted of Thornton, Colman, Lloyd, Cowper, James Bensley, and two other members whose identities remain uncertain.[1] Contemporary references to the club's existence occur only in Cowper's letters. On 9 June 1786, after receiving a letter from Colman, Cowper wrote to Joseph Hill:

Such notices from old friends are always pleasant, and of such pleasures I have received many lately. They refresh the remembrance of early days, and make me young again. The noble Institution of the Nonsense Club will be forgotten when we are gone who composed it, but I often think of your most heroic line, written at one of our meetings, and especially think of it when I am translating Homer.—
To whom replied the Devil yard-long-tailed.[2]

Cowper had earlier (1785) written of 'a Club of seven Westminster men to which I belonged, who dined together every Thursday'.[3] These two passages contain all we know of the club: it met each Thursday, it consisted of seven Old Westminsters, it was called the Nonsense Club, and it was an organization given to literary activity (especially burlesque). Cowper's two other references are valuable mainly in determining the membership of the club. Writing in 1777 of Gray, he said, 'he did not belong to our Thursday Society & was an Eaton man'.[4] And in 1765 he moralized on the early deaths of James Bensley and Robert Lloyd: 'The Tragedies of Loyd & Bensley are both very deep. If they are not of use to the surviving part of the Society, it is their own Fault.'[5]

The identities of the members besides Cowper, Thornton, Colman, Lloyd, and Bensley remain the subject of conjecture. The strongest candidates are certainly Joseph Hill and Chase Price. Hill, we know, was present and writing at the meeting. But he was not an Old Westminster. And Cowper, in the third letter quoted above, has to tell him that Gray was not a member. A strong case for Chase Price's membership has been made by Charles Ryskamp, who demonstrates that Price was the 'Toby' and 'C. P., Esq.' of Cowper's early poems and letters. He was also an Old Westminster, a resident of the Inner Temple, and a friend of all the other members.[6] He was a great clubman and wit—'the *Falstaff* of the present age'—and at the Beefsteak Society, he and Churchill are said to have 'kept the table in a roar'.[7] Certainly he seems a likely candidate for the club.

And what of Charles Churchill? It is certain that he was not an original member of the club, which seems to have been founded during 1755–7, years when Churchill was still in the country. He was probably never an 'official' member of the club at all. (Cowper's letters indicate that he and Churchill were not close.) But once he got within easy visiting range of London, Churchill undoubtedly attended club meetings and, like Hill, wrote club literature.[8] At first, Churchill's visits must have been infrequent; in 1757, he was curate of his father's living at Rainham, Essex, a town about fifteen miles from London. But his father also held a town living, and on his death in September 1758, Charles was elected to fill the vacant curacy and lectureship of St John's, Westminster.[9] From that moment, he became a dedicated student and then master of the Nonsense Club's literary idiom.

As Cowper's remark about Hill's 'heroic line' indicates, the Nonsense Club meetings seem to have revolved around the writing of comic poetry and prose. From what can be gathered from the surviving poems and letters, an active correspondence between the club members seems to have been encouraged; a correspondence that required the exchange of humorous verses and essays, as well as gossip and news. Cowper, for instance, in his 1754 epistle to Lloyd, admits that besides writing to alleviate an attack of depression, 'there is another reason yet':

> Which is, that I may fairly quit
> The debt, which justly became due
> The moment when I heard from you:
> And you might grumble, crony mine,
> If paid in any other coin.
>
> (22–6)[10]

And Lloyd, himself obsessed with writing epistles to his friends, talks incessantly about his need to versify, as in a 1756 epistle to Colman:

> You know, dear George, I'm none of those
> That condescend to write in prose;
> Inspir'd with pathos and sublime,
> I always soar—in doggrel rhyme,
> And scarce can ask you how you do,
> Without a jingling line or two.[11]

In addition to their common experience of Westminster School, such literary trivia, the more foolish the better, seem to have been the glue that held the Nonsense Club together. As Lloyd writes in the closing lines of 'A Familiar Epistle to *******', 'in writing to a friend / A man may any nonsense send, / And the chief merit to impart, / The honest feelings of his heart.'[12] In such epistles, we sense the 'honest feelings' and experience the literary whimsy that united these friends.

An extended example of the Nonsense Club's whimsical correspondence survives in a strange, humorous piece called a 'Letter from an owl to a bird of paradise' that John Johnson says was written 'when Cowper was a young man in the Temple, as a contribution to the Nonsense Club'.[13] In it, Cowper, pretending to be an owl, complains that the 'nights being short at this time of year, my epistle will probably be so too; and it strains my eyes not a little to write, when it is not as dark as pitch.'[14] Expanding this conceit, Cowper seems to allude to the Nonsense Club's nocturnal pastimes of writing and drinking:

I am likewise much distressed for ink: the blackberry juice which I had bottled up having been all exhausted, I am forced to dip my beak in the blood of a mouse, which I have just caught; and it is so very savoury, that I think in my heart I swallow more than I expend in writing. . . . As you are constantly gazing at the sun, it is no wonder that you complain of a weakness in your eyes; how should it be otherwise, when mine are none of the strongest, though I always draw the curtains over them as soon as he rises, in order to shut out as much of his light as possible? We have had a miserable dry season, and my ivy-bush is sadly out of repair. I shall be obliged to you if you will favour me with a shower or two, which you can easily do, by driving a few clouds together over the wood, and beating them with your wings until they fall to pieces.[15]

Although a good deal of this letter seems pure fantasy, there is reason to believe that some of it, at least, carries an allegorical meaning. A 'bush', of course, was the traditional sign for a tavern, and, as Ryskamp points out, 'to look like an owl in an ivy-bush' was a proverbial phrase for 'to look ridiculous'.[16] The passages concerning blackberry juice, mouse blood, clouds, and showers undoubtedly have something to do with drinking, and I would suggest that the owl itself, as used by Cowper, seems not only a nonsense persona, but a symbol for a nocturnal dweller, writer, or drinker—in short, what we today would call a 'night owl'.

Indeed, for the Nonsense Club, the owl—with its nocturnal habits and sleepy ease—seems to have become a humorous symbol for all the things the club members loved best: nighttime conclaves, burlesque literature, easy writing, and drink. Cowper's reference to the owl's love of night life and night writing—'it strains my eyes not a little to write, when it is not as dark as pitch'—almost certainly alludes to the club's nocturnal literary sessions. In a peculiar adaptation of the Augustan use of the bird as an emblem of Dullness, the Nonsense Club makes the owl into a symbol of retreat from the 'rational' world of business and career—a persona at once rebellious and self-satirizing.[17] This paradoxical usage is exemplified in Churchill's *Night*—a poem in which the poet and Lloyd, like Cowper's owl, shun the 'daylight' world. From their night-time retreat (a tavern), they attack the hypocrisy of materialistic society and extol the virtues of pleasure and oblivion. But, at the same time, they seem palpably uneasy about their failure to cope with 'daylight' life:

> ROGUES justified and by success made bold,
> Dull fools and coxcombs sanctified by Gold,
> Freely may bask in fortune's partial ray,
> And spread their feathers op'ning to the day;
> But *thread-bare* Merit dares not shew the head
> 'Till vain Prosperity retires to bed.
> Misfortunes, like the Owl, avoid the light;
> The sons of CARE are always sons of NIGHT.
>
> (11–18)

Like Cowper's 'bird of paradise' (but more pernicious), the wealthy rogues preen their feathers in the sun; while the owl—

now not merely silly, but equated with 'misfortune'—hides and frets.

Though the Nonsense Club clearly did much writing during the first years of its existence, initially at least very little of this work found its way to the press. During the period between the demise of *The Connoisseur* and the Nonsense Club's outpouring of publications in 1760, only two verifiable pieces were published by its members: Thornton's contribution to Johnson's *Idler* (No. 15, 22 July 1758) and Colman's mock-critical *Letter of Abuse to David Garrick, Esq.* (1757). It was during this time, however, that Colman and Lloyd collaborated on a project that, upon its publication in 1760, became one of the more well known Nonsense Club productions: the *Two Odes* burlesquing the poetry of William Mason and Thomas Gray.

Scholars have generally agreed with Southey's conjecture that the *Two Odes* were written by Colman and Lloyd as a Nonsense Club prank. Possibly they were written as early as 1757, when Gray's exacting Pindaric imitations— *The Progress of Poesy* and *The Bard*—were first printed on Horace Walpole's Strawberry Hill press. The numerous accusations of 'obscurity' that plagued these poems certainly suggested to Colman and Lloyd their titles—'To Obscurity' and 'To Oblivion'—and determined their specific techniques of attack. But more generally, Colman and Lloyd's burlesques reflect the negative side of the mid-century mixture of enthusiasm and consternation that greeted the resurgence of the Pindaric ode.

While 'Pindaric' odes had been written in English since the time of Jonson, most had been composed under the mistaken assumption that the defining characteristic of the form was a marked irregularity of stanza and metre. Despite William Congreve's explanation in 1706 that 'the Liberty which he [Pindar] took in his Numbers, and which has been so misunderstood and misapply'd by his pretended Imitators, was only in varying the Stanzas in different Odes', very few works following the regular Pindaric model appeared during the early eighteenth century.[18] In the 1740s, however, the more exact Pindaric ode became a favourite vehicle of the so-called poets of Sensibility, chiefly because of its tradition of lyric intensity.[19] Collins, Warton, Mason, and Gray all wrote Pindaric odes with varying degrees of success (and with varying fidelity to Pindar);

however, it was Gray especially who took the greatest pains to reproduce the form and feeling of the Greek originals, strictly following the precept that, in Congeve's words, 'every Epode in the same Ode is eternally the same in Measure and Quantity, in respect to it self; as is also every Strophe and Antistrophe, in respect to each other'.[20] Yet it was not the form of the poems, but their epithetical idiom and magnified emotion that most offended the critics. Gray was accused (to use two representative phrases) of 'studied obscurity of composition' and 'vicious affectation of style'.[21] Because of their experimental nature and easily identifiable technical features, Gray's odes (like Fielding's *Amelia*) made ideal targets for burlesque.

The first of the *Two Odes* follows Gray's two Pindaric works very closely—though Colman and Lloyd purposely vary both the length and structure of their stanzas in order to exaggerate the traditional irregularity of the form. Mimicking the 'progress' metaphor of *The Progress of Poesy*, the 'Obscurity' ode charts the course of 'Fashion' as she first rides a weathercock—'Each blast that blows, around she goes'—and then begins to travel 'the fav'rite road / Of lofty cloudcapt Ode', while each modern 'Bard, with eager speed, / Vaults on the Pegasean Steed' in hot pursuit.[22] The introduction of Pegasus marks the beginning of a second 'progress'—this time a burlesque of the ancestry and adventures of the modern poets' steed. Needless to say, the contemporary model is 'not that Pegasus, of yore / Which th' illustrious Pindar bore, / But one of nobler breed'—a descendant, in fact, of great English racehorses. This 'new' Pegasus races at Newmarket and then is brought the short distance to Cambridge. There, the steed is ridden successively by Mason and Gray (both Cambridge men) in their distinctive manners. As Mason ambles and alliterates—'The whiles he wins his whiffling way, / Prancing, ambling, round and round, / By hill, and dale, and mead, and greensward gay'—Gray, accoutred in massive boots, and boasting a 'bushy peruke' and 'broad Mustachios', seeks 'not the level lawn, or velvet mead', but charges into the Welsh mountains. Stanza IV.1. of the mock ode imitates stanza II.1. of Gray's *Poesy* very closely: the original begins, 'Man's feeble race what Ills await', and laments the fate of mankind; the burlesque begins, 'Man's feeble race eternal dangers wait', and satirizes the bard's obliviousness to the 'Cambrian Gulph' he is approaching. In Gray's *Poesy* ode, Milton rides 'upon the seraph-wings of Extasy, the secrets of th' Abyss to spy'; in the mock ode, the poet soars to 'Lyrick Glory in the clouds', hits his head on the stars, and tumbles into a Welsh canyon—thus abruptly ending the 'progress' and burlesquing the conclusion of *The Bard* in one stroke.[23]

The second mock ode, 'To Oblivion', is modelled more closely on Mason's work—especially *To Memory* and *To Melancholy*—and is a lesser performance than the Gray parody. Its major device is simply the substitution of the goddess 'Oblivion' and all her accoutrements (poppies, pamphlets, pantomimes), for the goddess 'Memory' and hers (nectar, the lyre, Milton's poetry).

Both burlesque poems embody the criticisms most frequently raised against the modern ode. In April of 1763 William Cowper summarized many of these objections in his ironical 'Dissertation on the Modern Ode' written for Lloyd's *St. James's Magazine*. Taking as his opening topics the ode's contrived emotion and 'the great convenience of its irregular measure', Cowper praises all that is wrong with the form. 'There is nothing in creation', he writes, 'that will not afford matter for the Ode':

Whether the poet addresses himself to Wisdom or Folly, Mirth or Melancholy, he breaks out in a fine enthusiasm, with an 'Oh, or Hail,' or some such pathetic expression, which naturally leads him to a description in at least fourteen lines, of the person and dwelling of no matter whom, which, with some observations upon her equipage and attendance, no matter what, make two stanzas.[24]

Such 'fine enthusiasm' was repeatedly cited by critics as one of the Pindaric ode's major faults. Lloyd, for example, burlesqued the mandatory 'enthusiasm' of the form in his 'An Ode. Secundum Artem': 'Shall I begin it with *Ah*, or *Oh*? / Be sad? *Oh*! yes. Be glad? *Ah*! no.'[25]

In the second half of the dissertation, Cowper sets down two 'infallible rules, whereby a student may learn to build the lofty Ode'. The first is 'Pathos' ('get together a large quantity of Oh's and Ah's!') and the second, 'Classicality':

Take MILTON, read his shorter poems, and particularly LYCIDAS, COMUS and SAMPSON; wherever you meet with an epithet, more especially, if it be a compound one, put it in your notebook; for as MILTON copied the antients, the more you steal from MILTON, of consequence the nearer you come to the antients.

(p. 124)

While this ironic suggestion specifically satirizes the well-known propensity of writers like Gray, Mason, and Collins to lift lines from Milton's shorter poems, it more generally alludes to the highly adjectival, and much criticized, idiom that characterized the modern ode. To the critics, the 'epithetical' style cultivated by the ode writers was perhaps their greatest fault. Lloyd, in a number of pieces written for *The Monthly Review*, deplored the use of such epithets in modern odes and elegies: 'The *cloud-built height*, the *pebbled shore*, the *surging brook, flower-hid path*, pellucid stream, moss-grown bed, and quivering beam, are infinitely too pretty for the poetry of nature; a profusion of such epithets cloys the taste.'[26] And Cowper, in his dissertation, ironically recommends several epithets, drawing examples directly from the poetry of Mason and Gray. Three of the terms—'weeping', 'tinkling', and 'moss-grown'—are packed into two lines of Mason's *On Melancholy*: 'As drops this little weeping rill / Soft-tinkling down the moss-grown hill' (13–14). These same epithets also make their way into Colman and Lloyd's 'Oblivion' ode, which contains a 'tinkling, weeping rill' and a 'moss-green cell'.

The burlesque odes were well received—at least by Gray's critics. Samuel Johnson was quite happy with them: 'The first of these Odes is the best but they are both good. They exposed a very bad kind of writing.'[27] Another time, he was positively enthusiastic, saying of the first ode: 'A considerable part of it may be numbered among those felicities which no man has twice attained.'[28] The odes drew the approbation of other literary men. Dr James Grainger wrote that he had read the *Two Odes* 'with uncommon satisfaction, and hope they will produce a proper change in the future compositions of Mason and Gray.'[29] Mason and Gray, however, refused to be persuaded, and their admirers rose in vigorous defense. William Warburton, later the victim of Churchill's mock dedication, called them, in his usual graceful style, 'two miserable buffoon odes'.[30] Horace Walpole, years later, wrote that they were

'trash, that was squirted from the kennel against you both'.[31]
But Gray himself seemed more amused than angered by the
odes, and certainly felt no need to resort to scatological rejoinders. Instead, he humorously wrote to Mason that the 'Odes
sell no more than mine did, for I saw a heap of them lie in a
Bookseller's window, who recommended them to me as a very
pretty thing.'[32] His other references to the burlesque odes are
in the same light vein.

Of course, Colman and Lloyd were far from confirmed Gray-
haters. In his *Epistle to C. Churchill*, Lloyd praised Gray's poetry
in no uncertain terms:

> What Muse like GRAY'S shall pleasing pensive flow
> Attemper'd sweetly to the rustic woe?
> Or who like him shall sweep the Theban lyre,
> And, as his master, pour forth thoughts of fire?[33]

Joseph Warton recorded that Colman and Lloyd 'once owned
to me that they repented the attempt' to burlesque Gray's odes;
and Colman, years later, wrote:

These Odes were indeed a piece of boys' play with my schoolfellow
Lloyd, with whom they were written in concert, in those days when
we had so little grace as to ridicule our Poetical Masters, joking
perhaps too licentiously with the *Prettynesses* of one poet, and the
Obscurities of another. We were not however insensible to their real
merits and excellencies, nor desirous to depreciate them.[34]

Nevertheless, Colman and Lloyd's odes are representative of
the Nonsense Club's generally negative attitude toward what
they felt to be the new school of contrived obscurity and formally correct 'enthusiasm'. What struck them as most laughable
was the paradox of a poet *labouring* to write 'inspired' poetry, or
hoping by close formal imitation to capture the feeling of a poet
(e.g. Pindar) whose chief virtue was lyric intensity. Thus
Cowper, in his mock dissertation, ironically applauds the fact
that the modern 'student may learn to build the lofty Ode, with
as much regularity, and as true mechanical principles, as a
mason or bricklayer erects a wall'. And Lloyd, reviewing J.
Cunningham's *Elegy on a Pile of Ruins* for *The Monthly Review*,
contends that 'though we cannot suppose any species of Poetry
is written without labour, yet whenever it appears, it dis-
gusts'.[35]

The Nonsense Club's objections to such 'mechanical' poetry focused on two related practices. The first was the close imitation of a poetic model and the resultant stress on formal perfection at the expense of sense, spontaneity, and power. The second was the use of ornamental epithets and excessive alliteration. Charles Churchill, in *The Prophecy of Famine*, memorably summarizes these Nonsense Club *bêtes noires* when he laments (ironically) that he is one

> Who cannot follow where *trim* fancy leads
> By *prattling* streams o'er *flow'r-empurpled* meads;
> Who often, but without success, have pray'd
> For *apt* ALLITERATION's *artful aid*,
> Who would, but cannot, with a master's skill
> Coin fine new epithets, *which mean no ill*,
> *Me*, thus uncouth, thus ev'ry way unfit
> For *pacing* poesy, and *ambling* wit,
> TASTE with contempt beholds, nor deigns to place
> Amongst the lowest of her favour'd race.
>
> (83–93)

All of the faults of the ode are here: overwrought epithets ('prattling', 'flow'r-empurpled'); excessive alliteration; and what the Nonsense Club habitually called 'pacing' or 'ambling' verse—poetry written more with an ear to sound than to sense or vigour. This final problem is cleverly addressed by Churchill in *The Apology*, in a passage that marches unerringly to a brilliant closing simile:

> Verses must run, to charm a modern ear,
> From all harsh, rugged interruptions clear:
> Soft let them breathe, as Zephyr's balmy breeze;
> Smooth let their current flow as summer seas;
> Perfect then only deem'd when they dispense
> A happy tuneful vacancy of sense.
> Italian fathers thus, with barb'rous rage,
> Fit helpless infants for the squeaking stage;
> Deaf to the calls of pity, Nature wound,
> And mangle vigour for the sake of sound.
>
> (340–9)

It is excessively laboured poetry—whether the labour is expended on epithets, alliteration, or formal perfection—that most offends Churchill, Lloyd, and Cowper. Such writing is offensive to them precisely because it destroys, as it attempts to imitate, the spontaneity and natural vigour they feel to be the soul of poetry. Modern poetry is emasculated or, to use Lloyd's phrase, bound by 'mechanic chains', because the obsession with contrived effects cuts off the free flow of the writer's genius. But just how this genius should truly manifest itself in poetry was for them a problem considerably harder to solve.

II

The Nonsense Club was not alone in its criticism of rules and imitation, its abhorrence of the epithetical style and contrived emotion, and its praise for unconfined, if not uneducated, genius. But Cowper, Lloyd, and Churchill were the only mid-century poets seriously to accept—and practise—the aesthetic implied by this criticism. One of their most unusual criteria (and one held, certainly, half in jest) was actual speed of composition. Lloyd was well known for the speed with which he wrote. Kenrick says that he was gifted with a 'tenaciousness of memory and facility of composition, the productions of no writer perhaps, ancient or modern, being more truly said to be written *currente calamo* than those of our Author'.[36] (It will be remembered that the phrase *currente calamo*—'with pen on the run'—was used by Colman the younger to describe his father's writing of a *Connoisseur* essay). In his epistle of 1754 Cowper humorously emphasizes Lloyd's poetic facility. After comparing Lloyd and Matthew Prior—both masters of 'easy' poetry— Cowper asks 'Fame' to determine the better. Fame replies that Prior deserves the laurel because 'with endless pains', he 'smooth'd and refin'd the meanest strains'. But Cowper objects:

> Sure so much labour, so much toil,
> Bespeak at least a stubborn soil:
> Theirs be the laurel-wreath decreed,
> Who both write well, and write full-speed!
> Who throw their Helicon about
> As freely as a conduit spout!
> Friend Robert, thus like *chien sçavant*,
> Lets fall a poem *en passant*,

Nor needs his genuine ore refine;
'Tis ready polish'd from the mine.[37]

(81–90)

While Cowper's comparison of Lloyd to the 'learned dogs' of pantomime entertainments is a playful, if somewhat crude, dig at his old friend, the final couplet represents a concise statement of the Nonsense Club aesthetic.

The stress on speed of composition was naturally accompanied by a scorn for revision; and behind both of these practices stood the ideal of unrefined genius. Churchill regards the roughness of quickly written, unrevised verse as an indication of the strength and vigour of the poet. 'Perish my Muse', he declares, 'If e'er her labour weaken to refine / The generous roughness of a nervous line.'[38] And in *Gotham* he burlesques his own slipshod methods in lines whose energy decisively overrules his self-satire:

> Had I the pow'r, I could not have the time,
> Whilst spirits flow, and Life is in her prime,
> Without a sin 'gainst Pleasure, to design
> A plan, to methodize each thought, each line
> Highly to finish, and make ev'ry grace,
> In itself charming, take new charms from place.
> Nothing of Books, and little known of men,
> When the mad fit comes on, I seize the pen,
> Rough as they run, the rapid thoughts set down,
> Rough as they run, discharge them on the Town.

(II. 165–74)

Churchill's justification for his neglect of preparation and discipline is that only by following his natural flow of thought, without stopping to refine, or weakening later by revision, can the poet approach the spontaneity of genius. The result, Churchill expects, will be uneven poetry, but poetry whose intermittent dullness is more than made up for the brilliance of its periodic 'flights'. In fact, he defends his hero Dryden's poetry in just such terms:

> What if some dull lines in cold order creep,
> And with his theme the poet seems to sleep?
> Still when his subject rises proud to view,
> With equal strength the poet rises too.

·With strong invention, noblest vigour fraught,
Thought still springs up and rises out of thought.[39]

(378–84)

Churchill could easily be describing his own poetry here. His favourite poets were Dryden and Shakespeare: both writers who were famous for their unevenness, reluctance to blot, facility of composition, and spontaneous brilliance.[40] In the eyes of William Cowper, writing in 1780, these also were Churchill's defining characteristics:

He is indeed a careless Writer for the most part, but where shall we find in any of those Authors who finish their Works with the Exactness of a Flemish Pencil, those Bold & daring Strokes of Fancy, those Numbers so hazardously ventured upon & so happily finished, the Matter so compress'd and yet so clear, & the Colouring so sparingly laid on, and yet with such a beautifull Effect?[41]

For Churchill and Lloyd, however, spontaneity of expression meant something more than mere speed or lack of revision: it meant allowing the mind the freedom to roam where it would —and then following it. The result was a digressive style of poetry in which the act of writing, and the associations flowing through the mind during this act, were as important a subject as the actual topic of the poem. T. E. Blom has called this kind of verse 'self-reflexive process poetry', and has compared it to mid-century 'oracular process poetry' as defined by Northrop Frye:

Rejecting the depersonalizing and limiting effects of formal education and the doctrine of imitation, both oracular and self-reflexive process poets make use of techniques which they believe both facilitate and suggest unpremeditated expression. As Frye notes in *Anatomy of Criticism*, the element of subconscious, uncontrolled association that joins the sound, movement, and rhythm of words to produce oracular poetry is the same element that produces the metrical impulse of doggerel, and doggerel is the verse form which self-reflexive poets choose to achieve spontaneity in expression.[42]

As Blom later notes, this self-reflexive mechanism is particularly strong in the poetry of Robert Lloyd. Lloyd seems continually to be commenting on what he is doing while he is doing it. For example, in 'The Cobler of Tissington's Letter to David

Garrick, Esq.,' he writes:

> Cobling extends a thousand ways,
> Some coble shoes, some coble plays;
> Some—but this jingle's vastly clever,
> It makes a body write forever.[43]

Unlike the oracular poets, Lloyd's inspiration is not 'sublime imagination', but 'familiar emanations' in which 'thought appears in dishabille, / And fancy does just what she will'.[44] The poet rambles in loose four foot verse—digressing, interrupting, commenting upon his own writing—as he tries to express directly his immediate experience and emotion. He focuses on 'simple thoughts', 'just as they rise from head or heart, / Not marshall'd by the herald Art'.[45] Thus, when the poet loses his train of thought, he doesn't despair, he writes about it:

> First, for a thought—since all agree—
> A thought—I have it—let me see—
> 'Tis gone again—Plague on't! I thought
> I had it—but I have it not.[46]

> (35-8)

The emphasis on humorous spontaneity also affects the form of the poetry, characteristically producing open-ended works filled with digression. In one extreme example—a poem called simply 'A Tale'—Lloyd indulges in what amounts to free association. After beginning to describe a curiously cross-mythic visit of the goddess Venus to St Caecilia, Lloyd interrupts himself to determine what kind of sounding device was on Caecilia's door:

> But, truth to say, I cannot tell
> Whether it Knocker was or Bell,
> (This for vertù an anecdote is)
> Which us'd to give CÆCILIA notice,
> When any lady of the sky
> Was come to bear her company.
> But this I'm sure, be which it will,
> Thomas perform'd his part with skill.
>   Methinks I hear the reader cry—
> His part with skill? why, You or I,
> Or any body else, as well
> As Thomas, sure, could ring a bell.[47]

Lloyd uses this opening to slip into a two-page digression on the importance of different knocks in indicating the social rank of the caller. By the time he finally gets back to the visit, and begins describing the ladies' elaborate greetings, he is sounding like Byron at his most impatient:

> As *humble servant, how d'you do,*
> And in return, *pray how are you?*
> Enrich'd at ev'ry proper space
> With due integuments of lace,
> As Madam, Grace, and Goddeship,
> Which we for brevity shall skip.
>
> (p. 70)

The actual visit is sketched very quickly before Lloyd allows a metaphor for Caecilia's 'inspiration' to lead him rambling again—this time into three pages of digression on Methodists. Finally, to emphasize the extraordinary lack of order in the piece, Lloyd closes with a long catalogue describing just where his free association has taken him:

> But what can all this rambling mean?
> Was ever such an hodge-podge seen?
> VENUS, CÆCILIA, Saints, and Whores,
> Thomas, Vertu', Bells, Knockers, Doors,
> Lords, Rogues, Relations, Ladies, Cits,
> Stars, Flambeaux, Thunderbolts, Horns, Wits,
> Vulcan, and Cuckhold-maker, Scandal,
> Music, and Footman, Ear of Handel,
> Weather, News, Envy, Politicks,
> Intrigues, and Woman's Thousand Tricks,
> Prudes, Methodists, and Devotees,
> Fastings, Feasts, Pray'r, and Charities. . . .
>   Where's the connection, where's the plan?
> The devil sure is in the man.
> All in an instant we are hurl'd
> From place to place all round the world,
> Yet find no reason for it—mum—
> There, my good critic, lies the hum—
> Well, but methinks, it wou'd avail
> To know the end of this—A TALE.
>
> (pp. 75–6)

And that is the end of the poem. The critic is left empty-handed, and Lloyd flits away, fascinated and amused by the clutter of his own mind.

The value of such a piece, at least in the eyes of the Nonsense Club, was that besides being 'humorous' the nonsense and trifles more truly represented the natural instincts and workings of the author's mind than did the acquired patterns of thought and behaviour necessary for the writing of a serious, 'designed' work:

> . . . Trifles often shew the Man,
> More than his settled Life and Plan:
> These are the starts of inclination;
> Those the mere gloss of EDUCATION.[48]

By skimming the thoughts off the surface of his mind, Lloyd wanted not only to amuse his friends, but to give them the closest possible representation of his mental process—in effect, to reproduce himself as he would have been at a tavern or a Nonsense Club meeting. Like intimate conversation, his poetry ebbs and flows, branches off, loses its way, but the poet —the manipulator—remains constant. In his easy intimacy lies the value of the piece: 'in writing to a friend / A man may any nonsense send, / And the chief merit to impart, / The honest feelings of his heart.'[49]

When we speak of free association, humorous digression, and psychological self-portraiture, the names of Sterne and Byron come immediately to mind. Laurence Sterne was a contemporary of the Nonsense Club, and certainly the first four volumes of *Tristram Shandy* (1759–62) show a great affinity to the self-reflexive process poetry of Lloyd and Churchill. Sterne was, in effect, a self-reflexive process novelist. At the other end of George III's reign, the reflexive process tradition culminates in Byron's *Don Juan*: brilliantly spontaneous, unabashedly digressive, supposedly dictated by Byron each morning as he shaved. The delight in the process of the associative mind that characterizes both Sterne's and Byron's greatest works is also one of the most notable features of Charles Churchill's poetry. Although Blom unaccountably neglects Churchill in his discussion of self-reflexive process poets, it is in Churchill's work that this aesthetic is given a contemporary voice surpassed only by

Sterne's and a poetic articulation that remained unequalled until Byron.[50]

Eighteenth-century critics were quick to recognize the Shandean features of Churchill's poetry. *The Ghost*, without a doubt Churchill's most associational, process-oriented poem, was called by *The Monthly Review*, 'a digressive, incoherent production . . . which may not improperly be termed a kind of *Tristram Shandy* in *verse*'. But this incoherence (i.e. lack of unity) proved no drawback in the eyes of a latter *Monthly* reviewer, who praised both the poem and the novel: 'as in the inimitable work of his brother Sterne, there are a thousand moral, witty, and excellent passages scattered through this rambling performance; every part of which we have read with pleasure, without being well able to say what we were reading—such absolute command over use, such unbounded power hath GENIUS!'[51]

On a syntactic level, the self-reflexivity that characterizes *The Ghost* is most vividly exemplified by Churchill's incessant use of parenthetical statements. Short interjections alternate with longer, more complex parenthetical digressions—and digressions within digressions—that sometimes stretch a single sentence or phrase to truly 'incoherent' length. In a 1763 addition to Book I of *The Ghost*, Churchill begins a sentence, 'The HERO (who for brawn and face . . .)', writes thirty-five lines of digression on his looks, on honour, prudence, and discretion, throws in an additional parenthetical interjection—'(tho', save the mark, / That point is something in the dark)'—and finally concludes the sentence, 'Like DRUGGER comes, that magic pow'rs / May ascertain his *lucky* hours' (I. 201–38). The sentence—'The HERO . . . Like DRUGGER comes'—is suspended purposefully and obtrusively, in much the same way as Sterne suspends, for pages, Uncle Toby's famous comment on the 'noise' upstairs.[52] In fact, the use of parenthetical asides is such an integral part of *The Ghost*'s structure that by Book IV Churchill can joke 'that our drift (Parenthesis / For once apart) is briefly this' (IV. 123–4).

The Ghost appeared in three increments: Books I and II (March 1762), Book III (October 1762), and Book IV (November 1763). Because of the structure imposed on Book I by its earlier prototype—Churchill's unpublished 'Fortune Teller'—there is less digression in it than in the later books. Once free of

this restrictive model, however, Churchill begins to revel in
his own lack of direction. The spirit and style of this rambling is
typified by the opening of Book III. After writing a string of
clichés describing morning in the country—'These Images, or
bad or good, / If they are rightly understood, / *Sagacious*
Readers must allow, / Proclaim us in the Country now'—
Churchill abruptly begins again:

> IT WAS THE HOUR—tho' Critics frown,
> We now declare ourselves in TOWN,
> Nor will a moment's pause allow
> For finding when we came, or how.
> The Man who deals in humble Prose,
> Tied down by rule and method goes,
> But they, who court the vig'rous Muse,
> Their carriage have a right to chuse.
> Free as the Air, and unconfin'd,
> Swift as the motions of the Mind,
> The Poet darts from place to place,
> And instant bounds o'er Time and Space.
> Nature (whilst blended fire and skill
> Inflame our passions to his will)
> Smiles at her violated Laws,
> And crowns his daring with applause.

> (III. 25–40)

We may compare the second half of this proclamation with
Lloyd's description of Shakespeare:

> When Shakespeare leads the mind a dance,
> From France to England, hence to France,
> Talk not to me of time and place;
> I own I'm happy in the chace.
> Whether the drama's here or there,
> 'Tis nature, Shakespeare, every where.
> The poet's fancy can create,
> Contract, enlarge, annihilate,
> Bring past and present close together,
> In spite of distance, seas, or weather.[53]

In both passages, the emphasis is on the importance of the
poet's mental process and the spontaneous manipulation of his
materials. The poet does not plan his work in relationship to a
set of literary laws or purposes ('rule and method'); the work's

shape and subjects evolve directly from 'the motions of the Mind': a mind that can transform and violate reality, that 'bounds o'er Time and Space', that can 'Contract, enlarge, annihilate' the exterior world. Though they were conservative in their choice of subject and in their poetic idiom—preferring society and couplets to abysses and epodes, and damning at every opportunity the soaring obscurity of the 'oracular' poets —nevertheless, Lloyd and Churchill's position on poetic process was as radical as any of their time. They did not merely talk of spontaneity, they practised it with a vengeance.

Book III of *The Ghost* represents the high water mark of the aesthetic of spontaneity in the Nonsense Club's work. The mock description of morning and the proclamation of freedom quoted above are followed not by a return to the subject—The Ghost—but by a shifting digression on 'Rogues of Modesty' that continues until the poet realizes what he is doing:

> But hold—whilst thus we play the fool,
> In bold contempt of ev'ry rule,
> Things of no consequence expressing,
> *Describing* now, and now *digressing*,
> To the discredit of our skill,
> The main concern is standing still.

> (III. 59–64)

Imminent action is promised, but the poem stands still a good while longer as Churchill writes a twenty-five line digression on digressions, a one hundred line digression on method and methodical poets, a mock invocation of the methodical William Whitehead—'Damp ev'ry spark of genuine fire, / And langours, like thine own, inspire, / Trite be each Thought, and ev'ry Line / As *Moral*, and as *Dull* as THINE'—and, after all these expedients, is finally able to stop, 'Pois'd in mid-air' (III. 181). At least we think it is the poet poised in mid-air, until we find out at the bottom of a ten-line verse paragraph that the subject is now 'FAME'. A two-hundred line digression on 'FAME' follows, which ends with Churchill promising 'T'amaze the Readers with our skill, / To pour out such a flood of knowledge / As might suffice for a whole College' (III. 350–2). Luckily, the second item in this 'flood of knowledge' is a digression on cities—'A *City* once for Pow'r renown'd, / Now level'd even to the ground, / Beyond all doubt is a direction / To introduce some *fine* reflection' (III. 403–6)—in the course of which Churchill suddenly finds himself back in England '(for that's at last the Scene, / Tho' Worlds on Worlds should rise between, / Whither we must our course pursue)' and rising to the fortuitous occasion needs only two pages of political satire to bring him round to Dullman and his chaplain, Crape, waiting for the report of the three Ghost investigators, Pomposo, Plausible, and Moore.

In Book IV this digressive process continues, with Churchill becoming more and more self-conscious. It takes him 777 lines even to mention the Ghost, and he is quick to call attention to the fact:

> For instance—this book—the Ghost—
> Methinks I hear some Critic Post
> Remark most gravely—'The first word
> Which we about the Ghost have heard.'
>
> (IV. 777–80)

Churchill answers the critic's objection by claiming that he writes until the subject 'comes'; and he continues with a vivid description of the self-reflexive process:

> I wrote and wrote (perhaps you doubt,
> And shrewdly, what I wrote about,
> Believe me, much to my disgrace,
> I too am in the self-same case)
> But still I wrote, till FANNY came
> Impatient, nor could any shame
> On me with equal justice fall,
> If She had never come at all.
>
> (IV. 789–96)

There is, of course, a parody of the Muse 'coming' in all this, but the chief motive for the passage, I think, lies in Churchill's desire to describe his special style of writing. He literally did write and write until Fanny, the subject, by some quirk of association again entered his mind. But in this instance, as in so many others, Churchill quickly leaves her behind and once more digresses in a series of three verse paragraphs. In each paragraph (beginning with the identical, 'But to return'),

Churchill strives manfully to stop digressing, only to keep falling back into his old habits. He uses his failing as both a subject
and a comic structure:

> But to return—and this I hold,
> A secret worth its weight in gold
> To those who write, as I write now,
> Not to mind where they go, or how,
> Thro' ditch, thro' bog, o'er hedge and stile,
> Make it but worth the Reader's while,
> And keep a passage fair and plain
> Always to bring him back again. . . .
> But to return—if WIT, who ne'er
> The shackles of restraint could bear,
> In wayward humour should refuse
> Her timely succour to the *Muse*,
> And to no rules and orders tied
> Roughly deny to be her guide,
> She must renounce *Decorum's* plan,
> And get back when, and how she can. . . .
> But to return— . . .
>
> (IV. 813–43)

Here we have Churchill, as his wit runs away with him, talking
about his wit running away with him. The emphasis on the
untidiness of the process—both explicitly and through the
structure—is a humorous, but meaningful, aesthetic statement:
a statement that at least partially refutes critics like John
Forster, who censured Churchill as 'a writer who seized care-
lessly every incident of the hour; and who, knowing the enormous sale his writings could command, sought immediate vent
for thoughts and fancies too broken and irregular for a formal
plan.'[54] While this evaluation has a good deal of truth in it, it
ignores the aesthetic of spontaneity advocated by the Nonsense
Club. Churchill's economic and critical ideas may luckily have
coincided. But the critical ideals came first.

Churchill's fooling reaches its climax about a hundred lines
later when having digressed once again to speak of courtiers he
accidentally stumbles upon his main subject (Dullman and the
Ghost investigators) in the midst of his satire on the court. In
the space between stanzas, he seems to do a double take, and

then exclaims:

> Thanks to my Stars—I now see shore—
> Of Courtiers, and of Courts no more—
> Thus stumbling on my City Friends,
> Blind Chance my guide, my purpose bends
> In line direct, and shall pursue
> The point which I had first in view,
> Nor more shall with the Reader sport
> Till I have seen him safe in port.
>
> (IV. 963–70)

Here, at last, Churchill dismisses digression once and for all ('But hold—once more *Digression* hence— / Let us return to *Common-Sense*'), and through the City association works his way, in a relatively straight line, back to Dullman, to the more conventional satire on the Lord Mayor's procession, and, finally, to the end of the poem.

Certainly one would not pretend that Churchill thought that to produce valid poetry one had always to write at full speed without a plan. Much of this is humorous exaggeration. Churchill himself called *The Ghost*, 'A mere amusement at the most, / A trifle, fit to wear away / The horrors of a rainy day' (IV. 844–6). But anchoring the joke is the reality of Churchill's style. Some of his best effects are those available only to a mind working 'vigorously' and at full speed. In *The Ghost*, the constant shifting of subject and attitude is engendered by the varying ways in which key words or ideas strike Churchill as he hurries by. A concept can change shape in an instant. A case in point is Churchill's handling of 'Truth' in Book II. Initially, Churchill seems very much on the side of Truth, describing her as a goddess 'But little lov'd, or known on earth' (II. 124), a deity whose name is exploited and maligned. After describing some of these hypocritical usages, Churchill aligns himself with the genuine article:

> If, in the giddy hours of Youth,
> My constant soul adher'd to TRUTH;
> If, from the Time I first wrote Man,
> I still pursu'd thy sacred plan, . . .
> Hither, o hither, condescend,
> ETERNAL TRUTH, thy steps to bend,

And favour *Him*, who ev'ry hour
Confesses and obeys thy pow'r!

(II. 147–50, 157–60)

Churchill does not merely invoke Truth, he challenges her.
She need come only if he has fulfilled her 'sacred plan'. The
tenor of the passage seems serious, but immediately Churchill
begins to contaminate the ideal. He asks that Truth come not
'with that easy mien' that won Swift, nor with that 'arch
ambiguous face' that captured Cervantes, but in 'sacred ves-
ture clad, / Solemnly dull, and truly sad!' (II. 161–8). Within a
few more lines, we find Truth flanked by Dullness and Attention: 'With THEE, let formal DULLNESS come, / And deep
ATTENTION, ever dumb' (II. 179–80). And by the next
paragraph Churchill has come round completely from his
original position and is praising 'down-right *City* TRUTH'
(the very same hypocritical Truth he began by attacking). The
reversal comes about insidiously, as Churchill prepares the
reader for a straightforward discussion of 'ETERNAL
TRUTH' and then begins to substitute subversive words and
ideas. Schooled in irony, we stop, backtrack, and soon regain
orientation. But only for a moment. As soon as Churchill finishes his short section on '*City* TRUTH', he begins a new paragraph without a hint of irony:

By TRUTH inspir'd, *our* BACON's force
Open'd the way to Learning's source;
BOYLE thro' the works of NATURE ran;
And NEWTON, something more than Man,
Div'd into Nature's hidden springs,
Laid bare the principles of things.

(II. 213–18)

He goes on to praise Dr John Douglas, who had recently shown
that a charge of plagiarism raised against Milton was based on
a forgery:

By TRUTH inspir'd, when *Lauder's* spight
O'er MILTON cast the Veil of Night,
DOUGLAS arose, and thro' the maze
Of intricate and winding ways,
Came where the subtle Traitor lay,
And dragg'd him trembling to the day.

(II. 221–6)

But then just as we have again readjusted our perspective, the same unannounced and unexpected substitution of values occurs:

> By TRUTH inspir'd, our *Critics* go
> To track FINGAL in *Highland* snow,
> To form their own and others *CREED*
> From *Manuscripts* they cannot read.
> By TRUTH inspir'd, we numbers see
> Of each Profession and Degree,
> Gentle and Simple, Lord and Cit,
> Wit without wealth, wealth without wit;
> When PUNCH and SHERIDAN have done,
> To FANNY's *Ghostly Lectures* run.
>
>   (II. 233–42)

Churchill gradually degrades Truth from the inspirer of Bacon to the inspirer of Ghost mania, but he neither hints at nor acknowledges the transformation. While the satire of the latter sections is palpable, the consistency of Churchill's rhetoric leads the reader momentarily astray. This disjunctive method —commonly used by the Augustans in smaller units such as 'contaminating catalogues'—is for Churchill a central structuring device. He habitually moves through the many connotations of a given word or ideal without overtly taking sides. Meanings are not opposed as good or bad, true or corrupt, but merely *used* in the many ways that society actually uses them. In essence, Churchill shows us that, in Thomas Lockwood's words, 'the true basis of the associations evoked by moral abstractions such as Virtue, Vice, Reason, and Nature, lies not in morals but in language'.[55]

David Hume, writing in 1757, came to essentially the same conclusion:

It is indeed obvious, that writers of all nations and all ages concur in applauding justice, humanity, magnanimity, prudence, veracity; and in blaming the opposite qualities. . . . This great unanimity is usually ascribed to the influence of plain reason, which, in all these cases, maintains similar sentiments. . . . So far as the unanimity is real, this account may be admitted as satisfactory. But we must also allow, that some part of the seeming harmony in morals may be accounted for from the very nature of language. The word *virtue*, with its eqivalent in every tongue, implies praise, as that of *vice* does blame.[56]

But whether (using Hume's example) *virtue*, in its material application, involves the getting of money (work ethic) or the disdaining of money (monasticism), conservative politics or radical politics, coddling the child or beating him for his own good, depends entirely on the interpreter. In Churchill's poetry, no reconciliation of conflicting meanings is attempted, nor is there usually any overt condemnation of a specific meaning. In general, the structuring abstraction appears not as an absolute standard, but as a relativistic idea whose shape and value depend entirely on context.

The effects possible in this relativistic mode are well illustrated by the digression on Fancy in Book IV of *The Ghost*. Here Churchill's ability to reverse meaning and context with disconcerting agility is reminiscent of Swift's convoluted brilliance in *A Tale of a Tub*. But Churchill's ambiguity arises not so much out of a premeditated moral plan (as does Swift's), but simply by reflex; his speed and powers of association carry him into contradictory contexts; he moves reflexively from one pole of an argument to its opposite. In Book IV, he begins the digression by giving serious praise to Fancy—'Some for *Reality* may call, / FANCY to me is All in All'—and backs his praise with the very personal example of Fancy's offering him 'Deliv'rance from the gripe of Woe' during a dreadful period when he was overcome by 'Authority' (about to be jailed for debt). At the darkest moment, 'When Virtue shunn'd the shock, and Pride / Disabled, lay by Virtue's side', Fancy came like a saviour:

> Health in her motion, the wild grace
> Of Pleasure speaking in her face,
> Dull Regularity thrown by,
> And Comfort beaming from her eye,
> FANCY, in richest robes array'd,
> Came smiling forth, and brought me aid,
> Came smiling o'er that dreadful time,
> And, more to bless me, came in *Rhime*.

(IV. 339–46)

The catalogue of Fancy's comforts represents Churchill's grand desiderata, expressed many times elsewhere in his poetry. But Churchill seems compelled to push over to the

other side of Fancy. As his view expands beyond his personal
experience—'Nor is her Pow'r to Me confin'd, / It spreads. It
comprehends Mankind'—Churchill's tone changes. Moving
into an ironic mode, he describes Fancy's role in making George
III's coronation seem splendid to the viewers and participants.
Fancy quickly becomes the implied villain in a classic battle
between appearance and reality. It is Fancy that deludes the
absurd 'Whiffle' into thinking he is great and good. It is Fancy
that makes a superannuated court lady think herself young
again:

> FANCY, betwixt such eyes enshrin'd,
> No brush to daub, no mill to grind,
> Thrice wav'd her wand around, whose force
> Chang'd in an instant Nature's course . . .
> Quite alter'd was the whole machine,
> And Lady —— —— was fifteen.
>
> (IV. 605–8, 625–6)

Fancy, by the end of the coronation satire, seems a sham, a
way of counterfeiting life. But Churchill's earlier praise of
Fancy is never openly contradicted or qualified. The shift in
point of view is unannounced and unacknowledged. And even
when it is felt, we are left to ask ourselves, is there such a thing
as 'true Fancy'? Doesn't Fancy—whether Churchill's or the
populace's—deal in the same illusions? Or, if the illusions are
realities, then aren't Whiffle's as valid as Churchill's? Strange
as it may seem, Churchill's answer to this last question appears
to be 'yes'. He seems prepared to believe that men actually *are*
what they believe themselves to be simply because there is no
way to refute their belief: 'By his own Sense and Feelings
taught, / In speech as lib'ral as in thought, / Let ev'ry Man
enjoy his whim; / What's He to Me, or I to him?' (IV. 213–
16).[57]

A final example of Churchill's mastery of this relativistic
mode is notable also for its compression and 'weightless' brilliance. This is the transitional passage in *The Prophecy of Famine*
between the literary satire on academic verse and the political
satire on Scotland. Notice how the ideas of Art and Nature
seem to exchange places:

> Of false refinements sick, and labour'd ease,
> Which Art, too thinly veil'd, forbids to please,

By Nature's charms (inglorious truth!) subdued,
However plain her dress, and haviour rude,
To *northern* climes my happier course I steer,
Climes where the Goddess reigns throughout the year,
Where undisturb'd by Art's *rebellious* plan,
She rules the *loyal Laird*, and *faithful Clan*.

(103–10)

The opening statement on Art is part of a longer satire on highly artificial poetry that represents Churchill and the Nonsense Club's usual aesthetic position. But as the passage proceeds, the entire formula becomes ironic by association, as Churchill uses it to introduce a satire on Scotland—a land, even by his standards, *too* rude and plain. The reader begins by agreeing with something that is suddenly transformed into its opposite: effeminate 'Art' becomes a sorely needed 'plan' of life; Nature's 'charms' become the harsh, bestial reality of life in rural Scotland. Like 'Fancy', the abstractions 'Art' and 'Nature' must be judged in context. And the context, in the hands of Churchill, is constantly changing, slipping away, reversing itself. The response of the reader is usually a form of confusion —a confusion too often attributed to the failure of Churchill's poetic expression. But the disjunction of his poetry—caused in part by reflexivity and speed—is also a conscious attempt to convey the disjunction of the times and the inherent ambiguity of aesthetic and ethical abstractions. Rather than being guilty of confused expression, Churchill is guilty only of expressed confusion.

For the student of the mid-eighteenth century, this poetic practice says much about the period as a whole. It was a time when reflexivity and contradiction were not only blossoming novelistic and poetic devices but actual modes of perception and action. Running to extremes, cultivating incongruity, and all the time watching oneself with fascination—these are the characteristics of 'modern' mid-century man. Perhaps the most famous, and certainly the most vividly recorded case, is James Boswell's. One minute an 'Addison', the next a rake, a fledgling author, a guilty husband, a man-about-town, Boswell in his journals records with extraordinary immediacy and candour the incongruous, embarrassing flow of his mind as he drifts in and out of one social 'costume' after another. His life is

polarized and contradictory; his values dependent to an extraordinary degree on the context in which he is placed. In the
London Journal, he confesses to a fault that immediately calls to
mind the Nonsense Club's compulsive irreverence and propensity to laugh at or distort their own most deeply held values:
'Another shocking fault which I have is my sacrificing almost,
anything to a laugh, even myself; in so much that it is possible
if one of these my companions should come in this moment, I
might show them as a matter of jocularity the preceding three
or four pages, which contain the most sincere sentiments of my
heart; and at these would we laugh most immoderately.'[58]

Even Samuel Johnson, steeped as he was in conservative
values, was painfully aware of the contradictions of his life: the
force of his utterance and the ludicrousness of his appearance,
the strength of his will to believe and his inability to sustain
faith, his admiration of activity and addiction to sloth. Like
Churchill, Johnson recognized clearly the inability of abstractions to encompass the variety of nature. 'The works and operations of nature', he wrote, 'are too great in their extent, or too
much diffused in their relations, and the performances of art
too inconstant and uncertain, to be reduced to any determinate
idea.' This impossibility of absolute definition is most obviously
manifested in language: 'Things modified by human under-
standings, subject to varieties of complication, and changeable
as experience advances knowledge, or accident influences
caprice, are scarcely to be included in any standing form of
expression, because they are always suffering some alteration
of their state.'[59] Indeed, at mid-century, discourse theory was
steadily moving toward the conclusion 'that all writing is
necessarily tentative and ephemeral, subject to endless evolution
as additional data comes to light'—a formulation Churchill
sensed instinctively and portrayed in his work to a degree
unrivalled by any contemporary poet.[60]

It was to the shifting, incongruous, contextual life of real
human beings that Churchill dedicated his poetry. His fascination was with the immediate impression, the unpremeditated
expression, and the visceral reaction. Churchill, like Boswell,
was an empirical man; a man who tests and tries, adopts many
roles, and trusts only his own senses. Often this testing is done
in a humorous vein, but, as Martin Price notes, 'what seems to

us mere frivolity was often the detached experimental playfulness of men testing the nature of sensibility and the powers of response'.[61] And, as Walter Jackson Bate observes, this empirical, irreverent state of mind also had its dangers:

In its opposition to the universal, and its emphasis upon sensory and experiential proof, it [empiricism] is also essentially anti-rationalistic: it turns in distrust upon the generalizations which the 'meddling intellect' is prone to make for the sake of convenience; in the reasoning process itself, as in other phenomena, it accepts that alone which is constant and direct experience can verify; and, if carried far enough, its extreme results may easily become a skeptical relativism, and a final inability to rely on much more than individual sentiment.[62]

Churchill, certainly, carried his 'empiricism' about as far as one could, and a sceptical, relativistic, disjunctive poetry was the result.

III

The lives of all of the Nonsense Club members were deeply marked by the same qualities that characterize Lloyd and Churchill's poetry: contradiction, moral and aesthetic relativism, rebellion against established forms, a love of spontaneity, and an extreme consciousness of self. By 1762, four of the five friends (Cowper only excepted) had essentially given up the professions dictated to them by their families and training, and were attempting to live by their literary wits in London. This was a risky business, to say the least: the 'starving author' was an eighteenth-century commonplace. Of course, Thornton expected a substantial inheritance, and Colman had at least the grudging support of the Earl of Bath and the hope of a legacy, but both Lloyd and Churchill were entirely on their own—a situation of which they were very much aware.

After receiving his MA from Cambridge in 1758, Lloyd had become an usher at Westminster School. The job proved irksome, the pupils unruly, and the pay meagre (typically 4s. to 8s. per week plus board). Feeling trapped, and no doubt spurred on by Colman and Thornton's success with *The Connoisseur*, Lloyd soon resigned his position to undertake a literary career. In his 'Apology' he described the indignities and frustrations that pushed him to this drastic and, as it eventually proved, fatal step:

> For, not to dwell upon the toil
> Of working on a barren soil,
> And lab'ring with incessant pains
> To cultivate a blockhead's brains,
> The duties there but ill befit
> The love of letters, arts, or wit.[63]

In a succeeding passage, Lloyd ties his love of 'letters, arts, and wit' to a plea for intellectual freedom that, while referring specifically to the teaching position, recalls the Nonsense Club's more general ethical and aesthetic preoccupations:

> For me, it hurts me to the soul
> To brook confinement or controul;
> Still to be pinion'd down to teach
> The syntax and the parts of speech;
> Or, what perhaps is drudging worse,
> The links, and joints, and rules of verse.

The confinement of the job and the confinement of the curriculum were both unbearable. One can easily understand Lloyd's unhappy reaction when he found himself not only tied down by his job, but in the hypocritical position of having to teach imaginative restrictions ('rules') to his pupils.

Churchill's reasons for neglecting and then resigning his duties as curate and lecturer of St John's, Westminster, were likewise based on hatred of 'confinement or controul'. He had come to Westminster in 1758 with a wife, two children (there would soon be a third), and little money. (He would later characterize the duty of the English clergy as 'To pray, and starve on forty pounds a year'.)[64] During his first two years there, he ran deeply into debt. In imminent danger of debtors' prison, he was saved only by the intercession of Pierson Lloyd, who prevailed on his creditors to accept a composition of five shillings in the pound—a deed Churchill never forgot and one which he repaid as soon as his literary success allowed.

Faced with the impossibility of making ends meet on a curate's stipend, Churchill had earlier tried to supplement his income by teaching at Rainham, and later tutoring at a ladies' boarding school in Queen's Square, Bloomsbury. During this time, he may also have edited, with Lloyd, the poetical section of *The Library*. Such drudgery must have been particularly oppressive to a man of Churchill's temperament, and it certainly did nothing to mitigate the rebellious streak already detectable in his early, imprudent marriage and his premature withdrawal from the university. When none of his money-making expedients worked, when bankruptcy finally became a reality, Churchill, in a rejection of orthodox responsibilities, began to ignore both his family and clerical duties in order to devote himself wholly to poetry. On 14 March 1761, *The Rosciad* was published, and Churchill became at once notorious and solvent. This new-found freedom and reputation, however, only further fuelled his rebelliousness. In January 1763 he resigned his curacy. Sometime earlier, he had separated from his wife.

Undoubtedly, the belatedness of Churchill and Lloyd's rebellion contributed greatly to its magnitude. Unlike Thornton, whose inheritance allowed him to neglect medicine from the beginning, or Colman, whose allowance made it possible for him to move gradually out of the law and into the theatre, Lloyd and Churchill were stuck—economically—in positions they found intolerable. Whereas Thornton and Colman had both been publishing since their early twenties, Lloyd (except for his *Connoisseur* pieces) and Churchill had seen their literary efforts go unrecognized and unrewarded until nearly the age of thirty. An explosion was imminent, and in the early 1760s it came.

Drawn together by their defiance and their uncertainty, Churchill and Lloyd began habitually to sit late in taverns: comforting and reassuring each other, cultivating oblivion from a bottle, and denouncing the outside world for its hypocrisy. This paranoiac isolation is strikingly captured in Churchill's *Night: An Epistle to Robert Lloyd* (1761); a poem that, while overtly defending an imprudent lifestyle, is perhaps most interesting for its tone of doubtfulness, and for the implicit insecurity it reveals.

Several critics of *Night* have been content merely to stress the more overt themes of the poem. Kenneth Hopkins calls it a defence of libertinism, while Raymond Smith emphasizes its praise of individualism and its attacks on establishment hypocrisy, thereby linking it with Churchill's later satires.[65] But I think these critics miss an essential quality of the poem, one defined in a glimmering of brilliance by William Kenrick when, in his preface to the 1774 edition of Lloyd's *Poetical Works*, he wrote of Lloyd and Churchill's 'suicide genius'. Such genius, by 'railing at others . . . thinks to excuse itself; imputing to ignorance or malevolence the cause of that ruin in which, against its own better knowledge, it is inevitable as unpardonably involved.'[66] John Forster recognized this same self-destructive defensiveness in Churchill's behaviour when he noted that he 'would resist or he would succumb: in the one case, boasting exemption from vice, would become himself the victim of the worst vices; and in the other, with a violent recoil from the hypocrisies, would outrage the proprieties of life.'[67] These two comments summarize the dubious mood of *Night*. It is a defence of libertinism, a plea for personal liberty, and a satire on false propriety—but more than that, it is a portrait of Churchill and Lloyd in the midst of their rebellion: at once bold and doubtful, boisterous and self-destructive, cheerful and afraid.

The poem opens with a short jab at Churchill's enemies, but then dissolves into a strangely poignant lament and an implicit admission that the relief that night affords is as much from the poet's own 'sorrow' and 'care' as from the hypocrisies of the 'daylight world':

> WHEN foes insult, and *prudent* friends dispense,
> In pity's strains, the worst of insolence,
> Oft with thee, LLOYD, I steal an hour from grief,
> And in thy social converse find relief.
> The mind, of solitude impatient grown,
> Loves any sorrows rather than her own.
>   LET slaves to business, bodies without soul,
> Important blanks in Nature's mighty roll,
> Solemnize nonsense in the day's broad glare,
> We NIGHT prefer, which heals or hides our care.
>
>   (1–10)

The poet's 'sorrow' and 'care' are only obliquely caused by the hypocritical 'daylight' world he attacks. It is not the insults of foes nor the insolence of prudent friends, nor even the chicanery of public life, that most deeply distress Chuchill—these can, and through the length of the poem, *will* be combated—but it is some more personal perplexity that is aggravated by solitary contemplation: 'The mind, of solitude impatient grown, / Loves any sorrows rather than her own.' Again, in the second stanza, it is the 'important blanks' of the daylight world that are satirized, but the poet's own 'care' that night 'heals or hides'. What 'sorrow' and 'care' refer to becomes clearer in the third stanza, when Churchill contrasts the prosperity of the hypocritical worldlings to his own, and Lloyd's, equivocal position:

> ROGUES justified and by success made bold,
> Dull fools and coxcombs sanctified by Gold,
> Freely may bask in fortune's partial ray,
> And spread their feathers op'ning to the day;
> But *thread-bare* Merit dares not shew the head
> 'Till vain Prosperity retires to bed.
> Misfortunes, like the Owl, avoid the light;
> The sons of CARE are always sons of NIGHT.
>
> (11-18)

'CARE' would seem, then, to refer to poverty or some sort of economic distress; but since at the time of the poem Churchill was not in monetary straits (having recently made a killing on *The Rosciad*), I would suggest that 'CARE' alludes more accurately to Churchill and Lloyd's fateful decision to abandon what today would be called the 'rat race'.

Having rejected the conventional world, Churchill and Lloyd vigorously attacked its hypocrisy; but at the same time, they regretted their inability to challenge the power of the daylight rogues. Driven by impulse and bravado (and perhaps conviction) to renounce conventional careers, they nevertheless were not content in their retirement. The 'pity' of friends and the supercilious stares of the 'great' heated them to retaliation. But their power of retaliation (outside satiric poetry) was limited, by the very act of their rebellion, to the committing of more and more flagrant social improprieties. William Kenrick characterized their 'progress': 'The truth seems to be that, however eagerly these sons of Anacreon might enter on the career of these jovial amusements, they continued their race, out of pique at the worldy disrespect, which they had unadvisedly and perhaps unexpectedly incurred.'[68] What was once both fun and daring became—with the throwing over of their jobs and responsibilities—a crusade for self-justification; and because the fun had been based on drink and irresponsibility, the crusade would continue in this 'career' to its logical self-destructive end. It is in an implicit recognition of the desperation of his situation that Churchill drowns 'in Oblivion's grateful cup . . . / The galling sneer, the supercilious frown, / The strange reserve, the proud affected state / Of upstart knaves grown rich and fools grown great' (85–8). If the rich knaves and fools are the apparent villains, it is Churchill's self-imposed impotence and self-destructive rebellion that are the real causes of his 'CARE'.

If Churchill and Lloyd's responses to criticism were both, to a degree, self-destructive, Lloyd added to his a substantial dose of self-effacement. The more passive of the two men, he seemed content that posterity should forget him. This bluff lowering of expectations is found everywhere in his poetry. 'You say I shou'd get fame. I doubt it: / Perhaps I am as well without it', Lloyd writes.[69] And in another place:

> I cannot strive with daring flight
> To reach the bold *Parnassian* HEIGHT;
> But at its foot, content to stray,
> In easy unambitious way,
> Pick up those flowers the muse's send,
> To make a nosegay for my friend.
> In short, I lay no idle claim
> To genius strong, and noisy fame.
> But with a hope and wish to please
> I write, as I would live, with ease.[70]

This lowering of sights was not limited to Lloyd. Cowper expressed the same lack of ambition in a letter of 2 September 1762 to his friend, Clotworthy Rowley:

If a great Man struggling with Misfortunes is a Noble Object, a little Man that despises them is no contemptible one; And this is all the Philosophy I have in the World at present. . . . Upon the whole my dear Rowley, there is a degree of Poverty that has no Disgrace belonging to [it, th]at degree of it I mean in which a man enjoys clean Linnen and good Company, & if I never sink below this degree of it, I care not if I never rise above it.[71]

We know that Lloyd and Cowper were very close during these years and it is not hard to image them recklessly convincing each other of the worthlessness of conventional endeavour and success. Genteel indolence was their expressed ideal: 'Ambition, splendour may be thine; / Ease, indolence, perhaps, are mine.'[72] In a vivid self-reflexive vignette, Lloyd combined the idea of ease in life and the critical standard of ease in poetry:

> And will my friend for once excuse
> This off'ring of a lazy muse,
> Most lazy,—lest you think her not,
> I'll draw her picture on the spot.
> A perfect ease the dame enjoys;
> Three chairs her indolence employs:
> On one she squats her cushion'd bum,
> Which would not rise, tho' kings should come;
> An arm lolls dangling o'er another,
> A leg lies *couchant* on its brother.
> To make her look supremely wise,
> At least like wisdom in disguise,
> The weed, which first by *Raleigh* brought,
> Gives thinking looks instead of thought,
> She smokes, and smokes; without all feeling
> Save as the eddies climb the ceiling,
> And waft about their mild perfume,
> She marks their passage round the room.
> When pipe forsakes the vacant mouth,
> A pot of beer prevents her drowth,
> Which with *potations pottle deep*
> Lulls the poor maudlin muse to sleep.
> Her books of which sh'as wond'rous need,
> But neither pow'r nor will to read,
> In scatter'd tomes lie all around
> Upon the lowest shelf—the ground.
> Such ease no doubt suits *easy* rhyme
> Folks walk about who write SUBLIME.[73]

Although the love of ease and disregard of ambition described in this passage can have a therapeutic value, Lloyd's self-indulgent version of what Churchill would later call 'My damn'd Indolence, and Lloyd's Mutability'[74] suggests a deeper and more destructive impotence: the poet has 'neither pow'r nor will to read', his books lie 'scatter'd' on the ground, he drinks to lull himself into oblivion. Despite the humorous details of the vignette, there is in it an implicit recognition that such 'maudlin' self-diminution can only lead to failure. 'Vacant mouth' is not only a description of Lloyd's expression; it is a metaphor for his achievement as a poet.

For Cowper, too, such indolence held strong temptations. He enjoyed being a man of the town, writing slight poetry, and carrying the name of 'genius'. In the letter to Rowley quoted above, it appears that he is looking for a rationale that would allow him to forsake the requirements of ambition for a more dissipated lifestyle. But unlike Churchill and Lloyd, he could not break away. Only a full year later, after months of anguish caused by just this dilemma—the dilemma of the choice of life —was he compelled to make a decision. In December of 1763, rather than stand for a public examination for a position in the House of Lords (Clerk of the Journals) being offered him by a kinsman, Cowper tried several times to kill himself. When he failed, he lost his sanity. Cowper's suicidal mania has usually been attributed to his extreme shyness, to his fear of public exposure, to the lingering after-effects of his having been refused in marriage by his cousin Theodora. But I would argue that his suicide attempts were something more: they were his form of escape from the 'daylight world'. They were his rebellion.[75]

Churchill, on the other hand, rebelled in more aggressive ways. He advocated a life, and a poetry, not so much of ease and self-effacement as of vigour, eccentricity, and spontaneity. In his attack on 'Method' and methodical men in *Night*, we get a sense of how closely these aesthetic and ethical qualities were linked in Churchill's mind:

> The Wretch bred up in Method's drowsy school,
> Whose only merit is to err by rule,
> Who ne'er thro' heat of blood was tripping caught,
> Nor guilty deem'd of one eccentric thought,
> Whose soul directed to no use is seen
> Unless to move the body's dull Machine;
> Which, clock-work like, with the same equal pace,
> Still travels on thro' life's insipid space,
> Turns up his eyes to think that there should be
> Among God's creatures two such things as *we*.
>
> (19–28)

Churchill's ethical radicalism is quite evident in these lines. He does not rail against 'Dullness' in the Popean sense, but against dull men. (Indeed, the chief satiric target of *The Ghost* is named 'Dullman'.) The negative qualities that Pope ascribed to 'Dullness'—eccentricity, self-fixation, dissipation—become Churchill's virtues. Even 'Oblivion', the great *alter ego* of 'Dullness', is for Churchill a desirable state. And here again we touch upon the central theme of *Night*: oblivion is cultivated not only because it brings nocturnal happiness, but because it blanks out the threatening realities of the day:

> Exempt *we* sit, by no rude cares opprest,
> And, having little, are with little blest.
> All real ills in dark oblivion lye,
> And joys, by fancy form'd, their place supply,
> NIGHT's laughing hours unheeded slip away,
> Nor one dull thought foretells approach of DAY.
>
> (281–6)

Churchill not only despises day, he fears it.

In emphasizing the undercurrent of despair in *Night*, I do not wish to diminish falsely the poem's major themes. The strongest is an intermittent satiric attack on the 'important blanks' of the daylight world and the institutions that they represent: government, business, the military, and the church. The second is a defence of individualism and the development of a philosophy of conscience. Personal integrity and conscience (in this poem speciously called 'Reason') form the moral bases of Churchill's poetry. For him, they are the only standards left in a world where all moral codes are hypocrisies. Churchill, in fact, develops a kind of situation ethics, wherein all actions are relative, and context alone determines their moral and ethical weight:

> If RUPERT after ten is out of bed
> The fool next morning can't hold up his head,
> What reason this which *me* to bed must call
> Whose head (thank heaven) never aches at all?
> In diff'rent courses diff'rent tempers run,
> He hates the Moon, I sicken at the sun.
> Wound up at twelve at noon, *his* clock goes right,
> *Mine* better goes, wound up at twelve at night.
>
> (77–84)

This would seem to be Churchill's answer to the 'bourgeois' maxim given memorable form about this time by Benjamin Franklin: 'Early to bed and early to rise / Makes a man healthy, wealthy, and wise.'

For Churchill there are no valid universal or homogeneous rules of behaviour. He advocates a doctrine of individual conscience and judgment, rejecting traditional wisdom for a more spontaneous response based on context and intuition—an ethical stance that bears both an analogous and affective relationship to the structure of his poetry. The people, or poets, who follow traditional forms without testing them against experience are men of 'prudence'—soulless blanks who merely perform the required task at the required time, and whose sole motive is gain. This is a position Churchill utterly rejects, and in the final lines of *Night* his advocacy of individualism approaches what can only be termed a kind of heroic solipsism: 'If to thyself thou canst thyself acquit, / Rather stand up assur'd with conscious pride / Alone, than err with millions on thy side' (380–2). In Churchill's poetry, the requirements of society and tradition—so important to the 'Augustan' ethic and aesthetic—take a distant second place to the needs of the individual.

With such individualism, necessarily, came a close scrutiny of self, not only because of the reliance on conscience, but because the self was intrinsically interesting. Churchill and Lloyd's poetry is not only self-reflexive: it is self-fixated. The character of the poet and his poetry forms by far its major subject. Lloyd especially, seems obsessed with discussing, or defending, his verse. The self-deflating lines quoted above can be duplicated in almost any of his poems. Always we hear of 'easy rhyme', lack of ambition, the rejection of fame, the poet's humility, and subsequently, his exploitation by the powers that be. Churchill, too, was fascinated with himself. The slightly ridiculous figure he cuts in a blue coat with gold buttons, the way he bashes out verse, his love of women and drink, his pride —all are charted carefully in the furious, half-amused style that itself recreates Churchill's meteoric personality.

Churchill and Lloyd were 'geniuses', and, with the other members of the club, subject to all the genius's remarkable (and recordable) oddities. Though in *The Connoisseur* Thornton and Colman had satirically discussed the characteristics and absurdities of the contemporary 'genius', still, with each passing year, the lives and values of the Nonsense Club members conformed more and more closely to this half serious, half satiric paradigm. In 1763, Boswell would call them the 'London Geniuses', and in the same year Kenrick, in a review of Thornton's burlesque St Caecilia's Day ode, would tellingly connect the ideas of genius, spontaneity, and dissipation: 'There is something so peculiar even in the extravagancies of true genius, something so seductive in its wildest flights and vagaries, that the fruits of its very dissipation are more esteemed by Readers of taste, than the most elaborate lucubrations of plodding industry.'[76] Certainly the Nonsense Club's fondness for speed and spontaneity of composition represented a practical, sublunary adaptation of the unpremeditated 'flow' of thought so often attributed to great genius. And even their behaviour fit the personification of 'GENIUS' that Lloyd pictured as a 'bustling lad of parts':

> Who all things did by fits and starts,
> Nothing above him or below him,
> Who'd make a riot, or a poem,
> From excentricity of thought,
> Not always do the thing he ought.[77]

They were not unaware of the paradox of their behaviour. Colman, in an essay on the 'Genius' for the *St. James's Chronicle*, facetiously admits that 'I am myself an acknowledged genius', and ironically describes the virtues of the breed:

The GENIUS . . . needs neither diligence nor assiduity. Supported by confidence, he disdains to halt along the crutches of application. So far from being vested merely in one science, he runs round the whole circle of his pleasure. . . . Almost every man is an adept in every art; acquires learning without study; improves good sense without meditation; writes without reading; and, being full as well acquainted with one thing as another, is unquestionably a GENIUS.[78]

In typical Nonsense Club style, Colman parades before us, as examples of wayward genius, himself and his friends: first, the academic genius—'If he is entered at either of our universities, the tameness of an academical life being ill adapted to the vivacity of his disposition, he will spend all his time in Covent

Garden'—then the genius of the Inns of Court:

The lively student at the inns of court has too sublime a turn of mind
to follow his profession. He gives the attornies a contempt for him by
endeavouring to convince them facetiously, and is seen walking the
streets in an illegal bag-wig, instead of prudently wearing a business-
following bob. He may be found oftener behind the scenes of the
playhouse, than in the courts of justice; and if he is a prodigious
GENIUS indeed, he even writes for the stage.[79]

This is a description of Colman himself. At the time of its writing (11 June 1761), he was 'a prodigious GENIUS indeed'.
Neglecting the law to write for the stage, he had that winter
seen his first major comedy, *The Jealous Wife*, become a popular
success.

Colman, with the theatre at Drury Lane in which to exert his
'genius', could afford to laugh at himself. But in 1761–2,
Churchill, Lloyd, and Cowper were still very much adrift. In a
certain sense, their lives followed their aesthetics. In life as in
art, these members of the Nonsense Club exhibited a love of
spontaneity and a corresponding hatred of any rules or conventions that confined that impulse. So they cast about—trying out
subjects, flaunting conventions, running to extremes, yet all
the time scrutinizing themselves for clues as to their proper
course. A meaningful course in life was, in the last analysis,
essential. Beneath their brash exteriors, they each recognized
that spontaneity was as dangerous as it was desirable. They
knew very well the fateful dichotomy of genius—the difference
between creative power and superficial facility. Their impulse
to create needed to be channelled, focused, condensed to
produce anything of consequence. They needed a compelling
object on which to focus their energies.

Lloyd, at least, believed that choice was the key; the eccentric
'genius' of his poetry works by 'fits and starts', and would as
soon 'make a riot as a poem', but 'was it once his own election,
/ Would bring all matters to perfection'.[80] This was clearly
Lloyd's hope, and the hope of the others: to exercise their full
freedom of choice in finding a proper activity or cause to which
to dedicate themselves. Lloyd, perhaps the saddest case, would
never find an anchoring ideal, and would fritter away his life

on drink and mediocre verse. But Cowper, after a cleansing spell of madness, would find Evangelical Christianity. And Churchill would meet John Wilkes.

5 Signs and Instruments

I

Witty, eccentric, and well-heeled, Bonnell Thornton was neither as rebellious, nor as vulnerable, as Churchill and Lloyd. After *The Connoisseur*'s passing, he continued his humorous exploration of the clash of social classes and idioms, contributing squibs and essays to various London periodicals. One of these essays, No. 15 of Johnson's *Idler* (22 July 1758), along with his burlesque pamphlet *City Latin* (1760), form a prologue to Thornton's major burlesque projects of 1762–3: the Sign Painters' Exhibition and the *Ode on Saint Ceacilia's Day*.

Idler No. 15 is interesting because it is another indication of Thornton's affinity with Hogarth. As W. J. Bate points out, the essay—which describes the indignities suffered by one 'Zachary Treacle', a tradesman, at the hands of his wife— resembles in theme and, at times, in detail Hogarth's satiric print 'Evening', from his *Four Times of the Day* series (1738).[1] This print shows a tradesman and his wife leaving Sadler's Wells after an exhausting outing. While the stout, commanding wife carries only a fan, the harried husband is left to carry a sleeping child home. Mr Treacle is in a similar predicament; after dinner he 'is sure to be dragged out by her [the wife] either to Georgia, or Hornsey Wood, or the White Conduit House':

Yet even these near excursions are so very fatiguing to her, that, besides what it costs me in tea and hot rolls, and syllabubs and cakes for the boy, I am frequently forced to take a hackney-coach, or drive them out in an one-horse chair. At other times, as my wife is rather of the fattest, and a very poor walker, besides bearing her whole weight upon my arm, I am obliged to carry the child myself.

The gardens and resorts mentioned by Treacle—Hornsey Wood, the White Conduit House, the Georgia—were all lesser equivalents of Sadler's Wells: watering places and entertainment parks for the middle classes. In Thornton and Hogarth's eyes, they were also the ideal habitat in which to stalk the affectations of this segment of society. In his print, Hogarth specifically emphasizes the upper-class yearnings of the trades-man's family: the wife affects gloves, a fan, and a pearl neck-lace, and the small boy, crying over a scolding administered by his sister, is accoutred like a miniature London fop—right down to the cane he uses as a hobby horse. Thorton likewise gives the wife upper-class airs: she will not work, 'but walks all the morning sauntering about the shop'; she disdains business, and when Treacle does his day books, he finds her 'lolling over the counter, and staring at it, as if I was only scribbling or drawing figures for her amusement.' The son too is given a decidedly aristocratic license: 'The brat must be humoured in every thing: he is therefore suffered constantly to play in the shop, pull all the goods about, and clamber up the shelves to get at the plums and sugar.'

Although Thornton's primary purpose may be to provoke the reader to laughter at Treacle's expense, the very behaviour he describes acts to expose a secondary level of meaning in the essay: its identification of the frustration of the industrious tradesman in the face of insouciant upper-class attitudes. Treacle's wife, besides being a comic figure, becomes a kind of covert symbol for the corruptive effect of upper-class values on middle-class virtue.

The affectations of the middle class—more specifically, aspiring cits—also form the central topic of Thornton's next identifiable literary venture, *City Latin, or Critical and Political Remarks on the Latin Inscription on Laying the first Stone of the Intended New Bridge at BLACK FRIARS*, a satirical essay prompted by the 'inscriptions in large plates of pure tin' unveiled on 31 October 1760 during the ceremony alluded to in the pamphlet's title.[2] The Latin of the inscriptions was universally acknowledged as bad. Churchill, in *The Ghost*, ironically praised the author, John Patterson, for having produced 'inscriptions, worthy found / To lie for ever under-ground' (IV. 1084–6). Thornton's approach was more elab-orate. Adopting the persona of a public school master, the 'Rev. Busby Birch' (an allusion, of course, to Westminster and whipping), he took apart Patterson's Latin line by line. Thorn-ton was known as an accomplished Latinist, and while his grammatical criticism is far too subtle for anyone not blessed with a classical education, it appears to have been accurate because the pamphlet appeared in a second edition in 1761.[3]

For the unlettered, perhaps the most interesting section of *City Latin* is Thornton's discussion of the impropriety of putting English words into Latin—a discussion in which Thornton's humorously ambivalent position with regard to the native British versus the classical idiom is plainly evident. On the one hand, he satirizes the cits for their pretension in using Latin rather than their native tongue; on the other, he comments in an ironic, but nevertheless significant way, on the essentially rough, vulgar quality of the English language. Here is his handling of the name 'William Pitt':

> But to come to the Name *Pitt*. . . . O what a glorious Opportunity was here let slip of naturalizing an *English* Name into the *Latin* Tongue, by a *Latinization* of it. . . . *Pitt! Pitt!* a low *English* Word! *Sink, Ditch, Bog, Quagmire*, would sound equally noble. But if, instead of this, it had been written *Fossa*, how grandly would that have sounded! And, surely, every Admirer of antique learning will agree with me, that *Fossa! Guilelmi Fossae!* . . . would have made the illustrious Name of the *Fossas* adored and remembered to all Posterity.[4]

A bit farther on, the Revd Busby Birch delves into the etymology of common English names, finding that those 'which have any Meaning at all, are borrowed from the lowest, and sometimes the most ridiculous, as well as offensive Objects. Thus, for Instance, what can be more shocking to a delicate Ear, than *Mangey, Rag, Belcher, Gorge, Grub, Trollop, Nanny, Hussey*, &c. &c. &c. Not to mention some others that border very nearly on Indecency.' Birch's denunciation of these vulgar names is surprisingly similar to Matthew Arnold's famous tirade on the child murderer 'Wragg' in 'The Function of Criticism at the Present Time': 'Wragg! If we are to talk of ideal perfection, of 'the best in the whole world,' has anyone reflected what a touch of grossness in our race, what an original shortcoming of the more delicate spiritual perceptions, is shown by the natural growth amongst us of such hideous names, —Higginbottom, Stiggins, Bugg!'[5] But while Arnold's assumption seems to be that the names in fact define the people they signify and thus indicate the 'grossness in our race', Thornton's ironic banter implies a certain sympathy and identification with the names (after all, Birch's criticisms are being satirized, not the names themselves). The importance of this distinction becomes evident in light of Paulson's questions regarding the name of Tom Idle in Hogarth's *Industry and Idleness* series: 'Have others been prejudiced against Idle by his name and so discouraged him that he has taken on the qualities which his name assigned him? Or, as the sophisticated audience would assume, is the name an indication of what he essentially *is*, an emblem of him?'[6] Arnold would presumably choose the second alternative; Thornton perhaps the first. The underclasses too would choose the first, recognizing implicitly that names can be an instrument of social oppression.

In the case of *City Latin*, I would suggest at least three significant points of view. The first, and most overtly satirized, is that of an affected middle class. It is this group, presumably, which endorsed the idea of inscribing the tablets in Latin, and which would agree with Busby Birch that Fossa is preferable to Pitt. The second would be that of either a distinctly lower class or of a sympathetic member of the sophisticated audience. Such a view recognizes that the mere existence of such names presupposes a history of wretched social conditions, and that their continued usage is a way of enuring certain classes to their traditional mode of life: there could be no 'Mangey' without mange, no 'Rag' or 'Wragg' without beggars and rag-pickers, no 'Trollop' or 'Hussey' without wide-spread prostitution. The final pair of names suggests a third possible reading, one that recognizes the lower class's disrespectful attitude toward the establishment 'code' and consequent support of defiant (or deviant) social behaviour in defence of the traditional, unwritten 'code' of the populace. As E. P. Thompson observes, 'rarely have the two codes been more sharply distinguished from each other than in the second half of the eighteenth century. One may even see these years as ones in which the class war is fought out in terms of Tyburn, the hulks and the Bridewells on the one hand; and crime, riot, and mob action on the other.'[7] In such a social context, names like 'Hussy', 'Trollop', 'Tom Idle', 'Betsy Careless', or 'Jonathan Wild' could take on heroic, even revolutionary, overtones.

As a student of the semiotics of the popular culture, Thornton usually took a non-partisan view of the socio-political problem.[8] His fascination with popular events and symbols for themselves tended to neutralize the conventional upper-class, satirical point of view from which his analysis of culture often begins. Although Busby Birch's criticisms of Patterson's Latin are accurate and funny, his supercilious manner parodies cultural snobbery in all its forms. Birch's exaggerated distaste points up the symbolic richness of common English names: a richness that could make 'Will Pitt' an extraordinary propaganda asset and 'Lord Chatham' an instant propaganda liability. In the guise of a Westminster pedant, Bonnell Thornton defines in his curious way the distinctive strength and ugliness of the English language.

II

In 1760 London was served by four dailies and five or six evening tri-weeklies, as well as four weeklies carrying some news.[9] Supported by advertising revenues and sales, these newspapers represented not only viable economic concerns, but a material expression of the interaction of the values of politics, commerce, and wit. The gradual incorporation of political and social essays as features in commercial advertisers was a particularly noteworthy trend: *The Craftsman* had carried advertisements, but *The Public Advertiser* carried 'Junius'.[10] The newspapers also increasingly carried letters, squibs, and pieces of wit and humour along with their usual stock prices, ship arrivals, news, and commercial information.[11] A significant manifestation of this trend occurred in 1760 when *The Public Ledger* became the first daily paper to adopt a sixteen-column format. A competing daily, *The Gazetteer*, soon converted from twelve to sixteen columns, in the process adding substantially to its entertainment and commentary columns.[12] In 1763 *The Public Advertiser*, in a move in which Thornton seems to have played a central role, followed suit.

Thornton's involvement with the daily and tri-weekly press was his chief literary and economic preoccupation. In March 1761 he became a founding partner of the joint-stock company formed to publish *The St. James's Chronicle*—a sixteen-column (four pages folio, four columns per page) tri-weekly that achieved both reputation and longevity, lasting well into the nineteenth century. Although many accounts of the paper (including,

unfortunately, my own) state that Thornton along with
Colman and Garrick held controlling interest and that
Thornton was 'titular manager', the recently discovered
minute-books of the joint-stock company give a somewhat dif-
ferent picture of the publishing and editorial arrangements.[13]
Thornton was one of a consortium of ten (then almost immediately twelve) investors—among them Garrick, Colman, Thomas
Davies, Ralph Griffiths, and the printer and prime mover,
Henry Baldwin—who backed the paper. Of the twenty available shares, Thornton held two himself and two in trust for an
unknown third party; Colman and Garrick held one each.[14]
The stock holders met quarterly (often at the Globe Tavern in
Fleet Street, or the Bedford Head in Covent Garden) to divide
profits and discuss troublesome issues; an appointed five-
member committee met monthly to oversee the books. The
editor was a young Oxonian named Nathaniel Thomas.

Although Thornton cannot be described as 'titular manager',
there can be little doubt that he, along with Colman and Garrick,
had a substantial influence on *The St. James's Chronicle*. The three
wrote essays (including Colman's 'Genius' series), letters, and
puffs for the paper, which, according to Southey, 'at once
assumed a literary character far above that of its rivals'.[15]
Colman and Garrick's 1763 reference to Thornton as the
paper's 'grand conductor' would seem to indicate that he was
more than an occasional contributor.[16] And if the paper was not
a Garrick/Nonsense Club organ, it was widely recognized by
their contemporaries as a vehicle for advancing the Nonsense
Club's interests and views.[17] Indeed, the Articles of Agreement
provided that the printer (Baldwin) would be 'at Liberty to
insert Partners Advertisements, not exceeding two per Week of
each Partner's, charging such Partners Advertisements with the
Duty only'—thus offering each partner a cheap form of publicity. The paper appeared on 14 March 1761, and played an
important role in the paper war swirling around *The Rosciad*; and
it continued to provide a convenient instrument through which
Thornton, Colman, and Garrick could comment on the various
dramatic, artistic, literary, and political controversies of the day.

Excepting the theatrical war, the most significant artistic controversy of 1761 centred on two exhibitions of paintings that
opened in London that spring—exhibitions that were to inspire

Thornton's most original burlesque. The exhibitors were the Society for the Encouragement of Arts, Manufactures, and Commerce ('Society of Arts') and the Society of Artists of Great Britain ('Society of Artists'). The former association—though founded to encourage native British artists—had fallen into disfavour with Hogarth and other influential painters because of its heavy-handed directorship and its insistence on hanging amateur and professional pictures side by side.[18] The latter society was founded in 1761 by the artists dissatisfied with the Society of Arts. Its first exhibition was meant as a kind of answer to the alleged false connoisseurship of the Society of Arts show.

The Society of Arts exhibition of 1761 opened on 27 April and the Society of Artists exhibition on 9 May, but as early as 23–5 April *The St. James's Chronicle* was commenting on both. In a letter from one 'John Oakley' (presumably Colman or Thornton), we find a restatement of all the old Hogarthian complaints against 'the Tribe of Auctioneers, Connoisseurs, Picture-Brokers, Dealers, Menders, Cleaners, &c. &c. &c.' who drew the public away from native British artists. Naturally, Oakly uses Hogarth as his prime example of English genius— 'We have now living as great a Genuis as any Time or Nation has produced. He stands by himself, as the great Original of Dramatic Painting'—and generally sides with the Society of Artists against the Society of Arts. This initial piece set the tone for the art criticism found in *The St. James's Chronicle.* Throughout the early spring, every issue carried some reference to the dispute, and always the bias was against the Society of Arts. In the issue of 7–9 May, a pamphlet was announced supporting the Society of Artists. The next issue (9–12 May) carried some quotations from it, which, of course, praised Hogarth and attacked the connoisseurs. The issue of 12–14 May contained some verses by Roubiliac satirizing connoisseurs, and the following issue (14–16 May) held a second letter from John Oakly.

In the midst of this campaign on behalf of Hogarth and the Society of Artists, *The St. James's Chronicle* ran the following burlesque advertisement:

The projected Exhibition of the BROKERS and SIGN-PAINTERS of *Knaves-Acre, Harp-Alley,* &c. &c. &c. is only postponed, till a Room spacious enough can be provided, as the Collection will be very numerous. In the mean Time the several ARTISTS (Natives of Great-Britain) are invited to send the Printer of this Paper, a List of those Capital Pieces, which they intend to submit to the public Judgement. N.B. No Foreigners, and *Dutchmen* in particular, will be allowed a Place in the Exhibition.

Appearing in the 23-6 May issue of the paper, this mock announcement seems to mark the first glimmering of what a year later was to become Thornton's Sign Painters' Exhibition. One further notice about the exhibition appeared in the 30 May–2 June issue of *The St. James's Chronicle*, but no more was heard after that. At this point the notion of a Sign Painters' Exhibition seems to have been a literary *jeu d'esprit* and nothing more.

By the time the two exhibitions came round again in the spring of 1762, two things had happened that might have inspired Thornton to bring his hoax to life. First, Hogarth was no longer exhibiting with the Society of Artists, and perhaps had reasons for supporting a burlesque of art exhibitions in general. Second, the idea of 'exhibits' had seized the public imagination, especially after the extravagant show of George III's coronation in September 1761. (In fact, writing in *The St. James's Chronicle* of 11–13 August 1761, 'the facetious Cobler of Cripplegate'—probably Colman—compared the prospective coronation to an exhibition, and Westminster Abbey to the exhibition halls in the Strand and Charing Cross.) Perhaps prodded by these developments, in the early spring of 1762 Thornton began to realize his scheme. The first notice for the exhibition appeared in *The St. James's Chronicle* of 13–16 March:

GRAND EXHIBITION

The Society of SIGN PAINTERS beg Leave to give Notice, that their GRAND EXHIBITION will be some Time next Month. A large commodious Room is provided for that Purpose, and their Collection is already very numerous. In the mean Time they shall be obliged to any Gentleman who will communicate to them where any curious Sign is to be met with in Town or Country, or any Hint or Design for a Sign, suitable to their Exhibition.
Letters will be received by the Printer of this Paper.

From this notice and subsequent reports it appears that the majority of the signs displayed at the exhibition were authentic;

that is, they were gathered from the town or countryside rather than painted especially for the occasion. The Nonsense Club, under Thornton's direction, undoubtedly did a good deal of the collecting.

A second important hint contained in the above announcement has to do with the connection between *The St. James's Chronicle* and the exhibition. There seems to me a distinct possibility that the scheme originated, at least in part, as a way of increasing the paper's circulation. First of all, the original idea for the exhibit appeared in *The St. James's Chronicle* soon after the paper commenced publication in 1761. Information about the developing exhibition of 1762 always appeared first in *The St. James's Chronicle* and then in other papers; communications concerning signs were to be sent to the printer; and, in the exhibition catalogue itself, the purported sign painters turn out to be journeymen in Henry Baldwin's print shop. *The St. James's Chronicle* minute book indicates that Thornton had taken a substantial loss by publishing a collection of pieces from the 1761 *St. James's Chronicle* under the title of *The Yearly Chronicle*.[19] It is possible that The Sign Painters' Exhibition was an attempt to promote the paper and, at the same time, recoup his losses.[20]

William Hogarth, a master of promotion in his own right, seems to have played a significant part in the preparation for the exhibit. Southey writes that he 'entered into the humour of the adventure, and gave a few touches in chalk where effect could be added by it: thus in the portraits of the King of Prussia and the Empress Maria Theresa, he changed the cast of their eyes so as to make them leer significantly at each other.'[21] Paulson makes a strong case for an even more meaningful participation by Hogarth. He views the exhibition as another manifestation of Hogarth's campaign against the Society of Arts, and assigns him the role of co-creator with Thornton.[22] During 1762, the Hogarth–Nonsense Club relationship was particularly close. Besides being allies in the fight against the connoisseurs, Hogarth and the Old Westminsters enjoyed a warm social companionship; Churchill, in a later satire against Hogarth, recalled often sitting with his friends and listening to Hogarth talk (interminably, Churchill implies) about art.[23] It is not surprising, then, that the first fully articulated prospectus for the Sign Painters' Exhibition (23–5 March) should be satirically juxtaposed with an announcement of Hogarth's anathema, the Society of Arts Exhibition:

INTELLIGENCE EXTRAORDINARY

Strand. The Society of Manufactures, Arts, and Commerce, are preparing for the Annual Exhibition of Polite Arts, hoping, by Degrees, to render this Nation as eminent in Taste as War; and that, by bestowing Praemiums, and encouraging a generous Emulation, among the Artists, the Productions of Painting, Sculpture, &c. may no longer be considered as Exoticks, but naturally flourish in the Soil of Great Britain.

Grand Exhibition. The Society of Sign Painters are also preparing a most magnificent Collection of Portraits, Landscapes, Fancy-Pieces, Flower Pieces, History Pieces, Night-Pieces, Sea-Pictures, Scripture-Pieces, &c. &c. &c. &c. designed by the ablest Masters, and executed by the best Hands, in these Kingdoms. The Virtuosi will have a new Opportunity to display their Taste on this Occasion, by discovering the different *Stile* of the several Masters employed, and pointing out by what *Hand* each Piece is drawn. A remarkable *Conoscente* who has attended at the Society's great Room *with his Glass* for several Mornings, has already piqued himself on discovering the famous Painter of the *Rising Sun*, (a modern *Claude Lorraine*) in an elegant Night-Piece of *the Man in the Moon*. He is also convinced, that no other than the famous Artist who drew the *Red Lion at Brentford*, can be equal to the bold Figures in *the London 'Prentice*; and that the exquisite Colouring in the Piece, called *Pyramus and Thisbe*, must be by the same hand as *the Hole in the Wall.*

While the Society of Arts' actual position in support of the British arts is given in the first advertisement, the announcement is undermind by the succeeding squib on the Sign Painters' Exhibition. This second piece addresses again the issue of the 'science' of the connoisseur and harks back to the Rembrandt hoax perpetrated by Hogarth and Wilson on Thomas Hudson. This time, of course, the paintings in question are mere sign boards, but the egregious pride of the 'remarkable *Conoscente*' remains. The clear implication is that for the connoisseur any art exhibition is merely an excuse for the ostentatious display of Taste. Without directly attacking the Society of Arts, Thornton casts a satiric shadow of false connoisseurship over its exhibit.

As the date of the exhibition drew closer, letters and squibs multiplied. In *The St. James's Chronicle* of 25–7 March, Thornton

refuted, in the name of the Sign Painters, 'the malicious Suggestion, that their GRAND EXHIBITION . . . is designed as
a Ridicule on the Exhibitions of the Society for the Encouragement of the Arts, &c. and of other Artists', claiming instead
that their 'sole View is to convince Foreigners, as well as their
own blinded country men, that how ever inferior this Nation
may be unjustly deemed in other Branches of the polite arts,
the Palm for SIGN PAINTING must be universally ceded to
us'—a nice combination of burlesque humour ('the Palm for
SIGN PAINTING') and serious commentary on the public's
neglect of British polite art. A correspondent (probably Thornton) to the issue of 3–6 April described a meeting with the
devil, who admits that he has spread falsehoods about Lloyd's
recently published *Poems* and Colman's latest play, and is cur-
rently trying to convince the town that the Sign Painters' Exhibition is meant to ridicule the Society of Arts. In the issue of 8–10
April there is a burlesque advertisement for an 'Exhibition of
Cosmetick Artists in Painting' and, in the issue immediately
preceding the scheduled opening on Thursday, 20 April, a letter
from one 'Philo-Mides' inquiring whether the exhibition is real
or a hoax. This last question must have occurred to many
people when at the last minute the exhibition was abruptly
postponed. In announcing the delay in *The St. James's Chronicle*,
Thornton tried to put the best face on the matter, assuring
the public 'that every Thing is completely ready for their
EXHIBITION, which will commence on *Thursday next*'.[24] In
The Daily Advertiser (20 April 1762), he was more candid:

The Society of SIGN PAINTERS think it better to give the real and
true Reason for deferring their Exhibition, than to invent any
Excuse, how plausible soever. They cannot complete fitting up the
Rooms, placing their Signs, and making out their Catalogue, till
Thursday next; when the Publick may be assured, that everything
shall be ready for the Admittance of those who please to honour them
with their Presence.

On Thursday, 22 April, the Sign Painters' Exhibition opened
'at the large Rooms, the Upper End of Bow-street, Covent-
Garden, nearly opposite the Play-house Passage' (Thornton's
chambers). It could be visited from 9 a.m. to 4 p.m., admission
one shilling. The exhibition spread through a passage room

and a paved courtyard, culminating in 'a large and commodious Apartment, hung round with green Bays, on which this curious Collection of Wooden Originals is fixt flat . . . and from whence hang Keys, Bells, Swords, Poles, Sugar-Loaves, Tobacco-rolls, Candles, and other ornamental Furniture, carved in Wood, that commonly dangles from the Penthouses of the different Shops in our Streets.'[25]

The exhibition catalogue contained a list of the sign boards, 13 in the passage room, 8 in the passage, and 76 in the grand room, along with 25 carved figures and busts. The signs themselves were just those that could be found hanging over any London street or country inn-yard, with the humour residing either in the comic title or in some added touch to the sign itself. Hogarth, under the name of 'Hagarty', seems to have been responsible for the retouching or original execution of eleven signboards, and there is reason to think he had a hand in many more.[26] Two signs credited to 'Bransley'—No. 71, *Shave for a Penny, Let Blood for Nothing* and No. 72, *Teeth drawn with a Touch*—almost exactly duplicated the comic juxtaposition of barber, victim, and sign ('Shaving, Bleeding & Teeth Drawn wth a Touch') in the print *Night* from Hogarth's *Four Times of the Day* series (1738). And No. 61, *The Robin Hood Society, a Conversation; or Lectures on Elocution* by 'Barnsley' (a misprint for 'Bransley'?) was praised by a reviewer in the *London Register* for execution 'almost worthy of Hogarth—they are full of a Variety of droll Figures, and seem indeed to be the Work of a great Master, struggling to supress his Superiority of Genius, and endeavouring to paint down to the common Stile and Manner of the School of Sign-Painting.'[27]

A number of signs in the exhibition carry important connotations for the Nonsense Club. In terms of both image and theme, No. 19, *Nobody, alias Somebody* and No. 20, *Somebody, alias Nobody* bear a close relationship to Churchill's self-definition in *Night*. *Nobody, alias Somebody* showed 'a Figure . . . all Head, Arms, Legs and Thighs', while *Somebody, alias Nobody* represented 'a rosy Figure, with a little Head, and a huge Body, whose Belly swags over, almost down to his Shoe-Buckles'.[28] Paulson remarks: 'the Somebody–Nobody tradition is an old one. . . . Somebody is the representative of 'knaves or fools, in coat or gown'—what Fielding, Gay, and

Hogarth thought of as "the great".'[29] 'Jolly Nobody', on the
other hand, is the nonconformist—one who 'during his Life
does nothing at all / But eat and snore / And drink and roar, /
From whore to tavern, from tavern to whore.'[30] Using
Churchill's terminology, Somebody is the man of 'Prudence',
who reaps the benefits of society by unquestioningly following
its rules; Nobody is the independent underdog, who because he
unashamedly acts out his physical desires—eating, drinking,
fornicating—can see through the pretentious sham of the
hypocritical Somebody. Somebody follows the establishment
code, Nobody the unwritten popular code; Somebody supports
the institutions of Tyburn, the Fleet, and Bridewell, Nobody
understands the reason for crime, riot, and mob action. In
Churchill's poem, Somebody is an 'Important blank' in the
daylight world, and Nobody is a 'son of Night'. *Night*, in
essence, is a poem written by a Nobody against the
Somebodies.

Besides painted signboards, the exhibition also included
carved symbols ('Keys, Bells, Swords', etc.) and wig blocks.
The wig blocks played a dual role, providing a burlesque equivalent of sophisticated sculpture and commenting on society's
equation of costume with worth (e.g. No. 9, 'A Block, done
from the Life'). In a sense, they were the popular type of the
Somebody: 'blanks' given social status only by the wigs that
covered them. The role of wigs as social symbols was well
recognized in the eighteenth century: 'a wig is as much a Mark
of Distinction as any other Point of Dress, or any other Circumstance in Life: It is not more ridiculous, in my Opinion, for
a Commoner to fix Coronets upon his Coach, than for a Person
to wear a Queue-wig, or Tye-wig, that is not entitled to it from
his Station.' So wrote a correspondent to *The St. James's Chronicle* of 25–7 May 1762. Several months later 'AN ANTI
PERUKIST' (possibly Thornton) wrote to the same paper
facetiously documenting the breakdown of social distinctions
implied by wig styles: in medicine, for example, the 'Solemnity
of the Tye-Wig was formerly adjudged only to belong to the
Physician; the Surgeon was allowed a less degree of Seriousity
in one or two Tails; and the whole Wisdom of the Apothecary
was confined to the Full-Bottom. But now all Orders are confounded: You cannot know one from t'other by his Head

alone.'[31] In 1768, Thorntons's last published work would be a satire on a doctors' dispute entitled *The Battle of the Wigs*. Hogarth, too, recognized the potential of wigs and wig blocks as vehicles of social commentary; a potential he exploited in *Five Orders of Periwigs, The Bruiser* (see below), and other prints.

Another sign that warrants comment is No. 30, *The Dancing Bears. A sign for N. Dukes, or A. Hart, or any other Dancing-Master to Grown Gentlemen* by Hagarty. This sign showed 'four Bears on their hind Legs, drest in different characters, one with a Gold Chain round his Neck, giving Right Paw and Left, gravely practising Country-Dances, under the Tuition of a Monkey, drest like a Dancing-master, and fiddling on a KIT-ten.'[32] Although Dukes and Hart were indeed dancing masters (Colman mentions them in *Terrae-Filius* No. 4; Churchill in *The Ghost*, III. 249–54), the dancing bear motif in Hogarth's work consistently carries political overtones. In plate 4 of the *Election* series, for example, the muzzled bear is the type of the crowd that has been manipulated into a political procession or 'dance', but whose raw power is barely kept under control. In signboard No. 30, the bears would seem to suggest an ignorant but powerful populace (the gold chain signifying the City?) taught to 'dance' by an upper-class manipulator (the fashionably dressed monkey). The motif is particularly significant in that it appears again in *The Bruiser*, Hogarth's satiric portrait of Churchill. In the inset print (added to state six), Churchill is shown as a muzzled dancing bear and Wilkes as a foppish monkey. Interestingly, their fiddler, Lord Temple, is portrayed as a wig block: the Somebody who has persuaded the Nobody Churchill to dance to his tune.

The Sign Painters' Exhibition received high praise in *The London Register*; and *The St. James's Chronicle* quickly reprinted the review as part of its advertising campaign. Of Thornton, the reviewer wrote:

The original Paintings, &c. the Catalogue of which now lies before us, are the Project of a well-known Gentleman, in whose House they are exhibited; a Gentleman, who has in several Instances displayed a most uncommon Vein of Humour. His Burlesque-Ode on St. Cæcilia's Day, his Labours in the Drury-Lane Journal, and other Papers, all possess that singular Turn of Imagination, so peculiar to himself. This Gentleman is perhaps the only Person in England (if we

except the Artist above-mentioned [Hogarth]), who could have projected, or carried tolerably into Execution, this Scheme of a Grand
Exhibition. There is a whimsical Drollery in all his Plans, and a comical Originality in his Manner, that never fail to distinguish and
recommend all his Undertakings. To exercise his Wit and Humour in
an innocent Laugh, and to raise that innocent Laugh in others, seems
to have been his chief Aim in the present Spectacle. The Ridicule on
Exhibitions, if it must be accounted so, is pleasant without Malevolence; and the general Strokes on the common Topics of Satire are
given with the most apparent Good-humour.[33]

Yet, despite the emphasis on good humour, in some quarters
the exhibition was criticized as nothing more than a money-
making scheme, and in others interpreted as a direct attack on
the Society of Arts and the Society of Artists. One contemporary print showed Hogarth as Don Quixote, urged on by
Thornton and opposed by a mob of artists, many of them
recognizable caricatures of Society of Artists members.[34]
Another print gives us our only graphic representation of the
Nonsense Club. This etching, *A Brush for the Sign-Painters* (BM
3841), shows Hogarth in the shape of a pug, sitting on a close
stool and painting his much-maligned history piece, *Sigismunda*,
on a signboard. Grouped prominently around the back of his
easel are four figures: Thornton, Colman, Lloyd, and Churchill.
Thornton, the most prominent, is given the head, tail, and legs
of an ass (a reference, presumably, to No. 8, *The Vicar of Bray*,
'a Ass in a Feather-topped Grizzle, Band, and Pudding
Sleeves'), while a bat—exclaiming 'OH HA HA—HE HE
HE'—is shown bespattering his head. The bat's peculiar laugh
is a reference to Nos. 49 and 50, which were covered by blue
curtains after the manner of 'indecent' pictures in some collec-
tions. When the curious viewer requested that the curtains be
lifted, he was confronted with two signs reading 'HA! HA!
HA!' and 'HE! HE! HE!'[35] In front of Thornton stands Colman, looking very boyish and short, his breeches down,
holding a pallet reading 'Four feet nothing'. To his left, Lloyd
appears in profile, his long (and much remarked upon) nose
the distinguishing mark. Next to Lloyd is Churchill, with his
round, beefy face and clerical collar. That Churchill appears in
the print is particularly interesting in that it shows how intimate, at least in the public eye, his and Hogarth's relationship

4. *A Brush for the Sign-Painters.* Anonymous engraving, 1762

must have appeared in the first half of 1762. The print calls the group 'four Eminent Master Sign-Painters, Compilers of a twelvepenny Catalogue, Retailers of Stale Wit, and Commentators on their own folly Vide. St. James Cron.'[36]

It has been assumed that the Sign Painters' Exhibition ran only as long as the Society of Arts show (less than one month) and thus closed the same day that the exhibition of the Society of Artists opened at Spring Gardens: 'The Society of Arts exhibition ended on 17 May; on the same day the Society of Artists of Great Britain opened their exhibition at Spring Gardens. The sign painters' exhibition ended the same time and the *St. James' Chronicle*, as if to clarify their position, published a complimentary essay on the Society of Artists' exhibition.'[37] This finding, however, conflicts with an advertisment in the *Daily Advertiser* of 17 May announcing the 'Grand Exhibition of the Society of Sign Painters / This Day, and all Week': 'The Society intended to have closed their Exhibition with that in the Strand; but finding genteel Company still resort, they are determined to continue their Exhibition as long as that of the Artists is kept open at Spring Gardens. And, for the convenience of many, they have extended the Hours of Admittance from Ten in the Morning till Six in the Evening.' This extension is confirmed by a letter of 3 June 1762 that Thornton, *en route* to Manchester, wrote to Henry Baldwin. In it, he asked Baldwin to place an advertisement in *The St. James's Chronicle* announcing that 'as the Exhibition at Spring Gardens closes Tuesday next, the Sign Painters exhibition will close also, for the present Year'.[38] The Sign Painters' Exhibition, then, closed the same day as the Society of Artists exhibition: Tuesday, 8 June 1762. The lengthening of the exhibition's run and the extension of the hours of admittance are the strongest indications of the exhibition's overall success.[39] But what is perhaps more revealing is Thornton's use of the phrase 'for the present Year', implying as it does that he was at least toying with the idea of a revival in 1763.

In both conception and execution, the Sign Painters' Exhibition represented an art world turned upside down; one in which shop signs were hung in a sophisticated setting and people paid admission to see them. Although any analogy between an eighteenth-century burlesque exhibit and the more self-conscious 'pop' art movement of the 1960s (also incorporating signs and advertisements) must be carefully qualified, the impact on the audience must have been in many ways similar: a forced recognition of both the graphic and semiotic richness of the ubiquitous commercial 'art' pervading everyday life. The effect of the exhibition was to stress the 'signedness' of the ordinary signboard. Already bearing an often incongruous or ironic relationship to its object (as Thornton had pointed out in *Adventurer* No. 9), the shop and tavern signs in the exhibition underwent a further modification in being physically divorced from their usual referents. They stand as detached—though necessarily conditioned—signifiers requiring from the audience an active negotiation of meaning within the possible and often conflicting alternatives of a transforming social/visual vocabulary. Their meanings depend on the viewer's understanding of current social relationships as well as conventional or traditional emblems. In this context, the alterations by the 'Sign Painters' can be seen essentially as an exaggeration of the normal modification of functional signboards to reflect or exploit current events. Horace Walpole, for example, commented on the alteration of signboards after the '45': 'I observed how the Duke's head had succeeded almost universally to Admiral Vernon's, as his had left few traces of the Duke of Ormond's. I pondered these things in my heart, and said unto myself, "Surely all glory is but as a sign."'[40] Unlike polite paintings, signboards were subject to continual alteration in light of changing circumstances: the hero of today replaced the hero of yesterday on the same piece of board in front of the same tavern. In a sense, then, signboards formed a ubiquitous, highly visible lexicon to the 'text' of the popular culture: one that documented the continuing social process and its transforming effect on signification and meaning.[41]

Hogarth, of course, had long recognized the value of signboards as an element of his artistic vocabulary; in his popular prints, modified shop signs were frequently used as vehicles of topical or satirical meaning. The satirically-altered signboards of the Sign Painters' Exhibition represented in a certain sense the signs in the popular prints 'come to life'. Where art had first imitated life, now life (i.e. physical signboards) imitated art.[42] A similar paradox informed the occupation of sign painter. Despite the seemingly burlesque connotations of 'sign painter as serious artist', in fact, in the early eighteenth century, the sign-painting and allied trades often served as training grounds for serious artists.[43] William Kent, before he left to seek his fortune in London, was apprenticed to a coach painter in Yorkshire; Hogarth himself is rumoured to have painted signs in his early days.[44] For all these reasons, it is helpful to think of the Sign Painters' Exhibition as 'carnivalesque' rather than simply 'satiric'.[45] Its signs are not merely a set of signifiers capable of humorous application to various manifestations of contemporary culture (although they are indeed that), but an implicit critique of the potentially exclusive ideology of artistic 'decorum', polite 'taste', and the 'science' of the connoisseur. The Sign Painters' Exhibition, in effect, 'uncrowns' polite exhibitions and fills the exhibition hall with the everyday, commercial art of the populace.

III

Within a year of the Sign Painters' Exhibition, Thornton had become an influential force on another of London's major newspapers: *The Public Advertiser*. The paper was conducted by the twenty-three-year-old Henry Sampson Woodfall, who in the late 1750s had been given full editorial control by his father (also named Henry).[46] Although Thornton may have contributed to the *Public* previously, it is only in the spring of 1763 that positive evidence of his influence on the paper becomes available. In the light of certain structural changes the paper undergoes at this period and of its central importance to John Wilkes's media strategy later in the year, I would like to examine Thornton's relationship with *The Public Advertiser* in its broader cultural and political contexts.

At the beginning of 1763, the *Public* remained primarily a vehicle for commercial advertisement. It was a twelve-column paper (four pages, three columns per page) consisting of a first page devoted to advertisements, and a second page of ship news, London news, and foreign news. Pages three and four contained primarily advertisements, except for a short listing of stock prices and bankrupts, and usually (on page four) a one-column letter, extract, or poem. In approaching the *Public* and the changes it undergoes, I will be concerned most immediately with what might be called the semiotics of format—that is to say, the signifying value of the paper's structure, rather than the meaning of the disposable texts that are fitted daily into that structure. Unlike most other literary works, including essay journals and magazines, the *Public* was not intended for repeated reading. As its editors humorously emphasized, it was by definition a disposable product; one that had to be replaced everyday. As one writer put it, 'This animal . . . will exist four and twenty hours, if accident or inward decay, do not destroy him sooner.'[47] It was, of course, just this aspect of the periodical press—its transitory, throw-away nature—that so irked Swift and Pope. But from a commercial point of view the cycle of disposal and renewal was absolutely vital to the solvency of the paper: one might go so far as to say that the newspaper was the first product in history which depended on planned obsolescence to remain profitable.

The initial impression given by the twelve-column *Public* is of somewhat chaotic commercial plentitude. The format of page one—its almost exclusive orientation toward commercial advertisements, especially publishers' advertisements—signifies what the paper is and what its audience expects of it. Even the news section on page two tends to focus on items of commercial interest—ship arrivals, the freezing over of the Thames, the newest prizes seized by American privateers—although these items are leavened with court news, notable accidents, births, deaths, and marriages. The listing of goods and services is the paper's *raison d'être*, taking up, even if we exclude the news, about three-quarters of the paper's available space. Letters and literature comprise about one-twelfth of the whole and are usually found on the final page.

The twelve-column *Public Advertiser* was clearly a paper catering for the commercial classes; that segment of society so often ridiculed in the higher literary forms of the era. Over the previous decade the paper had pretended to very little in the way of wit or political acumen, but on 14 March 1763 it underwent a major restructuring, expanding to sixteen columns and relocating an enlarged letters and literature section permanently to a spot just after the first set of advertisements. Subsequently, the proprietors sought to explain and justify their innovations (which included raising the price from twopence to twopence halfpenny) in a series of puffs, editorials, and planted letters. It was probably at this point that Thornton became the paper's 'grand . . . adviser', as Colman and Garrick were to call him in a poem published one month later.

The expanded *Public Advertiser* immediately took on a lighter, more cosmopolitan tone, while it simultaneously sought to defend its innovations to an established readership. In a planted letter of 23 March, for example, one 'John Wollar' wrote that 'I have a Family of Girls, who are not contented with reading news merely, but they want something else, as they say, to divert them over their Morning's Tea; though, for my part, I confess I take more Pleasure in looking over the Advertisements and Price of Stocks, than in reading any of your Essays, as they call them, or Pieces of Wit and Humour.' He goes on to say that his girls had forced him to drop the *Public* in favour of the *Gazetteer*, an advertiser which had gone to a sixteen-column mixed format in 1760, but now 'as your present paper comprehends everything that is given in any other Daily Paper, you are reinstated in your usual Place at our Breakfast table.' What is emphasized about the *Public*'s altered format, then, is not its uniqueness, but on the contrary its attempt to retain all that was right about the old format while adapting to the changing taste of the audience. This is not to say, however, that the new variety doesn't get its share of attention. In a squib of 8 April entitled 'Our Plan', a writer sounding suspiciously like Thornton facetiously set forth the paper's ambitions:

Firstly the first, We shall present to our Readers some Sense or Nonsense, as it happens to turn out,—as it is written by the most learned, witty, humorous Writers of the present Age, which beats all Ages, past, present, and to come.

Firstly the second, We have engaged *Scotchmen* to write Politics in Praise of the Ministry.—That we hope will be acceptable to all our Readers. J. H. D. M. A. B. C. &c.

Firstly and thirdly, We have engaged *Englishmen* to write against the Ministry.—That we hope will be acceptable to all our Readers. J. W. C. C. A. B. C. &c.

Firstly the fourth, We have engaged an *Irishman* to be of no Side at all, that is, of all sides, that is, on his own Side. A. M.

Lastly the first, We are promised the Assistance of Gentlemen, superior in Learning, Wit and Humour, far superior to the

Authors (*ingenious* we should call them) of the RAMBLER, the ADVENTURER, the WORLD, the CONNOISSEUR, and the immortal   . *Addison* and *Steele* are unfortunately dead—but A. B. and C. D. and E. F. and G. H. and I. K. and L. M. and the rest of the Gentlemen that assort together for the Encouragement of *Letters*, will do all in their Power to promote *this* Paper.

Besides the obvious appeal to a more sophisticated readership, this puff is particularly interesting for its cryptic allusions to some of the chief political writers of the moment: J. H. (John Home), D. M. (David Mallet), J. W. (John Wilkes), C. C. (Charles Churchill), A. M. (Arthur Murphy). Thornton, if it is he, implicitly addresses not only the audience's interest in wit and politics, but their taste for personal controversy and scurrility.

Although the expanded *Public* promised 'to maintain the Character, which they flatter themselves this paper has ever borne, of Decency and Truth', the kind of irreverence and indecency usually associated with satirical magazines (e.g. *The Drury-Lane Journal*) and political propaganda quickly began to find its way into the paper. On 26 March, for example, one 'Sall Scribble' contributed a poem entitled '*Better OUT than IN*' —a satire in which William Pitt's relationship to Britannia is compared to a certain physical problem experienced by decorous ladies:

> Madam, you see at least one Time,
> When Modesty became a Crime,
> BRITANNIA might have po-p'd before,
> And sav'd herself the Pain she bore;
> But Fear of Censure kept that *in*,
> Which *out* had sooner chang'd the Scene.
> From her Disaster then take Heed,
> Nor blush to f—t when you have need.

Despite the larger truth of Stephen Botein's suggestion that the commercial papers wished to present a 'positive image of an independent and thriving middle order of society—respected and respectable', the concerns of the *Public* were clearly not limited to respectability, decency, and truth.[48] In its new format, *The Public Advertiser* mixed both the irreverent wit of sophisticated satire and the scurrility of the streets into a kind of daily *heteroglossia*: a paper structurally embodying the democratic interplay between the commercial language of the advertisements and stocks, the chat and horror of the news, the irreverent wit of certain contributions and the serious moralizing of others. [49] Such a medium, by ceaselessly stressing its 'impartiality' in matters of class and politics, served both to highlight the individual salience of clashing idioms and to suggest their potential reconciliation in the pursuit of goods, services, entertainment, and up-to-date news.

The *Public*'s claims of 'presentness' and participation—concepts which, as I will suggest below, link the press to the middling people in the production of a commercialized 'folk' culture—are adumbrated in a column entitled 'TO-DAY', which first appeared on 12 April 1763. Again, the style and substance seem to point to Thornton's authorship. The writer opens with an acknowledgement of his 'unlearned Readers (he hopes he has very many of them)' and then expands the metaphor of the animal who lives only twenty-four hours:

Such an Animal is a NEWS-PAPER. Its utmost Hopes must be, to live its Day out: But it has the Comfort to reflect, that its Life is renewed from Day to Day. . . .

No Animal can live without being fed. The PUBLIC ADVERTISER expects to have its daily Food. The Lions in the Tower, and the Ducks in the Canal in St. James's Park, have many a nice Bit thrown to them from those who like to see them, besides what the Keepers chuse to allot them. To drop the Allusion, and yet to keep it up in some Measure, the Four Columns of this Paper will swallow a great deal: This Paper is not, therefore, afraid of being overgorged: Nobody need, therefore, be shy of sending to us, from Fear of our not having Room.

As this squib indicates, the *Public*'s proprietors sought not only to bring 'sophisticated' wit and 'popular' politics into the commercial sphere, but to bring its readers voluntarily into the media process as contributors to what at bottom was a commercial enterprise: the daily filling of 'the enormous Four Columns'. This dialogue between the media and the audience (based primarily on letters, replies, rejoinders, etc., from the readership) began quickly to achieve both symbolic and real parity with the paid advertisements, commissioned articles, and news that had formed the paper's primary content: after 14 March even the printer's information at the bottom of page four was altered to solicit letters first, and give advertising rates afterwards. The paper's emphasis on its transitory, up-to-date quality; the implied importance of being current and in-the-know; the solicitation of contributions from the readership: all helped to create a public hungry for news, ready for change, and accustomed to thinking of themselves as part of the process. In the 1760s, to an unprecedented degree, the commercial press became the 'parliament' of the people: whether the communication was gossip or politics, commerce or wit, the dailies and tri-weeklies provided a forum for public discussion and an instrument of social ferment and control.[50]

Thornton appears to have had an advertising arrangement with *The Public Advertiser* similar to that with *The St. James's Chronicle*, because the *Public* became the chief vehicle for the promotion of his next burlesque extravaganza, the production of the mock *Ode on Saint Cæcilia's Day*. The original version of this ode—'Adapted to the Ancient British Musick'—had been written and published in 1749, while Thornton was still at Oxford, but it had never been set to music or performed. Presumably the success of the Sign Painters' Exhibition in 1762 had something to do with Thornton's decision to bring it to life the following year.

The advertising campaign mounted for the performance of the ode was an extensive one. Announcements began appearing in *The Public Advertiser* as early as 17 May 1763 and in the week before the performance were a daily, front-page feature. In the early advertisements, the ode was identified as 'Timotheus' by a 'learned OXONIAN' and was scheduled to be performed on Friday, 10 June 1763, at Ranelagh House.[51] The date remained constant, but the title changed eventually to 'A GRAND BURLESQUE ODE' by 'BONNELL THORNTON, Esq.'—the first time Thornton had allowed his name to be used in connection with an original work. Supplementing these advertisements were a number of letters that took the forthcoming performance as their subject. The most important of these was a long epistle from 'CROMATIC' that appeared in the *Public* on 26 May.

In this letter, Thornton sets forth his theory of burlesque. Typically, he begins by addressing 'the polite, as well as the ordinary, Part of the Public', assuring his audience that his remarks are meant for 'Readers of every Class'.[52] He then divides burlesque into two kinds. The first is achieved by 'dressing Characters in Heroic Garb, and making them awkwardly imitate the Stile and Manners of Great Personages. Where Characters are not introduced, a Mean Subject, treated in that Manner, and carried on with affected Solemnity, will have the like droll Effect' (i.e. high burlesque). The second is 'where Kings, Queens, Princes, Princesses, Heroes, or Persons celebrated for Wisdom and Learning, &c. think, speak, and act like Vulgar People; or where lofty Subjects are displayed in that ludicrous Stile' (low burlesque). By combining a literary satire on the musical ode with an orchestral parody of these odes' usual settings, Thornton produced a piece that is, by his own definition, at once high and low burlesque. On the mock-heroic (or high) side, a vulgar subject—street instruments—is made the content of an elevated literary form, the musical ode. On the travesty (or low) side, a serious subject—the power of music—is described in ludicrous lyrics sung to the accompaniment of street instruments. According to CROMATIC, the chief purpose of the burlesque ode is 'to ridicule the Affectation of Writers for, as well as Composers of *Music*, in harshly, inharmoniously, injudiciously labouring to convey Sound by Sense, or Sense by Sound' and to 'laugh at the amazing Powers attributed to Music by the Ancients'. Like the Nonsense Club's critique of the 'mechanical' Pindaric ode (from which the musical ode derives), the burlesque ode attacks the highly affected and derivative nature of what is supposedly a 'passionate' genre. And, like the Sign Painters' Exhibition, it offers in burlesque form an essentially serious infusion of vitality from the rough arts of the populace.

Just as the signboards of the Sign Painters' Exhibition and the commentary surrounding them had implied a disordering or breaking down of the stultified conventions of sophisticated painting and exhibiting, so Thornton's burlesque ode implicitly challenged the cosmic and social order that served the traditional St Cecilia's Day ode both as a subject and a structure. The 'power of music' odes which were annually purveyed for the St Cecilia Society, and of which Dryden's 'A Song for St. Cecilia's Day' is perhaps the best known example, celebrated the harmony of music as the type and cause of the order of the universe. In Dryden's poem, it is from 'Harmony, heav'nly Harmony / This universal Frame began', as unordered Nature, 'a heap / Of Jarring Atomes', is given organization and relationship by music: 'Then cold, and hot, and moist, and dry / In order to their stations leap / And MUSICK's pow'r obey' (1–10). This order, of course, extends from the elements to human society—a 'Diapason closing full in Man'. By replacing the conventional instruments of the ode with the Jews harp, hurdy-gurdy, salt box, and marrow bones and cleavers, Thornton implies a disruption of this conventional harmony that is most immediately manifested in the social order. The burlesque ode suggests that the dissonant strength of popular culture may be superior to the effete order of sophisticated culture. Symbolically, the vulgar 'rough music' of the unsophisticated populace temporarily replaces the effete, conventional 'music' of the sophisticated classes as the ordering (or disordering) force in society. In eighteenth-century street slang, it should be remembered, the phrase 'rough music' denoted 'frying-pans, pokers and tongs, marrow-bones and cleavers, bulls' horns, &c. beaten upon and sounded in ludicrous processions'.[53] Such performances of 'rough music' (although common at marriages and other joyous occasions) often occurred in conjunction with popular protests against deviant or exploitative social behaviour, and, as E. P. Thompson has shown, were in many ways analogous to the French *charivari*: temporary manifestation of popular 'misrule', which, as Natalie Zemon Davis suggests, both 'reinforce order and suggest alternatives to the existing order'.[54] In Thornton's ode, then, we find what amounts to a musical dialogue between popular and sophisticated elements of society—a dialogue that resonates in several social contexts.

A heretofore unnoticed article (presumably by Thornton) in *The Public Advertiser* of 10 June describes in detail a rehearsal of the ode and gives a clear sense of the nature of the work in performance. The ode is structured as a conflict between the conventional instruments and their vulgar equivalents. It begins with an overture performed by the ordinary instruments, 'after which an *Extraordinary* Singer rises up in favour of the *Extraordinary* Instruments, and bawls out (in excellent Recitative) 'Be Dumb, be Dumb, ye inharmonious Sounds.''[55] Then

standing up 'in Defense of OLD *English* Music', another singer
reverses the usual aesthetic hierarchy, calling the conventional
instruments 'vulgar': 'The meaner Melody we scorn, / Which
vulgar Instruments afford; / Shrill *Flute*, sharp *Fiddle*, bellow-
ing *Horn*, / Rumbling *Bassoon*, or tinkling Harpsichord.'[56] As
this part is sung, the conventional instruments 'are in a violent
Agitation. The Flutes are outrageously blown up, so that one
would think they would break their Wind. The Fiddlers are in
a woeful Scrape, there is such a Working of their *Cat-Guts.* The
Horns swell with Indignation; the Bassoons grumble greatly,
and the Harpsichord [is] in the sharpest Key.' This 'Opposition' (as the writer calls it) is silenced by the beating of the salt
box, and an 'AIR is sung to the *Clattering* and *Battering* of this
noble Instrument . . . by a Lady, long practised in *Culinary*
Music, and remarkable for her Execution in *the Roast Beef of Old
England.*' This air marks the cessation of conflict and is incidentally the one that Samuel Johnson repeated to Boswell:

> In Strain more exalted the SALT-BOX shall join,
> And Clattering and Battering, and Clapping combine;
> With a Rap and a Tap while the hollow Side sounds,
> Up and down leaps the Flap, and with Rattling rebounds.[57]

The remainder of the burlesque instruments are then introduced, with each performer taking a solo at the appropriate
time, and the 'whole concludes with a most grand, and con-
sequently, most noisy Chorus, in which the whole Band, Vocal
and Instrument, ordinary and extraordinary, join together in
universal Concord and perfect Harmony.'[58]

> Now to CAECILIA, heav'nly Maid
> Your loud united Voices raise:
> With solemn Hymns to celebrate her Praise,
> Each Instrument shall lend it's Aid.
> The SALT-BOX with Clattering and Clapping shall sound,
> The IRON LYRE
> Buzzing twang with wav'ring Wire,
> With heavy Hum
> The Sober HURDY-GURDY thrum
> And the Merry Merry MARROW-BONES ring round.[59]

There is clearly in this musical assemblage a humorous
analogy to political disruption, conflict, and *rapprochement*

between upper and lower segments of society—a political subtext that is increased in popular significance by the traditional connotations of the vulgar instruments themselves. For the Jews harp, salt box, hurdy-gurdy, and marrow bones and cleavers were the instruments of the London 'mob'; the usual accompaniment to anti-government street ballads; the background noise for all large gatherings of the populace—whether at Southwark Fair or Tyburn 'Fair'. While I do not wish to imply that Thornton's ode was in itself a piece of political propaganda, its structure and symbolism encoded a political message readily accessible to a contemporary audience.

The ode's more immediate context, however, was the concerts that formed the chief attraction of London's pleasure gardens. As Percy Young remarks, the gardens' music was 'the lowest common denominator among an infinite series of social grades': the repertoire included bits from 'oratorio, Italian opera, ballad opera, folk song . . . and adaptations of favourite instrumental tunes'.[60] Thornton's ode was linked to this tradition not only by its eclectic nature and place of performance, but by its beneficiary. The concert was arranged for the benefit of Charlotte Brent, a soprano who commonly sang at the pleasure gardens and the theatres; it was purportedly scored by Thomas Arne, Brent's mentor and a chief supplier of songs to the gardens.[61] Given this context, the ode can hardly be seen as an attack on the music of the gardens, but rather a somewhat lower scale, and for that reason humorous, variation of them. The pleasure gardens offered a spectrum of music favoured by the broad, middle-brow London audience; Thornton simply shifted the spectrum to the left by composing his ode for the instruments of the lower class of Londoner. But this shift, however innocuous, carried with it symbolic implications easily exploited by propagandists.

The propagandistic possibilities of the ode are exemplified by its treatment in *The St. James's Chronicle* of 11 June 1763. Reviewing the performance, the writer notes that Ranelagh 'never was honoured with a more truly *British* Company than last Night, to hear the Performance on mock old British Instruments, the Jews-Harp, Salt-Box, Marrow-Bones and Cleavers, and the Hurdy-Gurdy, for Miss Brent's Benefit'. In the era of Wilkes, Bute, and the Scottish 'invasion' of London, any reference to a 'truly *British* Company' necessarily carried anti-Scottish, anti-ministerial overtones. But the reviewer is not content to stop there. 'I believe', he continues, 'those truely South British Instruments, the Marrow-bones and Cleavers, had made every person in the room errant Rebels, if Mr. Wilkes, who was present, had not convinced them it would be a Breach of Privilege.' In linking the marrow bones and cleavers with Wilkes, the reviewer plays on the widespread tradition that these were the instruments of English Liberty. The marrow bones and cleavers had long been associated with 'rough music', the skimmington, and other manifestations of popular discontent or approbation.[62] Because of their connection with the Roast Beef of Old England (and the literal nourishment of the English people), they frequently found their way into both official and unofficial processions and often took on a symbolic role in public expressions of 'Liberty'. In *The St. James's Chronicle*'s review, these 'truely South British' instruments are portrayed as rousing the 'truly *British* Company' in support of Wilkes.

This review may have been written by Thornton himself. It plays on the idea of entertainment as politics and politics as entertainment so central to the newspaper's coverage of the Wilkes phenomenon. At the time of the ode, Thornton was deeply involved with Wilkes, who was himself just out of the Tower, facing an administration bent on discrediting him. With the help of Thornton, Churchill, and Lloyd, he was waging a fight for his political life.

6 *Wilkes and Libertines*

I

As early as the summer of 1762, Churchill, Colman, Lloyd, and Thornton were names well known in the London literary world. On 4 March, Lloyd had published an edition of his poems; on 6 March, Colman's third play, *The Musical Lady*, opened at Drury Lane; the first two books of Churchill's *Ghost* appeared the same month; and Thornton's Sign Painters' Exhibition of 22 April proved a popular success. But the libertarian impulses so pronounced in the Nonsense Club's literary work were increasingly being translated into the members' lives, with disruptive and often dangerous results.

Colman, sometime late in 1761, had begun a liaison with one Sarah Ford, a former servant girl and part-time actress. She was far below Colman in social status, but worse, at least in the eyes of society, she was the cast mistress of the actor Henry Mossop, one of Garrick's secondary players. Mossop, who had 'seduced and debauched' her and left her with a daughter, had himself left for Ireland in 1760.[1] Had Colman simply 'kept' Sarah Ford (as a mistress), there would have been no problem; but in 1762 he began living with her, and on 21 October she bore him a son, later to achieve dramatic fame as George Colman the Younger. This event cemented the relationship between Colman and his mistress, much to the chagrin of some of Colman's friends and relatives.[2] The entire episode takes on a particularly ironic cast when viewed in the light of some observations made in *Connoisseur* No. 51 on the 'kind keeper' whose mistress bears him a child. Rather than dispose of it in the ordinary way (by farming it out to a wet nurse), the keeper's mistress 'could not bear the dear infant out of her sight; and it would kill her not to suckle it herself':

The father was therefore obliged to comply; and an acquaintance caught him the other morning, stirring the pap, holding clouts before the fire, and (in a word) dwindled to a mere nurse. Such is the transformation of this kind keeper, whose character is still more ridiculous than a fondlewife among husbands. The amours, indeed, of those

fond souls commonly end one of these two ways: they either find
themselves deserted by their mistress, when she has effectually ruined
their constitution and estate; or after as many years of cohabitation,
as would have tired them of a wife, they grow so dotingly fond of their
whore, that by marriage they make her an honest woman, and
perhaps a lady of quality.

(304–5)

The latter fate was to be Colman's—he married Sarah Ford
on 12 July 1768.[3] As in the case of the 'genius', one of the
Nonsense Club's humorous examples seems once again to have
come back to haunt them.

Unlike Colman, Robert Lloyd was blessed with neither a
steady income nor a faithful female companion. By 1762, his
financial straits had become so bad that he had to publish his
Poems despite the fact that he had not written enough of them to
fill a volume. (He padded with an altered version of Colman's
'The Law Student', with the *Two Odes*, and with several Latin
translations.) Lloyd and his friends seem to have solicited hard
for subscriptions. Subscribers—besides Thornton, Churchill,
Colman, and Cowper—included Johnson, Sterne, Garrick,
Hogarth, Newbery, Reynolds, the Earl of Bath (ten volumes!),
and scores of others. Ominously, one missing name was that of
Robert's own father, Pierson Lloyd. The volume was dedicated to William Fitzherbert, squire and MP of Tissington,
Derbyshire. There is evidence that Lloyd developed a close
(possibly professional) relationship with Fitzherbert. One of his
poems 'To George Colman', was 'Written Jan. 1, 1761. From
Tissington in Derbyshire', and contains a familiar reference to
Fitzherbert as the 'Squire'. Lloyd's self-chosen pseudonym in
'The Cobler of Tissington's Letter to David Garrick' (1761)
would also seem to refer to a residence in Derbyshire during
that year. Both Lloyd and Colman used 'Cobler' as a burlesque
equivalent of 'writer' ('Some cobble shoes, some cobble plays'),
and Colman himself adopted the pseudonym 'The Cobler of
Cripplegate' (i.e. the poor London parish of St Giles–Cripplegate, home of Grub Street) in a 1763 epistle to Lloyd. Whether
Lloyd served Fitzherbert as a tutor to his children or simply as
a friend is not known, but Fitzherbert was one of the circle of
wits and men-about-town within which the Nonsense Club
moved, and his personality, as described by Johnson, reveals

strong parallels to Lloyd's: 'He made every body quite easy, overpowered nobody by the superiority of his talents, made no man think worse of him by being his rival, seemed always to listen, did not oblige you to hear much from him, and did not oppose what you said. Every body liked him; but he had no friend.'[4] Fitzherbert later would serve as an important go-between in negotiations between Wilkes and the government. He hanged himself in his London stables in 1772.

During the period of 1762-4, Lloyd was deeply under Churchill's influence—an influence that was to last as long as his life—but neither his talent, constitution, nor pocketbook were equal to the excesses of the satirical clergyman. Unable to rival Churchill's success or means, Lloyd nevertheless tried to duplicate his lifestyle. As a consequence, he fell ever deeper into debt and drink, and by September 1762 was forced to begin his own periodical, *The St. James's Magazine*, in order to generate some income.

In an introductory poem called 'The Puff: A Dialogue Between the Bookseller and Author', Lloyd set forth his hopes for the magazine. It would contain none of the worn out attractions of the ordinary monthly:

> No pictures taken from the life,
> Where all proportions are at strife;
> No HUMMING-BIRD, no PAINTED FLOWER,
> No BEAST just landed in the TOWER,
> No WOODEN NOTES, no COLOUR'D MAP
> No COUNTRY-DANCE shall stop a gap.[5]

What Lloyd counted on to take the place of these staples were the contributions of his friends. The Bookseller asks, 'There's CHURCHILL—will not CHURCHILL lend / Assistance?'

> AUTHOR
> Surely—to his FRIEND.
> BOOKSELLER
> And then your interest might procure
> Something from either CONNOISSEUR.
> COLMAN and THORNTON, both will join
> Their social hand, to strengthen thine:
> And when your name appears in print,
> Will GARRICK *never* drop a hint?

The Author's hopeful answer is again yes; and Lloyd's confidence on this point was such that he could promise in his advertisement that 'the Public, in this collection, will at least be sure to meet with ORIGINALS'.[6] Lloyd's high hopes were partially fulfilled. *The St. James's Magazine* retained its innovative format for some time and was one of the first magazines to specialize in original literary material rather than reprints from other periodicals. Among those lending a 'social hand' were Thornton, Colman, Churchill, Cowper, and Garrick.

Of all their contributions, by far the most interesting (for our purposes) is Colman and Garrick's *The Cobler of Cripplegate's Letter to Robert Lloyd, A.M.* (April 1763)—a poem that contains vivid portraits of the Nonsense Club, and a timely warning to Lloyd on the consequences of literary drudgery. In it, we get a taste of the Nonsense Club's acute consciousness of their group identity and individual reputations:

> I hate the stile, that still defends
> Yourself, or praises all your friends,
> As if the club of wits was met
> To make eulogiums on *the Set*;
> Say, must the town for ever hear,
> And no *Reviewer* dare to sneer,
> Of THORNTON's humour, GARRICK's nature,
> And COLMAN's wit, and CHURCHILL's satire? . . .
> CHURCHILL! Who ever loves to raise
> On slander's dung his mushroom bays:
> The priest, I grant, has something clever,
> A something that will last for ever.
> Let him, in part, be made your pattern,
> Whose muse, now queen, and now a slattern,
> Trick'd out in ROSCIAD rules the roast,
> Turns trapes and trollop in the GHOST,
> By turns both tickles us, and warms,
> And, drunk or sober, has her charms. . . .
>   And COLMAN too, that little sinner,
> That essay-weaver, drama-spinner,
> Too much the comic *Sock* will use,
> For 'tis the law must find him *Shoes*.
> And tho' he thinks on fame's wide ocean
> He swims, and has a pretty motion,
> Inform him, LLOYD, for all his grin
> That HARRY FIELDING holds his chin.

Now higher soar, my muse, and higher,
To BONNEL THORNTON, hight Esquire!
The only man to make us laugh,
A very PETER PARAGRAPH:
The grand conductor and adviser
In CHRONICLE, and ADVERTISER,
Who still delights to run his rig
On *Citizen* and *Periwig*!
Good sense, I know, tho' dash'd with oddity,
In THORNTON is no scarce commodity:
Much learning too I can descry,
Beneath *his* periwig doth lie.—
—I beg his pardon, I declare,
His grizzle's gone for greasy hair. . . .
But why neglect (his trade forsaking
For scribbling, and merry-making,)
With tye to overshade that brain,
Which might have shone in WARWICK-LANE?
Why not, with spectacles on nose,
In chariot lazily repose,
A formal, pompous, deep physician,
HIMSELF A SIGN-POST EXHIBITION?[7]

After thus summarizing Lloyd's friends, the 'Cobler' addresses the poet directly, chiding him for neglecting his art in order to edit a magazine. In truth, by this time the editorship of *The St. James's Magazine* had become exceedingly onerous to Lloyd, who had squandered what little talent he once possessed in churning out fables and filler for the publication; he admits as much in 'A Dialogue Between the Author and his Friend':

Continual plagues my soul molest,
And *Magazines* disturb my rest,
While scarce a night I steal to bed,
Without a couplet in my head,
And in the morning, when I stir,
Pop comes a *Devil*, 'Copy sir.'
I cannot strive with daring flight
To reach the bold *Parnassian* HEIGHT.[8]

In light of this, the 'Cobler's' closing admonition is extremely pointed, but unfortunately too late to save Lloyd:

Rouse then, for shame, your ancient spirit!
Write a great work! a work of merit!

> The conduct of your friend examine,
> And give a PROPHECY OF FAMINE;
> Or like yourself, in days of yore,
> Write ACTORS, as you did before. . . .
> Learn not a shuffling, shambling, pace,
> But go erect with manly grace;
> For OVID says, and pr'y thee heed it,
> *Os homini sublime dedit.*
> But if you still waste all your prime
> In spinning Lilliputian rhyme,
> Too long your genius will lie fallow,
> And ROBERT LLOYD be Robert SHALLOW.

Despite the implied irony, this warning was too sharp to be laughed off, and Lloyd's response to the entire piece was equivocal. Colman, who reprinted the poem in his *Prose on Several Occasions* (1787), left a description of Lloyd's confusion, consultation, and final decision. The poem, Colman wrote, 'was written in concert with Garrick, and with Churchill's knowledge and privity sent to Lloyd for insertion in his monthly publication. Lloyd . . . consulted Churchill on the propriety of printing such an attack upon himself and his friends. In that point, says Churchill drily, you must judge for yourself. He did judge for himself, and published it.'[9]

Lloyd's adviser, Churchill, was by mid-1762 the most famous satirist and one of the most remarked upon libertines in London—and each day he seemed bent on surpassing his previous day's reputation. It was during this time that his intimacy with John Wilkes began. Wilkes, the son of a wealthy Westminster distiller, was in his person, morals, and ideology a man after Churchill's own heart. Strikingly ugly (a feature Churchill never tired of pointing out about himself), Wilkes was nevertheless extremely successful with women, and he cultivated his talent to the fullest. A man of extraordinary charm and wit, he was at once cunning and unusually forthcoming about his vices and ambitions. In the spring of 1762 Wilkes was about to embark on a typically self-serving, but bold and historically crucial campaign against the policies (and personalities) of the Earl of Bute and George III, a campaign that would eventually tie his name forever with the word 'liberty' in the annals of English history. Churchill, the poet of liberty, was his natural ally.

Wilkes and Churchill's friendship seems to date from 1761–2, though George Nobbe points out that they may have known each other as early as 1759.[10] The two men genuinely liked each other, and they were certainly held together by more than political ideals. Both were addicted to the pursuit of pleasure. In the first surviving letter between the two (15 June 1762), Wilkes mentions both editorial matters connected with his opposition paper, *The North Briton*, and a forthcoming meeting of the Monks of Medmenham—a meeting that Churchill (and perhaps Lloyd) was to attend.

The Monks of Medmenham—or the 'Order of St Francis', as they called themselves—espoused a philosophy summed up by the motto over the door of their meeting place at Medmenham Abbey: FAY CE QUE VOUDRAS. Such an injunction would seem a sufficient explanation for Churchill's attraction to the group, even disregarding the more explicitly pleasurable activities that were carried on within the abbey's walls. The order was headed by Sir Francis Dashwood, an extremely imaginative sensualist, and besides Wilkes included Lord Sandwich, the poet Paul Whitehead, and approximately eight other 'monks'. (Churchill, though a visitor, was never a fully-fledged member.) The activities of the order ranged from the singing of bawdy catches to the celebration of elaborate Black Masses.[11] One relatively constant ingredient were the 'nuns' brought in for sexual recreation. Wilkes's short reference to the order in his first letter to Churchill—'next monday we meet at Medmenham'—implies that the poet already was familiar with these goings-on, and had probably attended at least one previous meeting. That he was more than casually acquainted with the activities of the order is made clear by a satirical description of its rituals (replete with the political allusions of a later, and more acrimonious, period) in *The Candidate*:

> Whilst Womanhood, in habit of a Nun,
> At M[EDMENHAM] lies, by backward Monks undone;
> A nation's reck'ning, like an alehouse score,
> Whilst PAUL *the aged* chalks behind a door,
> Compell'd to hire a foe to cast it up;
> [DASHWOOD] shall pour, from a Communion Cup,
> Libations to the Goddess without eyes,
> And *Hob* or *Nob* in Cyder and excise.

$$(695-702)^{12}$$

Churchill and Wilkes did not confine their libertine activities to Medmenham Abbey. Their letters to each other were filled with references to their sexual adventures—some seemingly written on the spot:

By the way my Dear Wilkes, did you ever know a man, who rail'd at Fornication unless he was old or impotent? If you know such a one set him down—hic niger est, hunc hii Romani cavito. In your's you tell me you engaged with—I could not understand it, my Lindamira says it must be with Old Scratch, with whom, judging you by me, she supposes us both to be on good terms. I rather think you meant it a hint for me to fill up a blank, and she seems to like the interpretation, and looks towards the Bed.[13]

In another letter, Wilkes tantalizes Churchill: 'I am just summon'd about my house and my girl—I shall return in less than an hour—If you will wait, you shall kiss the *lips*—if you will dine, you shall suck the sweetest *bubbies* of this hemisphere.'[14] Such adventures naturally could end a good deal less attractively than they began. In one striking instance, Churchill wrote to Garrick what appears to be a 'morning after' letter: 'Half drunk—Half mad—and quite stripped of all my Money, I should be much obliged if you would enclose and send by the Bearer five pieces.'[15]

It is this self-destructive element of Churchill's libertinism that becomes more and more apparent as he runs through the course of his pleasures. He seems to have contracted syphilis early in 1762, and by autumn the disease was severely affecting his health. Wilkes wrote expressing concern on 9 September, and Churchill answered the next day; 'I am infinitely obliged to you for the kind Concern you express for my Health, but what account to give you of it I can't well tell. What I imagined to be St. Anthony's fire turns out to be St. Cytherea's. I am better as to acuteness of pain but next week make . . . for Salivation.'[16] But Churchill's disease grew progressively worse. On 12 December, he wrote to Wilkes that 'My teeth begin to loosen but yet I think they could bite the proud Scot', and the following day: 'The Spitting comes on me so fast that I have not one moment to set pen to paper—My Body is weak, but my heart is good yet—tho' faith I was devilishly Low Spirited last Night—I shall not write to you what when present I will say, that I would not forego the pleasures arising from that dear handful of Delight, tho sure to be salivated once a Quarter.'[17] This letter captures Churchill's essential attitude toward his pleasures and their ill consequences: he refused to forego the former in order to avoid the latter. There is a strong element of self-destructiveness in his response, but it is the same kind of disregard of self that in a more elevated context makes the hero or the matyr. About a year later, in better health, Churchill would sum up his hedonistic but somehow courageous philosophy in an epigrammatic sentence worthy (if 'pleasure' were but replaced by 'honour' or 'freedom') of a figure of heroic romance: 'My Life I hold for purposes of pleasure; those forbid, it is not worth my care.'[18]

Such dedicated libertinism was an outgrowth of Churchill's outspoken love of personal liberty; and both the ideal and the more sordid reality combined to provide the motive and effectuating force behind some of his strongest satire. While his unswerving dedication to individual freedom provided a philosophical rationale for his support of John Wilkes, and his love of pleasure drew him close to Wilkes the man, the disease and pain resulting from his libertine dalliances indelibly coloured his satire. During the composition of *An Epistle to William Hogarth*, Churchill wrote to Wilkes: 'I have laid in a great stock of gall, and I do not intend to spare it on this occasion—he shall be welcome to every drop of it, Tho' I Thought, which I can scarce think, that it would never be schew'd. I hope it will not go off in an obliging Gonorrhea, Which (from which Communicated I know not) is at present ravaging the Constitution of Mrs. J. and playing the Devil with your humble.'[19] Some time later, after quoting to Wilkes the first 52 lines of the attack on Hogarth, Churchill reiterated the part disease played in his satire: 'I am most confoundedly bad, Confin'd to my room with an Eruptio Veneris. . . . The Scot's Pastoral arose from a pox, but this will be rather of a milder Nature, and Hogarth is much oblig'd to the agreeable Mrs. J. for being so merciful in her distributions.'[20] Though the equation of disease with satire is partially meant as a joke, it is also an essentially accurate statement of one of Churchill's most powerful motivations to satire. Certainly, he wrote his political satires because of loyalty to Wilkes and liberty (and for money)—but their particularly corrosive tone, their imagery of disease, waste, and impotence,

arose in large measure from the psychological and physiological
effects of Churchill's recurring venereal infections.

II

The social context of Churchill's early political satire was
adumbrated by Robert Lloyd in 'Chit-Chat', a poem that
records an imaginary conversation between spectators watching George III's procession to Parliament on 25 November
1762. The procession was notable for two attractions: the gaudy
new state coach, and the king's Scottish 'favourite', John
Stuart, Earl of Bute. As two women ask, 'Which is the King?
. . . Which is the coach?', a Scotsman and another bystander
focus on the chief spectacles of the procession:

SCOTCHMAN.

Which is the noble EARL OF BUTE,
Geud-Faith, I'll *gi* him a salute.
For he's the *Laird of aw our clan*,
Troth, he's a *bonny muckle man*.

MAN.

Here comes the Coach, so very slow
As if it ne'er was made to go,
In all the gingerbread of state,
And staggering under its own weight.

MRS. SCOT

Upon my word, its *monstrous* fine!
Would half the gold upon't were mine!
How gaudy all the gilding shews!
It puts *one's* eyes out as it goes.
What a rich glare of various hues,
What shining yellows, scarlet, blues!
It must have cost a heavy price;
Tis like a mountain drawn by mice.[21]

The ridicule of the new coach (still in clumsy service today) and
Lord Bute was not confined to Lloyd's poetry: the procession
in question was punctuated by the crowd's attacking Bute and
nearly killing him before he could make his escape.

Bute's extraordinary unpopularity was the result of a mix of
factors ranging from aristocratic envy to popular xenophobia,

but the major charges can be summarized under three heads.[22] First, Bute was a Scot and was thought to be using his influence over the king to prefer fellow Scotsmen to lucrative and powerful places throughout the government. Second, Bute was a Stuart and was assumed to be encouraging the king's supposed absolutist tendencies. Third, Bute and the king were together pushing for an immediate end to the Seven Years' War with France—a war William Pitt had conducted with brilliant success. In the popular mind, Bute's ascendancy threatened not only the jobs and status of Englishmen, but political stability and national prestige. In 1762 prints and satires against the Scottish 'invasion' became a growth industry, and the most vilified figure in them was inevitably the Earl of Bute.

The anti-Bute sentiment had begun to gather momentum in October 1761 when Pitt resigned as Secretary of State after failing to win Parliamentary support for a pre-emptive declaration of war on Spain. Although Bute was actually rather uneasy about the resignation, Pitt's fall was publicly blamed on the favourite. The resignation sparked an outraged response from the chauvinistic London populace and powerful segments of the City, who supported a policy that might today be called 'peace through strength'. Their derision of the administration—nominally headed by the Duke of Newcastle at the Treasury—grew even more strident when Spain's alliance with France forced England to declare war anyway, on 4 January 1762. Newcastle, his position impossibly precarious, resigned on 26 May, and George III immediately replaced him with Bute—thus providing a clearly defined target for one of the most intense campaigns of anti-ministerial propaganda in English history.[23]

For the Nonsense Club, these political goings-on mainly provided journalistic and satirical fodder (Churchill, for example, attacked Bute's influence over George III in *Night*), but for John Wilkes the fall of Pitt was an unmitigated disaster. In 1757, Wilkes had been launched in politics by the Pitt–Grenville connection when they supported him in a parliamentary election he bought in Aylesbury for £7,000 (this after losing his first bid for Parliament in 1754 at a cost of £4,000). Thus Wilkes's financial future, as well as his future in politics, was inextricably bound up with that of Earl Temple of Stowe and his brother-in-law, William Pitt. This is not to say that

Wilkes was a mere puppet. After his earliest political appointment, he had written to a friend: 'You see, I declare myself a
friend of liberty and will act up to it'.[24] But his financial well-
being certainly received a shock with the October resignations
of Pitt and Earl Temple (Lord Privy Seal).

For his part, Bute, immediately after his appointment,
brought to fruition a long-considered plan to set up a political
journal in defence of himself and his administration. It was a
move fraught with danger. Dr John Campbell, Bute's friend
and a veteran propagandist, warned of the potential consequences on 5 June 1762, only six days after the paper commenced publication: 'There is no doubt that you will receive
many provocations. Papers will be set up to libel your measures.
But, my Lord, that signifies little if you set up no paper to
defend them, for in that case a paper war would commence and
as in all wars those who live by [them] will study to continue
them.'[25] Bute's error was immediately compounded by his
choice of an author and title for the paper. In a move that
seems inexplicably insensitive, Bute hired Smollett, perhaps
the most well-known and controversial Scottish writer in
London, to conduct a weekly journal to be called *The Briton*. If
the irony was lost on Bute, it did not escape his enemies, and
The Briton instantly succeeded in provoking the paper war that
Campbell had dreaded.

The initial target of Smollett's paper was *The Monitor*—a
weekly essay paper supported by William Beckford and other
'independent' merchants which since its inception in 1755 had
championed City Toryism, most notably in its 'interest in
trade and its hostility to monopolies, large-scale merchants,
financiers and capitalists, its concern for the welfare of the
middling sort and its defence of the citizens of London and
their governing bodies against disparaging attacks.'[26] *The
Monitor*'s anti-plutocratic, anti-oligarchical bias was soon
turned to the purposes of the 'patriot-minister' William Pitt,
and throughout the Seven Years' War it served as a vital instrument in maintaining Pitt's power base among the middling
sort of the City and insuring his continued popularity in other
sectors of society. With the widespread defection of Tories from
Pitt over the issue of continuing the war, and the subsequent
redefinition of political labels this move entailed, *The Monitor*

became stridently anti-Bute and thus anti-'Tory' in the term's new (or revived) propagandistic sense.[27] Conducted primarily by Arthur Beardmore, *The Monitor* in 1762 served as a mouth-piece for the Pitt–Temple interest, and on 22 May ran the first of its continuing series on court favourites—an essay by Wilkes describing a stereotypical favourite (Bute) and cataloguing the pernicious effects of Count Bruhl's recent ascendancy in Saxony. It was a piece that raised eyebrows at court and mirth in the coffee-houses.[28]

The inaugural issue of Smollett's *Briton* (29 May 1762) attacked Wilkes's essay directly, promising to 'convict' the author of *The Monitor* 'not barely of fallacy, but of fraud, not of a weakness only, but of wickedness also'.[29] Temple immedi-ately suggested that Wilkes answer Smollett with a paper of his own. Well aware of Churchill's fearsome power and literary reputation, Wilkes seems to have enlisted him to help with a quick three-paper counter-attack to be entitled ironically *The North Briton*. The fact that Churchill's old literary antagonist Smollett was the enemy undoubtedly helped to draw him into the controversy, as did Wilkes's arrangement for Churchill to receive the profits of the paper.[30] The promise that a notable like Earl Temple was giving financial support to the project was probably another inducement.

On 5 June 1762 the first issue of *The North Briton* appeared, and one week later Churchill's old enemy, Arthur Murphy, began his own pro-administration paper, *The Auditor*. Churchill was now indeed in congenial company. When *The North Briton*'s irreverent appeal for 'liberty of the press' caught the mood of the town the original three-issue plan was abandoned, and Churchill became editor of and occasional writer for one of the most notorious opposition papers yet to appear in English politics.

From the beginning, the Nonsense Club was in tacit support of *The North Briton*. On the day the first *North Briton* was pub-lished, *The St. James's Chronicle* contemptuously dismissed Smollett's *Briton*—'on examining it, we found the Execution, besides some very exceptionable Points in the *real* Intent of the Piece, to be infinitely beneath either our Notice or Criticism'—and at the same time praised Wilkes's essay: 'This Day the Public has been presented with another new Paper, entitled the

North Briton, written in Answer to the foregoing. It opens with some very sensible Reflections on the Liberty of the Press, which having within these late Years endured many unjustifiable Attacks from ministerial Pens supported by ministerial influence, we shall here lay an Extract of what the Author says on this Subject before our Readers, there being nothing, in our Opinion, more deserving their careful Attention and Notice.'[31] The writer then applauds the way the new paper exposes the tactics and assertions of *The Briton* and comments finally that 'The *North Briton*'s Triumph . . . would have been much more glorious, had his Antagonist approved himself a greater Hero'.

Smollett seems to have earned the abuse that was promptly heaped upon *The Briton*.[32] Writing from the point of view of the court and in defence of an essentially rigid hierarchical order, he incessantly belaboured the City, the middling men, and their defenders as (to take a sampling) 'the dregs of the people', 'the base, unthinking rabble', 'coffee house politicians, bankrupt mechanics soured by their losses, and splenetic sots', and, in a series that anticipates the vitriolic catalogues of *Humphrey Clinker*, 'forlorn Grubs and Garetteers, desperate gamblers, tradesmen thrice bankrupt, prentices to journey-men, understrappers to porters, hungry pettifoggers, bailiff-followers, discarded draymen, hostlers out of place, and felons returned from transportation.'[33] 'These are the people', Smollett writes, 'who proclaim themselves free born Englishmen, and transported by a laudable spirit of patriotism, insist upon having a spoke in the wheel of government.' One can imagine the effect of such statements on the independently minded tradesmen, merchants, and artisans of the metropolis. As the merchant William Temple wrote in *North Briton* No. 19, in Smollett's eyes 'the present citizens, merchants, traders, and commonalty of LONDON are just such another rabble as the mob under *Wat Tyler* and Jack *Straw* was formerly. . . . You neither want for capacity to discern his insults, nor for spirit to resent the abuse: no; for to do you justice, I must say . . . the *merchants of London*, in their collective capacity, possess more honest, useful, political knowledge, and understand more the true interest of their country, than all the ministers of state ever discovered, or were masters of.' Given Smollett's consistently derogatory view of the great majority of the middling people, it is not surprising that Earl Temple should quickly conclude 'that The Briton left to himself is left to his own worst enemy'.[34]

In *The North Briton*, Wilkes and Churchill engaged in their own versions of slander, most of it directed upwards. Early on, for example, Wilkes 'tried the temper of the court' by publishing in No. 5 an essay Temple had forbidden him to print in *The Monitor*: his famous comparison of the relations of Bute and the Princess Dowager with those of Roger Mortimer and Queen Isabella in the reign of Edward III.[35] Since the 1750s there had been a suspicion that the Princess Augusta (George III's mother) and Bute were engaged in an illicit love affair. Rumours of the affair, though false, became popular 'facts' in the period after 1761, achieving expression in prints, poems, and songs.[36] In this context, the peroration of Wilkes's essay may be read as a garish bit of innuendo masquerading as exemplar history:

O may Britain never see such a day again! when the power acquired by profligacy may lord it over this realm; when the feeble pretensions of a *court minion* may require the prostitution of royalty for their support; or if, which heaven avert! such a day should come, may a Prince truly jealous of the honour of his House, and armed with the intrepidity of EDWARD THE THIRD, crush the aspiring wretch who mounts to power by such ignoble means.

The phrases 'prostitution of royalty' and 'aspiring wretch who mounts to power' are typical of the sexual references that pervaded anti-Bute propaganda and took graphic form as 'The Scotch Broomstick and Female Besom' or 'Gisbal's Staff' in the popular prints. Wilkes's grandiloquence, in effect, becomes a kind of gaudily decorated window revealing Bute and the king's mother in a compromising position.[37]

Churchill seems to have had no hand in *North Briton* No. 5, but he is credited with writing at least nine others: Nos. 7, 8, 10, 18, 21, 22, 26, 27, and 42.[38] His greater contribution was as editor of the paper. Wilkes, as Colonel of the Buckinghamshire Militia, was stationed in Winchester during the summer of 1762 and was forced to send his drafts to London for publication. Churchill corrected them and saw them through the press. The first paragraph of the first surviving letter between the two men (written from Winchester) neatly summarizes and dramatizes the editorial dynamics: 'As the Devil wou'd have it, no contrivance of mine wou'd answer till now to send you the North Briton. . . . As to this number, add, subtract, multiply and divide it, as you like.'[39] (The paper in question is No. 3.)

Because of his conspicuous London activity on behalf of *The North Briton*, and his fame as a poet (far surpassing any notoriety Wilkes had yet gained as a politician), Churchill at the outset received the lion's share of attention from contemporary controversialists and cartoonists. Murphy in *The Auditor* of 22 July satirically suggested that if the opposition regained power Churchill would be made Archbishop of Canterbury, and he imagined the new pontiff's behaviour as reflecting the philosophy expressed in *Night*: 'The archbishop of Canterbury preached yesterday before the house of Lords; *as his head never akes at all*, he had sat up at a tavern the whole preceding night; the congregation allowed it to be one of Tristram *Shandy's* best sermons, and said it was a pity his grace was so drunk.' Wilkes wrote to Churchill five days later, 'I congratulate you on being mention'd in such terms by the *Auditor*. May he write in the spirit of prophecy!'[40] By early September, Churchill had appeared as a character in two political prints. In *The Fishermen* (BM 3876), he was shown with Smollett, Murphy, and Beardmore, fishing in the 'waters of sedition'. A copy of *The Rosciad* protrudes from his pocket, and he cries, 'Rare Sport, by G–d! Ill be d——d if this is n't better than preaching.' A print of 2 September, *John Bull's House sett in Flames*, was more sympathetic to Churchill, and expressed the strong anti-Scot sentiment of most Londoners. The print shows the poet carrying a bucket of water marked 'NORTH BRITON' as he helps Pitt and others put out a blaze at St James's Palace begun by Bute, 'Smallwit' (Smollett), and other Scots.[41]

Churchill's first essay for *The North Briton* was a relatively mundane exercise of the paper's ironic Scottish persona, whose praise served to damn the ambitious North Britons threatening to 'overrun' London. Writing in *The North Briton* No. 7 as 'BLUESTRING MAC STUART' (an allusion to Bute's anticipated installation in the Order of the Garter, not, as Neil Schaeffer seems to assume, a misprint for 'Blustering'), Churchill asks Mr North Briton to 'suffer me to intermingle tears of joy with you on our present happy situation, and to heighten your satisfaction, give me leave to exhibit to you a glimpse of futurity.'[42] To achieve this prophetic end, 'Mac Stuart' composes 'The FUTURE CHRONICLE or The Nova Scotia Intelligencer': a parodic newspaper containing announcements ('Mr. John Bull, a very worthy, plain, honest gentleman, of Saxon descent . . . was choaked by inadvertently swallowing a thistle') and advertisements ('O! the ROAST BEEF! or, The Case is altered, A Prose Poem in the modern Taste. By LAZARUS MAC BAREBONES of Scotstarvit Esq.') of an England under Scottish domination.

Churchill's relatively simplistic manipulation of the food / nationality metaphor and his prophecy of a future Scottish take-over of England are important because they anticipate the central themes of his first major political satire, *The Prophecy of Famine*. In a letter to Wilkes describing the germination of another idea, Churchill alluded to the close relationship between *The North Briton* and *The Prophecy*: 'The plan of the next N.B. I have chang'd, and for this reason—On pursuing it I find it the best Subject for a Poem I ever had in my life. The Prophecy of Famine you may remember took its rise from a similar circumstance.'[43] By 23 October, Churchill had a total design in mind. He wrote to Wilkes that 'It is split into two Poems—the Scottish Eclogue which will be inscrib'd to you in the Pastoral way—and another Poem—which I think will be a strong one—immediately address'd by way of Epistle to you—This way They will both be of a piece.'[44] By the time the poem was finally published in January 1763, it had taken on a new design: an opening section of literary criticism, followed by a 'defence' of the Scots, an apostrophe to Wilkes, and the Scottish eclogue.

The Prophecy of Famine is Churchill's key transitional work. In its programme of subjects and rhetorical approaches, it duplicates Churchill's own progress from satire concerned chiefly with aesthetic and personal issues to satire motivated primarily by political events. The poem opens with a description of the tyro's humble and often romantically inspired approach to pastoral versifying, then contrasts this foolish ignorance with the equally foolish pedantry of the more sophisticated ode and elegy writers. In typical Nonsense Club style, Churchill accuses these poets of discarding the 'workings of the heart' and banishing nature for 'mechanic art'. Then, to close the literary section, Churchill names Nature as his 'goddess', only to suddenly and deftly subvert this terminology by equating Nature with the brutal way of life in Scotland (see above, Chapter 4, Section III).

Churchill's transition from satiric ridicule to ironic praise marks the opening of the second section of the poem: a mock defence of the Scots in the manner of *The North Briton*. His allusion to '*waggon-loads* of courage, wealth and sense' (113) takes its context from the popular prints showing caravans of Scots on their way south (e.g. 'We are all a comeing', BM 3823) and parallels Johnson's famous rejoinder to Boswell's 'I come from Scotland, but I cannot help it'. But more importantly the mock praise exemplifies—as it intensifies—the semantic confusion engendered by the propagandistic appropriation and reversal of the terms 'Briton' and 'North Briton'. Here is Churchill's topsy-turvey apostrophe to Wilkes:

> Oft have I heard thee mourn the wretched lot
> Of the poor, mean, despis'd, insulted *Scot*,
> Who, might calm reason credit idle tales,
> By rancour forg'd where prejudice prevails,
> Or starves at home, or practises, thro' fear
> Of starving, arts which damn all conscience here.
> When *Scriblers*, to the charge by int'rest led,
> The fierce *North-Briton* foaming at their head,
> Pour forth invectives, deaf to candour's call,
> And, injur'd by one alien, rail at all;
> On *Northern Pisgah* when they take their stand,
> To mark the weakness of that *Holy Land*,
> With needless truths their libels to adorn,
> And hang a nation up to public scorn,
> Thy gen'rous soul condemns the frantic rage,
> And hates the faithful, but ill-natur'd, page.
>
> (179–94)

There is more than simple ironic reversal here: there is the kind of chaos of signification found in the contradictory juxtaposition of praise and blame, definition and counter-definition, that filled the pages of the newspapers. A Scot writes *The Briton* in defence of a Scot minister; an Englishman writes *The North Briton* attacking the Scots; the formerly 'Tory' *Monitor* attacks the new court 'Tories' (the conjunction of 'court' and 'Tory' itself being a radical displacement of traditional Hanoverian politics); a 'Patriot Minister' is driven from office by a 'Patriot King'. Labels break free of their referents; signifiers turn back on their signifieds. It is a commonplace of political history that the period immediately following the accession of George III marked a watershed in English politics: an era of instability, atomization, and reconfiguration, the dynamics and consequences of which continue to provoke heated debate among professional historians who (bringing political history into the academic present) accuse each other of harbouring 'Whig' or 'Tory' points of view.[45] My point is that Churchill not only reproduces in his satire the propaganda of the era, but that he captures rhetorically the essential ambiguity of reference and confusion of meaning that characterized the political and social theatre of the 1760s. The intensely self-conscious quality of Churchill's 'confusion' is especially evident in the final four lines of the above passage: Wilkes is praised for condemning his own paper, which is said to add 'needless truths' to 'libels' and thus present 'faithful, but ill-natured' charges. The Scots are simultaneously defended ('it is all unfortunate') and damned ('but it is all true') in a passage which itself bears an ironic relationship to actual events: Wilkes is in fact the fomenter of the 'frantic rage' he is said to condemn. In the apostrophe to Wilkes, Churchill's irony is not merely a partisan weapon: it is an irreverent exemplification of how language is manipulated and the motives which drive men to distort meaning.

As suggested above, one of the factors contributing to Churchill's vivid imagery in *The Prophecy of Famine* may have been his veneral disease. In the latter part of the poem, as the shepherds Sawney and Jockey parody the conventions of the pastoral eclogue, Churchill places his chief political concerns against a strongly imagined background of waste, loathesomeness, starvation, and disease. To appreciate the potential effect of Churchill's physical affliction on his artistic temperament, one need only turn to the description of the cave of Famine:

> All creatures, which, on nature's earliest plan,
> Were form'd to loath, and to be loath'd by man,
> Which ow'd their birth to nastiness and spite,
> Deadly to touch, and hateful to the sight . . .
> Found place *within*; marking her noisome road
> With poison's trail, *here* crawl'd the bloated Toad;

There webs were spread of more than common size,
And half-starv'd spiders prey'd on half-starv'd flies;
In quest of food, Efts strove in vain to crawl;
Slugs, pinch'd with hunger, smear'd the slimy wall;
The cave around with hissing serpents rung;
On the damp roof unhealthy vapour hung,
And FAMINE, *by her children always known,*
As proud as poor, here fix'd her *native* throne.

(319–22, 325–34)

The preoccupation with debility ('Efts strove in vain to crawl')
and discharge ('smear'd the slimy wall'), with 'hissing snakes'
and 'bloated' toads, with poison and starvation, seems to me to
be a direct consequence of Churchill's physical condition. At
the risk of indulging in the biographical fallacy, I would further
suggest that the influence of disease is the strongest single factor
behind his striking close description of Famine:

Pale FAMINE rear'd the head; her eager eyes,
Where hunger e'en to madness seem'd to rise,
Speaking aloud her throes and pangs of heart,
Strain'd to get loose, and from their orbs to start;
Her hollow cheeks were each a deep-sunk cell,
Where wretchedness and horror lov'd to dwell;
With double rows of useless teeth supplied,
Her mouth, from ear to ear, extended wide,
Which, when for want of food her entrails pin'd,
She op'd, and cursing swallow'd nought but wind.

(407–16)

At the time he wrote this description, Churchill was himself
suffering from a form of starvation. During the mercury-
induced 'salivation' treatment for venereal disease, one could
scarcely eat: Churchill refers to the spitting and the loosening
of the teeth in which it resulted in a letter to Wilkes (quoted
above, Section I of this chapter). Churchill's letters describing
his continuing illness are directly preceded by letters from
Wilkes asking him about the poem and urging him to finish it:
'I have not read a word of *Eclogue*, or *Epistle*—therefore I suppose you have set your hand to something better'; and some
days later, 'I hope you will now indemnify me for this long
absence by *eclogue* and *epistle* too'.[46] Never, it seems, had Churchill felt so helpless or full of gall. In a sense, Famine's sickbed

prophecy of future greatness re-enacts Churchill's drawing of satiric power from the confinement and disgust caused by his illness.

III

As the atmosphere surrounding *The North Briton* grew more electric, one of the friends from whom Churchill and Wilkes must have expected support was William Hogarth. By nature a Whig, and a xenophobic advocate of English talent and liberty, Hogarth had every reason to distrust Bute. But Hogarth was also a long time supporter of the Leicester House faction and he had close friends who supported Bute's policies in Parliament.[47] The violence of Wilkes and Churchill's propaganda must have been enough to turn Hogarth against them when, in the summer of 1762, the artist decided to execute a topical engraving in order to 'stop a gap' in his income (though he also said that the print was meant to urge 'peace and unanimity').[48] The print—*The Times*—contained an attack on both Wilkes and Churchill; and it transformed Hogarth, their one-time friend, into a hated enemy.

Wilkes and Churchill, in their later attacks on Hogarth, told of earlier days when they had sat and listened to the painter hold forth on the state of the arts; and we have seen how closely the entire Nonsense Club was identified with Hogarth during the period of the Sign Painters' Exhibition (April–May 1762). Paulson comments that Hogarth and 'Garrick's friends Colman, Thornton, Wilkes and Churchill . . . were drinking, talking, plotting, practical joking, and propagandizing companions, whose basic stance was irreverence—a group analogous to the Medmenham Brotherhood in this as in their splintering on the rock of the peace negotiations.'[49]

It is not surprising that Wilkes and Churchill were appalled to find that Hogarth was planning a print against their cause. Wilkes, as he tells it, send word 'to Mr. Hogarth, that such a proceeding would not only be unfriendly in the highest degree, but extremely injudicious'.[50] Hogarth responded to this veiled threat by saying that he would only attack Temple and Pitt. This, of course, did not satisfy Wilkes, who replied that 'if his friends were attacked, he should then think he was wounded in the most sensible part, and would, as well as he was able, revenge their cause'. Hogarth's further response may be inferred from the fact that when *The Times*, plate I, appeared on 7 September, it satirized Temple, Pitt, Churchill and Wilkes.

The Times, plate I, shows Pitt standing on stilts, fanning a flaming sign of the world (representing the Seven Years' War), while King George, dressed in fire-fighting clothes, tries to put the fire out (an allusion to the continuing peace negotiations). Pitt is surrounded by a crowd which includes City merchants and butchers sounding their marrow bones and cleavers; the King is impeded by three figures armed with clyster pipes, who lean out of the windows of a building marked 'TEMPLE COFFEE HOUSE' and squirt their sovereign. The lone figure in the lower window is Temple; the two garreteers are Churchill and Wilkes. Appearing only four months after the Sign Painters' Exhibition, the print shows Hogarth working deep within the idiom promulgated by the Exhibition—an idiom that must have taken on a sadly ironic meaning when turned against his old friends. In the left foreground are no less than four large pictographic signs representing (clockwise from bottom left) 1. the exploitation of America by City merchants; 2. George Townshend's Norfolk militia; 3. the resignation of the Duke of Newcastle; 4. Pitt's political supporters ('The Patriots'). In the background hang carved symbols of an eagle and a fleur-de-lis (alluding to Germany and France) and a sign depicting two men shaking hands (an allusion to the French–Spanish alliance).[51] The burning world that Pitt fans and George III tries to extinguish is an adaptation of the familiar *World's End* sign (seen in the Sign Painters' Exhibition as No. 21) and alludes not only to the present war, but to Hogarth's increasingly pessimistic view of the world. (The sign would appear again in Hogarth's farewell piece, *The Bathos*.) And the figure of Lord Temple, usually described as being 'faceless', seems in fact to be a wig block: a popular icon that plays on the Somebody–Nobody paradigm so prominent in the Exhibition.

'Hogarth has begun his attack today', Wilkes wrote to Churchill on 9 September, 'I shall attack him in hobbling prose, you will I hope in smooth-pac'd verse.'[52] Soon after, Churchill wrote to Garrick, 'I have seen Hogarth's print. . . . I am happy to find that he hath at last declar'd himself, for there is no

5. *The Times*, Plate 1. Engraving by William Hogarth, 1762

credit to be got by breaking flies upon a wheel. But Hogarths are Subjects worthy of an Englishman's pen. Speedily to be published, An Epistle to W. Hogarth by C. Churchill.'[53] But Churchill's satire was not speedily published, nor was it mentioned again for over half a year. Instead, Wilkes launched an immediate counter-attack in *North Briton* No. 17. Using his insider's knowledge he mercilessly probed Hogarth's art and life, disparaging his forays into history painting, accusing him of holding a 'professed enmity' toward his fellow painters, and laughing at his position as Serjeant Painter to the King. Hogarth's royal office, Wilkes wrote, should be considered little more than that of a '*house*-painter; for he is not suffered to *caricature* the royal family. The post of portrait painter is given to a *Scotsman*, one *Ramsay*. Mr. *Hogarth* is only to paint the wainscot of the rooms, or, in the phrase of the art, may be called their *pannel-painter.*'[54]

A print of 23 October, *The Boot & The Block-Head* (BM 3977), attributed *The North Briton* No. 17 to Churchill. Playing on the same store of popular images that formed the basis of the Sign Painters' Exhibition, the print shows Bute as a wig block, crowned by a Scotch bonnet with a long serpentine queue labelled 'Tail of Beauty'. The wig block is on a pole anchored in a single large boot (i.e. Bute). While on one side the 'Auditor' and his allies bow to the idol, on the other Churchill —*North Briton* in hand—chastises a shaken and elderly Hogarth. 'Il spare none of you from the top of the Bonnet to the sole of the Boot,' Churchill exclaims; to which Hogarth feebly replies, 'Dam it Charles what have you done to me you'l make me run mad.' In private, Hogarth admitted that the attack affected him deeply; as he wrote in his journal, 'it could not but hurt a feeling mind'.[55]

During the period of the exchange with Hogarth, Robert Lloyd began to take an active role in the production of *The North Briton*. On 7 October he was working as Wilkes's editor out of William Flexney's book shop near Gray's Inn Gate. Flexney was Churchill's first publisher, but more importantly for Lloyd he was the publisher of *The St. James's Magazine*. We know Lloyd edited at least two *North Britons*, Nos. 19 and 20, for Wilkes wrote to Kearsly about No. 19: 'Send the whole as soon as you can to Robert Lloyd Esqr. at Mr. Flexney's near

6. *The Boot & The Block-Head.* Anonymous engraving (possibly by George Townshend), 1762

Gray's Inn Gate, who is so kind to take care of and correct this Paper. I will send you the next in very good time . . . Send the MSS, too, to Mr. Lloyd.'[56] Another Wilkes letter of about this time finds 'Mr. Churchill, Mr. Lloyd, and myself . . . waiting here [Wilkes's house in Great George Street] for the proof'.[57]

Wilkes had tried to enlist Lloyd's aid as early as 27 July. In a letter to Churchill soliciting some 'Scotch verses', Wilkes requested that 'you . . . send me Lloyd's fable'.[58] On 22 August Lloyd wrote a long letter to Wilkes containing the beginnings of an ironic essay on Scotch fir and thistle (intended for the *North Briton*, but never used) and a poem satirizing the panegyrics written to celebrate the birth of George III's first son.[59] But even before this letter, Lloyd was identified with *The North Briton*. Smollett, in *The Briton* of 21 August, described him as 'PAEDAGOGUS LATRO': 'In his halcyon days, he enjoyed the important post of deputy usher to an academy, whence being driven, for reasons best known to himself, he now keeps a shred of existence together by begging subscriptions, and spunging on school-boys. Sometimes he feeds on Bruin's [Churchill's] Offal, whom he frequently follows, and helps out with scraps of blasphemy, ribaldry and treason.'[60]

On 30 October the first half of Lloyd's satire on the royal birth poems was published in *The North Briton* No. 22 as *The Poetry Professors*: an anti-rules, anti-academic exercise in the typical Lloyd style. The remainder of the verses served Wilkes and Churchill well during a publishing crisis later in the autumn. In early November 1762, a warrant was issued by the Secretary of State for the arrest of Arthur Beardmore of *The Monitor*. Two weeks later, on 18 November, a general warrant was handed down for the apprehension of the authors, printers, and publishers of *The North Briton*. The warrant was never served, but the printer William Richardson was frightened off and Wilkes and Churchill had to find a new press to work for them. The relative innocuousness of Lloyd's verses seems to have made them an ideal stop-gap, for Wilkes asked Churchill on 22 November to 'tell Lloyd we depend on him for next saturday, and ought to have his verses to-morrow'. Lloyd was late delivering, and Wilkes wrote again to Churchill on 24 November: 'The Printer of the N B has absolutely refus'd the having any more concern in that paper. . . . I wish we had

Lloyd's verse for fear our new printer shou'd not be ready at so short a warning. The other man [Dryden Leach] will print the remainder of the verses.'[61] On 27 November, Lloyd's remaining verses duly appeared in *North Briton* No. 26 and were eventually reprinted in a pamphlet topped by a print of two scrawny Scotch bards (BM 3869). On the same Saturday, Churchill wrote to Kearsly informing him that he and Wilkes had 'provided a Printer' and asking 'whether You will chuse to continue as the Publisher'.[62] Kearsly decided to stay on, but Leach dropped out, and Richard Balfe soon became *The North Briton*'s printer. In the next issue of *The North Briton* (No. 27, 4 December 1762), Churchill reflected on these goings-on, and reacted with characteristic bravado:

Almost every man I meet looks strangely on me—some industriously avoid me—others pass me silent—stare—and shake their heads.— Those few, those very few, who are not afraid to take a lover of his country by the hand, congratulate me on my being alive and at liberty—They advise circumspection—for, they do not know—they cannot tell—but—the times—Liberty is precious—Fines—Imprisonment—Pillory—not indeed that they themselves—but—then in truth —God only knows. . . . Let them point out if they can, and if they dare, from whom, and on what account, I am in danger, before they produce it as a motive to affect my conduct; and plainly shall they prove that I have deserved punishment, before they shall oppress me with the fear of it.

Churchill's mixture of apprenhension and self-righteousness is probably an accurate expression of the warring passions within the mind of many a writer and publisher at this time. The government had openly attempted to suppress a dissident press. But *The North Briton* had survived.

While *The North Briton* duelled with the government, *The St. James's Chronicle* maintained its policy of impartiality. It ran excerpts from both opposition and administration papers, treading gingerly to provide ostensibly balanced coverage and to avoid prosecution. In a representative gesture, Colman contributed a parodic 'North Briton Extraordinary' to the issue of 16–19 October 1762 and followed it up with an 'Auditor Extraordinary' in the issue of 28–30 October. In his preface to the latter, he alluded facetiously, but with an underlying seriousness, to the precarious position not only of his publisher, but of all publishers faced with the possibility of general warrants:

> I was at first very glad to find that nobody questioned [the North Briton Extraordinary's] authenticity, but soon began to tremble for its consequences. Some said, that the Messengers had seized you, your Compositors, Pressmen, Devils, &c. Some foretold Motions in the Court of King's Bench providing Vengeances, and letting all the Terrors of the Law loose upon you. . . . I would advise you, at all Events, to give the World fresh Proofs of your Impartiality, and so balance the Account fairly between both Parties. Expel one Poison by another! Or, to speak more respectfully of our controversial Writers, let Diamond cut Diamond![63]

Thornton, too, was writing humorous letters and squibs for the paper, but because of his penchant for anonymity we can only speculate about his contributions. An example of the kind of squib he might have written is a letter of 16–18 November from 'Nebuchad Razor', Mr Monitor's barber. Nebuchad, an illiterate but outspoken member of a working man's club, finds Mr Monitor scanning the index of the History of England for 'Favourites' and crying 'Mor, Mor, Mor, Mor, Mort, Mortimer'. 'I supposed', Nebuchad says, 'when he was crying Mor, Mor, that we were to have more Favourites. I know not what your Favourite is, but I take him to be a Man with a large Wig.' Here Thornton—if it is he—brings together in humorous juxtaposition the literate opposition's identification of Bute as Mortimer (a sophisticated literary and historical symbol) and the underclass's perception of any 'Favourite' as a 'Man with a large Wig', or, in modern times, a bigwig.

Sometime in early December 1762, Wilkes and Churchill wrote an anonymous letter to Arthur Murphy's *Auditor* extolling Florida as a 'well-improved and richly-cultivated Country', and noting in particular the economic advantages of sending Florida peat to be burned in the fireplaces of planters in the British West Indies.[64] Florida, a negotiated acquisition from Spain, was the subject of much controversy: the government argued that it was an attractive prize; the opposition held it was a barren wasteland. Murphy, anxious for any reason to praise Florida and the peace, printed the letter (signed 'Viator') in *The Auditor* No. 31, affixing his own remark that this information was supported by the 'full Authority of all Writers'.[65] *The St. James's Chronicle* quickly reprinted this part of *The Auditor* in the issue of 18–21 December, and then, after waiting a seemly two days, followed up with a letter from 'Observator' (probably Churchill and Wilkes) that gleefully exposed Murphy's gullibility. 'Has this Man lost all Sense of Shame?' the correspondent asks incredulously, pointing out that Florida 'never contained 500 Families through its whole Extent, and except in one or two very small Spots, is known to be a barren inhospitable Desert.' Warming to his task, he takes up the peat question:

With much Appearance of Compassion he assures us, that our Planters in the West-Indies, have no Fires in their Parlours or Bedchambers, and very soberly proposes the supplying them with Peat from the Bogs of Florida, as one of the capital Advantages of that boasted Acquisition.

Did any Man, before this egregious Wight, ever think of kindling Fires, or as he calls them, *comfortable Fires*, in a Country, where every Art is tried to moderate the perpetual, unremitted, and almost intolerable Heat of the Climate? His next Complaint will be, I suppose, for want of Ice houses, in Nova Zembla or Greenland; and his next Scheme will be to transport Ice to these Countries from Canada.[66]

This letter was the first in a flood of ridicule that effectively destroyed Murphy's credibility. On 8 February *The Auditor* ceased publication, and four days later Smollett's *Briton* joined its ally in the great compositor's case. But while Wilkes and Churchill were claiming journalistic victory, Bute had won the political war. On 10 February 1762 England had signed the GRAND DEFINITIVE TREATY between His Britannick Majesty, the most Christian King, and the King of Spain'.[67] Although hindered more than helped by *The Briton* and *The Auditor*, Bute had nevertheless controlled Parliament and decisively defeated a fragmented if raucous opposition.

Bute's success seems to have goaded Wilkes to even more audacious efforts. On 17 March, two days before the full text of the treaty was printed in the newspapers, Wilkes republished the old play, *The Fall of Mortimer*, with an ironic dedication to the Earl of Bute. He even went so far as to have a specially bound copy delivered to Bute's house in South Audley Street.[68] Bute, a man sensitive to personal attacks, had for some time been pressing the king to allow him to resign. The unrelenting personal abuse in the press seems finally to have persuaded the king. On 8 April 1763 Bute stepped down.

At the moment of the resignation Wilkes was in France, but Churchill quickly suspended publication of *The North Briton* and waited for Wilkes's return. On the following Monday, *The Public Advertiser* (noting the failure of *The North Briton* to appear on the preceding Saturday) published 'A NEW NORTH BRITON' —a full-length essay which catalogues, exaggerates, and laughs at all of the major political themes and symbols of the conflict between Wilkes, Churchill, and the government.

If this essay is not by Thornton (and I feel that many things about it—from a title reminiscent of 'A New Chapter in Amelia' to its appearance in *The Public Advertiser*—mark it as his), he certainly cleared it for publication. Its mimicry catches the essence of the symbolic battle playing itself out between *The North Briton* and Lord Bute, and serves as a kind of coda to a struggle that was now suddenly and drastically to change. The essay begins with an impudent address to Bute:

I AM not afraid, nor (I flatter myself) shall I be ever ashamed of the following BOLD Address to your Lordship; and to convince your Lordship, that I have not the least Dread of your Power, I have BOLDLY subscribed my Name to it. I set at Defiance (I will modestly say, *at this present writing*) Mr. *Carrington* the Prime Messenger, the Master of the Board of Works for erecting Pillories, the Receiver-general of Fines, the Marshal of the King's Bench, the King's Bench itself, and that *Scotchman*, Lord M [Mansfield] who presides there.[69]

The Scottish problem is then analysed: 'What is to become of those numberless *Sawneys*, who are now upon the *North* Road, hastening up in hopes of Preferment? They must go *back* again to the *Cave of* FAMINE.' The Cider Tax is said not to 'affect YOUR Country, as the poor, meagre, barren, and uncultivated Soil will allow nothing to grow upon it but Thistles.' The definitive treaty is called 'a Peace, "that passeth all Understanding" '. As the essay proceeds, the major propaganda themes—Bute's patronage of Scottish writers, the liberty of the press ('the Liberty of ALL Liberties, most dear to ME'), *The Fall of Mortimer*—all are paraded in an only slightly exaggerated rendition of *The North Briton*'s usual manner. The essay—signed 'JOHN CAESAR WILKES'—is something of a propaganda lexicon: it emphasizes the entertainment value of political conflict and freezes in high relief the most prominent political symbols of the early Wilkes era.

Two days later, Wilkes and Churchill published a legitimate announcement ascribing *The North Briton*'s silence to a fear 'of falling into involuntary errors', then sat back to wait for the government to reveal itself. On 19 April, George III in his speech from the throne made certain references to the peace that indicated that the new Grenville administration (headed by Earl Temple's brother and containing two former Medmenhamites) would offer little in the way of change. Possibly after consulting with Temple and Pitt, Wilkes attacked the speech in *The North Briton* No. 45.[70]

Although the speech from the throne, as Wilkes was careful to point out, had 'always been considered by the legislature, and by the public at large, as a *Speech of the Minister*', *The North Briton* No. 45—with characteristic boldness—couched its protest in terms that not so subtly implied that to endorse such policies George III must be either a knave or a fool: 'Every friend of this country must lament that a prince of so many great and amiable qualities, whom England truly reveres, can be brought to give the sanction of his sacred name to the most odious measures, and the most unjustifiable public declarations, from a throne ever renowned for truth, honour, and unsullied virtue.' Halifax, the Secretary of State, immediately concluded that the paper was actionable; and the legal machinery was set into motion which led to Wilkes's arrest.[71]

On 26 April, a general warrant was issued for the arrest of 'the Authors, Printers & Publishers of a Seditious, & Treasonable Paper, intitled, The North Briton, Number 45.' Three days later, after legal consultations by the government, several printers and the publisher, George Kearsly, were apprehended and examined. Kearsly revealed what was of course an open secret, 'that John Wilkes of Great George Street, Westminster, is the author of most of the said Papers called the North Britain, and that Charles Churchill, Clerk, of Mill Bank, Westminster, is the author of some others'.[72] The next morning (30 April) Wilkes was apprehended as he returned from Balfe's print shop, and held prisoner for some time in his own house before being taken up the street to the Earl of Halifax's. Churchill's fate is less clear. *The Public Advertiser* of 2 May stated that the

'Rev. Mr. Churchill was also carried to the E of H.'s Office, and after Examination was discharged'. But Wilkes's version of the events is more entertaining. 'I had heard', Wilkes later wrote, 'that their verbal orders were likewise to apprehend him, but I suspected they did not know his person.' On Churchill's suddenly entering Wilkes's house, 'I accousted him, "Good morrow, Mr. Thomson. How does Mrs. Thomson to-day? Does she dine in the country?" Mr. Churchill thanked me, said she then waited for him, that he only came for a moment to ask me how I did; and almost directly took his leave. He went home immediately, secured all his papers, and retired into the country.'[73]

The Public Advertiser and other papers broke the story of Wilkes's arrest on Monday and continued to give it daily coverage.[74] On Tuesday, 3 May, Wilkes was taken from the Tower to the Court of Common Pleas in Westminster Hall, where, according to the *Public*, he refused bail, 'pleading by his Council, Mr. Serjeant Glynn, for his Discharge'.[75] Glynn offered three lines of defence: Wilkes was arrested on insufficient evidence; general warrants were illegal; the offence was covered by Parliamentary privilege. Wilkes himself concentrated on a single and—for the press and people—far more emotional theme: the government's attempted destruction of individual English liberty.

On Thursday, 5 May, *The Public Advertiser* gave front-page coverage to the first of Wilkes's post-arrest handbills. Boldly headed 'MAGNA CHARTA', it contained a detailed, biased version of his arrest and confinement, and a 'true Copy' of the warrants. An editorial note appended to the handbill perfectly exemplifies the mixture of caution and alertness for the chance of commercial gain that would continue to characterize the relations between Wilkes and the media:

The above printed Hand-bill was sent us with a particular Desire that it should be inserted in our Paper. The Request, indeed, was a Sort of Demand upon us, as we profess an Impartiality on every Occasion. Not one of our Readers, we presume, can be displeased at our catching the Opportunity to insert what possibly he may be desirous to see, and which might not otherwise come to their Sight at all,—we are sure, none of them so soon.

In emphasizing its up-to-date coverage, while carefully distancing itself from Wilkes, *The Public Advertiser* suggests the importance of the commercial press to Wilkes's media strategy. For, in stressing their political independence, such papers—as opposed to the blatantly partisan *Briton, North Briton, Auditor*, and, in an earlier era, *Craftsman*—staked their claim to represent objectively the crosscurrents of public debate. This idea of press objectivity—so central to today's debate concerning the media and its manipulation of public opinion—is in many ways an invention of the mid-eighteenth century. Although earlier papers had naturally professed truthfulness, the dailies and triweeklies of the 1760s represented, as far as I can ascertain, a degree of actual objectivity unprecedented in the history of political controversy. (The closest analogy would be the monthly *Gentleman's Magazine*'s long-time practice of digesting opposing political papers.) And yet, of course, they were not wholly objective: their search for newsworthy items, their solicitation of letters from their readers, and their inherent commitment to freedom of the press, all made them the ideal vehicle for Wilkes, the clown prince of politics and defender of free expression, to ride to public notoriety and acclaim. With Thornton in place as the *Public*'s chief adviser, and the strong Nonsense Club influence on *The St. James's Chronicle*, the vaunted 'impartiality' of these papers more often than not worked decidedly to Wilkes's advantage.

On Friday, 6 May, Wilkes was again brought to Westminster Hall and this time prefaced his remarks to the judges with a speech specifically designed for newspaper consumption. 'My Lords,' he said, 'the LIBERTY of all Peers and Gentlemen, and what touches me more sensibly, that of all the middling and inferior Class of People, who stand most in Need of Protection, is in my Case this Day to be finally decided upon: A Question of such Importance as to determine at once whether ENGLISH LIBERTY be a Reality, or a Shadow.'[76] When, after weighing the evidence, Chief Justice Pratt discharged him on the grounds that libel was indeed covered by privilege, Wilkes once again addressed the bench, and in so doing assured everyone within hearing (and the next day's readership) 'that I feel it far less sensibly on *My own Account*, than I do for THE PUBLIC. The Sufferings of *an Individual* are a *trifling object*,

when compared with the WHOLE, and I should blush to feel
for *Myself* in comparison with considerations of a nature so
TRANSCENDENTLY SUPERIOR.'[77] At this, the Duke of
Portland recorded, the crowd 'could no longer refrain from expressing their approbation in the loudest & strongest terms'.[78]
The cheering shopkeepers, craftsmen, and gentlemen followed
Wilkes into the street and formed a jubilant procession to Great
George Street. On all sides, the common cry of 'Whigs for
ever, no Jacobites' merged with a new slogan: 'Wilkes and
Liberty!'[79] These must have been heady moments for Wilkes
and Churchill. They had won their first legal skirmish, they
were free, and their popularity with the people of London was
high. But in the midst of the celebration, one old friend was not
cheering. William Hogarth, during the proceedings, had—in
Wilkes's words—'skulked behind in a corner of the gallery of
the court of common pleas' and executed a sketch that would
become the satirical portrait, *John Wilkes, Esq.*[80]

IV

What were the dynamics of the political situation into which
the Nonsense Club members were thrust by their association
with Wilkes? The answer to that question is one of the more
hotly debated in English political history, but some answers
may be attempted here. In the 1760s, the House of Commons
was as controlled and exclusive as at any time since the Glorious
Revolution. The Septennial Act of 1716 had greatly increased
the period between elections and allowed eventually for the
formation of relatively permanent ministerial majorities in
Commons. The 'aristocratization' of constituencies, the increased control and organization of elections, and the very
human propensity to narrow the circle within which the prizes
were distributed, all, as W. A. Speck writes, 'coincided in the
years 1714 to 1760 to transform a divided elite into a ruling
class'.[81] At its most cynical, Georgian high politics had two
goals: to protect the interests of the Parliamentary classes and
to exploit society at large.[82] At the same time, however, this
arrangement depended to a remarkable degree on the consent
of the people and their continued agreement that the balanced
power enshrined by the Glorious Revolution—'that admir-

able and singular mixture of a hereditary limited monarchy, and splendid aristocracy, without the power of oppressing, and of an equal democracy without its unsteadiness and confusion', as a writer put it in 1758—was the most perfect system yet devised for preserving individual liberty and preventing arbitrary rule.[83] The aristocracy knew that it could only continue its comfortable existence by extolling the people's rights and liberties. The people, though they often resented the splendour and corruption of the great, believed that under the English system their freedoms and standard of living were the envy of Europe. Balance was the ideological key. The great destabilizer was the perception that any single element was attempting to seize power.

·The ideological orchestration possible under this system perhaps reached its zenith during Pitt's prosecution of the Seven Years' War. Pitt had demonstrated (and continually reiterated through his propagandists) his 'independence' from strictly oligarchical influence: he was, to the people at least, the 'Great Commoner'. George II, though wielding more power than has traditionally been accorded him by historians (especially those of whiggish persuasion), was firmly committed to the idea of limited monarchy: he entertained no dreams of absolute or arbitrary rule.[84] In the late 1750s, despite lingering jealousies, public feeling about the political dynamic was overwhelmingly positive: Newcastle took care of Parliamentary manipulation and domestic policy, Pitt won battles, and the populace cheered.[85]

The accession of George III in late 1760 promised more of the same. Here was a young monarch born a 'Briton', educated in the arts and sciences, and dedicated to moral, constitutional government. But the new king believed that the Old Corps 'machine' (still humming along nicely despite its age and numerous technical adjustments) and the increasingly dominant oligarchy it produced were neither ethically right nor conducive to the maintenance of constitutional balance. The monarch must reassert his rightful authority within the system; and George III was determined to do so. To this end, he began —with the help and guidance of Bute—to undermine the political establishment: not with the motive of imposing arbitrary rule, but of building a better establishment. Bute became

Secretary of State, then First Lord of the Treasury; Tories were welcomed back to court; Pitt resigned; the 'Pelhamite Innocents' were 'massacred'.[86] All this, from a certain point of view, was strictly right and constitutional; court propaganda and 'Tory' history as practised by Namier and his followers begin with this proposition. From the 'Whig' point of view, however, such machinations looked suspiciously like the resurgence of personal rule and government by favourites; at least, Whig historians argue, it was a breach of those unwritten 'proprieties' circumscribing the monarch's role in the system.[87] The constitutional arguments on both sides are complex and continuing, but one undisputed effect of the political fragmentation at the top was an enormous outpouring of propaganda and commentary directed at the people in the middle.

It was this tidal wave of political writing that swept up the Nonsense Club and which Churchill rode so dexterously—a feat which would have been hard to predict from earlier evidence. For the Nonsense Club members had always affected a dismissive, cynical view of politics: from Thornton's facetious banning of political writing from *The Student*, to *The Connoisseur's* laughter at the Oxford election and subsequent war fever, to the generally bantering tone of their writings related to the *Briton–North Briton* dispute, their stance had been that of amused bystanders (excepting, of course, Churchill's pivotal connection with Wilkes). As Vincent Carretta has demonstrated, in the 1740s the public's view of political integrity had deteriorated markedly following the cynical alliance of several well-known 'Patriots' (e.g. Pulteney) with Old Corps Whigs after Walpole's fall: 'Pope and Poetry are dead!' Horace Walpole had written in 1746, 'Patriotism has kissed hands on accepting a place.'[88] Given the Nonsense Club's proximity to the actors and locations of that drama, such cynicism was an inescapable part of their education: one can imagine the teenaged Colman and his friends perusing the prints and diatribes against turncoat Uncle Pulteney at Westminster Hall.

But the issue of Wilkes's arrest tapped more instinctive political and personal fears. Smollett's diatribes against the rabble and Wilkes's against the favourite were one thing; the arrest and imprisonment of a well-known political writer and Member of Parliament was another. With the signing of the peace and the resignation of Bute, old opposition targets had suddenly grown problematic; with the arrest of Wilkes all became clear in a new and more vivid way. An Englishman had been imprisoned and his property ransacked because he had published against the government. Many of those who had disapproved of Wilkes the gadfly became supporters of Wilkes the martyr.

The Public Advertiser lost no time in capitalizing on the strong upsurge of political interest. On 9 May, Woodfall—presumably with Thornton's advice and encouragement—initiated a new column called 'Political Intelligence Extraordinary'. 'Under this Head', ran the editorial note, 'we shall with strictest Impartiality insert any Articles or Letters, on either Side of the Question, which are not improper for our Paper.' Besides helping to feed the 'enormous Four Columns', this innovation provided for the first time a daily, semi-permanent forum for public political discussion. It was a forum that Wilkes and his friends in the Nonsense Club would use to great effect.

As early as 11 May, we find Thornton cajoling Woodfall to insert a potentially dangerous handbill describing the Parliamentary divisions and petitions relating to the Cider Bill. Thornton's personal stake in its publication may be measured by the fact that he gave Woodfall a written indemnification against 'all Expenses, that may accrue from Prosecutions or otherwise, on Account of your inserting a Printed Paper, entitled, Important Petitions and Protests, dedicated to all true Englishmen'.[89] The document was witnessed by Robert Lloyd and Thornton's servant, John Evans. 'Important Petitions and Protests' appeared in the next day's paper and must have caused some concern in the administration, because Lovell Stanhope, law clerk to the Secretaries of State, was dispatched to investigate the business. At this, young Woodfall became very nervous, and Thornton had to chide him in a note that conveys perfectly the risk and excitement of the moment:

Harry,

Your answer to Stanhope is simply no more, than that you took it in as a common Advertisement, of which you have a Proof. (Keep it, Keep every Thing in a snug Place.)

Don't be Afraid. (If you funk, good bye to you.) Don't shew my Indemnification to any Body, not even to *Father*.[90]

Besides the very interesting implications of Thornton's using a 'common Advertisement' as an alibi for printing incendiary material, this note epitomizes the role Thornton played in getting Wilkes's propaganda into the daily press. By mid-May, he and Lloyd (who was living at his house) seem to have been running something of a clearing house for Wilkite material. During the third week in May, for example, Wilkes sent Lloyd four sheets containing twenty-one 'Queries' pertaining to his arrest and imprisonment. Lloyd did some quick editing and wrote at the bottom of the last sheet, 'I am clear for the Insertion—RLL'.[91] The 'Queries' appeared under the heading 'Political Intelligence Extraordinary' on 23 May 1763. The next day, James Boswell, *en route* to his first visit to Johnson's chambers, seems inadvertently to have witnessed the beginning of a strategy session at Thornton's rooms. Dropping by to meet Thornton (whose writing he greatly admired) for the first time, he found 'a well-bred, agreeable man, lively and odd. He had about £15,000 left him by his father, was bred to physic, but was fond of writing. So he employs himself that way.' Boswell lingered for a time:

In a little, Mr. Wilkes came in, to whom I was introduced, as I was also to Mr. Churchill. Wilkes is a lively, facetious man, Churchill a rough, blunt fellow, very clever. Lloyd too was there, so that I was just got into the middle of the London Geniuses. They were high-spirited and boisterous, but were very civil to me, and Wilkes said he would be glad to see me in George Street.[92]

One suspects that once Boswell left, they got down to the real business of planning and propaganda.

On 28 May, Wilkes's 'Queries' were answered in the *Public*, reply by negative reply, and Wilkes immediately composed a letter 'To the Printer of P.A. Under P.I.E.' (i.e. *The Public Advertiser* under Political Intelligence Extraordinary). These sheets, pointing out the *'infamous Fallacies'* of the reply, were also channelled through Lloyd, who scratched out Wilkes's closing line and signature, and added 'The rest is not worth notice. I am yrs'—the closing that appeared when the letter was printed on the front page of the *Public* on 30 May.[93] The next day Lloyd wrote a letter to Wilkes that vividly illustrates the extent to which the group worked to saturate the press in the

weeks following Wilkes's arrest. After thanking Wilkes pro-
fusely for what must have been a monetary gift (something he
could always use), Lloyd added a postscript discussing the
propagandistic activities of the moment: 'P:S: Condamine's
Letter is excellent—Le Barbare Anglois.—we promise a translation of it for Wednesday. Have you finished Ld Despencers
Gardens. &c? . . . I write this from Thornton's where any
thi[ng or] any body will certainly find me.'[94]

The piece that Lloyd called 'Ld Despencers Gardens'
appeared in the *Public Advertiser* on 2 June. It was a long anonymous letter describing the villa and gardens of Wilkes's one-
time friend and present enemy, Francis Dashwood (Lord Le
Despencer), Chancellor of the Exchequer and former monk
of Medmenham. Posing as a traveller through Buckinghamshire (between which county and London, in fact, he and
Churchill travelled frequently during May), Wilkes satirically
describes Dashwood's estate at West Wycombe, pausing to
dwell on 'one remarkable Temple' of licentious import: 'the
Entrance to it, is the same Entrance by which we all come into
the World, and the Door is what some idle Wits have called the
Door of Life. It is reported that, on a late visit to *his*
Chancellor, Lord Bute particularly admired this Building, and
advised the noble Owner to lay out the 500 l. bequeathed to
him by Lord *Melcombe's* Will *for an Erection*, in a *Paphian
Column* to *stand* at the Entrance.'[95] The other item mentioned
by Lloyd, 'Condamine's Letter', appeared in the *Public* on 3
June. It was a translation of a letter from the visiting French
author, Charles Marie de La Condamine, who on 26 May had
been seized in his London lodgings by two 'brutal officers' with
a questionable warrant. They would not allow him to write to
the French minister until he bribed them; then they
disappeared. La Condamine wrote an angry letter (in French)
to the press about the incident, in which he emphasized his
shock that in the land of the English, 'who pique themselves
upon knowing and repeating the rights of humanity', he should
have been 'exposed in the capital itself, to an insult, which he
never suffered amongst barbarians'. Quick to recognize the
parallels between this and Wilkes's arrest, Lloyd translated
the letter for the *Public Advertiser* and later saw it widely
reprinted.[96]

In combination with the recurrent mention of Churchill's poetry, Colman's plays, Lloyd's *St. James's Magazine*, and Thornton's burlesque ode, the Nonsense Club's heightened political activity gave them inordinate (if often pseudonymous) space in the daily and tri-weekly press during the summer of 1763. It is almost impossible to find an issue of the *Public* or the *St. James's Chronicle* that does not in some way or another underscore their presence on the literary–political scene. How many of the squibs, letters, questions, and answers that fill the 'Political Intelligence' columns are theirs it is impossible to know, but all the indications are that during the spring and summer of 1763, the group carried out a well-co-ordinated propaganda campaign on behalf of John Wilkes and had a substantial influence over not only the political but also the literary content of *The Public Advertiser* and *The St. James's Chronicle*. On 5 May, for example, the *Public*, carrying Wilkes's first handbills, also reprinted Cowper's 'Dissertation on the Modern Ode'. On the same day, Colman and Garrick's *Cobler of Cripplegate's Letter to Robert Lloyd* (gleaned, like the 'Dissertation', from Lloyd's *St. James's Magazine*) appeared after Wilkes's handbills in *The St. James's Chronicle*. Thornton's dual roles as 'adviser' and regular contributor to the *Public*, and shareholder and writer for *The St. James Chronicle*, made him a pivotal figure in Wilkes's media strategy. To aggrandize and give symbolic weight to essentially commonplace events; to entertain the readership with jibes and insults against the administration; to keep the populace believing that the government's actions against Wilkes were actions against the people: these were the basic goals of early Wilkite propaganda.

The next burst of publicity was to be Churchill's. On 16 May, Hogarth had published his famous satirical portrait of Wilkes. It provoked a great deal of commentary in the political columns and set Churchill seriously to the task of composing his long-promised satire on Hogarth. The story that this satire grew out of an argument between Churchill and Hogarth at their shilling rubber club at the Bedford Arms may be true; but, at most, this squabble was a contributing rather than determining factor in Churchill's decision to attack.[97]

During the time that the poem was developing, Churchill was often with Wilkes. In early June the two travelled to Aylesbury, whence Wilkes wrote to Temple: 'I have most successfully got through the fine list of patriotic toasts, and the nasty wine of this borough. I have only a little headache, but poor Churchill is half dead.'[98] Churchill remained in Aylesbury after Wilkes's return to London and may have been visited by Thornton and Lloyd. Writing from London on 9 June, Wilkes jokingly referred to the '3 thirsty Parsons' at Aylesbury and asked Churchill to give his 'compliments to the two others'.[99]

By mid-June, Churchill was working furiously on the *Epistle to Hogarth*. Back in London, he promised Wilkes, 'I will—positively will—have it out on the twentieth'.[100] The promised publication date of 20 June also appeared in an advertisement in the *Public Advertiser*, but Churchill missed his deadline. Boswell, writing on 25 June, noted that 'Churchill's *Epistle to Hogarth* is not come out'; and the *Public* printed two letters chiding him for tardiness.[101] But, by the end of the month, the long awaited revenge satire was in the bookshops.

An Epistle to William Hogarth is a personal satire not only in the sense that it attacks Hogarth the man (rather than the artist), but because it encompasses so many of Churchill's personal concerns, drawing its literary devices and vehicles of attack from the entire range of his experience. In the context of Churchill's own psychological make-up, the major target of the piece is not Hogarth, but the personified abstraction 'Candour', whom Churchill engages in a debate lasting half the poem. 'Candour', as Churchill uses it, takes its meaning from a definition now obsolete: 'freedom from malice, favourable disposition' (*OED*). Churchill, however, twists the term to mean 'hypocritical tact', and uses it to refer to those who would ignore the reality of evil for the sake of kindness or peace of mind. In *An Epistle to Hogarth*, Candour argues with Churchill over the validity of satire: while Churchill describes the jealousy and envy that stain mankind, Candour contends that the only achievement of the satirist is 'To make good seem bad, and bad seem worse'—that satire is merely a form of false 'zeal', which 'tends to aggravate and not to heal' (67, 70).[102]

This is undoubtedly an argument Churchill had used on himself during the period following the publication of *The Times*, plate I, when, at the urging of Garrick and perhaps Thornton, he had held back from attacking Hogarth. In a letter from this period, Churchill indicates that his was a long-pent-up dislike, one which he felt he would never express: 'I have laid in a great stock of gall, and I do not intend to spare it on this occasion—he shall be welcome to every drop of it, Tho' I Thought, which I can scarce think, *that it would never be schew'd*' (my emphasis). In the first half of the *Epistle*, Churchill works through the various arguments and counter-arguments he had no doubt experienced himself in relationship to Hogarth. In so doing he produces not only a justification, but an ethical staging area for his attack.

As the argument develops, Candour—at first a rather convincing voice—dwindles to a mere advocate of Prudence, a shift that allows Churchill to compare his political activity and personal integrity to that of the false sycophants surrounding the King:

> Had I spar'd those (so *Prudence* had decreed)
> Whom, God so help me at my greatest need,
> I ne'er will spare, those vipers to their King
> Who smooth their looks, and flatter whilst they sting, . . .
> Had I thus sinn'd, my stubborn soul should bend
> At CANDOUR's voice, and take, as from a friend,
> The deep rebuke; Myself should be the first
> To hate myself, and stamp my Muse accurs'd.
>
> (147–50, 153–6)

Becoming more specific, Churchill lists by name a number of corrupt ministers and placemen—including Bute, Webb, and Hogarth's friend Samuel Martin: a rogue's gallery that forces Candour to admit that with 'such Men before Thee . . . I, thy foe misdeem'd, cannot condemn, / Nor disapprove that rage I wish to stem' (213, 219–20). But Candour is not yet through. Quickly shifting the argument, she uses the very wickedness of these politicians to denounce the hyperbole of Churchill's satire:

> BAD as Men are, why should thy frantic rimes
> Traffick in Slander, and invent new crimes?
> Crimes which, existing only in thy mind,
> Weak spleen brings forth to blacken all Mankind.
>
> (235–8)

With growing confidence, Candour blasts away at Churchill's 'foul gall of discontent' until finally, swollen almost to bursting with self-righteousness, she issues Churchill an outright challenge to 'Prove that in One, which you have charg'd on All. / Reason determines, and it must be done; / 'Mongst men, or past, or present, name me One' (306–8). Now, at last, having prepared a rhetorical atmosphere in which his charges will carry the greatest possible force (and having, along the way, got in attacks on various of his political adversaries), Churchill answers back:

> HOGARTH—I take thee, CANDOUR, at thy word,
> Accept thy proffer'd terms, and will be heard . . .
> HOGARTH stand forth—Nay hang not thus aloof—
> Now, CANDOUR, now Thou shall receive such proof,
> Such damning proof, that henceforth Thou shalt fear
> To tax my wrath, and own my conduct clear—
> HOGARTH stand forth—I dare thee to be tried
> In that great Court, where Conscience must preside.
>
> (309–10, 315–20)

Exhibit A—Hogarth—is, as it were, dragged in by the scruff of the neck in answer to Candour's challenge. This scene contains some of Churchill's best writing, as he stands between Candour and Hogarth, turning from one to the other, refuting and accusing, breathlessly pleading the cause of conscience and honour. His dramatically broken phrasing perfectly fits the 'trial' motif—a motif that may have been inspired by the 'court of honour' at Westminster School, and which was undoubtedly reawakened by Wilkes's bravura performance in Westminster Hall. In the first half of the poem, Churchill is the one on trial; in the second half, Churchill vindicates himself by displaying Hogarth to the court.

Once Hogarth is in the dock, Churchill shifts to straightforward accusation and brings two major charges against the painter: he is jealous of all genius, past and present (a charge already brought by Wilkes in *North Briton* No. 17); and he is an enemy of liberty, as demonstrated by his satirical portrait of Wilkes at the Court of Common Pleas:

> Lurking, most Ruffian-like, behind a screen,
> So plac'd all things to see, himself unseen,

VIRTUE, with due contempt, saw HOGARTH stand,
The murd'rous pencil in his palsied hand.
What was the cause of Liberty to him,
Or what was Honour? let them sink or swim,
So he may gratify without controul
The mean resentments of his selfish soul.
Let Freedom perish, if, to Freedom true,
In the same ruin WILKES may perish too.

(409–18)

The mere memory of Hogarth's attack on Wilkes and Liberty
seems to have been enough to release the 'great stock of gall'
Churchill had 'laid in' while meditating his revenge. For immediately following the Wilkes scene comes a scathing portrait
of the aging painter, in which Churchill combines images of
disease and decay in a passage reminiscent of his earlier description of Famine:

WITH all the symptoms of assur'd decay,
With age and sickness pinch'd, and worn away,
Pale quiv'ring lips, lank checks, and falt'ring tongue,
The Spirits out of tune, the Nerves unstrung,
Thy Body shrivell'd up, thy dim eyes sunk
Within their sockets deep, thy weak hams shrunk
The body's weight unable to sustain,
The stream of life scarce trembling thro' the vein,
More than half-kill'd by honest truths, which fell,
Thro' thy own fault, from men who wish'd thee well,
Can'st thou, e'en thus, thy thoughts to vengeance give,
And, dead to all things else, to Malice live?
Hence, Dotard, to thy closet, shut thee in,
By deep repentance wash away thy sin,
From haunts of men to shame and sorrow fly,
And, on the verge of death, learn how to die.

(419–34)

This attack was made all the more brutal by the fact that
Hogarth was indeed terribly ill at the time of its writing. The
description horrified Garrick, who wrote to Colman: 'Pray
write to me, & let me know how yᵉ Town speaks of our Friend
Churchill's Epistle—it is yᵉ most bloody performance that has
been publish'd in my time. . . . I am really much, very hurt at
it—his description of his Age & infirmities is surely too shock-

ing & barbarous—is Hogarth really ill, or does he meditate revenge?'[103]

Hogarth was both really ill and meditating revenge. On 1 August he published *The Bruiser*, a satirical portrait of Churchill as a bear, holding a large club and a flagon of ale. But, as Paulson notes, underlying the portrait was an implicit resignation and readiness for death: to execute the print Hogarth had rubbed out his own face from the plate of his famous self-portrait with pug and had replaced it with the powerful bear, the 'Russian Hercules' Charles Churchill.[104]

The exchange between Hogarth and Churchill provoked substantial commentary in the press. Lamentations, strictures, and squibs appeared in the letter columns; poems about the 'dog' and 'bear' were common; the print makers were again busy. Aside from Churchill and Hogarth's own work, perhaps the most interesting of these productions is *The Bruiser Triumphant. A Farce* (BM 4085), a print that reviews many of the issues and symbols of the dispute. In a composition reminiscent of *A Brush for the Sign-Painters*, Hogarth, as an ass, is shown designing *The Bruiser* while Churchill and Wilkes laugh at him. The print is littered with references to earlier events and relationships: a satyr holds a tablet inscribed '*Ha! Ha! Ha! said* Old Will, *Now You shall see yᵉ boasted Work of all the Antient & Modern PAINTERS, Your Raphael, Rubens, Carrach, OUTDONE!*'; a curtain behind Wilkes and Churchill reads, 'THIS CURTAIN HANGS HERE *to preserve from Vulgar Eyes the Beauty of that inestimable PICTURE representing a* HARLOT *blubbering over a BULLOCK's HEART*'; a paper resting on Churchill's lap rhymes, '*Since Willie has shewn us the* Dog *& the* Bear, / *Who scruples to own but They're much on a par? / The* Bear *has been baited & terribly bang'd, / And the* Dog, *when his Day comes, deserves to be* H—gd'. The *Bruiser Triumphant* is not only a well executed and highly detailed piece of graphic satire, it is a text which emphasizes the degree to which Churchill (as bruiser and bear) had himself become part of the iconography of the popular culture.

In early June 1763, while Hogarth was still meditating revenge, Churchill, Thornton, and Colman became involved in another well-publicized skirmish when they attended Encaenia at Oxford. Churchill's arrival—in a 'broad gold laced hat'— created a sensation, and in the Sheldonian Dr John Burton

7. *The Bruiser.* Engraving by William Hogarth, 1763

8. *The Bruiser Triumphant*. Anonymous engraving, 1763

delivered a Latin oration attacking Wilkes and Churchill in open 'defiance of this *formidable satirist*'.[105] When Churchill threatened to write a satire in return, Burton responded on 16 July with a long letter to the press ridiculing Churchill's threat and mentioning Colman and Thornton: 'I am informed, upon good Authority, that two of his Cronies who had left the *severe* Studies of *Law* and *Physic* to join the Festivities of their *Alma Mater*, did, out of pure Compassion for the place of their Education, use all the Rhetoric they were Masters of to dissuade him from his Purpose.'[106]

Colman, for his part, used the visit to Oxford as the subject of four essays entitled *Terrae-Filius*, after the tradition of 'a Student, who writes a Satyr upon the Members of the University during the Festival'.[107] In No. 2, anticipating speculation as to the authorship of the essays, he celebrated himself and his friends in their role as well-known writers and political celebrities:

Should it be the first of these wags, it is pretended that the company may expect a *Sign Post Exhibition*, or that the solemn Oratorios . . . will be turned into ridicule by a *grand Burlesque Ode*, and a masked Band from Ranelagh: and in case it should be the other *Little Wit*, it is supposed that, besides threatning the University with a TERRAE-FILIUS, he means . . . to present us with new JEALOUS WIVES, and new POLLY HONEYCOMBES, of his own composition. . . .

Others again . . . will have it that I am one or the other of the supposed Authors of the *North-Briton*; since it is generally reported that the *Reverend Gentleman*, having snapped the last cord of poor Hogarth's heart-strings, will come down in his laced hat, like *General* Churchill. . . . At the same time too the News-papers having already informed us that *the Member of Parliament for Aylesbury* will be here in his way to Stowe, the Squire is hourly expected with a grand retinue of Compositors, Pressmen, Devils, and *his own extempore travelling Press* from Great George Street, Westminster.[108]

Colman's picture of the group as a kind of travelling media event was not that far from the truth. Soon after his return from Oxford, Thornton received a note from Boswell, who, as always, was anxious to shore up his intimacy with the reigning celebrities of the day. In answering it, Thornton picked out a metaphor that neatly summed up the group's incessant movement and public showmanship during the period:

Your Note came to my eyes this night, or I might rather say in the Hibernian dialect, tomorrow morning, for the watchman has just told me, it is past twelve o'clock. Messieurs Wilkes, Churchill, and myself are to be Aylesbury on Wednesday next, and Colman is already in the Country. The time of my return is quite uncertain; and when I return, to use the language of Shew-folks, my stay will be but short in this Town. However, I will take the first opportunity of collecting together as many of the friends you mention as I can; and I make no doubt but that they will be happy to meet Mr. Boswell.[109]

On the following Friday, Wilkes reported from Aylesbury that 'Mr. Churchill, Mr. Thornton, and I came to this renowned borough Wednesday noon', and all indications are that this group, along with Lloyd, continued to form the Wilkes inner circle in the months that followed.[110]

7   Independence

I

On Tuesday, 8 November 1763, Wilkes sent Thornton a volume of *The Parliamentary or Constitutional History of England* with an inserted note:

My dear Sir,

It is of importance to me to have to-morrow or thursday in the *Public* from this mark in the Parliamentary History Vol. 3 page 185 to the same mark in page 189—the whole is innocent and safe—Let me beg you return the volume to

your affectionate friend,

John Wilkes

Below this, Thornton scribbled a note to Woodfall:

Harry,

If you can possibly squeeze this in, into to-morrow's, any part of the paper, you know 'twill oblige one who has laid under obligation frequently, and I hope will [*MS torn*] -tly those interested in your paper.[1]

The excerpt Wilkes marked concerned a Member of Parliament named George Ferrars who, during the reign of Henry VIII, was arrested for debt while Parliament was in session. This violation of privilege so incensed the House of Commons that they 'would sit no longer without their Brother Member, but rose up and went in a Body to the House of Lords, where their speaker informed the Chancellor what a great Indignity was upon them'. As a result, Ferrars was released and his captors imprisoned, 'the Sheriffs and *White*, the Prosecutor, were committed to the *Tower*, and the rest to Newgate'. The excerpt ends with Henry VIII giving the entire proceeding his unqualified approval: 'This I hope will be a good Example to others, to learn better Manners, and not to attempt any thing against the Privilege of this High Court of Parliament.'[2] The excerpt appeared on the front page of the *Public Advertiser* on Thursday, 10 November 1763.

Wilkes's motive in circulating this story was to prepare the public for his anticipated complaint of a breach of privilege when Parliament gathered on 15 November. The summer had been a good one. In the courts, the numerous law suits Wilkes had encouraged his printers to bring against the administration were proceeding successfully. In the papers and the forum of public opinion, his reputation as a defender of English liberty was secure. Wilkes had every right to believe that the opening of Parliament would provide him with another opportunity to confront the administration, and he methodically set about preparing the atmosphere for his performance.

The administration, however, had not been resting. Its writers and defenders had provided a steady counterpoint to the Wilkite material in the press, and the enormous power and influence of the government had begun to work against Wilkes in both open and secret ways. Wilkes's incessant irreverence—and what some saw as rabble rousing—had served to alienate many in opposition who were initially inclined to support him. And government agents had succeeded in bribing a printer who worked at Wilkes's private press to deliver to them a copy of a lewd poem, *An Essay on Woman*, that he had printed for circulation among his friends. Both sides had their cases ready when Wilkes attempted to raise the question of privilege on 15 November.

The government beat him convincingly. Before Wilkes could make his complaint, Grenville delivered a message from the king asking that the House consider the case against *The North Briton* No. 45. By the time the Commons adjourned late that night, Sir Fletcher Norton, the Attorney-General, had succeeded in having *The North Briton* No. 45 voted 'a false, scandalous, and seditious libel', thereafter condemned to be burned by the common hangman. At the same time, in the Upper House, the Earl of Sandwich and William Warburton, Bishop of Gloucester, attempted to sully Wilkes's character by reading and denouncing *An Essay on Woman*. But even more dangerous to Wilkes was the personal attack by Samuel Martin, who in the Commons debate disparaged the author of *The North Briton* in terms clearly intended to provoke a duel. The next day Wilkes responded with a note acknowledging his authorship and Martin quickly replied with a challenge. They met at noon in Hyde Park. The first shots were inconsequential, but Martin's second shot hit Wilkes in the side and left him badly wounded. When it was later discovered that Martin had practised with a pistol all summer, the 'duel'—at least to Wilkes's supporters—began to look like part of a larger plot.[3]

For Churchill, the three seemingly concerted attacks against Wilkes became an obsession, and left alone to fight Wilkes's battle after the latter's secret departure for France on 24 December, he made the four attackers—Martin, Sandwich, Warburton, and Norton—the major villains of his political satires of 1764.

But in November of 1763 Churchill had troubles enough of his own. Sometime during the autumn, he had eloped with Elizabeth Carr, who was aged fifteen and the daughter of a respected Westminster stonemason. The girl's family threatened legal action and undertook violence. On 3 November, Wilkes wrote to Churchill, who was then living with the girl at Aylesbury: 'I hear many schemes against your life, if you persevere—The father, brother, and a servant, went with pistols charg'd, to Kensington Gardens, in consequence of an anonymous letter, to have assassinated you.'[4] To this letter, Churchill replied in a note that fairly reeks of bravado, but that in a more subtle way reveals the depth of his concern for Elizabeth Carr:

Your advice And the illness of Mrs. Carr more than the fears of Assassination brought me to Town. Assassination—a pretty word, fit for boys to use, and men to laught at—I never yet play'd for so deep a stake, But if call'd on think I dare set my life on a cast, as that rash Young Man her Brother shall find if he puts me to the proof. My Life I hold for purposes of pleasure; those forbid, it is not worth my care.[5]

Despite his outward bluster, Churchill seems truly concerned about the effects of his affair with Elizabeth Carr, both in relation to his own reputation and because he sincerely cared for the girl. When he speaks in the letter of playing 'for so deep a stake', he is, of course, referring to his life; but the expressed concern for the 'illness of Mrs. Carr' in the preceding sentence continues to hover over the metaphor: the 'stake' is not merely his life, but his life as a payment for her.

As it turned out, Churchill was never chastised, legally or physically, for the affair, and he soon returned the ailing Elizabeth to her home, where she was forgiven. But the girl ran away again, eventually settling down with Churchill in Richmond and then in the more rural setting of Acton Common. The two seem to have been on good terms at the time of the poet's death. Describing that occasion in his unfinished autobiography, Wilkes wrote: 'Mr. Churchill was at that time on the happiest terms with Miss Carr, and she had consented to a tour in the South of France and Italy, which Mr. Wilkes had projected for his friend.'[6]

Colman, for his part, had since Garrick's departure for the continent in mid-1763 become one of the three men with complete operational control of Drury Lane Theatre. By mid-1764 he must have realized that the role of dramatist and manager—so attractive an escape from that of lawyer—had itself become his profession; a profession that would have to provide for him for the rest of his life. The Earl of Bath had died in July, leaving his entire estate in the trust of his brother, a man with a fixed dislike of Colman.[7] Although Colman did receive an annuity of £900—no paltry sum—the stipend was dwarfed by the huge Bath estate, which reportedly reached a million pounds. The 'brisk heir to forty thousand pound' had become a professional man of the theatre, with all the anxieties, responsibilities, and uncertainties that accompanied that most public of jobs. In early 1764, Thornton too entered a new phase of life. On 3 February he married Sylvia Brathwaite, daughter of Colonel John Brathwaite, governor of Cape Coast Castle in Africa.[8]

But it is in Churchill and Lloyd's strongly contrasting, yet ultimately identical fates that the story of the final year of the Nonsense Club resides. Lloyd, labouring under the onerous burden of *The St. James's Magazine*, had grown more and more dependent on alcohol. A quiet, malleable man, who 'took much snuff . . . and would often sit the auditor of conversation rather than the promoter', he sought solace in 'the pleasures of the table, particularly of the bottle, in which he was induced to indulge himself too freely for his constitution'.[9] By following his more talented and well-heeled friends, Lloyd became entrapped in snares from which he had neither the means nor strength to extricate himself. His health, his writing, and his pocket suffered. Boswell, even on short acquaintance,

recognized both Lloyd's failure and its source. He left this doggerel portrait:

> Than Robert Lloyd no stranger Blade
> Eer undertook the writing trade
> The Muses very well he knows
> But Bachus leads him by the nose
> And hence it is so wond'rous long
> For Bachus' grips are mighty strong.[10]

Lloyd himself was only too aware of his predicament. In February 1764 he was arrested for debt, and became an inmate of the
Fleet Prison.

Once in prison, Lloyd was forced to relinquish the editorship
of *The St. James's Magazine* to William Kenrick (who would later
become the editor of his posthumous *Poetical Works*). On the
occasion of his giving up of the magazine, Lloyd addressed a
poem to Kenrick entitled 'The Temple of Favour'—a work
that describes the vicissitudes of the poet's life using the same
nautical metaphor of abandonment and despair that his friend
Cowper would make famous years later in *The Castaway*.
Though 'pilot of the ship no more', Lloyd asks if he may come
aboard as 'passenger' and tell his tale:

> On ink's calm ocean all seems clear,
> No sands affright, no rocks appear;
> No lightnings blast, no thunders roar;
> No surges lash the peaceful shore;
> Till, all too vent'rous from the land,
> The tempests dash us on the strand:
> Then the low pirate bounds the deck,
> And sons of theft enjoy the wreck.
>   The harlot muse so passing gay,
> Bewitches only to betray;
> Tho' for a while, with easy air,
> She smooths the rugged brow of care,
> And laps the mind in flow'ry dreams,
> With fancy's transitory gleams.
> Fond of the nothings she bestows
> We wake at last to real woes.[11]

In a sense, this poem represents Lloyd's awakening from the
drink and poetry-induced escapism of Churchill's *Night*. But
the strong independence advocated in the earlier poem remains,

as Lloyd goes on to condemn those writers who become slaves
and hypocrites for the sake of 'Favour', and then summarizes,
once again, his lack of ambition, his self-reflexive style, and his
love of liberty:

> For me, by adverse fortune plac'd
> Far from the colleges of taste,
> I jostle no poetic name;
> I envy none their proper fame;
> And if sometimes an easy vein,
> With no design, and little pain,
> Form'd into verse, hath pleas'd a while,
> And caught the reader's transient smile,
> My muse hath answer'd all her ends,
> Pleasing herself, while pleas'd her friends;
> But, fond of liberty, disdains
> To bear restraint, or clink her chains.[12]

But, in the Fleet, Lloyd had to 'bear restraint'. Since no one
discharged his debts, we must assume that either they were
extremely heavy or that he was considered a hopeless case.
Colman and Thornton, both of whom had considerable funds,
did not help. Kenrick later claimed that Thornton became
Lloyd's 'most inexorable creditor', but this may be an exaggeration.[13] A likely possibility, as Southey suggests, is that
Thornton had already provided Lloyd with large sums and,
with his new bride to support, felt he could do no more.[14] Even
Pierson Lloyd, who had rescued Churchill from debt, could do
nothing for his own son. Nor could Churchill, who was making
a substantial living from his poetry, offer more than a servant
and the sum of one guinea a week. It seems clear that Lloyd's
debt or his irresponsibility must have been extraordinary if
neither his father nor his friends could (or *would*) secure his
freedom.

In a poetic epistle to James Bensley first published in October
1762, Lloyd had described his personal alienation in terms that
seemed to anticipate the feelings of regret and betrayal caused
by his imprisonment. He saw himself 'from wordly friends
estrang'd, / Embitter'd much'; and after railing, in the body of
the poem, at the hypocrisy of 'Connections at a public School',
he closed with a bitter passage cursing his muse:

> —Oh! had it pleas'd my wiser betters
> That I had never tasted letters,

Then no Parnassian maggots bred,
Like fancies in a madman's head,
No graspings at an idle name,
No childish hope of future fame,
No impotence of wit had ta'en
Possession of my muse-struck brain. . . .
    —O! for a pittance of my own,
That I might live unsought, unknown!
Retir'd from all this pedant strife,
Far from the cares of bust'ling life;
Far from the wits, the fools, the great,
And all the little world I hate.[15]

Lloyd's estrangement from Thornton, at least, is confirmed in a letter to Wilkes written after Churchill's death: 'Thornton is what you believed him', he wrote, 'I have many acquaintance but no friends here.'[16]

II

While Lloyd languished, Churchill prospered, entering a period of literary productivity that led to the writing of twelve individually published poems in less than a year. A much-revised memorandum from late autumn 1763 indicates the kind of arrangement Churchill had with his publishers and the prices he was receiving for his work. This extremely interesting document records that Churchill was offered an advance of £150 by George Kearsly and William Flexney to deliver two poems on the following dates: 'the said Poem called the Author on the 21st Day of December 1763 & the said Poem called the Duellist on the 4th Day of January . . . 1764'.[17] Upon delivery of the poems, Kearsly and Flexney promised 'the said C: Churchill to pay him the further sum of 300£'. The agreement includes a stipulation that the publishers retain the copyright to the poems for five years.

Whether such an agreement actually went into effect is unknown, but the document suggests that Churchill was making a substantial living from his writing. If the figure of £450 for two poems is at all indicative, then the poems of Churchill's last year would have brought roughly £2,250. Churchill made no secret of his new wealth, dressing ostentatiously, setting up as a country gentleman, and flaunting his solvency in a way that seems to have endeared him the more to his readers.

Churchill delivered *The Author* far ahead of schedule, but lagged behind on *The Duellist*. The reason for this precipitance and delay is suggested by an item in *The St. James's Chronicle* of 6–8 December 1763 (the same issue that carried the first advertisement for *The Author*): 'On Tuesday last the celebrated Mr. Charles Churchill set out from his House in Parliament-street, in his way to Paris'. Scholars have tended to dismiss this notice —along with later testimony placing Churchill in France in late December—as unconfirmable gossip, but an unpublished letter from Churchill to Flexney dated 15 January 1764 proves that the poet was indeed in France on that date. Because it has not heretofore appeared in print, I transcribe the letter in full:

Calais—Jan.ʳʸ 15. 17[*illegible*].

Dʳ F/

I am this moment arrived here from the most unpleasant Journey I ever undertook thro' all Flanders—I find I shall not be able to be in Town by the 19 *Ins.*'—on which day my bill of 50.£ becomes due— my delay is in consequence of the weather *only*—for tho' a hard journey it has proved *profitable*—as soon as the Trader sails, I bend my course for England—at all events, you will See me by the 25. certainly; I therefore desire you will Shew this note to the person who presents the bill;—& I will pay any expence on that day—viz 25 this month—I hope your Sauce [*?*] proved good—'till I see you Adieu!—

Yrs Sc. C. Churchill[18]

Since the first advertisement for *The Duellist* appeared on 20 January 1764, the note suggests that Churchill worked on *The Duellist* while in France and delivered the completed poem to Flexney immediately upon his return; this I take to be his meaning when he describes the journey as being 'profitable' (£300 of profit, to be exact). The dates of Churchill's stay in France, then, can be set with reasonable certainty at 7 December 1763 to approximately 20 January 1764; dates which would account for the early publication of *The Author* and the late appearance of *The Duellist*.

The question of why Churchill went to France is more difficult to answer. In England, the seriousness of Wilkes's wound and his increasingly bleak prospects for justice in Parliament were already causing him to consider the flight to France he eventually undertook on 24 December. Out of doors, however, things went well. On 3 December the public hangman and officials attempting to burn *The North Briton* No. 45 had been roughly handled by an indignant crowd, and on 6 December a favourable verdict in Wilkes's suit against Under-Secretary Wood had again brought a 'Wilkes and Liberty' crowd into the streets.[19] Why Churchill should leave at such a crucial moment is a mystery. It is doubtful, especially since he spoke no French, that he was sent to prepare the way for such an experienced traveller and Francophile as Wilkes. It does not seem likely that the trip had anything to do with his affair with Elizabeth Carr. The only clue would seem to be the Earl of Hertford's communication to Horace Walpole of 28 December, in which he reports that 'Churchill is said to be here [Paris] after having sworn that he was the author of the infamous paper ascribed to Wilkes, but as I have not seen him nor do not imagine such a trick would save the latter, I do not believe it.'[20] It is just possible, then, that Churchill went to Paris to be out of the range of government prosecution as he attempted to deflect the responsibility for *An Essay on Woman* from Wilkes to himself. If so, it is a measure of the desperation of Wilkes's situation that Churchill would even consider such a move.

But Wilkes was threatened by more than simply government prosecution. The duel with Martin had been only the most definitive of a series of challenges and assassination attempts that had punctuated Wilkes's career as a political controversialist. In October 1762 he had fought an inconclusive duel with Earl Talbot over remarks made in *The North Briton* No. 12. On 15 August 1763 he was challenged in Paris by Captain John Forbes, a Scots Officer in the French service, and it was reported in the London papers that he had been killed. Although the reports of Wilkes's death were greatly exaggerated, the challenge and subsequent attempt to portray Wilkes as a coward became a scandal, and led to the suspicion that Forbes was in Sandwich's pay.[21] Then, on Tuesday, 7 December—the very day that Churchill apparently left for Paris—another Scots officer, Alexander Dunn, was overheard by the printmaker Mathias Darly boasting, as Darly quickly wrote to Wilkes, 'his Intentions of massacring you the first Opportunity, and that

there was thirteen more Gentlemen of Scotland of the same
Resolution . . . who was resolved to do it, or die in the
attempt.'[22] Dunn, who seems to have been mentally ill, later
arrived at Wilkes's house, threatened his servant, and was
eventually taken into custody. Again the incident was widely
discussed in the newspapers and the suspicion raised that Dunn
had been employed by Sandwich. These events formed the
material basis for Churchill's poem of conspiracy and assassination, *The Duellist.*

The Duellist (January 1764) is devoted to telling in octosyllabics a kind of gothic horror story about the plot of Sandwich,
Warburton, and Norton to assassinate Wilkes—using as their
instrument, naturally, Samuel Martin. In the first two books,
Churchill develops a running contrast between the disinterested
'Old Patriots' of England and the self-interested politicians of
the present, whose 'partial ties' and 'dependant stations' corrupt the allegorical 'Temple' of English liberty:

> Such were the Men, in days of yore,
> Who, call'd by Liberty, before
> Her Temple, on the sacred green
> In Martial pastimes oft were seen—
> Now seen no longer—in their stead,
> To laziness and vermin bred,
> A Race, who strangers to the cause
> Of Freedom, live by other laws,
> In other motives fight, a prey
> To interest, and slaves for pay.
>
> (II. 389–98)

As is evident in this passage, Churchill's octosyllabics are not
the ideal instrument for making a compelling allegorical case
for England's corruption by hypocrisy and dependence. The
allegory is too pat; and while Churchill does have some interesting things to say about supposedly 'objective' law as an
ideological tool of oppressive government (III. 625–42),[23] he
does not achieve real satiric insight or power until, deep within
the corrupted temple, he finds Sandwich, Warburton, and
Norton plotting Wilkes's death. At this point, Churchill aban-
dons allegory to execute vivid satiric portraits of Wilkes's
enemies. Of these, the most notable is his portrait of William
Warburton.

Churchill despised Warburton not only because he had attacked Wilkes, but because he represented the most obvious
and odious example of a man who had risen to power through
connections, sycophancy, and guile. As Melvyn New has
pointed out, Warburton was considered the literary 'Dictator'
of mid-century England; 'a primary symbol of the gravity and
prudery' against which the Nonsense Club and others (among
them Laurence Sterne) reacted so vehemently.[24] To Churchill,
Warburton became the supreme embodiment of all the Nonsense Club hated—the ultimate 'dependent', who 'would
cringe, and creep, be civil, / And hold a stirrup for the Devil
. . . / Who basely fawn'd thro' all his life, / For *Patrons* first,
then for a *Wife*' (677–82). He was the finished hypocrite, who
'drank with drunkards, liv'd with Sinners, / Herded with In-
fidels for dinners' (727–8), yet still kept up the character of the
devout and learned divine—writing defences of Scripture, as
well as criticisms of Pope. Churchill's portrait of Warburton
provides not only a vivid personification of 'Dependence' in
action, but also a context constructed of unequivocal invective
from which to view his later ironic picture of the Bishop in the
'Dedication' to the *Sermons*.

The contrast between dependence and independence sketched
in *The Duellist* forms a continuing preoccupation in the poems
of Churchill's last year. In Churchill's political poetry, the
condition of independence takes on something of an interpret-
ative function: one that leads to an incessant questioning and
defence of the poet's motives and, at a propagandistic level, to
a series of scathing attacks on men at any social level who opt
for the safety of interest-motivated dependence rather than the
riskier freedom of conscience-motivated independence. The
kinds of question inherent in the debate between dependence
and independence had been evident in Churchill's poetry since
the time of *Night*, with its dubious defence of a free if anxiety-
ridden bohemianism, but in the poems of late 1763 and 1764
the political dimension becomes increasingly important as it
indexes the economic conundrums and psychological pressures
faced not only by the poet but by his audience.

Perhaps the most straightforward exposition of the putative
choice confronting Churchill, and by extension all Englishmen
in his position, occurs in *The Conference* (November 1763), a

dialogue between the poet and a cynical lord. The 'proud Landlord, and his threadbare guest' discuss the quality and fate of 'Virtue' (in Churchill's usage not so much 'morality' as the more archaic 'Manly strength' or 'integrity') as it is affected by 'Interest', 'Prudence', economic circumstance, and human self-deception. 'What is this boasted Virtue, taught in Schools', asks the lord:

> Can She the pittance of a meal afford,
> Or bid thee welcome to one great Man's board?
> When Northern winds the rough December arm
> With frost and snow, can Virtue keep thee warm?
> Canst Thou dismiss the hard unfeeling Dun
> Barely by saying, Thou art Virtue's Son?
>
> (133–8)

These are hard and crucial questions for someone with Churchill's history and social standing, especially in light of Lloyd's incipient economic failure. Churchill's initial answer is a hubris-tainted, 'Rogues may grow Fat, an Honest man dares starve', but the lord quickly punctures this rhetoric:

> L. These stale conceits thrown off, let us advance
> For once to real life, and quit Romance.
> Starve! pretty talking! but I fain would view
> That man, that honest man would do it too. . . .
> Cowards in calms will say, what in a storm
> The Brave will tremble at, and not perform.
> Thine be the Proof, and, spite of all You've said,
> You'd give Your Honour for a crust of bread.
>
> (81–4, 89–92)

Churchill's incisive refutation of his own naive bluster indicates the kind of radical ambiguity that characterizes his attempts to negotiate a middle ground between independence and economic necessity. He presents himself not as a Horace (or Pope) lashing the times from the comfort of his villa, but as a middling man caught between the ideal of personal integrity and the imperatives of physical survival. Despite the specious declarations of independence that necessarily punctuate the play of

the argument, Churchill's most interesting poetry suggests that
the issue is still, and will always be, in doubt:

> C. What Proof might do, what Hunger might effect,
> What famish'd Nature, looking with neglect
> On all She once held dear, what Fear, at strife
> With fainting Virtue for the means of life,
> Might make this coward flesh, in love with breath,
> Shudd'ring at pain, and shrinking back from death,
> In treason to my soul, descend to bear,
> Trusting to Fate, I neither know, nor care.

> (93-100)

In the verse paragraph that follows, Churchill's own brush
with debtors prison and rescue by Pierson Lloyd serve to exemplify the tenuous status of independence and the importance of
horizontal mutuality in providing the security necessary to
support personal integrity. Churchill's newly achieved independence becomes symbolic of the proper relations between the
public and the individual: at once a reward for merit and an
obligation to aid others caught in the trammels of the system:

> That I no longer skulk from street to street,
> Afraid lest Duns assail, and Bailiffs meet;
> That I from place to place this carcase bear,
> Walk forth at large, and wander free as air . . .
> That, from dependence and from pride secure,
> I am not plac'd so high to scorn the poor,
> Nor yet so low, that I my Lord should fear,
> Or hesitate to give him sneer for sneer . . .
> That, kind to others, to myself most true,
> Feeling no want, I comfort those who do,
> And with the will have pow'r to aid distress;
> These, and what other blessings I possess,
> From the indulgence of the PUBLIC rise;
> All private Patronage my Soul defies.
> By Candour more inclin'd to save, than damn,
> A gen'rous PUBLIC made me what I am.

> (129-32, 137-40, 143-50)

From his middle state ('not plac'd so high . . . / Nor yet so low
. . .'), Churchill surveys the temptations of aristocratic patronage and the threat of debt and ruin, then throws himself at the
feet of a 'gen'rous PUBLIC'. By placing himself in the open

market place, rejecting 'private Patronage', and vaunting his independence, Churchill appeals to the ideology of the 'middling' sort: an ideology which encouraged independence from aristocratic influence and promoted the horizontal self-help (as in benefit societies and charitable associations) necessary to maintain it.[25]

Indeed, it was precisely during this period that the term 'independence' itself began to expand from its traditional 'country' connotations of land-based self-sufficiency to the more democratic and generalized Wilkite notion that 'to be independent was to some extent a matter of choice which was open to nearly all men, and certainly to the male householder'.[26] For the City interests (whose property tended to be moveable rather than landed) and for those with little or no property, the idea of independence carried important psychological associations: it was a way of expressing self-worth in a society that could still be rigidly hierarchical. It is from this atmosphere of newly-defined independence that Churchill's political satires derive their ethical foundation. Despite the poems' great variation in subject matter and tone, this concept—what might be called 'independence in a new key'—remains at the centre, anchoring Churchill's response to the world.

The theme of independence appears in its most highly mediated form in *Gotham* Book I (March 1764)—a poem most critics have referred to as 'lyrical' and have tended to interpret as Churchill's playful break from the rigours of political satire.[27] The central fiction of the poem is Churchill's imagining himself the monarch of an island of perfect bliss, where all citizens (and even inanimate objects) gather to sing the praises of his benevolent reign. Informing this comic/utopian vision are two interrelated motifs: an extensive use of popular elements, grotesque imagery, and natural cycles to create a 'festive' perception of the world; and a burlesque interpretation of the role of monarchy itself.

The popular motifs which inform *Gotham* Book I are suggested by the poem's title. As has often been noted, Churchill's kingdom is named for a village in Nottinghamshire famous for its foolish inhabitants. The phrases 'As wise as a man of Gotham' and 'the wise men (or fools) of Gotham' were proverbial in England, and the stories of the Gothamites' ridiculous behaviour were part of most Englishmen's mental furniture. Boswell, for example, remarked in 1763 that '*The Seven Wise Men of Gotham*, and other story books . . . in my dawning years amused me as much as *Rasselas* does now'.[28] What is often overlooked, however, is the political dimension of the Gothamites' actions. The story goes that King John was about to pass through the meadows belonging to Gotham, which would have made them forever a public road. The Gothamites prevented him and then 'thought of an expedient to turn away his Majesty's displeasure from them':

When the messengers arrived at Gotham they found some of the inhabitants engaged in endeavouring to drown an eel in a pool of water; some were employed in dragging carts upon a large barn, to shade the wood from the sun; others were tumbling their cheeses down a hill, that they might find their way to Nottingham for sale; and some were employed in hedging in a cuckoo which had perched upon an old bush . . . in short they were all employed in some foolish way or other, which convinced the King's servants that it was a village of fools.[29]

By resorting to inverted behaviour, the Gothamites avoided expropriation and punishment by government authority.[30] The 'wise fools of Gotham' were not so foolish after all.

Such traditions of popular resistance were still very much alive in the eighteenth century and, through a skillful combination of media and commercial interest, could be invested with continuing political significance. The most immediate example of such updating was the traditional election of the 'mayor' of Garret, a small community near Wandsworth which had at one period elected a 'mayor' to defend the local commons against enclosure. The struggle was successful, and thereafter a new mayor was elected whenever there was a Parliamentary election. The tradition was promoted by the publicans of the area who put up money for candidates 'dressed like chimney sweepers on May Day, or in the mock fashion of the period'.[31] In the 1760s, the election at Garret took on a renewed political importance when Samuel Foote's afterpiece *The Mayor of Garret* was produced at the Haymarket. The date of the first performance, 20 June 1763, coincided precisely with the public uproar over Wilkes and liberty; and the play achieved immediate and continuing popularity. So did the election. In 1768, 'the road within a mile of Wandsworth was so blocked up with vehicles, that none could move backward or forward during many hours'. It was asserted that Foote, Wilkes, and Garrick 'actually wrote some of the addresses for the candidates, including in the material popular or radical grievances'.[32]

My purpose in reviewing these traditions—and their political implications—is to provide a context for understanding what Churchill is about in *Gotham* Book I. For although the poem is clearly a humorous exercise, it is also a fiction which, drawing on popular tradition, asserts the notions of independence, good-feeling, and mutuality as the bases of a well-regulated society.

The central movement of *Gotham* Book I—a playful description of the country's inhabitants, social structures, and love for Churchill—is introduced by a searing attack on European imperialism. Although Churchill's ostensible topic is the treatment of colonial peoples, the implication of his argument is that such economic oppression and ideological window-dressing is the stock-in-trade of governments both foreign and domestic.

> Happy, thrice happy *now* the Savage *race*,
> Since EUROPE took their *Gold*, and gave them *Grace*! . . .
> The Worth of Freedom strongly She explains,
> Whilst She bows down, and loads their necks with Chains;
> Faith too She plants, for her own ends imprest,
> To make them bear the worst, and hope the best;
> And whilst She teaches on vile int'rest's plan,
> As Laws of God, the wild decrees of man,
> Like PHARISEES, of whom the Scriptures tell,
> She makes them ten times more the Sons of Hell.
>
> (I. 67–8, 81–8)

The notion of 'Freedom' as a social placebo, of religious law as a tool of secular oppression and exploitation, and of those who most strictly adhere to that law (the 'PHARISEES') as the chief architects of a living hell for the people, all anticipate to some degree Blake's later critique of imperial Britain. This insight, however contradictory in light of Churchill's connection with both aristocratic and trading interests, is not diminished but given a kind of bitter poignancy by the poet's ironical use of the same precedent to justify his claim to Gotham:

> But whither do these grave reflexions tend?
> Are they design'd for any, or no end?
> Briefly but this—to prove, that by no act
> Which Nature made, that by no equal pact
> 'Twixt Man and Man, which might, if Justice heard,
> Stand good, that by no benefits conferr'd,
> Or purchase made, EUROPE in chains can hold
> The Sons of INDIA, and her mines of gold.
> Chance led her there in an accursed hour,
> She saw, and made the Country her's by pow'r;
> Nor, drawn by Virtue's Love from Love of Fame,
> Shall my rash Folly controvert the claim,
> Or wish in thought that title overthrown,
> Which coincides with, and involves my own.
>
> (I. 89–102)

Here Churchill, in effect, mimics the cynical lord of *The Conference* and disclaims the love of virtue for the imperatives of interest.

Once he has entered the world of Gotham, Churchill begins a humorous naming of all the elements of his kingdom. In a kind of carnivalesque imitation of official fanfare, Churchill imagines the musical instruments of his kingdom joining together magically to praise his happy rule. His emphasis, like Thornton's in the burlesque ode, is on the combination of diffuse elements and their *rapprochement*, the mixing of separate forms and levels into a general harmony:

> All, from the Fiddle (on which ev'ry Fool,
> The pert Son of a dull Sire, discharg'd from School,
> Serves an apprenticeship in College ease,
> And rises thro' the *Gamut* to degrees)
> To Those which (tho' less common, not less sweet)
> From fam'd *Saint Giles's*, and more fam'd *Vine-Street*, . . .
> THORNTON, whilst HUMOUR pointed out the road
> To her arch cub, hath hitch'd into an ode;
> All Instruments (attend Ye list'ning Spheres,
> Attend Ye Sons of Men, and hear with ears) . . .
> All Instruments, *self-acted* at my name
> Shall pour forth harmony. . . .

Rejoice, Ye happy GOTHAMITES, rejoice!
Lift up your voice on high, a mighty voice,
The voice of gladness, and on ev'ry tongue,
In strains of gratitude, be praises hung,
The Praises of so great and good a King;
Shall CHURCHILL reign, and shall not GOTHAM sing?

(I. 139–44, 147–54, 159–64)

As *Gotham* progresses, Churchill moves through the ages of man, the symbolism of flowers and tress, the divisions of the day and year, in each emphasizing the most common popular and official associations:

MARCH various, fierce, and wild, with wind-crack'd cheeks,
By wilder Welchmen led, and crown'd with leeks!
APRIL with fools, and MAY with bastards blest;
JUNE with White Roses on her rebel breast;
JULY, to whom, the Dog-Star in her train,
Saint JAMES gives oysters, and *Saint* SWITHIN rain;
AUGUST, who, banish'd from her *Smithfield* stand,
To *Chelsea* flies, with DOGGET in her hand;
SEPTEMBER, when by Custom (right divine)
Geese are ordain'd to bleed at MICHAEL's shrine,
Whilst the Priest, not so full of grace as wit,
Falls to, unbless'd, nor gives the Saint a bit . . .
All, One and All, shall in this Chorus join,
And dumb to others' praise, be loud in Mine.

(I. 387–98, 406–8)

Just as the official holiday calendar would later be mimicked and subverted by grand celebrations marking Wilkes's birthday, his release from prison, and other opposition landmarks (a practice that had already begun with special meetings and toasts commemorating his release from the Tower), so Churchill playfully expropriates the ordering symbols and calendar of English society for his own utopian kingdom: a spontaneous, egalitarian society stressing mutuality and independence; a society philosophically not unlike the 'free and easy' tavern and business clubs so central to the support and ritual of the Wilkite movement.[33] Over this society, Churchill places himself as a benevolent, aware monarch: a role that at once parodies and seriously parallels the traditional 'patriot' view of monarchy as protector of the people against oligarchic exploitation.

This central inversion—Churchill's creation of himself as carnivalesque monarch—finds its analogue in the popular culture's creation of 'alternative rulers' as focal points for popular grievances and misrule. Such a role could be filled by the condemned felon, or rural outlaw, or popular local politician (e.g. the mayor of Garret), but the extreme national manifestation in eighteenth-century England was undoubtedly John Wilkes, who inspired not only processions and tumults, but shouts of 'God save great Wilkes our King' and the posting of handbills urging church-goers to pray not for George III but for Wilkes and liberty.[34] Brewer has gone as far as to see in Wilkes the figure of a 'lord of misrule' presiding over irreverent, disruptive, but essentially therapeutic nonsense and inversion.[35] It is this tradition, I would suggest, that informs Churchill's comic fiction in *Gotham* Book I: a fiction that allows him, first, to present himself as an alternative 'monarch'—a somewhat burlesque, but accessible and sympathetic, focal point of popular celebration—and, secondly, to introduce playfully the central subject of the remaining two books of *Gotham*: a discussion of the proper relationship of the monarch, his ministers, and the people.

Having made a rather unimpressive transition in *Gotham* Book II from a discussion of poetical (and, by implication, personal) style to a propagandistic history of the Stuart monarchy, Churchill in Book III again presents himself as the king of Gotham in order to explore socio-political relations at the apex of power. Rather than the carnivalesque motifs and popular symbolism that characterize the utopian society of Book I, we find in *Gotham* Book III (August 1764) a relatively conventional exposition, along lines traditional to the 'country' opposition, of the dangers of the king's dependence on his ministers and the virtue of an independent, 'patriot' stance. The importance of the 'patriot' ideal to the arguments of the earlier opposition to Walpole has been thoroughly explored by Kramnick, Skinner, Carretta, and others.[36] Put briefly, the patriot king—like the patriot commoner—was an individual who transcended party entanglements and who asserted his independent judgement against the often self-interested views of his ministers. According to Bolingbroke's distillation of the topic in *The Idea of a Patriot King* (written 1738, commercially published 1749), a monarch with these qualities would be 'the common father to his people'; one who could 'distinguish the voice of his people from the clamour of faction', and 'redress grievances, correct errors, and reform and punish ministers'.[37] Bolingbroke, in short, advocated an independent monarchy as a means of restoring the 'balanced government'—monarchy, aristocracy, and democracy—that he argued had been destroyed under the oligarchical rule of Walpole and his creatures.[38]

Whether George III actually read Bolingbroke is not known, but he was greatly affected by patriot ideals, especially as defined by his political tutor, Lord Bute. When he took the throne, the new king immediately began to assert his independence of the dominant Old Corps Whigs, to install men of various party persuasions to places of power, to—in his own words—'put an end to those unhappy distinctions of party called Whigs and Torys'.[39] Theoretically his move was consistent with the ideal, but in the real world of politics it brought him head to head with men who had made their reputation as independent 'patriots'—most notably the 'patriot minister', William Pitt, and his supporters in the City of London. While George III was acclaimed by Bute's propagandists as the promised 'patriot king', his new government was attacked by City interests and the fragmented opposition as a revival of government by personal favourites: rather than being held in thrall by party, the king was held in thrall by Bute. Thus a king who professed and practised political independence to a degree unprecedented in Georgian politics was criticized by writers such as Wilkes and Churchill, and by the majority of the urban populace, for his dependence on an unpopular—even, indeed, 'foreign'—minister.

Churchill's discussion in Book III, then, advocates essentially the same theory of monarchy that George III thought he was following, and the questions that Churchill asks himself as monarch are precisely those which preoccupied George III:

> What, to myself and to my State unjust,
> Shall I from ministers take things on trust,
> And, sinking low the credit of my throne,
> Depend upon dependants of my own?
> Shall I, most certain source of future cares,
> Not use my Judgement, but depend on their's,

Shall I, true puppet-like, be mock'd with State,
Have nothing but the Name of being great,
Attend at councils, which I must not weigh,
Do, what they bid, and what they dictate, say,
Enrob'd, and hoisted up into my chair,
Only to be a royal Cypher there?

(III. 249–60)

Although both George III and Churchill would answer 'no' to these questions, the former's solution was to purge the Old Corps Whigs, the latter's to vilify Lord Bute and his dependents.

How then to prepare oneself for the arduous choices of monarchy? Churchill's answer is to banish 'IGNORANCE':

The Soul, with great and manly feelings warm'd,
Panting for Knowledge, rests not till inform'd,
And shall not I, fir'd with the glorious zeal,
Feel those brave passions, which my subjects feel,
Or can a just excuse from Ign'rance flow
To Me, whose first, great duty is—TO KNOW.
  Hence IGNORANCE—thy settled, dull, blank eye
Wou'd hurt me, tho' I knew no reason why—
Hence IGNORANCE—thy slavish shackles bind
The free-born Soul, and lethargy the mind—
Of thee, begot by PRIDE, who look'd with scorn
On ev'ry meaner match, of thee was born
That grave Inflexibility of Soul,
Which Reason can't convince, nor Fear controul,
Which neither arguments, nor pray'rs can reach,
And nothing less than utter Ruin teach—.

(III. 323–38)

Although this admonition is clearly directed at the king—an essentially typical example of the great body of propaganda urging George III to take heed of popular sentiment and repudiate both the Grenville administration and the supposed 'secret' influence of Bute—its metaphorical dimension addresses a larger audience: the audience of Englishmen hungry for political power and tired of their traditionally subordinate position in the political process. This was Wilkes and Churchill's constituency: the newspaper-reading, print-viewing, letter-writing middling sort who felt that their contribution to the nation and their increasing sophistication in matters cultural and economic continued to be ignored, belittled, and ridiculed by large segments of the ruling class. There is a sense in which Churchill's personification of Ignorance takes on the negative attributes of a selfish, hidebound aristocracy: its 'slavish shackles bind / The free-born Soul'; it looks 'with scorn / On ev'ry meaner match'; it demonstrates a 'grave Inflexibility of Soul', which causes it neither to hear nor to respond to popular grievances until it is too late. Churchill's implication is that in a nation where popular protest is ignored or suppressed (whether it be the protests of a Wilkes in *North Briton* No. 45, or of the poor rural labourer who in 1763 wrote, 'Your harts is Liftied up in Pride and You nowe that there is no Law for a pore man but If this is not alteard I will Turn Jusstis my salfe'),[40] such protests will eventually take the form of rebellion:

> When Stern REBELLION, who no longer feels,
> Nor fears Rebuke, a nation at her heels,
> A nation up in arms, tho' strong not proud,
> Knocks at the Palace gate, and, calling loud
> For due redress, presents, from Truth's fair pen,
> A list of wrongs, not to be borne by men,
> How must that King be humbled, how disgrace
> All that is royal, in his name and place,
> Who, thus call'd forth to answer, can advance
> No other plea but that of IGNORANCE.
>
> (III. 309–18)

Although Churchill should not be interpreted as *encouraging* rebellion, he is certainly advocating a far more open atmosphere of communication between the government and the governed: an atmosphere given utopian form in *Gotham* Book I and exemplified by Churchill's own rather cheeky advice to the king in Book III. The vehicle for creating such an atmosphere, of course, was the press: a press which, as both Churchill and the king well knew, still could not openly report Parliamentary debates nor criticize the government without fear of prosecution.

III

However attractive the possibility of 'knowing', it remained for Churchill a highly problematic and contradictory exercise. As the theoretical concurrence and practical division inherent in the notion of the 'Patriot King' demonstrates, to read political writing and newspaper commentary 'independently' was necessarily to enter a realm of logical contradiction and semantic confusion, especially for those readers not privy to the inner dynamics of government. The kind of media-shock that could be engendered by the incessant supply of contradictory information was wonderfully expressed by a writer to the *Public Advertiser* of 15 June 1763:

In the Course of the present political Disputes, I have been successively told, by Writers of undoubted Authority, that the Administration was wise and foolish, knavish and honest; the Peace advantageous and prejudicial, infamous and honourable; the Tax upon Cyder a wanton and necessary Tax, an Excise and no Excise, and oppressive and a constitutional Measure; the North Briton a Traitor and a Patriot, and that my dear Country is ruined and preserved by each and every of these Parties and Transactions. It was once, I remember, about the latter End of the last Century and Beginning of this . . . a received Axiom, that *'What is, is'*; from which original Proposition were deduced the two grand Corollaries concerning Truth and Falsehood, the Things which are and the Things which are not. But these Maxims are now out of Date, and I will venture to assert, from daily Experience, that *'Whatever is, is not'*, and whatever is true, is false. . . . I have by a gentle *Sorites* (you do or do not know what that means) deduced the following Conclusions; that there has been no Administration, no Peace, no tax upon Cyder, no such Paper as the North Briton, no such Place as Great Britain, and that I lie most truly when I tell you, I am your humble Servant, NOBODY.

In the playful exasperation of Mr 'Nobody'—and we must remember the social implications of that title—there lies an insight into the conscious confusion, contradiction, and relativism of Churchill's poetry. Michel Foucault, in an analysis of the psychological state of eighteenth-century middling man, has written that 'mercantile liberty . . . appears as the element in which opinion can never arrive at truth, in which the immediate is necessarily subject to contradiction, in which time escapes the mastery and certainty of the seasons, in which man is dispossessed of his desires by the laws of interest. In short, liberty, far from putting man in possession of himself, ceaselessly alienates him from his essence and his world.'[41] In *The Ghost* Book IV, Churchill put it more affirmatively:

> By his own Sense and Feelings taught,
> In speech as lib'ral as in thought,
> Let ev'ry Man enjoy his whim;
> What's He to Me, or I to him? . . .
>   Opinions should be free as air;
> No man, whate'er his rank, whate'er
> His Qualities, a claim can found
> That my Opinion must be bound,
> And square with his; such slavish chains
> From foes the lib'ral soul disdains,
> Nor can, tho' true to friendship, bend
> To wear them even from a friend.
>
> (IV. 213–16, 251–8)

In the interplay of these three related formulations—Churchill's assertive independence in thought and speech, Nobody's confusion and consequent nihilism in the face of incessant contradiction, and Foucault's exposure of the alienation implicit in the conjunction of liberty and interest—resides the central tension or, perhaps more accurately, conundrum of Churchill's political poetry. The tendency of his poetry to slide from extreme to extreme and to contradict previously held positions recalls the Nobody's (and, by implication, the reading public's) baffled response to the dialogue, or 'dialogism', of the daily newspaper.[42] His immediacy, topicality, and constant updating (Churchill ceaselessly emended and reissued his poems as a way of following current events and generating new sales) suggests the presentness, open-endedness, and confusion of the continuing political discussion. In a sense, Churchill's poetry acts as simulacrum of the problem of choice faced by men in a condition of independence; a problem central not only to the political arena but, as the history of the Nonsense Club demonstrates, to the 'choice of life'. Morse Peckham has described such framed disorder as human 'variability training': a 'rehearsal for those real situations in which it is vital to our survival to endure cognitive tensions' and a 'reinforcement of the capacity to endure cognitive disorientation'.[43] Churchill's rapid shifts in perspective and tone, his incongruous and unannounced juxtaposition of clashing, mutually debilitating points of view, his fascination with the problem of choice, all highlight what might be called the dark side of liberty: the necessity of making moral and ethical decisions in a ceaselessly changing and contradictory world; and the possibilities for alienation, cynicism, and nihilism attendant upon those decisions.

One of the most striking exemplifications of the problem of choice in Churchill's poetry occurs in the opposed portraits of *The Ghost* Book IV and *The Candidate* (May 1764). In these portraits, we find a radical development of Churchill's propensity to describe contradictory extremes of experience from what amounts to a phenomenological point of view: a view in which considerations of objective reality and of purely subjective response are temporarily left out of account, and the reader is left free to choose between all possible relations of meaning. It will be remembered that in *The Ghost* Book IV, 'Fancy' was simultaneously Churchill's saviour and Whiffle's delusion (or, by implication, Churchill's delusion and Whiffle's saviour); and that in *The Prophecy of Famine*, 'Nature' was both Churchill's goddess and the savage way of life in Scotland. In his opposed portraits, Churchill expands this approach by constructing seemingly non-ironic, contradictory descriptions of persons, with no tonal or structural management to direct the reader's response. At the close of *The Ghost* Book IV, for instance, there occur two consecutive portraits. The first is of an unnamed monster from Scotland obviously intended to suggest Lord Mansfield, Chief Justice of the Court of King's Bench. The second is of a saviour, also from Scotland, who will 'make this savage Monster tame' (IV. 1913). After execrating the Mansfield figure for over 100 lines, Churchill celebrates the 'Saviour' down to the final lines of the poem and then abruptly names him 'Mansfield': 'And, burning with the glorious flame / Of Public Virtue, MANSFIELD came' (IV. 1933–4). For the unprepared reader the cognitive shock is considerable: Mansfield as monster and saviour? Mansfield as object of invective and praise? . . . Or is this thing called 'Mansfield' simply the dual creation of administration and opposition propagandists? Is he, in fact, the 'media Mansfield': the utterly contrary juxtaposition of opinions about him that fill the columns of the newspapers and the shelves of the political bookshops? If, as Churchill writes, 'Opinions should be free as air', then art should perhaps, as Peckham suggests, provide a 'rehearsal' for dealing with those contradictions which necessarily define a 'free-opinion' society. But the question remains as to whether such cognitive dislocation in poetry acts to cure or merely to exacerbate the condition of alienation—and attendant nihilism—implicit in a cultural atmosphere where 'opinion can never arrive at truth' and where the only truth, perhaps, is opinion.

In *The Candidate*, Churchill's opposed portraits of Lord Sandwich as his 'virtuous' self and as the vice-ridden 'Lothario' again raise the kinds of epistemological questions discussed above—'how do I know?' and, perhaps more importantly in the world of politics, 'who do I trust?'—but the images that arrested contemporary readers were the sensational descriptions of Lothario's corruption:

> From his youth upwards to the present day,
> When Vices more than years have mark'd him grey,
> When riotous excess with wasteful hand
> Shakes life's frail glass, and hastes each ebbing sand,
> Unmindful from what stock he drew his birth,
> Untainted with one deed of real worth,
> LOTHARIO, holding Honour at no price,
> Folly to Folly added, Vice to Vice,
> Wrought sin with greediness, and sought for shame
> With greater zeal than good men seek for fame. . . .
> To whip a Top, to knuckle down at Taw,
> To swing upon a gate, to ride a straw,
> To play Push-Pin with dull brother Peers . . .
>
> (307–16, 325–7)

. . . these were the accomplishments of the Secretary of State for the Southern Department, and one of Wilkes's chief persecutors. The relativistic effects possible using the device of opposed portraits become evident in the succeeding verse paragraph as the dialectical play of Lothario against Sandwich comes together in a kind of synthesis of negation:

> Is this Nobility, which, sprung from Kings,
> Was meant to swell the pow'r from whence it springs?
> Is this the glorious produce, this the fruit,
> Which Nature hop'd for from so rich a root?
> Were there but two (search all the world around)
> Were there but two such Nobles to be found,

The very name would sink into a term
Of scorn, and Man would rather be a worm,
Than be a Lord; but Nature, full of grace,
Nor meaning birth, and titles to debase,
Made only One, and having made him swore,
In mercy to mankind, to make no more.
Nor stopp'd She there, but, like a gen'rous friend,
The ills which Error caus'd, She strove to mend,
And, having brought LOTHARIO forth to view,
To save her credit, brought forth SANDWICH too.

(399–414)

This is something like being rescued from the hangman in order to be thrown to the wolves: the ethical equation of one vicious and one virtuous lord adds up to the double horror of Sandwich. The implications for aristocracy as a class are clear: 'Were there but two such Nobles to be found, / . . . Man would rather be a worm, / Than be a Lord'.

The anti-aristocratic bias so evident in the Sandwich–Lothario comparison forms the negative counterpoint to the positive theme of independence in Churchill's work. In *The Farewell*, for example, Churchill raises the traditional fear of the patriot and the country that England will fall prey to a corrupt court oligarchy:

Amongst our British Lords should there be found
Some great in pow'r, in principles unsound,
Who look on Freedom with an evil eye,
In whom the springs of Loyalty are dry,
Who wish to soar on wild Ambition's wings,
Who hate the Commons, and who love not Kings,
Who would divide the people and the throne
To set up sep'rate int'rests of their own . . .
Let not a Mob of Tyrants seize the helm,
Nor titled upstarts league to rob the realm,
Let not, whatever other ills assail,
A damned ARISTOCRACY prevail.

(341–8, 361–4)

The threat of a 'Venetian oligarchy' was a central concern of the middling men, and one paid a good deal of lip-service by aristocrats in opposition. It was also, of course, a rationale informing George III's moves against the Old Corps Whigs, and amounted in a propagandistic sense to not much more than an all-purpose bogey used by various factions in attacks on each other. But as John Brewer has perceptively commented, 'Rather than asking, "is this contemporary view constitutionally correct?" . . . we should ask, "why is it that certain contemporaries put forward a particular view, and to what purpose?" Put another way, "what were they trying to do in articulating a particular line or mode of argument?" '[44] Viewed in this light, Churchill's anti-aristocratic attitude breaks down into two parts: first, the relatively 'classless' fear of take-over by closed, dictatorial oligarchy (the traditional country-party position used by elements of the ruling class against each other); second, a more personal resentment of aristocratic privilege and power at an individual level: an attitude that, I think, reflects rather accurately the feelings of those gentlemen and gentlemen-tradesmen with an independent turn of mind— the middling sort, the small masters, the urban professionals— whose status was based on moveable property, hard work, and good luck. This is not to say that these men did not aspire to landed wealth, but that in their present position they were keenly aware of the prestige accorded by society to birth as opposed to worth, to static title as opposed to dynamic self-development.

The most striking poetical example we have of the prejudices of these segments of society (as filtered through Churchill's intensifying consciousness) occurs in the aptly-titled *Independence* (October 1764), the last poem published during Churchill's lifetime. The structuring fiction of the poem is a celestial court room scene pitting the real worth of the independent, self-made 'Bard' against the unearned privilege of the hereditary 'Lord'. While the poem's overt subject is the difference between the literary powers of the Lord and the Bard, its allegorical thrust is unmistakably political.

Churchill's opening role-inversion immediately suggests the poem's aggressive, irreverent quality, as the Bard mimics in his dealings with the aristocracy their own condescending point of view:

> HAPPY the *Bard* (tho' few such *Bards* we find)
> Who, 'bove controulment, dares to speak his mind,
> Dares, unabash'd, in ev'ry place appear,

And nothing fears, but what he ought to fear.
Him Fashion cannot tempt, him abject Need
Cannot compel, him Pride cannot mislead
To be the slave of greatness, to strike sail,
When, sweeping onward with her Peacock's tail,
QUALITY, in full plumage, passes by;
He views her with a fix'd, contemptuous eye,
And mocks the Puppet, keeps his own due state,
And is above conversing with the great.

(1–12)

As the poem develops, always contrasting the Bard's earned
worth with the unearned privilege of title, three distinct layers
of reference become evident. The first represents a restatement
of the egalitarian impulses latent in Churchill's work from the
beginning. There is a native worth (or genius) stronger than
any inherited status; an individual claim to importance far out-
weighing any accident of social stratification:

A mere, mere *Lord*, with nothing but the name,
Wealth all his Worth, and Title all his Fame,
Lives on another man, himself a blank,
Thankless he lives, or must some Grandsire thank,
For smuggled Honours, and ill-gotten pelf;
A *Bard* owes all to Nature, and Himself.

(69–74)

Secondly, there is the conventional praise of the opposition
(the Parliamentary 'Minority' to whom Churchill addresses
the poem); praise which most often takes the form of disclaimer
or exception. Thus, in the midst of a long passage of unequivocal scorn for the aristocracy, Churchill tries (parenthetically)
to limit the scope of his condemnation:

A *Lord* (nor let the honest, and the brave,
The true, Old Noble, with the Fool and Knave
Here mix his fame; curs'd be the thought of mine,
Which with a B[UTE] and F[OX] should GRAFTON join)
A *Lord* (nor here let Censure rashly call
My just contempt of some, abuse of all,
And, as of *late*, when SODOM was my theme,
Slander my purpose, and my Muse blaspheme,
Because she stops not, rapid in her song,
To make exceptions as She goes along,

Tho' well She hopes to find, another year,
A whole MINORITY exceptions here) . . .

(57–68)

Finally, there is the vivid rendering of the relationship of the aristocracy and the common people that forms the most original and striking element of the poem. Employing once again a court room motif, Churchill brings the Bard and the Lord together before 'JOVE' to be weighed in Reason's scale. The Lord, although unnamed, has been identified as George Lyttleton; the Bard, of course, is Churchill.[45] But subsuming the more limited personal references to Lyttleton and Churchill, the fictional weighing of the Lord and the Bard constitutes a political allegory of unsurpassed vividness—one that draws its imagery from the heart of the popular culture and represents through a combination of personification and self-dramatization Churchill's essential vision of the composition, demeanour, and power of two antagonistic components of English society.

The Lord is presented first:

> The *First* was meagre, flimsy, void of strength,
> But Nature kindly had made up in length
> What She in breadth denied; Erect and proud,
> A head and shoulders taller than the croud,
> He deem'd them pygmies all; loose hung his skin
> O'er his bare bones; his Face so very thin,
> So very narrow, and so much beat out,
> That Physiognomists have made a doubt,
> Proportion lost, Expression quite forgot,
> Whether It could be call'd a face, or not;
> At end of it howe'er, unbless'd with beard,
> Some twenty fathom length of chin appear'd;
> With Legs, which we might well conceive that Fate
> Meant only to support a spider's weight,
> Firmly he strove to tread, and with a stride
> Which shew'd at once his weakness and his pride,
> Shaking himself to pieces, seem'd to cry,
> Observe good People, how I shake the sky.

(117–34)

More than simply the caricature of a Lord, this passage is an allegorical portrait of the political posture of the English aristocracy. As a class, it is 'Erect and proud', a 'head and shoulders taller than the croud', but 'meagre, flimsy, void of strength', with no 'breadth' of political support. It is a top-heavy social entity striving to tread 'firmly' on political 'legs' meant 'only to support a spider's weight'. The precariousness of the aristocracy's political position—virtually unsupported at the top of the hierarchy—is embodied in the precarious gait of the Lord as, forgetting the weak legs on which he stands, he claims to 'shake the sky'. The people, not taken in for a minute, join with the gods to laugh at his combination of weakness and pride: 'Each Goddess titter'd, each God laugh'd, JOVE star'd, / And the whole People cried, with one accord, / Good Heaven bless us all, is That a *Lord!*' (144–6).

The identification of this portrait as Lyttleton's is based on two pieces of evidence: first, the Lord's figure closely resembles Lyttleton's tall, 'slender uncompacted frame and . . . meagre face';[46] second, the '*Saint* Archibald' mentioned in line 138 is Archibald Bower, a writer patronized by Lyttleton.[47] Yet while there is doubtless a good bit of Lyttleton in the portrait, I would like to suggest that another, far more important political personage lurks in Churchill's imagery: the tall, aristocratic, thin-faced figure of William Pitt himself.

As is well known, Lyttleton and Pitt were close relations, original members of the Cobhamite faction or 'cousinhood' of the Whig oligarchy, and, until 1756, intimate friends. Although a serious breach had occurred between Lyttleton and the Temple–Pitt faction in 1756, it is important to remember that it was patched up in early 1764, before Churchill wrote *Independence*. More importantly, although contending that libel was covered by privilege, Pitt had many times expressed openly his dislike of Wilkes and *The North Briton*, most memorably in a speech of 23 November 1763 in which he characterized Wilkes as undeserving 'to be ranked among the human species—he was the blasphemer of his God and the libeller of his King'.[48] It was a piece of rhetorical hyperbole Wilkes would never forgive.[49] Indeed, Pitt's oratory, much more than Lyttleton's, would have been described as the type that attempted to 'shake the sky', and the reference to the Lord 'shaking himself to pieces' coincides closely with what we know of the effect on Pitt's health of his oratorical histrionics in the House of Commons.[50] Finally, the overall physical description of the Lord seems a precise literary rendition of the caricatures of Pitt to be found in the popular prints, the most famous perhaps being *The Distressed Statesman* (1757; repr. 1761). The 'drooping chin', the 'long, shapeless torso, the gangly arms, and the thin, spindly legs' that Herbert Atherton lists as Pitt's typical burlesque characteristics are just those features emphasized in Churchill's portrait of the Lord.[51] While I would not go so far as to suggest that the portrait is predominantly of Pitt, its very ambiguity strengthens the case for its not being simply a portrait of Lyttleton: it is the portrait of an attenuated ruling class as seen through the eyes of those staring up from the middle and lower rungs of the social ladder.

The succeeding portrait of the Bard is surely one of the most remarkable and underrated allegorical portraits of the eighteenth century. In it, Churchill, in effect, *becomes* the nation: he is the archetypal commoner, the prototypical John Bull, a personification of the 'people':

> Such was the *First*—the *Second* was a man,
> Whom Nature built on quite a diff'rent plan;
> A *Bear*, whom from the moment he was born,
> His Dam despis'd, and left *unlick'd* in scorn;
> A *Babel*, which, the pow'r of Art outdone,
> She could not finish when She had begun;
> An utter *Chaos*, out of which no might
> But that of God could strike one spark of light.
> 　Broad were his shoulders, and from blade to blade
> A H—— might at full length have laid;
> Vast were his Bones, his Muscles twisted strong,
> His Face was short, but broader than 'twas long,
> His Features, tho' by Nature they were large,
> Contentment had contriv'd to overcharge
> And bury meaning, save that we might spy
> Sense low'ring on the penthouse of his eye;
> His Arms were two twin Oaks, his Legs so stout
> That they might bear a Mansion House about,
> Nor were They, look but at his body there,
> Design'd by Fate a much less weight to bear.

(147–66)

In this portrait, we see Churchill's poetic self-definition consciously incorporating the physical and social characteristics of the lower spectrum of English society. Churchill conceives of the Bard as a *'Bear'* (with all its personal and social implications) whom his 'Dam despis'd, and left unlick'd in scorn'—an image that brings to mind the population of the London streets: the unwanted children, the social outcasts, the rough, the violent, the untended. The Bard's speech is vulgar and chaotic, a *'Babel'*, an 'utter *Chaos'*. Again the metaphor suggests the characteristics of the London 'mob': loud, unorganized, spontaneous, rootless. As Churchill's focus sharpens, the Bard emerges as a solid, burly figure, at once powerful and ridiculous. His physical strength is that of a chairman, or butcher, or day-labourer; his 'contentment' and 'broad' face recall the traditional caricature of a cit.[52] He seems the urban equivalent of the rural 'John Bull', whom John Arbuthnot had described in 1712 as 'ruddy and plump', a 'plain-dealing Fellow, Cholerick, Bold, of a very unconstant Temper . . . careless . . . a Boon-Companion'.[53] Indeed, the Bard's broad shoulders, vast bones and tightly-twisted muscles metaphorically support the English nation, an allusion made explicit in the closing lines of the portrait through Churchill's deft incorporation of popular symbolism. The Bard's arms are 'two twin Oaks', his legs 'so stout / That they might bear a Mansion House about'. The English oak, of course, had long carried symbolic associations: English sailors had 'hearts of oak', aristocrats were 'mighty oaks', and in the periodicals the name 'Oakly' had come to imply a solid, honest, and often exasperated defender of English values.[54] In giving the Bard arms of oak, Churchill not only alludes to his brawny physique, but presents himself as the type of the rough, genuine English citizenry. The same allusive range is evident in the following image of the Bard's legs bearing a 'Mansion House'. In a general sense, a mansion house was the home of any aristocrat or upper-class land-owner—whether in town or country, a seat of power and privilege. But the phrase 'the Mansion House' referred specifically to the mansion of the Lord Mayor of London and thus to the power base of the City magnates. By combining in the person of the Bard the images of 'two twin Oaks' and stout 'legs' which 'bear a Mansion House', Churchill metaphorically celebrates the common people as the basis of both landed and mercantile power: their arms do the work, their legs bear the burden.

But perhaps the most interesting aspect of Churchill's self-portrait is its liminal quality. For the Bard is an entity in transition, metamorphosing from an 'utter Chaos' to a solid, threatening social agent. He is a figure flaunting the conventional structures of society as he determines his own direction and development:

> O'er a brown *Cassock*, which had once been black,
> Which hung in tatters on his brawny back,
> A sight most strange, and aukward to behold
> He threw a covering of *Blue* and *Gold*.
> Just at that time of life, when Man by rule,
> The Fop laid down, takes up the graver fool,
> He started up a Fop, and fond of show,
> Look'd like another HERCULES, turn'd *Beau*.
>
> (167–74)

This picture should surely be entitled 'Bruiser at the Crossroads'. The movement from poverty to prosperity, from cleric to dandy, from 'graver fool' to 'fop' simultaneously mocks social proprieties and adumbrates the transformations of the self-made man. Churchill's literal 'defrocking'—his eschewal of clerical dress for gold lace and fringe—was one of the most remarked-upon symbols of his personal transformation.[55] In his own rendition of this alteration, Churchill paints himself as a kind of harlequin: the clown figure whose symbolic inversion posits a breakdown of static cultural roles and hierarchies, and their free recombination in new patterns.[56] In a sense, the Bard is a version of the folk 'changeling'—an agent who is 'free because his very existence is disjunction'.[57] But he is also a carnivalesque version of the bourgeois ideal: the self-made man whose very 'self-making' entails transformation in costume and status, and freedom of movement in a fluid social order. The Bard may, at times, appear ridiculous: an awkward combination of lower class belligerence, middle class aspiration, and upper class ostentation.[58] But his self-mockery is itself a form of independence: a defence against the 'grave' hypocrisy of the establishment; a defence of the Nobody against the Somebody. In this stance, Churchill essentially summarizes the Nonsense Club's complicated response toward the middling and inferior classes, and, in varying degrees, toward themselves. Over and over again in *The Connoisseur*, Lloyd and

Churchill's poetry, and Thornton's burlesque projects, the Nonsense Club's conventional 'gentlemanly' laughter at the middling and lower sort is modified by a sense that despite the awkward foolishness of these classes, they represent, even in their idiosyncrasy and insubordination, the real strength and character of the English nation. At the same time, the ability to laugh at oneself, to play the fool—however debilitating such a state of mind may eventually prove—allows the Nonsense Club members (particularly Churchill and Lloyd) to defy the authority and conformity of the power élite. In Churchill's poetry, the values of the people are defensive, irreverent, and genuine; those of the establishment, aggressive, conventional, and hypocritical: just the contrast Churchill had originally developed between himself (the Nobody) and the 'important blanks' in *Night*. It is this sense of protective irreverence—directed within and without—that links the state of mind of the common people and the Nonsense Club, and forms a defence against (to use Lloyd's phrase) the 'mechanic chains' of the establishment, whether those chains take the form of aesthetic, economic, or political oppression.

In *Independence*, the threat of political 'chains' becomes overt in the latter part of the poem when Churchill, as he rhapsodizes on the personal independence which 'cam'st upon me, like a second birth, / And made me know what life was truly worth' (515–16), is suddenly confronted by a tyrannical government determined 'To controul, and awe / Those saucy hopes, to strike that Spirit dumb' (524–5). Churchill acknowledges the intrusion —'Behold, in State, ADMINISTRATION come'—and then, taking his most defiant stance, dares his enemy to do its worst:

> Why let Her come, in all her terrors too;
> I dare to suffer all She dares to do.
> I know her malice well, and know her pride,
> I know her strength, but will not change my side.
> This melting mass of flesh she may controul
> With iron ribs, She cannot chain my Soul.
> No—to the last resolv'd her worst to bear,
> I'm still at large and *Independent* there.
>
> (527–34)

This manifesto of personal integrity and political resistance, the subversive tendencies of which are scarcely masked by subsequent praise of the Parliamentary opposition, represents the extreme moment of rebelliousness in Churchill's poetry. In his identification with the disgruntled commonalty, however, Churchill does not become, as has often been thought, 'simply the voice of the mob'.[59] Such a formulation neglects the complex make-up and mixed loyalties of those segments of society to which Churchill did appeal. As I have tried to show, Churchill attempted to blend in his political poetry the prejudices and symbolism of both the 'middling and inferior class of people'; to effect poetically just that alliance which Wilkes five years later would forge into an instrument of extraordinary political (and even greater symbolic) power.[60]

Churchill's poetry speaks to a certain state of mind. His own preoccupation with power and irreverence often brings to the poetry a militancy and violence of expression more characteristic of the lower classes than the *petite* or *haute bourgeoisie*. But it is the attitude of the broad English middle class—that mixed sense of suspicion and emulation in relations with the aristocracy—that forms the affective focus of his satire. Emulation and sycophancy, the tools of dependence, must be destroyed; suspicion and irreverence, the instruments of reform, must be tapped and refined (or, perhaps, coarsened) into an emotional indignation that does not shrink at the word 'rebellion' nor quail at the thought of bringing political protest into the streets. Like the Bard, the common people must recognize their strength and reject that 'foolish diffidence' which has made them accept subordination and oppression. As Churchill writes in a passage combining literary and social politics: 'Had *Bards* but truly known / That Strength, which is most properly their own, / Without a *Lord, unpropp'd,* They might have stood / And over-topp'd those Giants of the wood' (359–62).

It is in the service of independence, irreverence, and disorder that Churchill finds his true political voice—a voice conditioned by the simmering discontent of the middling people as well as the more focused complaints of the political opposition. The Nonsense Club, and its preoccupation with irreverence, spontaneity, self-consciousness, and personal rebelliousness, is the matrix from which Churchill's distinctive style of poetry grows. But in his later works these personal and aesthetic qualities are transformed into a political statement with a field of reference far more extensive than the glib, ironic domain of the town wit, or the ideologically circumscribed arena of the party writer. Churchill becomes *himself* a symbol of the common people. Their awkwardness, honesty, licentiousness, and resentment of authority take allegorical form in his lumbering figure. His personal contradictions and animosities are subsumed by the imagery of a larger struggle, and his irreverence gives literary expression to the irreverence of a large segment of the English people.

IV

On 1 October 1764 Thornton reviewed *Independence* for *The Public Advertiser*. His copy-text still exists, with marginal commentary scribbled next to those portions of the poem he has marked for insertion.[61] The commentary itself is perfunctory, but Thornton unerringly picks out the most important passages for transcription: the opening declaration of independence, the portraits of the Lord and the Bard, the trial scene, the outspoken defiance of the administration. At the same time, he passes 'over the intermediate parts of the poem, (in which the Author describes what was formerly true nobility, shews the difference between ancient and modern patrons, decries the servility of depending bards, and extolls the contrary character, &c. &c.) because we would not be thought to transcribe more than will serve to give our readers relish and desire for the whole.' What will give the readers 'a relish and desire for the whole' are the vividly irreverent, rebellious, egalitarian sections of the poem, just those sections truest to Churchill's unique style and point of view. What Thornton omits are the trite, half-hearted descriptions of true aristocracy and proper poet–patron relations, just those themes that Churchill inherits and never succeeds in making his own. Pope and Dryden, two greater poets, sought to correct aristocratic and middle class deviance, and to restore proper hierarchical relations. Churchill, at the level of deepest impulse, hated all aristocracy, all patronage, and all the deference, conformity, and exploitation such hierarchical relations imply.

While Churchill responds to the political situation of 1762–4 as a Wilkes partisan and an opposition propagandist, his response is conditioned by the subverted forms, self-fixation, and obsessive irreverence that characterize the early work of the Nonsense Club. The history of conversions that marks the transformation of the latter relationship to the former—the movement of politics from the background to the foreground of the Nonsense Club's collective consciousness—I have attempted to suggest in the preceding chapters. Central to this movement is Churchill's realization, however theoretically unarticulated it may have remained for him, that the inversion of order and hierarchy necessary to the Nonsense's Club's burlesque literature and projects was itself a process with political implications. Churchill's later satire throws into sharp relief the social implications of this aesthetic—an aesthetic which because of its stress on the flouting of rules and conventions re-emphasizes formally the political message of the text.[62] In 1764 a hostile writer for *The Monthly Review* momentarily caught the relationship in an ungrammatical series cataloguing the range of Churchill's independence: 'He writes as if he was independent of the rules of decency, the dictates of truth, the principles of justice, the laws of his country—and what, in a son of Apollo, may be deemed still greater presumption, he writes as if he was independent of the rules of poetry. A savage kind of Independence this!'[63]

Such a rejection of conventional order, whether in an aesthetic or social context, is necessarily the first step toward reconstituting either literature or society. But, as our critic implies, Churchill is characteristically obsessed with the rejection rather than the reconstitution. Although paying lip-service to the 'honest' aristocrats, the Patriot King, the well-mixed state, and other shibboleths of the system, the thematic and formal thrust of Churchill's poetry is essentially anarchistic: conceptual abstractions are hopelessly ambiguous, poetic forms restrictive and deadening, moral standards sterile and relative, social stratification arbitrary and tyrannical. It is perhaps this incipient nihilism that has kept Churchill from the first ranks of English poets and rebels: his inability to imagine a counter-order, except in terms of a 'return to the past' he has already psychologically rejected, to replace the conventional order he destroys. Instead he concentrates on the paradoxes of the present in verse satires whose structure is intentionally digressive and dislocative, and whose substance is marked by ambiguity, contradiction, and irreverence. Churchill's was a potentially radical art form; he was an early master of the 'estrangement' effect and the 'shock' of montage.[64] But his vision did not extend, except in the most fitful way, beyond the subversion of conventional meaning and order. For Churchill, there would seem to be no 'right reason' and no right reading: only an infinite series of temporary interpretations, each vulnerable to the deconstructive power of scepticism and irreverence. To adapt a phrase of M. H. Abrams's, Churchill, 'having deconstructed Humpty-Dumpty, cannot put Humpty-Dumpty together again'.[65]

Nor would he necessarily have wanted to. The basic thrust of Churchill's life was self-destructive. Driven by his sense of the unfairness of the conventional social system, and abetted by his lasting addiction to pleasure regardless of consequence, Churchill made his life a series of rejections: the rejection of education, of conventional marriage, of profession, of wife and family, of propriety in all its forms, and finally of life itself. In *Independence*, his characterization of himself as a 'melting mass of flesh' was far from a mere stroke of rhetoric. Afflicted by syphilis and still living hard despite his arrangement with Elizabeth Carr, he seems in his last few months to have recognized the end was near. In the posthumously published 'Dedication' to the *Sermons*, written at about this period, he refers to the time 'when this busy brain rests in the grave', and speaks of his bequests and his executor (16–19). And even as early as May 1764, in *The Candidate*, he had imagined his gravestone and its inscription: 'Life to the last enjoy'd, *here* Churchill lies' (152). A letter of 11 April 1764 from Garrick to Colman attests to the broken state of Churchill and Lloyd's health. Having mistakenly thought a notice in the *Public Advertiser* regarding the death of a Mr Lloyd referred to his friend Robert, Garrick wrote from Rome: 'poor Lloyd! & yet I was prepar'd—the death of any one we like don't shock us so much when we have seen them long in a lingring decay—Where is yᵉ bold Churchill? —What a Noble ruin!—when he is quite undone, you shall send him here, & he shall be shewn among yᵉ fragments of Roman Genius—Magnificent in Ruin!'[66]

Perhaps because of his health, Churchill had repeatedly put off a visit to Wilkes in France. But on 22 October 1764 he at last embarked for Boulogne, where he and Wilkes were to meet. After the two had been together about one week—no doubt carousing at their usual pace—Churchill was suddenly struck down by fever. Wilkes immediately sent a letter to Lloyd describing Churchill's situation. Lloyd's reply revealed its gravity: 'Your letters have given me inexpressible uneasiness concerning my friend Charles. . . . Indeed we are all much alarmed; for though the seeming spirits of your letter to me gave us hopes it might not be so bad with him, that which Jack [Churchill's brother] received, entirely squashes them.'[67]

Lloyd's fears were justified. Churchill never recovered, dying on Sunday, 4 November 1764. His death was greeted in London with the predictable mixture of eulogy and satire.[68] *The St. James's Chronicle* made much of the occasion, printing verses on the poet throughout the next several months. But there is evidence that the final state of Churchill's relations with Thornton and Colman were not good. Both men were conspicuously absent from the list of people to whom Churchill left mourning rings in his will, and Wilkes is said to have found among Churchill's papers a hundred lines of satire written against Thornton, Colman, and (unaccountably) Lloyd.[69]

For his part Lloyd did not, as legend would have it, take to his bed upon hearing of Churchill's death and never rise again, for on 20 November we find him writing to Wilkes about the possible publication of Churchill's works.[70] It was to this letter that Wilkes added the celebrated postscript, 'Mr. Lloyd soon after died in the Fleet prison, absolutely of a broken heart'. In fact, Lloyd died on 15 December, undoubtedly as much a victim of his own alcoholism as he was of despair over Churchill's death. But the coincidence was too great, and the legend flourished: in death as in life, Lloyd had loyally followed his friend.[71]

Before his death Churchill had been at work on two poems, *The Journey* and the 'Dedication' to the *Sermons*. The former poem was left unfinished and is memorable chiefly for the haunting aptness of the final line of its refrain: 'I on my Journey all Alone proceed'. The latter work, also left unfinished (although perhaps purposely so), was published with the *Sermons* in February 1765 and is usually regarded as Churchill's most complex satire.

The *Sermons* and their prefatory 'Dedication' were something of a booksellers' package: to get what promised to be an extraordinary satire, one had to buy a collection of very ordinary sermons.[72] In the 'Dedication' itself, Churchill played the role for which he had been conventionally trained: the poor clergyman, hopeful of preferment, dedicating his sermons to one of the ecclesiastical grandees of the land. Churchill, in effect, parodies the kind of dependent's exercise—or, to use his own phrase, 'Villain's art' (5)—that had brought Warburton to power.[73]

Churchill the clergyman begins by fawning and ends by complaining. Churchill the satirist begins by ironically praising and ends by threatening. But within this overall development, the conjunction of clergyman and satirist is casual: a product of circumstance and, one suspects, Churchill's whim.[74] The poem is in many ways about what the fawning clergyman does *not* want from Warburton and the worldly honours which are *not* the motives of his praise. As the clergyman peels back the veneer to expose the virtues of the 'inward man', Churchill dismantles the Somebody and finds nothing but ruthless ambition. In the end, the dedicator and Churchill agree that the inward man and ruthless ambition are one. But the tone is never consistent: invective, flat statement, and mock praise interact in an essentially random fashion:

> Think not, a Thought unworthy thy great soul,
> Which pomps of this world never could controul,
> Which never offer'd up at Pow'r's vain shrine,
> Think not that Pomp and Pow'r can work on mine.
> 'Tis not thy Name, though that indeed is great,
> 'Tis not the tinsel trumpery of state,
> 'Tis not thy Title, Doctor tho' thou art,
> 'Tis not thy Mitre, which hath won my heart.
> State is a farce, Names are but empty Things,
> Degrees are bought, and, by mistaken kings,
> Titles are oft misplac'd; Mitres, which shine
> So bright in other eyes, are dull in mine,
> Unless set off by Virtue; who deceives
> Under the sacred sanction of *Lawn-Sleeves*,
> Enhances guilt, commits a double sin;

So fair without, and yet so foul within.
'Tis not thy outward form, thy easy mien,
Thy sweet complacency, thy brow serene,
Thy open front, thy Love-Commanding eye . . .

(29–47)

. . . and so on in a long series of disclaimers. The clergyman's
thesis is that this outward show is *not* the essence of Warburton;
Churchill's point is that this is *all* that Warburton really is: and
the rhetorical relationship is not consistent nor easy to follow.
The reader is left to sort out the 'real' Warburton: to understand that *he* is power mad, that the 'farce' described by the
dedicator is Warburton's reason for existing, that Warburton's
mitre is *not* 'set off by Virtue', and that *his* lawn-sleeves hide a
hypocrite.

I do not mean to suggest, however, that Churchill and the
cleric are clearly separable. Quite the contrary. The cleric is
Churchill's naive, dependent self (the one with the brown
cassock hanging in tatters on his back) and the tonal shifts are
to some extent the satirist's spontaneous reaction to what might
have been. Throughout the poem the satirist's sneer intermittently punctuates the rather downtrodden capitulation that
forms the phenomenological basis for the cleric's panegyric.
Thus, for example, when the cleric laments Warburton's
having driven Wilkes into exile, he nevertheless professes to
understand his motivations:

O Glorious Man, thy zeal I must commend,
Tho' it deprived me of my dearest friend.
The real motives of thy anger known,
WILKES must the justice of that anger own;
And, could thy bosom have been bar'd to view,
Pitied himself, in turn had pitied you.

(145–50)

What begins as a seemingly ironic commendation—acknowledging the 'justice' of Warburton's 'real motives'—ends as a
staging area for an essentially straightforward attack: if Wilkes
had known the corruption of Warburton's heart, he would
have *had* to pity him. This shifting interplay of flattery and
exposure characterizes the major part of the 'Dedication' and
engenders its much-remarked-upon complexity of tone. But as

the poem moves toward its finale, Churchill's anger begins to
burn more steadily through the mist of indirection and to spot-
light Warburton as the stereotypical grandee, protecting his
perch above the multitude through a combination of bluster
and guile:

> *Doctor, Dean, Bishop, Gloster,* and *My Lord,*
> If haply these high Titles may accord
> With thy meek Spirit, if the barren sound
> Of pride delight Thee, to the topmost round
> Of Fortune's ladder got, despise not One,
> For want of smooth hypocrisy undone,
> Who, far below, turns up his wond'ring eye,
> And, without envy, sees Thee plac'd so high,
> Let not thy Brain (as Brains less potent might)
> Dizzy, confounded, giddy with the height,
> Turn round, and lose distinction, lose her skill
> And wonted pow'rs of knowing good from ill,
> Of sifting Truth from falshood, friends from foes;
> Let GLOSTER well remember, how he rose,
> Nor turn his back on men who made him great;
> Let Him not, gorg'd with pow'r, and drunk with state,
> Forget what once he was, tho' now so high;
> How low, how mean, and full as poor as I.

                                                      (163–80)

      As in *Independence*, Churchill envisions himself as the honest
commoner who 'far below, turns up his wond'ring eye' to the
aristocrat—in this case, the clerical equivalent of a peer—
balanced precariously on 'the topmost round / Of Fortune's
ladder'. The unsteady, corruptive quality of such power is embodied in the description of Warburton as 'Dizzy, confounded,
giddy with the height'; but more important is Churchill's focus
on the means by which Warburton rose. For Warburton is one
who has gained ascendancy through dependence and 'smooth
hypocrisy'. 'Gorg'd with pow'r, and drunk with state', he has
forgotten 'what once he was'. But Churchill never forgets
'what once he was' and the metaphorical thrust of his self-
presentation is emphatically downward: not merely to the level
of 'gentleman of comfortable means' into which he had written
his way, nor even to the class of lesser clergy into which he was
born, but to the social stratum where life is a constant struggle,
and irreverence and self-satire the only means of psychological

defence. Churchill ends his career portraying himself as the man at the bottom: not Horace at his villa, but Nobody trying to survive. His final, rather ominous, warning is directed not only to Warburton, but to all men of privilege:

> Let GLOSTER well remember, how he rose,
> Nor turn his back on men who made him great;
> Let Him not, gorg'd with pow'r, and drunk with state,
> Forget what once he was, tho' now so high;
> How low, how mean, and full as poor as I.

  * * * * * * * *

  * * * * * * * *

  * * * * * * * *

Cetera desunt.[75]

8 *Articulations of Irreverence*

I

. . . the tendency of historic Romanticism was away from authority toward liberty, away from acceptance of caked wisdom and toward the exploratory development of the individual, away from the secure fixities and toward the drama of the unforeseeable, away from monarchy and toward the sovereignty of the people. . . . This divergence of Classic and Romantic corresponds to that which obtains in the conception of the individual: the eighteenth century entrusts everything to the intellect and loves Man abstractly, as an archetype, whereas Romanticism studies sensation and emotion and embraces man as he is actually found—diverse, mysterious, irregular. . . .

Jacques Barzun, *Classic, Romantic, and Modern*[1]

If we say that a revolutionary era began about 1760, it is not because any persons or any organizations intended or worked in advance for a revolution. The modern conception of a revolutionary movement is the result, not the cause, of the revolutionary era that we are discussing. . . . By a revolutionary situation is here meant one in which confidence in the justice or reasonableness of existing authority is undermined; where old loyalties fade, obligations are felt as impositions, law seems arbitrary, and respect for superiors is felt as a form of humiliation; where existing sources of prestige seem undeserved, hitherto accepted forms of wealth and income seem ill-gained, and government is sensed as distant, apart from the governed and not really 'representing' them. In such a situation the sense of community is lost, and the bond between social classes turns to jealousy and frustration.

R. R. Palmer, *The Age of Democratic Revolution*[2]

The breakdown of traditional hierarchies and relationships in economic life and artistic genres that occurred in England during the middle and late eighteenth century has been often noted and variously interpreted. There was certainly a gradual dissolution of the traditional bonds of hereditary rank, moral

economy, and sense of 'place' in an ordered society that characterizes 'Augustan' nostalgia.[3] But if there was a breakdown in
order, there was also a breakdown in traditional tyrannies—or,
more accurately, a dispersion of tyrannies to a larger, less
tradition-bound segment of the population. It is common to
call these people the 'bourgeoisie' and to describe them in such
exaggerated phrases as the 'benevolently weeping bourgeoisie',
or, delving beneath the ideological surface, as that class which
'drowned the most heavenly ecstasies of religious fervor, of
chivalrous enthusiasm, of philistine sentimentalism, in the icy
water of egotistical calculation'.[4] While the first description is
easily refuted by an accurate knowledge of the varieties of
laughing comedy, ribald prints and poems, and personal vices
that continued to attract the middle classes throughout the
eighteenth century, the second description is a more complex
one. Certainly it is true that tradesmen and shopkeepers caught
up in a web of credit and debt, and often victimized by the
aristocracy, did seek to cultivate a trustworthy, civil, and,
perhaps, calculating demeanour toward their counterparts and
customers. Thus, as Brewer notes, foreign visitors to London
often 'remarked on the extraordinary civility of the shopkeepers
and tradesmen', while at the same time they 'were struck by
the rude, undeferential independence of the laboring poor'.[5]
But we must remember that in the breast of the greater part of
the English middle class beat a heart removed only by the thin-
nest veneer—a generation perhaps, a modicum of schooling, a
bit of luck in business—from the rough, independent, irreverent manner of the artisans and labourers. Francis Place has
left a remarkable set of descriptions of this hybrid middling
class—one that indexes the degree to which literary historians
especially have tended to project the idea of a careful, genteel
middle class backwards into the mid-eighteenth century.[6]
Writing in 1828, Place noted that 'for one careful attentive
discreet men [sic] some thirty years ago there are forty now',
and went on to record in striking detail 'the immorality, the
grossness, the obscenity, the drunkenness, the dirtiness, and
depravity of the middling and even of a large portion of the
better sort of tradesmen, the artizans, and the journeymen
tradesmen of London in the days of my youth': a group which,
on their hard-earned incomes, 'might have lived genteely, have

brought up their families respectably and placed them out in the world comfortably, but it was not the custom of that time to do so'.[7] This mixed character, this ability of the seemingly conscientious, hardworking middling sort to assume the vices and salacious irreverence associated with the lower classes and aristocracy, is a quality often ignored by leftist historians, who emphasize in the bourgeoisie a cold, prudent calculation masked by progressive, sentimentalist ideology, and by rightist historians, who find in the middle class an entrepreneurial spirit and energy which enhanced the freedom and standard of living of the majority. Yet the evidence of middle class irreverence is everywhere in the life, literature, and politics of the period—from the rather graphic spectacle of Hogarth (that great cultural entrepreneur and bourgeois ideologue) defecating on a church door for the edification and amusement of his middle-class friends (this during the 'Five Days' Peregrination' which he illustrated with the contrasting portraits of Mr Somebody and Mr Nobody) to the great popularity of a libellous poetry written by a notorious ex-clergyman in defence of a libertine politician named John Wilkes.[8]

There were, arguably, three broad ethical frames of reference available to the middle class: first, the ubiquitous temptations of social aspiration, 'dependence', and luxury, in which the middle class imitates the aristocracy; second, the essentially 'anti-aristocratic' values of hard work, prudence, and mercantile 'method'; third, the irreverence, rebelliousness, and clannish mutuality characteristic of the exploited. But the difficulty of trying to distinguish these forms of behaviour in practice becomes evident when we ask ourselves whether an essentially middle-class poet who becomes a vice-ridden *habitué* of taverns and brothels is aping the upper-class rake or reverting to the licentiousness of the 'mob'. The answer would seem to be *both*: Churchill seems to see himself simultaneously as a social pariah and the equal of a lord, as a bruiser and a fop, or, to use his own phrase, as a 'HERCULES, turn'd *Beau*'. As I have argued earlier, Churchill's self-characterization does not imply an irrevocable change from bruiser to beau, but a liminal condition: sometimes a cudgel player, sometimes a fop, sometimes a ridiculous but threatening combination of the two. T. J. Clark, in his illuminating study of Courbet and the 1848 revolution, has

pointed up the tendency of the bourgeois rebel sometimes to
affect the lower class trappings and attitudes of Bohemia and
other times to mimic the dandy—assuming in both poses a consciously ironic stance.[9] Such role-playing allows the rebel
simultaneously to parody the aristocratic aspirations of the
middling and lower classes, and to affront the essentially
middle-class values of prudence, method, and economic calculation. Churchill characteristically views both as conformist
systems that ignore—or suppress—individual worth in favour
of, on the one hand, social rank, and, on the other, money.
Carretta is, I think, essentially accurate in concluding that
Churchill 'was both attracted and repelled by England's rapid
economic and imperial growth, which the triumphs of the
Seven Years' War accelerated'.[10] In Churchill's eyes, the new
values and prosperity of the 'consumer society' were pernicious
because they caused middle-class upstarts to act like lords and
lords to act like middle-class upstarts. But they were also positive in that they broke down traditional barriers and deferences,
allowing people to dress, act, and express themselves as they
wished—in short, to exercise their liberty and achieve a feeling
of individual worth.

In the early eighteenth century, we characteristically find the
conditions of the marketplace and the prejudices of Augustan
literature moving in opposite directions. In an era of incipient
capitalism, Pope attacks 'paper credit'; in an era of expanded
literary industry, Swift and Pope abuse hack writers. But the
inclination of such conservative moralists to particularize their
targets tended often to work against their theoretical intent of
subordinating discrete detail to the universal moral purpose of
their works. Cibber may be immortalized as a dunce, but he *is*
immortalized. In Hogarth's work such aesthetic subordination
is even less complete, as the historical particular (individual
and object) threatens continually to subvert the universal moral
exempla Hogarth intends his 'modern history paintings' to
convey. Hogarth's central problem is trying to reconcile the
requirements of general moral applicability (history painting)
with the fascinating profusion and moral ambiguity of the
historical particular (modern history)—the objects, the slogans,
the signboards, the people of real life. Implicit in this egalitarian
aesthetic is a deepened sympathy for the plight of the aspiring

'middling and inferior' people confronted with the difficult choice of emulation or resentment in the face of upper-class privilege. Paulson notes that while, in most cases, the 'Augustans looked down from the point of view of the great lady or gentleman', Hogarth and Fielding 'look up from the point of view of [those] who have allowed themselves to lose their original and good selves and been corrupted by the ideals of great ladies and gentlemen into aping them'.[11]

It is the tradition of Hogarth and Fielding that the Nonsense Club most immediately inherits and which Churchill eventually stretches to its limits by focusing unapologetically on the historical moment and placing in an impossibly ambiguous context those general truths which that moment (or those particulars) once exemplified. Two decades after the poets of Sensibility had begun what John Sitter calls their 'flight from history' into the realm of the imagination, Churchill, translating the implications of the Nonsense Club's topical journalism into poetry, undertakes a complex, relativistic immersion *into* history—an immersion in which the moral and political presuppositions of the Augustans (already undermined by Hogarth and Fielding) are suspended in a medium of habitual scepticism.[12] Churchill's ethical relativism, in effect, frees the symbolic 'middling and inferior' classes from their traditional role as elements in a social allegory employed in 'high' political and cultural battles and allows their historical specificity and importance to assert itself free from the controlling hierarchical vision that lingers even in Fielding's and Hogarth's work. This is not, however, to say that Churchill actually believes that all men are created equal, but that the fictions of his poetry consistently imply that they are.

In Churchill's satirical poetry, we find a marked democratization of audience, coupled with a distortion of poetic form that reinforces Churchill's frequently expressed disdain for both literary and social authority.[13] Irreverence, independence, and impudence become the central values of an egalitarian, relativistic poetry which suggests, in content and form, the breakdown of stabilizing relations that Palmer defines as the 'revolutionary situation': 'old loyalties fade, obligations are felt as impositions, law seems arbitrary, and respect is felt as a form of humiliation . . . existing sources of prestige seem undeserved, hitherto accepted forms of wealth and income seem ill-gained, and government is sensed as distant, apart from the governed and not really "representing" them.'[14] I do not intend, certainly, to portray Churchill as a crypto-revolutionary: his connections to aristocratic power and his theoretical commitment to the English system are too strong to permit such an assessment. But I would contend that Churchill's irreverent rejection of conventional social roles and deferences, intensified by libertine energy and personal frustration, represents the most complex literary manifestation we have of the mood of discontent, effrontery, self-assertion, and hegemonic potentiality emerging in the English middling sort (and their allies above and below) during the middle years of the eighteenth century.

II

Perhaps these claims are too large for a body of poetry written rapidly by a profligate ex-clergyman, who, if Eric Rothstein is correct, 'roared in the void, and roared the more, perhaps, from fright at hearing his own lone voice'.[15] Yet I would have to suggest that out in the void someone was listening, for Churchill became almost overnight the most famous poet of his time, and earned, from poetry alone, an estimated £3,500 in two years.[16] That there was an audience for Churchill's poetry at all, let alone an audience that could and did pay good money for it, is perhaps the best contemporary evidence that the phenomenon of the 'benevolently weeping' but cold and calculating bourgeoisie was not as pervasive as some critics have implied. But it also suggests that rebelliousness and irreverence were profitable, and thus raises the vexing issue of the Nonsense Club's involvement with the print media as a business—a business that thrived on controversy.

Clearly, the Nonsense Club was deeply involved in the organization of the means of literary production in mid-century London. Not only did its members write and edit prolifically, but, as we have seen, Colman and Thornton were major shareholders in *The St. James's Chronicle*, and Thornton was chief adviser to Woodfall's *Public Advertiser*. Churchill received the profits from *The North Briton* and published his poems quickly in order to reap immediate benefits. Lloyd 'cobbled up' anything

he could to increase his income. The Nonsense Club wrote to
make money. Thornton, as the irreverent Roxana Termagant,
chided Fielding for his claims of disinterestedness and (with his
usual ambiguity) went to the heart of the business of writing in
a passage overtly linking literary production and the production of other saleable goods:

> I do not indeed pretend, with your Worship, to a spirit so disinter-
> ested, as to be entirely regardless of Profit, in the business.—Every
> one has a right to as much as he can earn: and the genius, whose
> brains spin materials for the mind, ought equally to be rewarded with
> the mechanick, whose hands furnish out the coarser stuff for the
> body.[17]

Again we are confronted with a basic truth underlying what
may or may not be an ironic example of Roxana's vulgar mer-
chandizing. At mid-century literary production was a burgeoning industry, replete with sophisticated advertising techniques
and specially targeted markets. Its clientele was no longer
merely the ruling élite or the literary coterie, but the beginnings
of what we today would call a 'mass audience'—an audience
(especially in London) including 'mechanicks', labourers, even
street urchins.[18] To capture this audience was to reap substantial profits.

It was common knowledge that controversy (literary or political) increased the market for papers, and that authors therefore
consciously provoked (and sometimes arranged) literary wars.
In the realm of politics, the situation was exacerbated by the
seriousness of the consequences hinging on what many commentators saw as simply a commercial gambit: the press was
accused of being 'a *political* way of trade' with a vested interest
in writing 'a whole nation into broils'.[19] The significance of
this issue to the Nonsense Club's history is that it exposes to
renewed scrutiny the question of the motives and commitment
behind the political stance discussed in the latter part of this
study.

The plain fact is that rebelliousness and irreverence were
profitable to certain segments of the middle class—printers,
engravers, publishers, writers—and that literary production as
a *business* was an important force in provoking and sustaining
political dissent regardless of the ideological sympathies of the

media-entrepreneurs themselves.[20] In this context, it is possible
to view Churchill as one who took great risks to earn big money:
challenging the government again and again in poems that
could easily have led to arrest and imprisonment, yet knowing
full well that imprisonment would have greatly increased the
sales of his already popular works. (In 1768 Wilkes in the
King's Bench Prison would once and for all prove the media
value of political incarceration.) But complicating, indeed re-
casting the entire situation is the fact that the government's
assault on Wilkes was viewed by many as an assault on the
freedom of the press itself—not only a threat to the free flow of
information and opinion, but to the livelihood of those whose
business it was to supply such information. The complex relationship of economics and ideology allows no definitive sorting
out of the Nonsense Club's motives beyond those alternatives—
psychological, economic, and political—explored during the
course of this study, but it does suggest that irreverence and
rebelliousness were perhaps more 'middling' even in their
economic motivations than it is customary to believe. The
ruling-class ideology of liberty had become through a series of
conversions the middle-class business of liberty, which when
promulgated through the commercial press produced a readership (or, in the illiterate, 'listenership') more likely to intern-
alize and insist upon the *reality* of liberty: the aristocratic sop
was transformed by middle-class marketing techniques into an
emergent rhetoric of underclass resistance.

   This underclass was not yet the incipient 'working class' that
E. P. Thompson has attempted so brilliantly to reconstruct,
but the 'middling and inferior class of people' to whom Wilkes
addressed his appeal, and whose attributes, in ironic combination, Churchill assumed in his last poems. It was this coalition
of the 'base, unthinking rabble' (to use a phrase of Smollett's,
but one which easily could have been Johnson's or Burke's),
small freeholders, 'patriot cits', and urban professionals that,
covered by a media barrage of unprecedented scope and effec-
tiveness, challenged in Wilkes's name the corrupt power of
Parliament in 1768–74.[21] The Wilkite movement was a movement suckled on irreverence, an irreverence simultaneously
descending from the sophisticated literary heritage of the
Augustans and ascending from the vulgar effrontery of the

London poor. In the Nonsense Club, we catch these traditions at a moment of tentative and ambiguous coalescence. The burlesque ode, the Sign Painters' Exhibition, *The Drury-Lane Journal*, *The Connoisseur*, all are preludes to a political point of view that, however contaminated by commercial considerations, acknowledges the power of the common people and the popular idiom in a newly-emergent cultural order. It was an order slow to achieve maturity: confused and splintered by the counter-revolutionary repression of the younger Pitt, and perhaps never achieving its full democratic potential in England.[22] But it speaks strongly to the American experience and ideology, just as Wilkite tactics and symbolism stirred the rebels already honing their pens against what they saw as the arbitrary rule of a Parliament across the ocean. And, in a sense, it may be seen as providing the ideological outlines for the myth of the American individualist: the proud, irreverent common man, brave to the point of rashness, spontaneous, independent, and self-aggrandizing. It was just these qualities that the London crowd celebrated in Wilkes, and that Cowper later recalled as the defining characteristics of the 'stout, tall captain' with whom he had once attended Westminster School:

> His pride, that scorns t' obey or to submit,
> With them is courage; his effront'ry wit.
> His wild excursions, window-breaking feats,
> Robb'ry of gardens, quarrels in the streets,
> His hair-breadth 'scapes, and all his daring schemes,
> Transport them, and are made their fav'rite themes.[23]
>
> (226–31)

Epilogue

After the deaths of Churchill and Lloyd, Colman remained Thornton's friend despite pressure to turn against him. In March 1765, Wilkes, taking up Lloyd's quarrel, wrote to the playwright, 'I find that [Lloyd] had subject of just indignation against *Thornton: so had Churchill.* I am a little inclin'd to revenge both their quarrels. Our dear friend wish'd I would. What is your opinion?'[1] Colman answered judiciously, though clearly favouring Thornton: 'I leave him to your justice, but recommend him to your mercy. Spare him I beseech you Good Wilkes!'[2] This equivocal reply seems to have satisfied Wilkes, for nothing more came of the quarrel. For his part, Thornton retained genuinely warm feelings toward Colman, as attested by his naming of his first son, born in 1765, Bonnell George Thornton.

For the next three years, Thornton lived in a state of domestic tranquillity; in the course of this four-year marriage his wife bore him three children: two boys and a girl. One of the old friends who watched them grow was the benignly mad Kit Smart, who in 1768 dedicated his *Parables of Our Lord and Saviour Jesus Christ* to Bonnell George. The dedication, 'To Master BONNELL GEORGE THORNTON, Of Orchard-Street, Westminster', concludes, 'I am with the greatest Sincerity and most inevitable Affection to the eldest Son of BONNELL and SYLVIA THORNTON, Your most hearty Friend, CHRISTOPHER SMART.'[3] Thornton's second son, Robert John, gained fame in his own right as a physician, scientific writer and illustrator, earning a place beside his father in *The Dictionary of National Biography*.

Thornton died on 9 May 1768, the year of his youngest son's birth. He was buried in the cloisters of Westminster Abbey, his monument bearing a Latin inscription written by his friend, Joseph Warton:

His genius, cultivated most happily by every kind of polite literature, was accompanied and recommended by manners open, sincere, and candid. In his writings and conversation he had a wonderful liveliness, with a vein of pleasantry peculiarly his own. In ridiculing the failings of men, without bitterness, and with much humour, he was singularly happy: as a companion he was delightful.[4]

As for Colman, he continued his managerial duties at Drury Lane even after Garrick's return from the Continent in 1765. That same year saw the publication of his translation of Terence, which like Thornton's later Plautus (1767) was well received.[5] In 1766, Garrick and Colman's joint work, *The Clandestine Marriage*, was produced after three years of intermittent writing, revision, and delay. It was an immediate success, and takes its place behind only the best work of Goldsmith and Sheridan in the history of late eighteenth-century drama.

In 1767, Colman took over the management of Covent-Garden Theatre. The following year he was elected to the Literary Club, and in that capacity makes intermittent appearances in Boswell's *Life of Johnson*. Colman managed Covent Garden from 1767 to 1774, and later became manager of the Haymarket Theatre, from 1777 to 1789. During his years in the theatre, he wrote or adapted over forty dramatic pieces, though none equal to *The Jealous Wife* and *The Clandestine Marriage*. In addition, he retained his interest in *The St. James's Chronicle* and wrote many periodical pieces, as well as translating Horace's *Ars Poetica* in 1783. It was about the time of this translation that he abruptly found himself in contact with a friend from whom he had not heard in thirty years: William Cowper.

Cowper's history following his destructive fit of madness is well known. Finding refuge in Evangelical Christianity, he lived as a recluse with the Unwin family, first at Huntingdon and later at Olney. After another violent attack of suicidal mania in 1773, he began to draw away from organized religion and to find comfort and distraction in pet animals, gardening, correspondence, and the composition of poetry. Through the latter two therapeutic occupations he gradually achieved the status of pre-eminent literary man of his time.

Cowper's attitude toward poetry never changed from his Nonsense Club days. He wrote easily and regarded verse as a mere hobby:

I have no more right to the name of a poet, than a maker of mousetraps has to that of an engineer; but my little exploits in this way have at times amused me so much, that I have often wished myself a good one. Such a talent in verse as mine is like a child's rattle,—very entertaining to the trifler that uses it, and very disagreeable to all beside. But it has served to rid me of some melancholy moments, for I only take it up as a gentleman performer does his fiddle.[6]

Following the publication of his *Poems* in 1783, Cowper sent a presentation copy to Colman. When Colman failed to acknowledge the gift or to send in return a copy of his Horace, Cowper was deeply hurt. He took out his resentment in a poem called 'The Valediction', in which he characterizes Colman as an 'Amusement-monger of a trifling age':

> Illustrious histrionic patentee,
> Terentius, once my friend, farewell to thee.
> In thee some virtuous qualities combine
> To fit thee for a nobler post than thine,
> Who, born a gentleman, hast stoop'd too low
> To live by buskin, sock, and raree-show.
> Thy schoolfellow, and partner of thy plays
> Where Nicol swung the birch and twin'd the bays,
> And having known thee bearded and full grown,
> The weekly censor of a laughing town,
> I thought the volume I presum'd to send,
> Grac'd with the name of a long absent friend,
> Might prove a welcome gift, and touch thine heart,
> Not hard by nature, in the feeling part.
> But thou, it seems (what cannot grandeur do,
> Though but a dream?) art grown disdainful too,
> And strutting in thy school of Queens and Kings,
> Who fret their hour and are forgotten things,
> Hast caught the cold distemper of the day,
> And, like his Lordship, cast thy friend away.
>
> (29–48)[7]

But on 27 December 1785 Cowper tried again, writing to Colman because he had heard that the playwright had enquired after him. This letter had a happier result: 'Colman . . . writes to me like a brother', Cowper rejoiced.[8] Once renewed, the friendship flourished, though only through correspondence, until ill health and mental decay struck down both men.

Colman was partially paralysed by a stroke in 1785 and by 1789 had become intermittently mad. Thereafter he lived in seclusion, under private care and observation. He died on 14 August 1794. Six years later, Cowper, having himself lapsed into terror and silence, followed his old friend to the grave. He was the last member of the Nonsense Club, and the most famous poet in England.

Appendix

THE CRAB

The Crab, an original poem in Charles Churchill's hand, is preserved in British Museum Add. MS 30878, fos. 66^r–67^v, a volume that contains the bulk of the Wilkes–Churchill correspondence. Although this correspondence was edited by Edward H. Weatherly in 1954, nowhere does Weatherly mention the existence of *The Crab*. Douglas Grant, editor of the Oxford edition of Churchill's *Poetical Works* (1956), seems also not to have known of the poem. As far as I can ascertain, *The Crab* has been overlooked, by accident or design, since the time Churchill wrote it.[1]

A parody of the poetical 'moral tales' (in the manner of La Fontaine and Gay) that Robert Lloyd was so fond of imitating, *The Crab* represents perhaps the best surviving example of the racy, humorous versifying that went on both at Nonsense Club meetings and at Medmenham Abbey. The most notorious literary artifact of the Medmenham brotherhood was undoubtedly John Wilkes's and Thomas Potter's *Essay on Woman* (1763), a lewd parody of Pope's *Essay on Man* with notes purportedly by William Warburton. Churchill, who would undoubtedly have known *An Essay on Woman*, was perhaps influenced in his choice of subject matter for *The Crab* by the first of 'Warburton's' supposed notes, in which he claims that 'it is not only lawful, but expedient for clergymen to eat crawfish, soup, lamphreys, &c., not to indulge their own inordinate appetites, but as provocatives to the *fuller discharge* of what is due to the dear Partners of our beds, according to the modus of Benevolence prescribed by St. Paul'.[2] *The Crab*, with its irreverent subject matter, rough phrasing, and parodic humour, is typical of the style of poetry practised at Medmenham, and it is possible that the poem was originally intended as a contribution to the merriment of that group.

The Crab contains two allusions to contemporary figures. The 'pious Stone' of line 8 is George Stone (1708?–64), Archbishop of Armagh and Anglican Primate of Ireland, whose alleged sodomitical practices were satirized in the 'Advertisement' to *An Essay on Woman* and who was credited by Wilkes with possessing the archetype of the phallus engraved on that poem's title page.[3] Churchill satirized one 'Stone' as a homosexual in *The Times* (ll. 475–6); and although Grant does not identify this reference except to say that it 'is impossible that it could be Andrew Stone', clearly this allusion is also to George

Stone.[4] Line 13 of *The Crab*, with its reference to a priest of 'more than Irish fame', would seem another hit at the same clergyman. The reasons for Wilkes and Churchill's animosity toward Stone are not entirely clear, but certainly his reliance upon connections to gain high position in the religious establishment and his being the brother of Andrew Stone, former tutor of George III and ally of Lord Bute, would have made him an unsympathetic figure to Churchill.[5] Stone was widely known to be both socially adept and morally tainted. Horace Walpole wrote that he 'ruined his constitution by indulgence to the style of luxury and drinking established in Ireland, and by conforming to which he had found the means of surmounting the most grievous prejudices and of gaining popularity, ascendant, power; an instance of abilities seldom to be matched.'[6] The second contemporary allusion (l. 34) is to 'Doctor' Joshua Ward (1685–1761), a well known and much satirized empiric, whose medicines (including the famous Ward's pill) were extolled by some, including Henry Fielding and George II, and cursed by others.[7]

The literary allusions to the 'great Pomonque Queen' (72) and 'Florimel in labour' (93) are more difficult to explain. The 'Pomonque Queen' is almost certainly Pomona, Roman goddess of fruit trees and gardens. Her flowing 'royal favours' possibly represent a scatological adaptation of lines 632–3 of Ovid's *Metamorphoses*, Bk.XIV, which contains the most widely known classical version of the story of Pomona and Vertumnus. The lines read, *'nec sentire sitim patitur biblaeque recurvas / radicis fibras labentibus inrigat undis'*—'Nor would she permit them to suffer thirst, but watered the twisted fibres of the thirsty roots with her trickling streams'.[8] Samuel Garth's translation of Book XIV, first published in 1717 and undoubtedly known by Churchill, renders the lines in a manner that seems to invite an obscene interpretation: 'Then opes her streaming Sluices, to supply / With flowing Draughts her thirsty Family'.[9] The allusion to 'Florimel in labour' presents similar difficulties. Florimell, of course, is one of the central figures of Spenser's *Faerie Queene*, Bks. III and IV, but she is a virgin and thus immune to 'labour' in the obstetric sense. However, if we read 'labour' as 'struggle' then Churchill would seem to allude to the episode in Book III in which Florimell is attacked and nearly raped by a fisherman in whose boat she takes refuge:

> Beastly he threw her downe, ne car'd to spill
> Her garments gay with scales of fish, that all did fill.
> The silly virgin stroue him to withstand,
> All that she might, and him in vaine reuild:
> She struggled strongly both with foot and hand,

To saue her honor from that villaine vild,
And cride to heauen, from human helpe exild.

(III. viii. 25–31)[10]

The allusion—like that to Pomona—is clearly an offhand one, but the combination of the images of struggle, sea creatures, and cries to heaven make it likely that this was the episode that Churchill had in mind. The final literary allusion (l. 131) is to Thomas D'Urfey (1653–1723), a prolific dramatist and poet whose *Tales* (1704) may have influenced Churchill's choice of verse form (see below).

The Crab is written in *rime couee*, a measure common in medieval romance, most notably Chaucer's burlesque romance, *Sir Thopas*.[11] The more immediate influence on the poem's form are probably the *rime couee* stanzas of 'The Broken Commands' in Thomas D'Urfey's *Tales, tragical and comical . . . From the prose of some famous antique Italian, Spanish, and French authors* (1704). *The Crab* is Churchill's only extended poem to take a form other than tetrameter or pentameter couplets.

In my transcription, I have followed Churchill's original spelling and punctuation. The Latin motto may be translated, 'For thee the blazing crab contracts its claws', and is an adaptation of Virgil's *Georgics*, I, 34–35: *'ipse tibi iam bracchia contrahit / Scorpios.'*[12] The original, interestingly, is a reference to the constellation of Scorpio making room in the heavens for Caesar Augustus' 'new star'; a parallel that Churchill perhaps meant as a complimentary allusion to the newly-won popularity of his friend, John Wilkes.

The Crab

——Tibi brachia contrahit ardens
Cancer——

Whoever studies Humankind
Devoid of prejudice, will find
    Whatever Priests pretend,
That they like us are flesh and blood,
And were before, and scince the flood,   5
    And will be to the end,

(2)

This truth scince all the Learned own,
Without excepting pious Stone,
    E'en let the Bigots rail
Their rage but shows them in the wrong,   10

Then not to make my prelude long,
Why here begins my Tale,

(3)

A priest of more than Irish fame
Tradition says, but hides his name,
 Who in his younger days   15
Instead of mumbling over beads,
Had done in Love surprizing deeds,
 And cropt immortal bays,

(4)

Began to find at fifty five
That though each member seem'd alive 20
 And each in vigour still,
Yet one would often droop its head,
And spite of what he did or said,
 Refuse to work his will,

(5)

A sad discovery you'll say   25
For one who in the Month of May
 Had fix'd upon a night
To meet an healthy buxom bride
Whose wants an Husband ill supply'd,
 And yet who knew her right,   30

(6)

Not go was to proclaim his case,
But then to suffer a disgrace!—
 'Ne'er fright yourself good Sir
(Said Doctor Ward) when Nature halts
Experience shews us certain Salts 35
 Will set her on the spur,

(7)

This Doctrine Cleopatra knew,
And thence luxuriously drew
 Exstatick draughts of pleasure,
Crabs, Cockles, when the Queen was lewd 40
The Roman's appetite renew'd
 And Oysters were a treasure,

(8)

In May th' inhabitants of Cloysters
Are too well fed to look for Oysters,
    Ay true but Crabs are plenty   45
So quick to Billingsgate he goes
And of the largest pick'd and chose
    And sent the Lady twenty,

(9)

So many Crabs the wond'ring wife
Had never seen in all her life   50
    Quick to her room she fled,
And not to leave them in the way
For fear of what the world might say,
    Hid them beneath the bed,

(10)

There long they lay in Silent state   55
'Till one impatient of his fate,
    Or urg'd by Lord knows what,
Crawl'd out with many an awkward stride,
And waiting the return of tide
    Stole in a neighbouring pot   60

(11)

The rest they stew'd with spice and wine
In proper time, and broil'd the chine,
    I'd swear no grace was said
He gave no respite to his jaws
By his advice she suck'd the claws,   65
        Then hurried up to bed

(12)

While he was fumbling at his hose,
Madam was whip'd between the cloaths
    And squat on that machine
(In vain we talk of style or mode)   70
From whence the royal favours flow'd
    Of great Pomonqué Queen,

(13)

And where the Crab lay snug and still
Who having quickly drank his fill
    Would eat as well as drink,   75
And fearless of the rattling shower
Stretch'd forth a claw with all his power
    And seiz'd the mossy brink

(14)

What stubborn Amazonian heart
But must have fail'd at such a smart,   80
    In such a tender spot,
Mercy! she shrieking cry'd dismay'd
O Man of God! quick lend me your aid,
    There's death within the pot,

(15)

The Priest to her assistance flew,   85
Pull'd up her shift in haste to view
    From whence those cries arose,
And whilst he mus'd on what he saw
The pendant Crab stretch'd th' other claw
    And caught him by the nose,   90

(16)

God's wounds he cry'd (for priests will swear)
Then groan'd as if his end was near
    Like Florimel in labour,
The Dame too now with fresh surprize
Redoubled quick her treble cries   95
    And fright'ned ev'ry Neighbour,

(17)

Both pull'd and tugg'd with might and main,
Us'd ev'ry art, but all in vain,
    To heighten their disaster
The more they pull'd the more they cry'd   100
The wicked Crab with cruel pride
    Still grip'd and clung the faster,

(18)

Now all the Street was in a clatter,
All wond'ring what could be the matter,
 Half drest ran Aunts and Cousins,   105
Some one thing some another swore
Howe'er at length they burst the door
 And tumbled in by dozens,

(19)

And now while all suppos'd a rape,
Or Murder in some dreadfull shape   110
 And ev'ry cheek grew pale
Imagine how at once they grinn'd
To see the Prelate's nostrils pinn'd
 So close to Madam's tail,

(20)

Imagine their surprize to hear   115
Such oaths which not a Turk would swear
 With now and then an Ave
While Madam wriggling to and fro
Now labour'd to dislodge the foe
 Now tired cry'd peccavi   120

(21)

Consider too the Husband's face
To find a Crab in such a place
 So curiously suspended
And then conceive—but what a jest
Without my aid you'll guess the rest   125
 And so my Story's ended.

(22)

Your Story ended! prithee friend
This never sure can be the end
 In spite of what you say
You stop because your spirits fail   130
Now Durfey would have told this tale
 In quite a diff'rent way,

(23)

We want to know the Prelate's shame
And of the Crab too what became
    And can't compound for less,   135
But you in strange pretended haste
For want of wit bid Men of Taste
    Conceive imagine guess

(24)

What Moral then would you infer?
A Tale Should have a moral Sir,   140
    A Moral! thus it flows,
On him misfortunes still attend
Who in the secrets of a friend
    Imprudent thrusts his nose.

Short Titles and Abbreviations

The Birth of a Consumer Society	*The Birth of a Consumer Society: The Commercialization of Eighteenth-Century England*, ed. Neil McKendrick (Bloomington, 1982).
Boswell, *Life of Johnson*	Boswell, *The Life of Samuel Johnson*, ed. George Birbeck Hill and L. F. Powell, 6 vols. (Oxford, 1934–50).
Brown, *Churchill*	W. C. Brown, *Charles Churchill: Poet, Rake, and Rebel* (Lawrence, Kan., 1953).
Carretta	Vincent Carretta, *The Snarling Muse: Verbal and Visual Political Satire from Pope to Churchill* (Philadelphia, 1983).
Chalmers	*The British Essayists*, ed. Alexander Chalmers (London, 1823).
Colman, *Prose on Several Occasions*	George Colman, *Prose on Several Occasions*, 3 vols. (London, 1787).
Colman's *Works*	*The Dramatick Works of George Colman*, 4 vols. (London, 1777).
Cowper's *Correspondence*	*The Correspondence of William Cowper*, ed. Thomas Wright, 4 vols. (London, 1904).
DLJ	*Have At You All: or, The Drury-Lane Journal* (London, 1752).
DNB	*The Dictionary of National Biography.*
Garrick's *Letters*	*The Letters of David Garrick*, ed. David Little and George Kahrl, 3 vols. (Cambridge, Mass., 1963).
Goldsmith's *Works*	*Collected Works of Oliver Goldsmith*, ed. Arthur Friedman, 5 vols. (Oxford, 1966).
Grant, Churchill's *Poetical Works*	*The Poetical Works of Charles Churchill*, ed. Douglas Grant (Oxford, 1956).

Letters and Prose Writings	*The Letters and Prose Writings of William Cowper*, ed. James King and Charles Ryskamp, 5 vols. (Oxford, 1979–86).
Lloyd's *Poetical Works*	*The Poetical Works of Robert Lloyd, A.M.*, ed. William Kenrick, 2 vols. (London, 1774, repr. New York, 1969).
London Journal	*Boswell's London Journal, 1762–3*, ed. Frederick Pottle (New York, 1950).
PA	*The Public Advertiser.*
Page	Eugene Page, *George Colman the Elder* (New York, 1935).
Party Ideology	John Brewer, *Party Ideology and Popular Politics at the Accession of George III* (Cambridge, 1976).
Paulson, *Hogarth*	Paulson, *Hogarth: His Life, Art, and Times*, 2 vols. (New Haven, 1971).
Peake	Richard Brinsley Peake, *The Memoirs of the Colman Family*, 2 vols. (London, 1811).
Poems (Baird–Ryskamp)	*The Poems of William Cowper*, ed. John D. Baird and Charles Ryskamp, 2 vols. (vol. I, Oxford, 1980; vol. II forthcoming).
Poems (Milford)	*The Poetical Works of William Cowper*, ed. H. S. Milford (4th edn., London, 1967).
Ryskamp, *Cowper*	Charles Ryskamp, *William Cowper of the Inner Temple, Esq.* (Cambridge, 1959).
SJC	*The St. James's Chronicle.*
Southey's *Cowper*	*The Works of William Cowper* (with Life), ed. Robert Southey, 15 vols. (London, 1836–7).
WCC	*The Correspondence of John Wilkes and Charles Churchill*, ed. Edward H. Weatherly (New York, 1954).
Wilkes's *Correspondence*	*The Correspondence of the Late John Wilkes*, ed. John Almon, 5 vols. (London, 1805).

Notes

INTRODUCTION

1. *London Journal*, p. 266.
2. George Sherburn, 'The Restoration and Eighteenth Century (1660–1789)', in *A Literary History of England*, ed. Albert Baugh (New York, 1948), p. 1052.
3. Ryskamp, *Cowper*, pp. 78–101.
4. For my definition of 'hegemony' I am indebted to the thought of Antonio Gramsci, especially as his work has been interpreted by Raymond Williams. 'Hegemony' has traditionally been defined as political rule or domination, but Gramsci distinguishes between 'rule' and 'hegemony', redefining the latter to include both the concepts of 'culture' as 'whole social process', and 'ideology' as 'meanings and values expressive of class interest'. As Williams writes, 'Hegemony is then not only the articulate upper level of "ideology", nor are its forms of control only those ordinarily seen as "manipulation" or "indoctrination". . . . It is a lived system of meanings and values—constitutive and constituting—which as they are experienced as practices appear reciprocally confirming. It thus constitutes a sense of reality for most people in the society, a sense of absolute because experienced reality beyond which it is difficult for most members of the society to move, in most areas of their lives. It is, that is to say, in the strongest sense a "culture", but a culture which has also to be seen as the lived dominance and subordination of particular classes.' *Marxism and Literature* (Oxford, 1977), pp. 108–10. Cf. Walter L. Adamson, *Hegemony and Revolution: A Study of Antonio Gramsci's Political and Cultural Theory* (Berkeley, 1980), pp. 114–201, *et passim*.
5. Stuart Hall in *Culture, Media, Language: Working Papers in Cultural Studies, 1972–79*, ed. Hall, Hobson, Lowe, and Willis (London, 1980), p. 138. The Centre for Contemporary Cultural Studies, University of Birmingham, has produced some of the most stimulating work of recent years in the area of interdisciplinary cultural studies.
6. Foucault, 'The Subject and Power', in Hubert L. Dreyfus and Paul Rabinow, *Michel Foucault: Beyond Structuralism and Hermeneutics* (Chicago, 1982), p. 219.

CHAPTER 1

1. John Carleton, *Westminster School* (London, 1965), p. 33. For another description of Cowper's Westminster, see Ryskamp, *Cowper*, pp. 14–35.

2. Herbert M. Atherton, *Political Prints in the Age of Hogarth: A Study in the Ideographic Representation of Politics* (Oxford, 1974), pp. 22–3, 122, *et passim*; Carretta, pp. 124–7, 178–84, *et passim*.

3. Richard Cumberland, *The Memoirs of Richard Cumberland* (London, 1806), p. 32.

4. Cumberland, p. 31.

5. For further examples of Nicoll's system, see Cumberland, p. 32, *et passim*.

6. Nicoll seems to have anticipated the relative independence of vertical authority and reliance on peer pressure that typified the English public schools in the early nineteenth century. See John Chandos, *Boys Together: English Public Schools 1800–1860* (New Haven, 1984), *passim*.

7. *Poems* (Milford), pp. 246–7.

8. Southey's *Cowper*, I. 3.

9. Cowper to William Unwin, 23 May 1781, in *Letters and Prose Writings*, I. 481. 'Translation of the Verses to the Memory of Dr. Lloyd (I)', l. 12, (Baird–Ryskamp), I. 442.

10. 'Table Talk', *Poems* (Baird–Ryskamp), I. 254–5.

11. Cowper to Unwin, Cowper's *Correspondence*, III. 80–1.

12. Cumberland, p. 34.

13. *The Annals of Westminster School* (London, 1898), p. 175.

14. *London Journal*, p. 63. Boswell did not understand the boys' Latin because in Scotland he was taught Continental pronunciation.

15. British Museum Add. MS 36593, fo. 70[r]. All quotations by permission of the British Library.

16. *Westminster School*, 2nd edn. (London, 1951), p. 54.

17. Grant, Churchill's *Poetical Works*, p. 452. All subsequent quotations are from this edition and are cited by line in the text.

18. Georg Christoph Lichtenberg, *Lichtenberg's Visits to England*, ed. Margaret L. Mare and W. H. Quarrell (Oxford, 1938; repr. New York, 1969), pp. 63–4.

19. 'Bonnell son of John Thornton by Rebecca his Wife', Register of St Paul, Covent Garden, 1703–39, p. 162.

20. The dormitory was originally designed by Sir Christopher Wren, but Lord Burlington's modifications were so extensive as to make the building virtually his. See Morris Brownell, *Alexander Pope and the Arts of Georgian England* (Oxford, 1978), p. 297.

21. 'Thornton's Burlesque Ode', *Notes and Queries*, 194 (July 1949), p. 322. See also Charles Ryskamp, 'Dr. Arne's Music for Thornton's Burlesque Ode', *Notes and Queries*, 202 (Feb. 1957), pp. 71–3.

22. McKillop, p. 322.

23. *An Ode on Saint Cæcilia's Day* (London, 1749); as quoted by McKillop, p. 322.

24. *The Reading Mercury*, 30 Dec. 1751. The advertisement from which this quotation comes originally appeared in a London paper on 28 Dec. and was cut out and saved by Henley himself. See Graham Midgley, *The Life of Orator Henley* (Oxford, 1973), p. 188. Thornton may have written the puff, cf. *DLJ*, p. 11: 'I must acknowledge that her Salt-box and Jew's-Harp have as much real *Reason* and *Casuistry* in them, as those unmeaning instruments, the HUMDRUMS, which are always to be met with at the bar and in the pulpit.'

25. Arthur Sherbo, *Christopher Smart: Scholar of the University* (East Lansing, Mich., 1967), p. 68.

26. For Chalmers's attribution, see his introduction to *The Connoisseur*, in *The British Essayists*, XXV. xxiii–xxiv. The poems signed 'B.T.' appear in *The Student* (London, 1750), I. 25–9, 80.

27. Colman, *Prose on Several Occasions*, I. 237.

28. This essay, 'On the Learning of Oxford Tradesmen and College Students', finds echoes throughout Thornton's *œuvre*. For example, the 'Student' writes that certain Oxford menials must be 'dignified with Latin appellations: our butler must be *promus*, our cook *coquus*, the porter at our gate *janitor*' (I. 53); Thornton, in *City Latin* (a satire on anglicized Latin), writes that 'the *Smiths* . . . might be stiled FABRICII, the *Gardeners* HORTENSII, the *Taylors* SARTORII, the *Drapers* TOGATI, the *Masons* AEDILES, &c.' (p. 28). The 'Student' writes of signboards (one of Thornton's favourite subjects), 'How sublime are the signs of our innkeepers: The *angel*, the *cross*, the *mitre*, the *maidenhead* with many others, are too well known to need mentioning'; Thornton, in *Adventurer* No. 9, writes 'but why must the *Angel*, the *Lamb*, and the *Mitre*, be designations of the seats of drunkenness and prostitution?' For the student of Thornton's style, 'Oxford Tradesmen' seems unmistakably a product of Thornton's early days with *The Student*. One other essay in *The Student* has been tentatively assigned to Thornton. Ronald Paulson ambiguously attributes the long explication of Hogarth's *March to Finchley* (II. 162–8) to 'Thornton or one of his colleagues', but in a note states that 'the published version is by Thornton'. See Paulson, *Hogarth*, II. 95, 433 n. 50. While in the light of Thornton's later connection with Hogarth the possibility is tantalizing, I can find no hard evidence to verify Paulson's claim.

29. *The Student* (London, 1750–1), II. 273.

30. Brown, *Churchill*, p. 18.

31. *The Student*, I. 34–5; Ryskamp, *Cowper*, pp. 226–7.

32. Boswell, *Life of Johnson*, I. 209.

33. *DLJ*, p. 10.

34. *The London Daily Advertiser*, 4, 6 Nov. 1751, 9 Jan. 1752. Cf. F. Homes Dudden, *Henry Fielding*, 2 vols. (Oxford, 1952), II. 888.

35. Midgley, pp. 185–92.

36. *The Covent-Garden Journal*, 2 vols. (New Haven, 1915), I, *passim.*
For additional information on the *DLJ*, see W. C. Brown, 'A Belated
Augustan: Bonnell Thornton, Esq.', *Philological Quarterly*, 34 (1955),
pp. 336–8; Lance Bertelsen, 'Have At You All: or, Bonnell Thorn-
ton's Journalism', *Huntington Library Quarterly*, 44 (1981), pp. 263–8;
and Bertelsen, 'Have At You All' in *British Literary Magazines: The
Augustan Age and the Age of Johnson, 1698–1788*, ed. Alvin Sullivan
(Westport, Connecticut, 1983), pp. 153–7.

37. *DLJ*, p. 7.

38. *DLJ*, p. 12. Other periodicals parodied in the journal include
The Gentleman's Magazine, The London Magazine, The Universal Magazine,
and Smart's *Midwife.*

39. Although each paper is dated Thursday, in actuality Thornton
had problems meeting his weekly deadline. *The London Daily Advertiser*
of Thursday, 30 Jan. 1752, carried an advertisement postponing the
publication of the third number of the *DLJ* until Saturday. A week
later, on 6 Feb., another advertisement appeared offering a 'Reward
of 100 Guineas, to be paid immediately on Conviction, at the Public
Register Office' to anyone 'that shall make Discover of the Villain,
who last Night knocked down her DEVIL, and took from him a Packet
of Papers, written in a fair Italian Hand, then carrying to the Printers
for the last half Sheet of her Journal', which, Roxana assures her
audience, will be published the following day.

40. *Henry Fielding: The Critical Heritage*, ed. Ronald Paulson and
Thomas Lockwood (New York, 1969), pp. 311–19.

41. *English Burlesque Poetry, 1700–1750* (Cambridge, Mass., 1932),
p. 14.

42. The 'New Chapter' appears in the *DLJ*, pp. 102–7; it is reprinted in *Henry Fielding: The Critical Heritage*, pp. 321–4.

43. *Henry Fielding: Tentative Realist* (Oxford, 1967), p. 128.

44. *Fun* (London, 1752), p. 32.

45. Orator Henley interpreted Smart's adoption of a female pseudonym and his donning of female costumes at the Old Woman's Oratory
as evidence of sexual deviance: 'Ah Molly Smart! . . . Pimlico Molly
Midnight translated to Rump-Castle! Hum-buggers-bougre.' There
is no corroborative evidence to support Henley's view. See Midgley,
p. 186.

46. The Drury Lane hundred was notorious for the high number of
prostitutes located in its vicinity. In her autobiographical sketch,
Roxana protests her innocence rather too often: 'I was born at a little
town in the West of England; no matter where, no matter when.—
'Tis an usual practice, I know, with the miserable creatures of the
Courtezan order (of which if any one suspects me to be, I here assure

him to the contrary) to incite the compassion of their casual gallants by pretending to be, what they call, Parson's daughters'—which is just what Roxana then pretends to be (p. 31). Her later story of how a young man was found by her bedside at school and caused her to be unjustly accused by her father only strengthens the reader's suspicion that Roxana is trying to hide precisely what Thornton wants to say.

47. *DLJ*, pp. 60–1.

48. To John Wilkes, Dec. 1769, Add. MS 30870, fos. 238^r–239^r; as quoted by Joel J. Gold, ' "Buried Alive": Charlotte Forman in Grub Street', *Eighteenth-Century Life*, 8 (Oct. 1982), p. 41.

49. On the unruly woman and 'women on top', see Natalie Zemon Davis, *Society and Culture in Early Modern France* (Stanford, 1975), pp. 124–52.

50. See n. 46 above.

51. *DLJ*, p. 5.

52. On the 'metalanguage' of the bourgeoisie, see Terry Eagleton, *The Rape of Clarissa: Writing, Sexuality, and Class Struggle in Samuel Richardson* (Oxford, 1982), pp. 25, 34–7.

53. *An Essay on the Increase and Decline in Trade* (1749); as quoted by M. D. George, *London Life in the Eighteenth Century* (London, 1925), p. 323 n. 2.

54. George, *London Life*, pp. 110–12; Raymond Williams, *The Country and the City* (New York, 1973), pp. 50–4, 145–7.

55. *The London Daily Advertiser*, 9 Jan. 1752.

56. Letter in *The London Chronicle*, 6 Apr. 1758; written in 1753.

57. *DLJ*, p. 49.

58. 'The Registry Office', No. 135, in Robert Wark, *Drawings by Thomas Rowlandson in the Huntington Collection* (San Marino, Calif., 1975).

59. *The Midwife, or The Old Woman's Magazine* (London, 1753), I. 7.

60. *The Spring-Garden Journal* was conducted by Roxana's eighteen-year-old relation, 'Priscilla Termagant'. It appeared in four weekly numbers from 16 Nov. to 7 Dec. 1752.

61. Of the eight *Adventurer* essays by Thornton, the most interesting for our purposes is No. 9 on the impropriety of signboards. In this essay, Thornton touches on several current concerns of the English art world and in certain ways looks forward to the Sign Painters' Exhibition of 1762. Thornton speaks through the persona of 'Philip Carmine', 'an humble journeyman sign-painter in Harp-alley', and thus all of the opinions expressed are not necessarily serious. Carmine's call for a 'more serious consideration' of the 'monstrous incongruities' of these 'pendant advertisements' seems to be meant ironically, but the following statement that 'the want of taste among my countrymen, and their prejudice against every artist who is

native, have degraded me to the miserable necessity, as Shaftesbury says, "of illustrating prodigies in fairs and adorning sign-posts" ', is a real attack on the connoisseurs who were already being criticized by English artists for neglecting native talent and squandering their money on the 'dark pictures' of the Old Masters. Hogarth was the leader of these anticonnoisseur forces, and he and Thornton were by this time acquaintances, if not close friends. Another of Thornton's *Adventurer* essays, No. 3 on a new pantomime entertainment, is interesting for its catalogue of current London freaks and oddities: a catalogue that finds a close parallel in the mock advertisement in *DLJ*, p. 22.

62. Lams, 'The "A" Papers in the *Adventurer*', *Studies in Philology*, 64 (1967), pp. 83–96. Cf. John Lawrence Abbot, *John Hawkesworth: Eighteenth-Century Man of Letters* (Madison, Wis., 1982), pp. 29–31.

63. *The Progress of Envy* was first published, as far as I can ascertain, in Lloyd's collected *Poems* (1762), pp. 206–21.

64. *The Poetical Works of Charles Churchill*, 2nd edn. (London, 1844), I. xxiii.

65. *Poems* (Baird–Ryskamp), I. 55.

CHAPTER 2

1. *The Connoisseur* (London, 1754–6). The first edition is available on University Microfilms Early British Periodicals series. Numbering is continuous and cited in parentheses in the text.

2. See Stuart Tave, *The Amiable Humorist* (Chicago, 1960).

3. *The Monthly Review*, 41 (May 1757), p. 444.

4. *English Art, 1714–1800* (Oxford, 1976), p. 4.

5. Walter Houghton, 'The English Virtuoso in the Seventeenth Century', *Journal of the History of Ideas*, 3 (1942), pp. 51–73, 190–219; but, for lingering positive usage of the term , see Brownell, *Pope and the Arts of Georgian England, passim.*

6. Richard D. Altick, *The Shows of London* (Cambridge, Mass., 1978), pp. 5–21; Joseph Levine, *Dr. Woodward's Shield* (Berkeley, 1977), *passim.*

7. *Tom Jones*, ed. Fredson Bowers and Martin Battestin (Middleton, Conn., 1975), p. 701.

8. Paulson, *Hogarth*, I. 351.

9. 'The Cit's Country Box', in Lloyd's *Poetical Works*, I. 44 (Lloyd's poems are not numbered by line in this edition.) Goldsmith, *The Citizen of the World* No. 25, in Goldsmith's *Works*, II. 90.

10. Peake, I. 44–5.

11. Peake, I. 42.

12. *Life of Johnson*, I. 420. On the general style of *The Connoisseur* and

The World, see John Butt, *The Mid-Eighteenth Century* (*The Oxford History of English Literature*, VIII; Oxford, 1979), pp. 316–19.

13. Herbert Randolph, *Life of General Sir Robert Wilson* (London, 1862), pp. 13–15; Paulson, *Hogarth*, II. 113–15.

14. Cf. Robert D. Spector, '*The Connoisseur*: a Study in the Functions of a Persona', *English Writers of the Eighteenth-Century*, ed. John H. Middendorf (New York, 1971), pp. 109–21.

15. *Keywords: A Vocabulary of Culture and Society* (New York, 1976), pp. 264–5.

16. See Peter Kivy, *The Seventh Sense: A Study of Francis Hutcheson's Aesthetics and Its Influence in Eighteenth-Century Britain* (New York, 1976), *passim*. For the French context, see R. G. Saisselin, *Taste in Eighteenth-Century France* (Syracuse, 1965), *passim*, and *The Rule of Reason and the Ruses of the Heart* (Cleveland, 1970), pp. 192–202.

17. *Letters Concerning Taste* (London, 1755), p. 3.

18. *Selling Art in Georgian London: The Rise of Arthur Pond* (New Haven, 1983), p. 55.

19. See, for example, Joan Hildreth Owen, 'Philosophy in the Kitchen; or Problems in Eighteenth-Century Culinary Aesthetics', *Eighteenth-Century Life*, 3 (1977), pp. 77–9. Early examples of the food–art equation include the epilogue to William Mountfort's (?) *King Edward the Third, With the Fall of Mortimer Earl of March* (London, 1691) and *The Spectator*, No. 409 (1712).

20. 'The Commercialization of Fashion', in *The Birth of a Consumer Society*, pp. 60–4, 95, *et passim*.

21. Roy Porter, *English Society in the Eighteenth Century* (Harmondsworth, 1982), pp. 218–26.

22. *The Pursuit of Happiness: A View of Life in Georgian England* (New Haven, 1977), p. 4.

23. *The Birth of a Consumer Society*, pp. 9–33; Porter, pp. 206–7.

24. *The Birth of a Consumer Society*, p. 98.

25. 'The Commercialization of Leisure', in *The Birth of a Consumer Society*, p. 273.

26. *Luxury: A Concept in Western Thought, Eden to Smollett* (Baltimore, 1977), p. 78. Cf. Robert D. Spector, *English Literary Periodicals and the Climate of Opinion during the Seven Years' War* (The Hague, 1966), pp. 23–4.

27. For a cogent discussion of the moral and economic theories informing this dispute, see Albert O. Hirschman, *The Passions and the Interests: Political Arguments for Capitalism before Its Triumph* (Princeton, 1977), *passim*.

28. T. W. Perry, *Public Opinion, Propaganda, and Politics in Eighteenth-Century England: a Study of the Jew Bill of 1753* (Cambridge, Mass., 1962);

Roy S. Wolper, 'Circumcision as Polemic in the Jew Bill of 1753: The Cutter Cut?' *Eighteenth-Century Life*, 7 (May 1982), pp. 28–36.

29. See Paulson, *Hogarth*, II. 199–200. Hogarth's series, *The Election*, was based on the Oxford contest.

30. *The Connoisseur*, No. 125 in Chalmers, XXVI. 313–14.

31. Cf. Samuel Johnson, *Preface to Shakespeare* (1765): 'The work of a correct and regular writer is a garden accurately formed and diligently planted, varied with shades, and scented with flowers; the composition of Shakespeare is a forest, in which oaks extend their branches, and pines tower in the air, interspersed sometimes with flowers and brambles, and sometimes giving shelter to myrtles and to roses.'

32. For an example of the more derogatory usage of 'genius', see George Colman, *The Genius*, No. 1, *Prose on Several Occasions*, I. 11–18.

33. In another essay, professional writing is described as 'one of the chief resorts of . . . Lawyers and Physicians without practice. There are, at present, in the world of Authors, Doctors of Physic who (to use the phrase of one of them) have no great fatigue from the business of their profession . . . and several Gentlemen of the Inns of Court, who, instead of driving the quill over skins of parchment, lead it through all the mazes of modern novels, critiques, and pamphlets' (No. 116; 700). See also No. 133 on literary law students.

34. Between 1747 and 1763 Drury Lane staged 29 new mainpieces and 58 new afterpieces. Covent Garden staged 10 new mainpieces and 20 new afterpieces. See George Winchester Stone, Jr. and George M. Kahrl, *David Garrick: A Critical Biography* (Carbondale, 1979), p. 160; and Stone, 'The Making of the Repertory', in *The London Theatre World, 1660–1800*, ed. Robert D. Hume (Carbondale, 1980), pp. 181–209.

35. For perhaps the most complete contemporary description of a pantomime in performance, see *DLJ*, pp. 114–17.

36. This scene was painted by Benjamin Wilson (of the Rembrandt hoax) as *Garrick and Mrs. Bellamy as Romeo and Juliet* (*c.*1752). The painting is now in the possession of the Yale Center for British Art. Cf. Lance Bertelsen, 'David Garrick and English Painting', *Eighteenth-Century Studies*, 11, (1978), pp. 320–4.

37. Suicide was a topic of great interest at mid-century. *The Connoisseur*, No. 50, for example, was reprinted in both *The London Magazine* of Jan. 1755 and *The Gentleman's Magazine* 1754 supplement, and during the same month (Jan. 1755) *The Gentleman's Magazine* ran a mock advertisement for a suicide service. For the intellectual background, see L. G. Crocker, 'The Discussion of Suicide in the 18th Century', *Journal of History of Ideas*, 13 (1952), pp. 47–72.

38. Page makes a rather unconvincing claim that the essays signed 'O' are Thornton's, those signed 'T' Colman's, and those signed 'W'

joint productions, but presents no evidence to support this theory. See *George Colman the Elder*, p. 27.

39. Peake, I. 347–8.

40. The single surviving piece of editorial correspondence is from Colman (who signs himself 'Town') to John Duncombe. It is printed in Peake, I. 49 (see note 45 below).

41. Appendix to *Critical Essays on the Performers of the London Theatres* (London, 1807), pp. 25–6.

42. Spector assumes that with the outbreak of the Seven Years' War it was only natural that 'the *Connoisseur* and the *World,* which had been in existence before the war, but which tended to ignore important occurences for the sake of mildly ironic social commentary, should quickly pass from the scene' (*English Literary Periodicals,* pp. 23–4). Mr Town lends some credence to this view when in No. 94 he admits that 'while this warlike disposition prevails in the nation, I am under some apprehensions, lest the attention of the public should be called off the weighty concerns of these papers' (566). However, John Butt suggests that Colman and Thornton, like John Hawkesworth of *The Adventurer,* might have brought their paper to a close once they had accumulated enough essays to fill a respectable number of bound volumes (*The Mid-Eighteenth Century,* p. 314). *The Connoisseur* appears to have been well received, achieving a reprint rate equal to that of its chief rival *The World* in both *The London Magazine* (*Connoisseur,* 50; *World,* 52) and *The Gentleman's Magazine* (*Connoisseur,* 13; *World,* 13). *The Connoisseur* was reprinted numerous times during the late eighteenth and early nineteenth centuries.

43. *Poems by Eminent Ladies,* ed. George Colman and Bonnell Thornton, 2 vols. (London, 1755), I, p. iii. The volumes were puffed in *The Connoisseur* No. 69.

44. To William Unwin, 6 Apr. 1780, *Letters and Prose Writings,* I. 330; William Hayley, *The Life and Posthumous Writings of William Cowper, Esq.* (Chichester, 1803–4), II. 394; Chalmers, p. xxii; Ryskamp, *Cowper,* p. 115.

45. Colman to Duncombe, in Peake, I. 49. This letter can be dated to the summer of 1755 because of Colman's references to the forthcoming duodecimo edition of *The Connoisseur*: 'we are printing the first four volumes in twelves'. The projected duodecimo edition is announced in *The Connoisseur,* No. 71, 5 June 1755.

46. See, for example, Irvin Ehrenpreis, *The Personality of Jonathan Swift* (Cambridge, Mass., 1958), p. 30.

47. Boyle had inherited the title of the Earl of Cork from Richard Boyle, third Earl of Burlington and fourth Earl of Cork, on the death of the latter in 1753.

48. Lloyd's *Poetical Works,* I. 170.

CHAPTER 3

1. Colman continued to be marginally connected with the law during the period of his transition to the theatre. He occupied chambers in Lincoln's Inn from 1755 to 1764, and travelled the Oxford circuit 'at least four or five times during the years 1758 to 1761'. See Page, pp. 42–3.

2. Colman, *Prose on Several Occasions*, II. 284–90. Lloyd altered and reprinted the poem to help fill out his *Poems* (1762).

3. *The Private Correspondence of David Garrick*, ed. James Boaden, 2 vols. (London, 1832), I. 83.

4. Garrick's *Private Correspondence*, I. 90.

5. Colman's *Works*, IV. 17–18.

6. Colman's *Works*, IV. 22, 54. The references, of course, are to characters in *Tom Jones, Clarissa*, and *Tristram Shandy*.

7. See Richard Bevis, *The Laughing Tradition: Stage Comedy in Garrick's Day* (Athens, Georgia, 1980), p. 115, *et passim*; cf. Robert Hume, 'Forms of Eighteenth-Century Comedy', in *The Stage and the Page: London's 'Whole Show' in the Eighteenth-Century Theatre* (Berkeley, 1981), pp. 6–7, 11–18.

8. Colman's *Works*, IV. 5–6.

9. *Polly Honeycombe* was given an 'indifferent' reception on 5 Dec., primarily because the players had not yet learned their parts. Its reputation grew quickly however, and when George III requested that it be played on 12 Dec. its success was assured. See *The London Stage, 1660–1800*, Part 4, ed. George Winchester Stone, Jr. (Carbondale, 1962), pp. 828–30.

10. Garrick's *Letters*, I. 332.

11. Colman's *Works*, I. 4–5.

12. Emily J. Climenson, *Elizabeth Montagu: The Queen of the Blue Stockings*, 2 vols. (New York, 1906), II. 226.

13. Garrick's *Letters*, I. 332.

14. Colman's *Works*, I. 2.

15. *The Plays of Hugh Kelly*, ed. Larry Carver (New York, 1980), pp. xxiii–xxiv.

16. Garrick's *Letters*, I. 333.

17. Colman's *Works*, I. 23–31.

18. 27 Mar. 1755, Peake, I. 48.

19. 'To George Colman, Esq. A Familiar Epistle Written Jan. 1 1761,' Lloyd's *Poetical Works*, I. 118–19.

20. For the divisions of the theatre audience, see for example, Henry Fielding, *The Tricks of the Town laid open: or, A Companion for the Country Gentleman*, 2nd edn. (London, 1747), pp. 27–8; and *Tom Jones*, p. 326.

21. *The Life of David Garrick, Esq.*, 2 vols. (London, 1801), II. 201. On the eighteenth-century theatre audience, see Leo Hughes, *The Drama's Patrons: A Study in the Eighteenth-Century London Audience* (Austin, 1971), and Harry William Pedicord, *The Theatrical Public in the Time of Garrick* (Carbondale, 1954).

22. Lloyd's *Poetical Works*, I. 10.

23. See William B. Worthen, *The Idea of the Actor: Drama and the Ethics of Performance* (Princeton, 1984), pp. 70–82, *et passim*. My thanks to Bill Worthen for allowing me to read his study in typescript.

24. *An Essay on the Art of Acting* in *Works*, 4 vols. (London, 1753), IV. 356.

25. *Memoirs of the Life of David Garrick*, 2 vols. (London, 1808), I. 349.

26. 10 Aug. 1763, Garrick's *Letters*, I. 382. In this same letter is the implication that Davies left the stage because of Churchill's satire: 'it has indeed been said, that the Stage became disagreeable to you from ye first publication of ye Rosciad, & that you were resolv'd to quit it.' Cf. Boswell, *Life of Johnson*, III. 223.

27. *The Theatrical Review* (1758), pp. 10–11.

28. Davies, I. 356.

29. Davies, I. 349–50.

30. *The Critical Review*, 11 (Mar. 1761), pp. 211–12.

31. Churchill suspected Murphy. See Brown, *Churchill*, p. 52.

32. *The Critical Review*, 11 (Apr. 1761), p. 339.

33. *The Letters of Tobias Smollett*, ed. Lewis Knapp (Oxford, 1970), pp. 97–8.

34. See, for example, Goldsmith's version of the battle in *The Citizen of the World* (14 Apr. 1761), in Goldsmith's *Works*, II. 436.

35. The epigram from which this quotation is taken appeared in *The Public Ledger* on 4 Apr. 1761; quoted in Goldsmith's *Works*, II. 438.

36. Davies, I. 357.

37. Samuel Foote, *Taste*, 2nd version (1761), Huntington Library MS LA 194, p. 2.

38. Weatherly, 'Foote's Revenge on Churchill and Lloyd', *Huntington Library Quarterly*, 9 (1945), p. 52, *et passim*; Brown, *Churchill*, p. 48.

39. *Taste*, p. 17.

40. *c.*May 1761, Garrick's *Letters*, I. 338.

41. Lewis Knapp, *Tobias Smollett: Doctor of Men and Manners* (Princeton, 1949), pp. 52–7.

42. Howard Dunbar, *The Dramatic Career of Arthur Murphy* (New York, 1946), p. 88 n. 1, 107.

43. Murphy, *Garrick*, I. 331.

44. For a more complete list, see J. M. Beatty, 'The Battle of the Players and Poets', *Modern Language Notes*, 34 (1919), pp. 449-61.

45. Murphy, *The Examiner* (London, 1761), p. 11. This poem was originally entitled *The Expostulation*. For Murphy's reasons for changing the title, see Dunbar, p. 118.

46. *The Triumvirate* (London, 1761), pp. 5-6.

47. Colman describes Jacky's 'Genius' as having 'carried him amongst under-actors, under-authors, and women of the town; in which company he soon converted his pertness to assurance, and wonderfully improved his natural talents for lying and defamation. . . . He is also a great writer of anonymous epistles from unknown friends, as well as incendiary letters from secret enemies.' See *Prose on Several Occasions*, I. 67.

48. *The Monthly Review*, 25 (Oct. 1761), p. 319.

49. Garrick's *Letters*, I. 348-9.

CHAPTER 4

1. Besides Joseph Hill and Chase Price—the two most likely candidates—other possible members of the Nonsense Club are listed by Ryskamp in *Cowper*, p. 83 n. 1: '(1) William de Grey by John S. Memes, ed. *The Miscellaneous Works of William Cowper* (Edinburgh, 1834), I. 59—a very unreliable source: see Southey's *Cowper*—accepted by Wright (*Letters*, I. 17), though only "possibly" in *Life* (1921), p. 25; (2) Richard Cumberland—"It is possible, though not probable"—by Stanley T. Williams, *Richard Cumberland* (New Haven, 1917), pp. 13-14. . . . (3) Edward Thurlow—by Memes and Eugene R. Page, *George Colman the Elder* (New York, 1935), p. 41, who bases this on Southey; but Southey nowhere suggests Thurlow, so far as I know.' The Nonsense Club was clearly a rather loosely-structured organization, and greater emphasis should be put on who was associated with the group than on who was actually 'in' it. Thus we know that Hill was present and writing at a meeting although he was not an Old Westminster. Churchill's lack of 'official' membership seems inconsequential in light of his important literary and political connections with the others.

2. *Letters and Prose Writings*, II. 563.

3. To William Unwin, 30 Apr. 1785, *Letters and Prose Writings*, II. 346.

4. To Joseph Hill, 20 Apr. [1777], *Letters and Prose Writings*, I. 268.

5. To Joseph Hill, 3 July 1765, *Letters and Prose Writings*, I. 99. Little is known of James Bensley, the one other certain member of the club. Places and dates are all we have. Bensley was elected with Lloyd from Westminster to Trinity College, Cambridge, in 1751, and after being rusticated for misbehaviour in 1754, returned to take his BA in

1755. He was admitted to the Inner Temple, but in 1756 transferred to Lincoln's Inn. In 1765, he died of injuries sustained while fox hunting. The sketchy record indicates a peripatetic, irresponsible man—living, and dying, for pleasure. Three of Lloyd's poetical epistles are addressed to him. See Ryskamp, *Cowper*, pp. 84–5.

6. Ryskamp, *Cowper*, p. 83.

7. William Combe, *The World As It Goes*, 2nd edn. (London, 1779), p. 27 n.; John Timbs, *Clubs and Club Life in London* (London, 1872), p. 114.

8. Brown, *Churchill*, p. 21, *et passim.*

9. For a cogent summary of Churchill's probable whereabouts between 1750 and 1758, see Churchill's *Poetical Works*, p. xii.

10. *Poems* (Baird-Ryskamp), I. 55.

11. Lloyd's *Poetical Works*, I. 165.

12. Lloyd's *Poetical Works*, II. 154.

13. *Private Correspondence of William Cowper* (London, 1824), I. xxi.

14. *Letters and Prose Writings*, I. 88.

15. *Letters and Prose Writings*, I. 88–9.

16. Ryskamp, *Cowper*, p. 196.

17. On Dullness and owls, see Thomas Faulkner and Rhonda Blair, 'The Classical and Mythographic Sources and Pope's *Dulness*', *Huntington Library Quarterly*, 43 (1980), p. 229.

18. 'A Discourse on the Pindarique Ode', in *The Mourning Bride, Poems, and Miscellanies*, ed. Bonamy Dobree (London, 1928), p. 130.

19. George N. Shuster, *The English Ode from Milton to Keats* (New York, 1940), pp. 146–85; Eric Rothstein, *Restoration and Eighteenth-Century Poetry, 1660–1780* (London, 1981), p. 93; Butt, pp. 65–78.

20. Congreve, 'A Discourse on the Pindarique Ode', p. 332.

21. *The London Magazine*, 29 (June 1760), p. 328.

22. Lloyd's *Poetical Works*, I. 120–8. For a cogent summary of the parallels between Gray's poems and *Two Odes*, see *The Monthly Review*, 23 (July 1760), pp. 57–63.

23. Quotations from Gray's odes are taken from *The Complete Poems of Thomas Gray*, ed. H. W. Stuart and J. R. Hendrickson (Oxford, 1966).

24. *The St. James's Magazine*, 2 (Apr. 1763), pp. 118–25. Cowper's 'Dissertation' seems to have been rather well received: it was reprinted in *The London Chronicle* (30 Apr.–3 May 1763); and twice in *The Public Advertiser* (5 May and 16 Aug. 1763).

25. *The St. James's Magazine*, 3 (Nov. 1763), p. 187. This poem was wrongly assigned to Cowper by Southey, but remains in Cowper's *Poems* (Milford), pp. 288–9; see Ryskamp, *Cowper*, p. 200.

26. *The Monthly Review*, 25 (July 1761), p. 62. See also Lloyd's

review of J. Cunningham's *An Elegy on a Pile of Ruins, The Monthly Review*, 25 (Nov. 1761), p. 328.

27. Boswell, *Life of Johnson*, II. 334–5.

28. *Johnsonian Miscellanies*, ed. G. B. Hill, 2 vols. (Oxford, 1897), II. 320. For an additional discussion of the odes, see Robert Halsband, 'A Parody of Thomas Gray', *Philological Quarterly*, 22 (1943), pp. 256–66.

29. John Nichols, *Illustrations of the Literary History of the Eighteenth Century*, 8 vols. (London, 1848), VII. 275.

30. To Richard Hurd, 17 June 1760, *Letters from a Late Eminent Prelate*, 2nd edn. (London, 1809), p. 305.

31. To William Mason, 22 Mar. 1796, *Horace Walpole's Correspondence*, ed. W. S. Lewis (New Haven, 1937–83), XXIX. 338.

32. 20 June 1760, *The Correspondence of Thomas Gray*, ed. Paget Toynbee and Leonard Whibley, 3 vols. (Oxford, 1935), II. 681.

33. Lloyd's *Poetical Works*, I. 94.

34. Warton's remark is recorded in *The Poetical Works of Thomas Gray*, ed. John Mitford (London, 1853), p. lxvii; Colman's comment is from *Prose on Several Occasions*, I. xi.

35. *The Monthly Review*, 25 (Nov. 1761), p. 328.

36. Lloyd's *Poetical Works*, I, pp. xvi–xvii.

37. 'An Epistle to Robert Lloyd, Esqr.', *Poems* (Baird–Ryskamp), I. 56–7.

38. *The Apology*.

39. *The Apology*.

40. See, for example, *The Rosciad*, ll. 217–26; Grant, Churchill's *Poetical Works*, p. 538 n.; Davies, *Garrick*, I. 325–6.

41. To William Unwin, *c.*Mar. 1780, *Letters and Prose Writings*, I. 320; cf. 'Table Talk', ll. 670–89. See also Morris Golden, 'Churchill's Literary Influence on Cowper', *Journal of English and Germanic Philology*, 58 (1959), pp. 655–65.

42. 'Eighteenth-Century Reflexive Process Poetry', *Eighteenth-Century Studies*, 10 (1976), p. 59.

43. Lloyd's *Poetical Works*, II. 92–3.

44. 'To George Colman, Esq.', Lloyd's *Poetical Works*, I. 111.

45. 'The Author: An Epistle to C. Churchill', Lloyd's *Poetical Works*, II. 18.

46. Cowper, 'An Epistle to Robert Lloyd, Esqr.'.

47. Lloyd's *Poetical Works*, I. 66.

48. 'A Familiar Epistle to J. B., Esq.', Lloyd's *Poetical Works*, II. 37.

49. Lloyd's *Poetical Works*, II. 154. Cowper's later poetry has often been cited for just these qualities; John Butt writes that Cowper 'dispenses with the too prescriptive directions of a literary kind in the

interest of a manner of writing that will allow ample latitude for his individual discursiveness. He will allow his mind to discover its own directions, zigzagging to and fro as one topic prompts another.' See *The Mid-Eighteenth Century*, p. 135.

50. For Byron on Churchill, see 'Churchill's Grave' (1816) in *The Poetical Works of Lord Byron*, ed. E. H. Coleridge (London, 1905), IV. 45–8. Cf. *The Quarterly Review*, 16 (Oct. 1816), pp. 203–4.

51. *The Monthly Review*, 27 (Oct. 1762), p. 316; *The Monthly Review*, 29 (Nov. 1763), p. 397.

52. Actually this suspended comment spans two books. See *The Life and Opinions of Tristram Shandy, Gentleman* (Boston, 1965), pp. 48–75.

53. 'Shakespeare: An Epistle to Mr. Garrick', Lloyd's *Poetical Works*, I. 78–9.

54. *Historical and Biographical Essays*, 2 vols. (London, 1858), II. 248.

55. Thomas Lockwood, *Post-Augustan Satire: Charles Churchill and Satirical Poetry, 1750–1800* (Seattle, 1979), p. 87.

56. *Of the Standard of Taste and Other Essays*, ed. John W. Lenz (New York, 1965), p. 4; cf. Lockwood, pp. 86–7.

57. Cf. Lockwood, pp. 85–6; see also W. C. Brown, 'Charles Churchill and Criticism in Transition', *Journal of English and Germanic Philology*, 43 (1944), pp. 161–9.

58. *London Journal*, p. 192.

59. *The Rambler* No. 125, ed. W. J. Bate and Albrecht Strauss, *The Yale Edition of the Works of Samuel Johnson*, IV (New Haven, 1969), p. 300.

60. Cyril M. Knoblauch, 'Samuel Johnson and the Composing Process', *Eighteenth-Century Studies*, 13 (1980), p. 248.

61. *To the Palace of Wisdom: Studies in Order and Energy from Dryden to Blake* (New York, 1964), p. 386.

62. *From Classic to Romantic* (London, 1946), pp. 93–4.

63. 'The Author's Apology', Lloyd's *Poetical Works*, I. 4.

64. *The Author*, l. 352.

65. Hopkins, *Portraits in Satire* (London, 1958), pp. 22–3; Smith, *Charles Churchill* (Boston, 1977), pp. 36–40.

66. Lloyd's *Poetical Works*, I, p. xxii; cf. Morris Golden, 'Sterility and Eminence in the Poetry of Charles Churchill', *Journal of English and Germanic Philology*, 66 (1967), pp. 333–46.

67. *Historical and Biographical Essays*, II. 219.

68. Lloyd's *Poetical Works*, I. xxi.

69. 'Epistle to the Same [J.B.], 1757', Lloyd's *Poetical Works*, I. 102.

70. 'A Dialogue', Lloyd's *Poetical Works*, II. 4.

71. *Letters and Prose Writings*, I. 90–1.

72. 'The Author's Apology', I. 8.

73. 'The Whim', Lloyd's *Poetical Works*, II. 168–9.

74. Letter to John Wilkes, 15 Oct. 1762, *WCC*, p. 19.

75. Cf. Ryskamp, *Cowper*, p. 45, *et passim*; Cowper, *Adelphi*, in *Letters and Prose Writings*, I. 13–25.

76. *The Monthly Review*, 28 (June 1763), p. 479.

77. 'Genius, Envy, and Time', Lloyd's *Poetical Works*, I. 48–9.

78. *Prose on Several Occasions*, I. 11–12.

79. *Prose on Several Occasions*, I. 17.

80. 'Genius, Envy, and Time', I. 49.

CHAPTER 5

1. *The Yale Edition of the Works of Samuel Johnson*, II (New Haven, 1963), pp. 48–50 n. 2.

2. The Black Friars Bridge was a subject of some controversy. Samuel Johnson wrote three letters to the *Gazetteer* arguing for its construction using the semicircular arches favoured by his friend John Gwyn, rather than the elliptical arches of the winning plan by Robert Mylne. Churchill satirized the bridge's design in *The Ghost* (IV. 1076–80) as another example of Scottish influence in London.

3. Thornton followed *City Latin* with a second pamphlet, *Plain English in Answer to City Latin* (London, 1761), but it is an inferior performance.

4. *City Latin*, 2nd edn. (London, 1761), pp. 24–6.

5. *Poetry and Criticism of Matthew Arnold*, ed. A. D. Culler (Boston, 1961), p. 249.

6. Paulson, *Popular and Polite Art in the Age of Hogarth and Fielding* (Notre Dame, 1979), p. 17.

7. E. P. Thompson, *The Making of the English Working Class* (New York, 1966), p. 60.

8. Cf. Paulson, *Popular and Polite Art*, pp. ix–x.

9. Ian R. Christie, 'British Newspapers in the Later Georgian Age', *Myth and Reality in Late-Eighteenth-Century British Politics and other Papers* (London, 1970), p. 314; Arthur Aspinall, 'Statistical Accounts of London Newspapers in the Eighteenth-Century', *English Historical Review*, 63 (1948), pp. 220–3.

10. The newspaper that carried the Junius letters was Henry Sampson Woodfall's *Public Advertiser*.

11. This was not true of *The Daily Advertiser*, which retained its predominantly commercial orientation and its twelve-column format.

12. Robert L. Haig, *The Gazeteer, 1735–1797: A Study in the Eighteenth-Century English Newspaper* (Carbondale, 1960), pp. 43–5.

13. Bertelsen, 'Have At You All: or, Bonnell Thornton's Journalism', p. 274; cf. Page, p. 71.

14. The Minute-Books of *The St. James's Chronicle*, Book A, Mar.

1761, Southern Historical Collection, Library of the University of North Carolina at Chapel Hill.

15. Southey's *Cowper*, I. 49.

16. See Ch. 6, Section I.

17. Richmond P. Bond and Marjorie N. Bond, 'The Minute Books of the *St. James's Chronicle*', *Studies in Bibliography*, 28 (1975), pp. 17–40, provide a valuable overview of the minute books and correct the entrenched view that Thornton, Colman, and Garrick controlled the paper. But they neglect to mention the substantial contemporary evidence that the paper was considered a mouthpiece for the Nonsense Club, Garrick, and Hogarth.

18. Paulson, *Hogarth*, II. 330, *et passim*.

19. Bond, 'Minute Books', pp. 38–9.

20. *SJC* did not take long to begin turning a profit. By 1763, the investors were earning a gradually increasing dividend.

21. Southey's *Cowper*, I. 54.

22. *Hogarth*, II. 335, *et passim*.

23. *An Epistle to William Hogarth*, ll. 457–62.

24. *SJC*, 17–20 Apr. 1762.

25. For a description of the exhibition, see *The London Register* (Apr. 1762), pp. 345–52. This description was partially reprinted in *SJC*, 29 Apr.–1 May, from which I take my quotations.

26. Paulson, *Hogarth*, II. 347–8.

27. Reprinted in *SJC*, 29 Apr.–1 May 1762. 'Plebian', writing to *SJC* 22–4 Apr., called this picture 'almost equal to Hogarth'.

28. *SJC*, 29 Apr.–1 May 1762.

29. *Popular and Polite Art*, p. 40.

30. Henry Fielding, *The Author's Farce* (London, 1730), air VII; as quoted in Paulson, *Popular and Polite Art*, p. 40. See also Hogarth's illustrations to 'Five Days' Peregrination', Paulson, *Hogarth*, I. 297; these illustrations also appear in *Popular and Polite Art* (plates 18 and 19) with captions reversed.

31. I have suggested that Thornton may be the author of the 'ANTI PERUKIST' letters (10–12 Aug. and 17–19 Aug.) for several reasons: his connection with *SJC*; his wearing of his own hair; his burlesque interest in the symbolic status of wigs, exemplified in his final work, *The Battle of the Wigs* (1768). On the political implications of abandoning one's wig, see Jennifer Harris, 'The Red Cap of Liberty', *Eighteenth-Century Studies*, 14 (1981), pp. 285–7.

32. *SJC*, 29 Apr.–1 May 1762.

33. *SJC*, 29 Apr.–1 May 1762.

34. The print, *The Combat*, is reproduced in Paulson, *Hogarth*, II. 350.

35. This motif figures prominently in a satire on the exhibition

entitled *HA! HA! HA! Or, The Laugher's Companion to the Grand Exhibition of the Sign Painters.* See the advertisement in *SJC*, 29 Apr.–1 May 1762.

36. For the identification of these figures as the Nonsense Club, see Lance Bertelsen, 'New Information on *A Brush for the Sign-Painters'*, *Eighteenth-Century Life*, 7 (1982), pp. 92–6.

37. Paulson, *Hogarth*, II. 352.

38. Letter to Baldwin, 3 June 1762, Beinecke Rare Book and Manuscript Library. Quoted by permission of Yale University. Thornton was accompanying his actor friend, David Ross, to Manchester.

39. See also *PA*, 5 May 1762: 'It is hoped that Ladies and Gentlemen do not take it ill, that no Person can be admitted with the same Catalogue twice; as otherwise it would be impossible to accomodate the Company.'

40. To Henry Seymour Conway, 16 Apr. 1747 OS, *Walpole's Correspondence*, XXXVII. 266. Walpole, of course, refers to the Duke of Cumberland's reputation as the hero (or 'butcher') who defeated the Scottish rebels at Culloden on 16 Apr. 1746; see, for example, Cumberland's reference to the '45' in the upper right-hand corner of *The Boot & The Block-Head* (Fig. 6).

41. Cf. Raymond Williams, *Marxism and Literature*, pp. 36–7; V. N. Volosinov, *Marxism and the Philosophy of Language* (New York, 1973).

42. Satirical prints sometimes provided models for commercial signboards. See Paulson, *Popular and Polite Art*, p. 48.

43. George, *London Life*, pp. 160–1 (see Ch. 1 n. 53 above).

44. Paulson, *Hogarth*, II. 335.

45. On 'carnival' and its socio-political implications, see Mikhail Bakhtin, *Rabelais and His World*, trans. Helene Iswolsky (Cambridge, Mass., 1968), pp. 1–58, *et passim*.

46. *DNB*: Woodfall.

47. *PA*, 12 Apr. 1763.

48. Stephen Botein, Jack R. Censer, and Harriet Ritvo, 'The Periodical Press in Eighteenth-Century English and French Society: A Cross-Cultural Approach', *Comparative Studies in Society and History*, 23 (1981), p. 489. My thanks to Jack Censer for acquainting me with this article.

49. The 'multiplicity of social voices and wide variety of their links and interrelationships (always more or less dialogized)' which Bakhtin stresses as 'the basic distinguishing feature of the stylistics of the novel' is at a less consciously artistic level the basic distinguishing feature of the newspaper. His description of the 'distinctive links and interrelationships between utterances and languages, this movement of the theme through different languages and speech types, its dis-

persion into rivulets and droplets of social heteroglossia' is precisely applicable to the treatment of notable events, political figures, *et al.*, in the juxtaposed columns of the dailies and tri-weeklies. 'Heteroglossia', as defined by Michael Holquist, is the 'base condition governing the operation of meaning in any utterance. It is that which insures the primacy of context over text. At any given time, in any given place, there will be a set of conditions . . . that will insure that a word uttered in that place and at that time will have a meaning different than it would have under any other conditions. . . . Heteroglossia is as close a conceptualization as is possible of that locus where centripetal and centrifugal forces collide; as such, it is that which a systematic linguistics must always suppress.' See M. M. Bakhtin, *The Dialogic Imagination*, ed. Michael Holquist, trans. Caryl Emerson and Michael Holquist (Austin, 1981), pp. 262–3, 428, *et passim*.

50. Cf. Botein *et al.*, p. 469.

51. The early advertisements included a burlesque catalogue of the various performers of the ode: 'The Vocal Parts by Mr. Cromatic, Mr. Demisemiquaver, Mr. Double-Bass, a college Youth, Miss Warble, and Miss Simpletone. The Choral Parts by Queer Figures. The above principal Singers, Chorus Singers, and additional Instrumental Performers, to be drest in suitable Characters.—The following exquisite Instruments, so highly esteemed by the Ancient Greeks and Romans for their amazing Effects on the Human Passions, will be necessarily made use of, and submitted to the Judgment of the Public. First Salt-Box by Mr. Rowling-Pin, First Jews-Harp by Mr. Twang-Lire, First Marrow-Bone and Cleaver by Mr. Ding-Dong, and First Hurdy-Gurdy by Mr. Bladder-Bridge.' See, for example, *PA*, 19 May 1763.

52. *PA*, 26 May 1763.

53. Francis Grose, *A Classical Dictionary of the Vulgar Tongue* (1796), ed. Eric Partridge (New York, 1963), p. 291.

54. Thompson, ' "Rough Music": Le Charivari Anglais', *Annales; économies, sociétés, civilisations* 27 (1972), pp. 285–312; Davis, *Society and Culture in Early Modern France*, p. 123.

55. *PA*, 10 June 1763.

56. *An Ode on Saint Cæcilia's Day* (London, 1763), p. 6.

57. *Ode*, p. 6; *Life of Johnson*, I. 420.

58. *PA*, 10 June 1763.

59. *Ode*, p. 11.

60. *The Concert Tradition* (London, 1965), pp. 141–2.

61. From the account of *SJC*, 9–11 June 1763, it would appear that Arne set the ode for the benefit of his pupil Miss Brent. Churchill, in *The Rosciad*, alludes satirically to their relationship: 'Let him [Arne] reverse kind Nature's first decrees, / And teach e'en BR[EN]T a

method not to please' (719–20). But because of a competing, though rather garbled claim by Charles Burney, the question of who set the ode remains unresolved. See Roger Lonsdale, *Dr. Charles Burney* (Oxford, 1965), pp. 486–90.

62. See, for example, Hogarth's *The Times*, plate 1; *Industry and Idleness*, plate 6; and the letter from Wilkes's supposed 'butcher' in *PA*, 13 May 1763. Grose writes that the marrow bones and cleavers were 'principal instruments in the band of rough music' (pp. 229–30).

CHAPTER 6

1. Captain Edward Thompson, Manuscript notes (private collection); quoted by Page, p. 75.

2. See, for example, the letter of 23 Aug. 1764 from Garrick to his brother: "I don't like ye wench . . . & yet would not offend Colman, who I fear will be much harrass'd wth her—an Idiot" (Garrick's *Letters*, II. 423).

3. *A Biographical Dictionary of Actors . . . in London, 1660–1800*, ed. Philip H. Highfil, Jr., Kalman A. Burnim, and Edward A. Langhans, (Carbondale, 1973–), III. 409.

4. Boswell, *Life of Johnson*, III. 148–9.

5. *The St. James's Magazine*, 1 (Sep. 1762), p. 4. The poem is reprinted in Lloyd's *Poetical Works*, I. 175–81, from which I take my quotations.

6. *The St. James's Magazine*, 1 (Sept. 1762), p. vi.

7. *The St. James's Magazine*, 2 (Apr. 1763), pp. 113–18.

8. *The St. James's Magazine*, 1 (Feb. 1763), p. 375.

9. *Prose on Several Occasions*, I. xiv.

10. George Nobbe, *The North Briton: A Study in Political Propaganda* (New York, 1939), pp. 13–14.

11. See Louis Jones, *The Clubs of the Georgian Rakes* (New York, 1942), pp. 116–41.

12. Wilkes's notes in *Correspondence*, III. 60–4, represent the most authentic description we have of the group. But see also the fictional account in Charles Johnstone, *Chrysal* (London, 1765).

13. Churchill to Wilkes, 13 July 1762, *WCC*, p. 6.

14. *c.*12 Nov. 1762, *WCC*, p. 33.

15. Houghton Library MS fms Eng 870 p. 63. All quotations from Houghton Library MSS by permission of the Houghton Library.

16. *c.*10 Sept. 1762, *WCC*, pp. 15–16.

17. *c.*13 Dec. 1762, *WCC*, p. 38.

18. *c.*6 Nov.1763, *WCC*, p. 75.

19. Weatherly tentatively dates this letter 16 Mar. 1763 (*WCC*, p. 48), but it seems much more likely that it dates from May—after Hogarth's print of Wilkes had appeared. Moreover, Churchill's

references to his gonorrhea and Mrs. J. would seem to put the letter very close in time to another epistle also mentioning the woman and the disease which Weatherly dates May (p. 52), and which I believe was written in either late May or early June. Douglas Grant dates both letters from the period following Hogarth's print of Wilkes. See Churchill's *Poetical Works*, p. 518.

20. *c*.May 1763, *WCC*, pp. 54–5.

21. Lloyd's *Poetical Works*, I. 192.

22. For prints and satires against the Scots, see Atherton, pp. 209–16 (see Ch. 1 n. 2 above); Carretta, pp. 227–47; and *Catalogue of Prints and Drawings in the British Museum: Division I, Political and Personal Satires*, ed. Frederick George Stephens and Edward Hawkins (London, 1883), IV. pp. lxiii–lxxxi. For Bute's reputation, see John Brewer, 'The Misfortunes of Lord Bute: A Case-Study in Eighteenth-Century Political Argument and Public Opinion', *The Historical Journal*, 16 (1973), pp. 3–43.

23. An illuminating discussion of the politics and propaganda of this era is John Brewer, *Party Ideology*. For the period immediately preceding that covered by Brewer, see Marie Peters, *Pitt and Popularity: The Patriot Minister and London Opinion during the Seven Years' War* (Oxford, 1980).

24. To John Dell, 15 Jan. 1754, Wilkes–Dell Correspondence, Aylesbury Museum; quoted by George Rudé, *Wilkes and Liberty: A Social Study, 1760–1774* (Oxford, 1962), p. 18.

25. Campbell to Bute, 5 June 1762, Bute MSS, Mount Stuart; quoted by Brewer, *Party Ideology*, p. 222.

26. Peters, p. 15.

27. For the redefinition of the terms 'Whig' and 'Tory', see Brewer, *Party Ideology*, pp. 39–54.

28. Peters, p. 241.

29. *The Briton* (London, 1762–63), p. 3.

30. On Churchill's receiving 'the profits arising from the sale', see Wilkes's *Correspondence*, I. 99.

31. *SJC*, 3–5 June 1762.

32. Sekora, pp. 155–211 (see Ch. 2 n. 26 above), explains Smollett's position in the context of traditional attacks on luxury; but he does not, to my mind, justify it.

33. Cf. Sekora, pp. 195–200.

34. *The Grenville Papers*, ed. W. J. Smith, 4 vols. (London, 1852–3), I. 457.

35. The Bute–Mortimer parallel was a typical example of the traditional use of exemplar history in political propaganda. The analogy had been used against Walpole in 1731 when the revised play, *The Fall of Mortimer*, was performed and then suppressed because of its

blatantly propagandistic theme. Mortimer and Isabella—Edward II's queen—were of course lovers who took England from Edward II and eventually had the king murdered. Isabella's son, Edward III, succeeded to the throne but was kept under the control of Mortimer and Isabella: an analogy opposition propagandists found particularly appropriate to the situation of young George III under the alleged spell of the Princess Dowager and Bute. Edward III's eventual overthrow of Mortimer was held up as a model for the young king, while the salacious implications of the 'affair' between Bute and the Princess became a favourite propaganda theme. As far as I can ascertain, *The North Briton*, No. 5 marks the first use of the analogy against Bute.

36. Rumours of the 'affair' had begun in the 1750s among those jealous of Bute's influence at Leicester House. The Prince of Wales first learned of the rumours in 1756 and wrote a letter to Bute promising to defend him against all such 'malice' and to 'remember the insults done to my mother, and never forgive anyone who shall offer to speak disrespectfully of her'. See *Letters from George III to Lord Bute, 1756–1766*, ed. Romney Sedgwick (London, 1939), pp. 3–4. For the prints on Mortimer/Bute, see BM *Catalogue*, Nos. 3867, 3966, 4048, 4150, 4442.

37. Wilkes's boldness in this attack earned him the lasting animosity of the king and those close to him. Horace Walpole summed up the reaction of the court and administration to *The North Briton*, No. 5: 'One of the first numbers was one of the most outrageous, the theme taken from the loves of Queen Isabella and Mortimer. No doubt but it lay open enough to prosecution, and the intention was to seize the author. But on reflection it was not thought advisable to enter on the discussion of such a subject in Westminster-hall; and, as the daring audaciousness of the writer promised little decorum, it was held prudent to wait till he should furnish a less delicate handle to vengeance: a circumspection that deceived and fell heavy on the author, who, being advised to more caution in his compositions, replied, he had tried the temper of the Court by the paper on Mortimer, and found they did not dare touch him.' *Memoirs of the Reign of King George the Third*, ed. G. F. Russell Barker, 4 vols. (London, 1894), I. 141.

38. Neil Schaeffer, 'Charles Churchill's Political Journalism', *Eighteenth-Century Studies*, 9 (1976), p. 410.

39. 15 June 1762, *WCC*, pp. 36–7.

40. 27 July 1762, *WCC*, p. 10.

41. Paulson, *Hogarth*, II. 361, suggests that this print was executed in anticipation of Hogarth's *The Times*, plate 1, in order that the fire motif of Hogarth's print might seem a plagiarism.

42. *The North Briton*, No. 7 (17 July 1762); Schaeffer, p. 414. Bute was installed in the Order of the Garter on 22 Sept. 1762.

43. *c*.14 Mar. 1763, *WCC*, p. 47.

44. 23 Oct. 1762, *WCC*, p. 24.

45. The best overview of these contrasting, and sometimes complementary points of view is in Brewer, *Party Ideology*, pp. 26–35. For the classic statements of the contrasting cases, see Sir Lewis Namier, *The Structure of Politics at the Accession of George III*, 2nd edn. (London, 1957) and Sir Herbert Butterfield, *George III and the Historians* (London, 1957).

46. 2, 5 Dec. 1762, *WCC*, pp. 36–7.

47. Among Hogarth's friends was Samuel Martin, who would later seriously wound Wilkes in a duel over the contents of *North Briton*, No. 40.

48. William Hogarth, Autobiographical Notes (unpublished version), p. 226; as quoted by Paulson, *Hogarth*, II. 363.

49. Paulson, *Hogarth*, II. 365.

50. Wilkes's *Correspondence*, III. 24.

51. A wooden fleur-de-lis (described as 'tarnished') appeared in the Sign Painters' Exhibition as No. 18 among the 'Busts, Carved Figures, &c.'

52. *WCC*, p. 15.

53. Hyde Collection; as quoted by Paulson, *Hogarth*, II. 374.

54. *The North Briton*, p. 102. Wilkes may have written No. 17 before Hogarth's print appeared. A note from Wilkes to Kearsly of 29 Aug. reads: 'Hogarth has a political Print which I am impatient to see—I am left Out, but he has Abus'd my dear friends Pitt and Lord Temple —I will therefore send you the best wrote N.B. I have been concern'd in, to pay my Compliments to him, as soon as ever the print appears' (Add. MS 22132, fo. 93^v).

55. Autobiographical Notes, p. 221 (see n. 48 above).

56. Add. MS 22132, fo. 94^r. Throughout this study I have used the spelling 'Kearsly' rather than the usual 'Kearsley' because George Kearsly himself used that spelling on all of his imprints and advertisements.

57. Add. MS 22132, fo. 90^v.

58. *WCC*, pp. 10–11.

59. Add. MS 30867.

60. *The Briton*, No. 13 (1762), p. 77.

61. 22, 24 Nov. 1762, *WCC*, pp. 34–5.

62. Houghton Library MS pfms Eng 131, p. 51.

63. Both the 'North Briton Extraordinary' and the 'Auditor Extraordinary' are reprinted in *Prose on Several Occasions*, II. 18–32.

64. In *The North Briton*, No. 30 (25 Dec. 1762), Wilkes and Churchill

tacitly admit that they wrote the letter: '*The* NORTH BRITON *presents his compliments to the* AUDITOR, *and returns his best thanks for the insertion of the letter concerning* FLORIDA, *signed* VIATOR, *in his last Paper, and for the* full credit *he has given to the several facts it contains.*'

65. As reprinted in *SJC*, 18–21 Dec. 1762.

66. *SJC*, 23–25 Dec. 1762.

67. *SJC*, 17–19 Mar. 1762.

68. Add. MS 22132, fo 91^v.

69. *PA*, 11 Apr. 1763.

70. On these possible consultations, see Nobbe, pp. 207–8.

71. Robert Rea, *The English Press in Politics, 1760–1774* (Lincoln, Nebraska, 1963), p. 43.

72. Add. MS 30883, fos. 45^v, 46^r.

73. Wilkes's *Correspondence*, II. 199–200. After being interrogated at Lord Halifax's house Wilkes was confined in the Tower of London. His insistence on obtaining a writ of habeas corpus from the Court of Common Pleas (presided over by the sympathetic Chief Justice Charles Pratt) delayed the granting of the writ and resulted in Wilkes's spending two days in close confinement with no visitors: a fact that was later made much of by Wilkes and his allies. At 7 p.m. on Monday, 2 May, his friends and counsellors were at last allowed to see him. An officer on duty that evening reported on the 'Insolence and Licentiousness of Mr. Wilkes Freinds', who were 'very disrespectful to the Crown and Unfit for a Royal Garrison'. (Add. MS 22132, fo. 86^r.) O. A. Sherrard, in *A Life of John Wilkes* (London, 1930), pp. 91–102, has suggested that an elaborate conspiracy existed between Pitt, Temple, Wilkes, Pratt, and the King's Messengers to have Wilkes arrested and brought before Pratt in Common Pleas. The theory remains unproved. For an administration's-eye view of these goings-on, see Phillip Lawson, *George Grenville: A Political Life* (Oxford, 1984), pp. 166–80.

74. *PA*, 2 May 1763, p. 2.

75. *PA*, 4 May 1763, p. 2.

76. *PA*, 7 May 1763, pp. 1–2.

77. *PA*, 7 May 1763.

78. Portland to Newcastle, 6 May 1763, Add. MS 32948, fo. 238^r.

79. George Onslow to Newcastle, 6 May 1763, Add. MS 32948, fos. 234^v–235^r; Rudé, *Wilkes and Liberty*, p. 27.

80. Wilkes's *Correspondence*, III. 26.

81. Speck, *Stability and Strife: England, 1714–1760* (Cambridge, Mass., 1977), p. 147.

82. Brewer, *Party Ideology*, p. 6; Porter, pp. 126–7.

83. Robert Wallace, *The Characteristics of the Present Political State of Great Britain* (London, 1758); as quoted by Speck, p. 20.

84. See John B. Owen, 'George II Reconsidered', in *Statesmen, Scholars, Merchants: Essays in Eighteenth-Century History Presented to Dame Lucy Sutherland* (Oxford, 1973), pp. 113–34.

85. Peters, pp. 143–52.

86. The 'massacre of the Pelhamite Innocents' refers to Bute's wholesale sacking of those Old Corps placemen who had failed to support the preliminaries of the peace. See Namier, *England in the Age of the American Revolution*, 2nd edn. (New York, 1966), pp. 403–14.

87. See Brewer, *Party Ideology*, pp. 26–35, *et passim*.

88. Carretta, pp. 173–210. Walpole to Horace Mann, 21 Mar. 1746, Walpole's *Correspondence*, XXIX. 229.

89. Add. MS 27780, fo. 2^r.

90. Add. MS 27780, fo. 1^r. 'Father' is Henry Woodfall, who still took an active interest in the family business. On paid advertisements as a vehicle of propaganda, cf. Smollett, *Humphry Clinker* (London, 1966), p. 102: 'the public papers are become infamous vehicles of the most cruel and perfidious defamation: every rancorous knave—every desperate incendiary, that can afford to spend half a crown or three shillings, may skulk behind the press of a newsmonger, and have a stab at the first character in the kingdom, without running the least hazard of detection or punishment.' *The Public Advertiser*'s rate for advertisements was three shillings.

91. James M. Osborn Collection. Beinecke Library, Yale University. ·

92. *London Journal*, p. 266. See above, Introduction p. 1. Thornton had favourably reviewed the Erskine–Boswell correspondence in *PA*, 15 and 19 Apr. 1763.

93. Osborn Collection.

94. Add. MS 30867.

95. *PA*, 2 June 1763. An abridged version of this letter was published as part of Wilkes's notes to Churchill's poems. See Wilkes's *Correspondence*, III. 55–9.

96. Robert Halsband conjectured that Lloyd was adapting part of La Condamine's *Histoire d'une jeune fille sauvage, trouvée dans les bois à l'âge de dix ans* (1755) into a satire on the Scots. La Condamine was a French traveller and geographer, who had travelled extensively in South America.

97. John Timbs, *Club Life in London* (London, 1866), I. 133; Brown, pp. 70–1.

98. Wilkes to Temple, 5 June 1763, *Grenville Papers*, II. 59.

99. *WCC*, p. 56. See above, Section I of this chapter. Wilkes and Churchill's whereabouts during the months of May and June are difficult to determine. It is clear that they spent a good deal of time outside London, though just how much is uncertain. Grant,

Churchill's *Poetical Works*, p. 518, says that Churchill was in Aylesbury from 6 May to 7 June—yet Boswell saw Churchill in London on 24 May (*London Journal*, p. 266). Weatherly, *WCC*, p. 52, states that Churchill spent all of June in Aylesbury, but again Boswell saw Churchill in London on 20 and 25 June. Churchill and Wilkes seem to have travelled very frequently between London and Aylesbury during these months.

100. *WCC*, p. 55.

101. Boswell to David Dalrymple, 25 June 1763, *The Letters of James Boswell*, ed. C. B. Tinker (Oxford, 1924), I. 13; *PA*, 22, 28 June 1763.

102. See Mary Clare Randolph, 'Candour in Eighteenth-Century Satire', *Review of English Studies*, 20 (1944), 45–62.

103. 10 July 1763, Garrick's *Letters*, I. 378.

104. Paulson, *Hogarth*, II. 393.

105. *The London Chronicle*, 14–16 July 1763.

106. *The London Chronicle*, 14–16 July 1763. Churchill advertised a satire entitled *Encaenia* in *Jackson's Oxford Journal*, 9 July 1763, but the poem never appeared. Churchill includes attacks on Oxford and Cambridge in *The Candidate*.

107. *SJC*, 7–9 July 1763.

108. *Prose on Several Occasions*, I. 237–9.

109. *c.*11 July 1763, Private Papers of James Boswell, Yale University Library MSS. Ryskamp tentatively dates this letter 25 July (*Cowper*, p. 146 n. 1). I believe 11 July is a more plausible date because Thornton, who had been in Oxford since 6 July, returned to town and then left again for Aylesbury, where he arrived on Wednesday, 13 July 1763 (see below).

110. *Grenville Papers*, II. 76–7.

CHAPTER 7

1. Huntington Library MS HM 22782.

2. *The Parliamentary or Constitutional History of England* (London, 1751), III. 186–9. This work, 'by Several Hands', appeared in increments. In an advertisement in *PA*, 21 Jan. 1754, the publishers Thomas Osborne and William Sandby announced five volumes just published in addition to eight already available. Twenty-four volumes eventually appeared.

3. *The London Magazine*, 32 (Dec. 1763), p. 653; Wilkes's *Correspondence*, II. 12–18; Walpole, *Memoirs of the Reign of King George the Third*, I. 252–3.

4. *WCC*, pp. 73–4.

5. *WCC*, p. 75. There were reports that Elizabeth Carr was the

daughter of the sculptor, Sir Henry Cheere, but no definite link has been established. See Brown, *Churchill*, pp. 78–80.

6. Add. MS 30865B, fos. 19ʳ–20ʳ.

7. Page, pp. 96–8.

8. Chalmers, XXV, pp. xxxi–xxxii.

9. Lloyd's *Poetical Works*, I, pp. xiv, xvii.

10. Among Boswell's papers from Holland, 1763–4; quoted in Ryskamp, *Cowper*, p. 90.

11. Lloyd's *Poetical Works*, II. 135–6.

12. Lloyd's *Poetical Works*, II. 143. On 13 Mar. Lloyd wrote a letter to Lord Hardwicke asking that he be released in order to attend the election at Cambridge. See Add. MS 35657. fo. 50ʳ.

13. Lloyd's *Poetical Works*, I, p. xxv.

14. *Southey's Cowper*, I. 104, n. 32; cf. Austin Dobson, *At Prior Park and Other Papers* (London, 1912), pp. 235–43.

15. 'A Familiar Epistle to J. B., Esq.', Lloyd's *Poetical Works*, II. 50. The poem originally appeared in *The St. James's Magazine*, 1 (Oct. 1762), 81–91.

16. 20 Nov. 1764, Add. MS 30868, fo. 147ʳ.

17. Draft agreement between Churchill, Kearsly, and Flexney; Osborn Collection, Beinecke Rare Book and Manuscript Library. Quoted by permission of Yale University.

18. Letter to Flexney, Beinecke Library. Quoted by permission of Yale University. The final two digits of the date are illegible but no year other than 1764 seems possible. Many contemporary rumours put Churchill in France in Dec. 1763–Jan. 1764. See Brown, *Churchill*, pp. 182–3.

19. For the issues of Wilkes vs. Wood, see Rea, pp. 68–9.

20. Add. MS 23218, fo. 112ʳ; quoted by Brown, p. 182.

21. See, for example, the report of Wilkes's death on *SJC*, 25–7 Aug. 1763, and the copies of letters concerning the challenge in *SJC*, 24–7 and 27–9 Sept. 1763.

22. Letter to Wilkes, 7 Dec. 1763; as transcribed in *SJC*, 10–13 Dec. 1763. Matt Darly sent the warning note to Wilkes immediately after having overheard Dunn.

23. For a stimulating but controversial discussion of the role of law as ideology in eighteenth-century England, see Douglas Hay, Peter Linebaugh, John G. Rule, E. P. Thompson, and Cal Winslow, *Albion's Fatal Tree: Crime and Society in Eighteenth-Century England* (New York, 1975), pp. 17–63, *et passim*.

24. 'Sterne, Warburton, and the Burden of Exuberant Wit', *Eighteenth-Century Studies*, 15 (1982), pp. 245–6. The term 'Dictator' is Edward Gibbon's; see *Memoirs of My Life*, ed. George A. Bonnard (London, 1966), pp. 144–5.

25. Cf. Brewer, *The Birth of a Consumer Society*, pp. 219–20, *et passim*; 'English Radicalism in the Age of George III', in *Three British Revolutions: 1641, 1688, 1776*, ed. J. G. A. Pocock (Princeton, 1980), pp. 345–6.

26. Brewer, 'English Radicalism', p. 345; cf. James E. Bradley, 'Whigs and Nonconformists', *Eighteenth-Century Studies*, 9 (1975), p. 25 n. 86.

27. See, for example, Smith, p. 97; Brown, p. 146. Churchill appears to have begun *Gotham* as early as Feb. 1763; see *WCC*, p. 44.

28. *London Journal*, p. 299.

29. W. Davenport Adams in *Old Nottinghamshire*, ed. John Potter Briscoe (London, 1884), p. 111.

30. On inverted behaviour as a form of popular resistance, see, for example, *The Reversible World: Symbolic Inversion in Art and Society*, ed. Barbara Babcock (Ithaca, 1978), pp. 39–116.

31. William Home, *The Every-day Book*, 2 vols. (London, 1825–7), II. 819–66; as quoted in Brewer, *The Birth of a Consumer Society*, p. 242.

32. For the material on the election of the mayor of Garret, I am indebted to Brewer, *The Birth of a Consumer Society*, pp. 242–3, *et passim*. Brewer, however, mistakenly records the first performance of *The Mayor of Garret* as having taken place in 1764.

33. Brewer, *The Birth of a Consumer Society*, pp. 203–62; 'The Number 45: A Wilkite Political Symbol', in *England's Rise to Greatness, 1660–1763*, ed. Stephen Baxter (Berkeley, 1983), pp. 349–80.

34. Brewer, *Party Ideology*, p. 185.

35. Brewer, *Party Ideology*, p. 190. The ritualized rebellion of carnival or saturnalia, of course, may act both to criticize and strengthen the established order through the irreverent mimicry of the rituals and forms of authority. Wilkite crowds, for example, were notable for their insistence both on liberty and loyalty to the Crown. Wilkes and Churchill likewise protested that they were loyal to the king and were only trying to save him from his corrupt ministers. Cf. Davis, p. 123; William Willeford, *The Fool and His Sceptre* (Evanston, Ill., 1969), pp. 226–7.

36. Isaac Kramnick, *Bolingbroke and His Circle: The Politics of Nostalgia in the Age of Walpole* (Cambridge, Mass., 1968); Quentin Skinner, 'The Principles and Practice of Opposition: The Case of Bolingbroke versus Walpole', in *Historical Perspectives: Studies in English Thought and Society in Honour of J. H. Plumb*, ed. Neil McKendrick (London, 1974), pp. 93–128; Carretta, pp. 33–61.

37. *The Idea of a Patriot King*, ed. Sydney W. Jackman (New York, 1965), pp. 45, 50.

38. Jeffrey Hart, *Viscount Bolingbroke: Tory Humanist* (London, 1965), p. 109.

39. George III, 'Memorandum', n.d., Royal Archives, Windsor, RA 15672; as quoted by Sir Herbert Butterfield, *George III, Lord North, and the People, 1779–80* (London, 1949), p. 3.

40. *The London Gazette* (Jan. 1763); as quoted in Thompson, 'The Crime of Anonymity', *Albion's Fatal Tree*, p. 276; cf. Thompson, *Whigs and Hunters: The Origin of the Black Art* (New York, 1975), *passim*.

41. *Madness and Civilization* (New York, 1973), p. 214.

42. Michael Holquist defines the socio-linguistic relationship that Bakhtin calls 'dialogism': 'Dialogism is the characteristic epistemological mode of a world dominated by heteroglossia. Everything means, is understood, as a part of a greater whole—there is a constant interaction between meanings, all of which have the potential of conditioning others. Which will affect the other, how it will do so and in what degree is actually settled at the moment of utterance.' *The Dialogic Imagination*, p. 426.

43. *Man's Rage for Chaos: Biology, Behavior, and the Arts* (New York, 1967), p. 314.

44. *Party Ideology*, p. 33.

45. See, for example, Grant, p. 553; Smith, p. 111.

46. The description is from Samuel Johnson, 'The Life of Lyttleton', *The Works of Samuel Johnson L.L.D.*, ed. Arthur Murphy (London, 1854), I. 362.

47. See Grant, p. 553.

48. See *DNB*, 'Pitt' and 'Lyttleton'; O. A. Sherrard, *Lord Chatham and America* (London, 1938), pp. 132–3.

49. For Wilkes's response and later opinion of Pitt, see the letter from Wilkes to the Duke of Grafton, 12 Dec. 1767, in Wilkes's *Correspondence*, III. 190–3. For a summary of the contrasting personalities of Wilkes and Pitt, see Sherrard, *Chatham*, p. 99.

50. See John Timbs, *Anecdote Lives of William Pitt, Earl of Chatham and Edmund Burke* (London, 1880), pp. 114–18, 130–8; cf. Basil Williams, *The Life of William Pitt, Earl of Chatham*, 2 vols. (London, 1913), II. 149.

51. Atherton, pp. 257–8 (see Ch. 1 n. 2 above). Pitt, although known as the 'Great Commoner', was notorious for his aristocratic hauteur and class consciousness, his personal irritability and ostentation. See, for example, A. S. Tuberville, *English Men and Manners in the 18th Century*, 2nd edn. (New York, 1967), p. 268; Sherrard, *Chatham*, p. 99.

52. Cf. Alexander Pope, *The Dunciad Variorum*, on the Lord Mayor's Procession: 'Glad chains, warm furs, broad banners, and broad faces' (I. 86).

53. Arbuthnot, *Law is a Bottomless-Pit* (London, 1712) and *John Bull*

Still in His Senses (London, 1712) in *The History of John Bull*, ed. Alan W. Bower and Robert A. Erickson (Oxford, 1976), pp. 9, 49.

54. See, for example, *SJC*, 23–5 Apr. 1761.

55. See, for example, *The Patriot Poet* (London, 1763), p. 32; *Churchill Defended* (London, 1765), pp. 13–15.

56. See Victor Turner, *The Forest of Symbols: Aspects of Ndembu Ritual* (Ithaca, 1967), p. 106; *Dramas, Fields, and Metaphors: Symbolic Action in Human Society* (Ithaca, 1974), p. 255; *The Ritual Process: Structure and Anti-Structure* (Ithaca, 1969), pp. 95–102.

57. Harold Bloom, 'The Breaking of Form', in *Deconstruction and Criticism* (New York, 1979), p. 3.

58. Cf. E. J. Hobsbawn on the 'social bandit': 'one of the chief attractions of the bandit was . . . that he is a poor boy who had made good, a surrogate for the failure of the mass to lift itself out of its own poverty, helplessness and meekness. Paradoxically therefore the conspicuous expenditure of the bandit, like the gold-plated Cadillacs and diamond-inlaid teeth of the slum boy who had become world boxing champion, serves to link him to his admirers and not separate him from them.' See *Primitive Rebels* (New York, 1959), p. 22.

59. Joseph Beatty, 'The Political Satires of Charles Churchill', *Studies in Philology*, 16 (1919), p. 308.

60. Churchill's enemies recognized the mixed nature of his audience clearly. See, for example, *The Patriot Poet* (London, 1763):

> If he but bawls for freedom—in a trice
> Commences patriot pure from ev'ry vice.
> Coblers, and all the brethren of the jacket,
> Huzza their champion, and enjoy the racket . . .
> The *city*, on *illiterate wealth's* pretence
> Assuming the prerogative of sense,
> Claiming, forsooth! *prescriptive right to low'r*,
> When her *vast sapience* dictates not to power.
> Auguments the tumult, ready, at command,
> To break o'er law in ruin on the land. (p. 31)

Cf. *Clodius, A Poem, Addressed to C. Churchill and the Writers in the Opposition* (London, 1764), which describes Wilkes and Churchill's supporters as 'the men, a common-council nam'd, / In London environs most justly fam'd / For wisdom and affection to the King, / Ready to set him right in every thing', (p. 13) and 'tribes of tradesmen', 'Foggers', 'Independent Whigs, True Englishmen / All furious to promote the faction's plan' (pp. 15, 21).

61. Churchill, *Independence* (London, 1764) with Thornton's notes in the margin. Beinecke Library, Yale University.

62. Cf. Frederic Jameson, *Marxism and Form* (Princeton, 1972), pp. 11, 335–57, *et passim*.

63. *The Monthly Review*, 31 (1764), p. 271.

64. I allude here, with tongue only slightly in cheek, to the criticism of Bertolt Brecht and Walter Benjamin. Brecht's emphasis on the necessity of discontinuity, internal contradiction, and rapid transition as ways of preventing illusion and encouraging in the audience a 'complex seeing' of his plays calls to mind the more radical elements of Churchill's poetic technique. Benjamin's analysis of the discontinuous 'shocks' with which modern urban society bombards the consciousness—crowds, advertisements, traffic, a montage of rapidly changing images—suggests the possible effects of the jostling crowds of the London streets (so vividly recorded by Lichtenberg, pp. 44–5, 64–5) on Churchill's poetic rhythm. Here, for example, is Benjamin's description of the experience of a modern city: 'Moving through this traffic involves the individual in a series of shocks and collisions. At dangerous intersections, nervous impulses flow through him in rapid succession, like the energy from a battery. Baudelaire speaks of a man who plunges into the crowd as into a reservoir of electric energy. Circumscribing the experience of the shock, he calls this man, "a *kaleidoscope* equipped with consciousness" '. I would suggest that in Churchill's 'nervous', discontinuous, kaleidoscopic poetry we may apprehend the incipient rhythm of an age about to be born. See Walter Benjamin, *Illuminations*, ed. Hannah Arendt (New York, 1978), pp. 174–5.

65. *A Glossary of Literary Terms*, 4th edn. (New York, 1981), p. 40.

66. Garrick's *Letters*, I. 412.

67. Lloyd's *Poetical Works*, I, p. xxxiii.

68. See Brown, *Churchill*, pp. 198–203.

69. Churchill left mourning rings to the Duke of Grafton, Earl and Countess Temple, Wilkes, Humphrey Cotes, Robert Lloyd, and Mr Walsh, the merchant in whose house he died. See Brown, *Churchill*, pp. 192–200; for the will, see Grant, Churchill's *Poetical Works*, p. xx.

70. Add. MS 30868, fo. 147[r].

71. Lloyd may have been attended in his last illness by Churchill's sister Patience ('Patty'). The traditional story is that Lloyd, upon hearing of Churchill's death, said, 'I shall follow poor Charles', took to his bed and died. For Lloyd's relationship with Patty Churchill, see Brown, *Churchill*, p. 185.

72. The sermons were possibly Churchill's father's; see Peake, I. 155–6. *The Critical Review*, 19 (1765) remarked that this 'dedication, we suppose, was intended to promote the sale of the book; as a piece of cork may be sometimes made use of to prevent a heavy body from sinking' (p. 117).

73. Although the dedication does not contain the word 'panegyric' in its title, the term does occur in line 10: 'But truth, *my Lord,* is panegyric here'. As James Garrison has shown, by mid-century 'panegyric' had come 'generically to imply its opposite, satire': thus the mere use of the term would have prepared Churchill's reader for mock or inverted praise. See Garrison, *Dryden and the Tradition of Panegyric* (Berkeley, 1975), pp. 15–18, 35–7.

74. Cf. Alan Fisher, 'The Stretching of Augustan Satire: Charles Churchill's "Dedication" to Warburton', *Journal of English and Germanic Philology*, 72 (1973), pp. 372–3; Yvor Winters, *Forms of Discovery* (Denver, 1967), pp. 131–45.

75. Churchill's continuing suspicion of all grandees—even those in the Parliamentary Minority who supposedly supported Wilkes—is exemplified by John Almon's report to Lord Temple (12 Nov. 1764) that before his death Churchill 'was very much out of humour with the Minority, and intended very soon to attack some of them upon their *moderation,* in a poem to have been called *Moderation,* inscribed to Mr Pitt'. Almon then vividly summarizes the opposition's attitude toward Churchill: 'yet his death will be felt as a real loss, for the public admired his writings, and whatever he might have said of the Minority, he would certainly have said much worse of the Ministry'. *Grenville Papers,* II. 459 (see Ch. 6 n. 34 above).

CHAPTER 8

1. J. Barzun, *Classic, Romantic, and Modern* (Chicago, 1961; repr. 1975), p. xv.

2. R. R. Palmer, *The Age of Democratic Revolution: A Political History of Europe and America, 1760–1800,* 2 vols. (Princeton, 1959–64), I. 21.

3. I place 'Augustan' in quotation marks to acknowledge suggestions that the term is inappropriate for describing the conservative literature of the late seventeenth and early eighteenth centuries. Although there are clearly ways in which the term 'Augustan' is misleading, I continue to believe that it is at least as accurate with regard to the literature it describes as other broadly classificatory terms: 'Metaphysical', 'Romantic', etc. See Howard Weinbrot, *Augustus Caesar in 'Augustan' England: The Decline of a Classical Norm* (Princeton, 1978).

4. Eagleton, *The Rape of Clarissa,* p. 17 (see Ch. 1 n. 52 above); Karl Marx and Friedrich Engels, *The Communist Manifesto* in *Essential Works of Marxism,* ed. Arthur P. Mendel (New York, 1965), p. 15.

5. Brewer, *The Birth of a Consumer Society,* p. 214.

6. See, for example, Ian Watt, *The Rise of the Novel: Studies in Richardson, Defoe, and Fielding* (Berkeley, 1965), pp. 158–61, *et passim.* Watt remarks that 'Pamela and her sex . . . with the exception of

a few wholly abandoned females, were reserved for higher things. The new ideology granted them a total immunity from sexual feelings.' One assumes that the '*few* wholly abandoned females' would include the thousands of London prostitutes as well as libidinous ladies of a higher order (e.g. Lady Vane). Also included in the 'few' would be the daughters of London tradesmen of whom Francis Place remarked: 'Want of chastity in girls was common. The songs which were ordinarily sung by their relatives and by young men and women and the lewd plays and interludes they occasionally saw were all calculated to produce mischief in this direction' (p. 57). Place later notes that 'each of my companions had a sweetheart who was the daughter of some tradesman, some of these girls were handsome, well dressed and in their general conduct respectable. With these girls I and my companions were as familiar as we could be, each with his own sweetheart. . . . I could name several of them now living long since married to young men who were as well acquainted with them before marriage as afterwards' (pp. 75–6). Perhaps the 'new ideology' was unknown to these young women. See *The Autobiography of Francis Place* (*1771–1854*), ed. Mary Thale (Cambridge, 1972), *passim.*

7. Place, pp. 14, 88–9, *et passim*; on Place, see D. J. Rowe, 'Francis Place and the Historian', *The Historical Journal*, 16 (1973), pp. 45–63.

8. For Hogarth's 'Peregrination', see Paulson, *Hogarth*, I. 294–8.

9. T. J. Clark, *Image of the People: Gustave Courbet and the 1848 Revolution*, 2nd edn. (London, 1982), pp. 18–20, 29, 34. Churchill's fundamental ambiguity in matters political suggests (in a burlesque, irreverent form) the incipient dilemma of those nineteenth-century advocates of 'middlingness'—'an uneasy alliance of liberal consciousness with conservative conscience'—when faced with the extremes of revolution or repression. See John P. Farrell, *Revolution As Tragedy: The Dilemma of the Moderate from Scott to Arnold* (Ithaca, 1980), pp. 18–19.

10. Carretta, p. 243.

11. *Hogarth*, I. 398. Cf. J. Paul Hunter, *Occasional Form: Henry Fielding and the Chains of Circumstance* (Baltimore, 1975), pp. 10–21.

12. John Sitter, *Literary Loneliness in Mid-Eighteenth-Century England* (Ithaca, 1982), p. 77. On the general shift towards a relativistic view of history at mid-century, see Carretta, pp. 211–26.

13. On the democratization of the satirist's audience, see Lockwood, pp. 152–66 and Carretta, pp. 232–44. Churchill's poetic and political stance recalls the Hegelian distinction between 'noble' and 'base' consciousness. The 'base' consciousness 'looks upon the authoritative power of the state as a chain, as something suppressing its separate autonomous existence, and hence hates the ruler, obeys

only with secret malice and stands ever ready to burst out in rebellion'. Trilling remarks that 'the relation of the individual self to wealth is even baser, if only because of the ambivalence which marks it—the self loves wealth but at the same time despises it; through wealth the self "attains to the enjoyment of its own independent existence", but it finds wealth discordant with the nature of Spirit.' See Lionel Trilling, *Sincerity and Authenticity* (Cambridge, Mass., 1972), pp. 35–7, 44.

14. Palmer, *The Age of Democratic Revolution*, I. 21. Cf. Gramsci's conception of a 'war of position' in which the ruling classes, though still dominant, are no longer hegemonic, and when insurgent classes exercise considerable hegemony without domination. See Adamson, pp. 225–8 (see Introduction n. 4 above).

15. *Restoration and Eighteenth-Century Poetry 1660–1780* (London, 1981), p. 125.

16. Peake, I. 130. Churchill's readership, however, was not limited to those who could afford to purchase his individual works. His poems were regularly reprinted in *The St. James's Magazine*, and excerpted in *The Gentleman's Magazine*, *The London Magazine*, *The Monthly Review*, *The Critical Review*, *SJC*, *PA*, and other papers. These periodicals, as well as the poems themselves, were often purchased by coffee-houses for the use of their patrons. Through all of these conduits, Chruchill's poetry reached a substantial readership.

17. *DLJ*, p. 4.

18. Despite Richard Altick's assertion in *The English Common Reader* (Chicago, 1957) that by 1780 'the national literacy rate was scarcely higher than it had been during the Elizabethan period' (p. 30), contemporary evidence consistently suggests that in London literacy was widespread. In plate 4 of Hogarth's *A Rake's Progress* (1735), for example, we find a bootblack avidly pouring over 'The Farthing Post'; in the opening plate of *Industry and Idleness* (1747), Tom Idle and Francis Goodchild are both provided with copies of *The Prentice's Guide*; in *Beer Street* (1751), a butcher enjoys the King's speech opening Parliament along with his beer, and two fishwives read 'A New Ballad on the Herring Fishery'. This is by no means to imply that the majority of mechanics, labourers, and urchins were literate, but to suggest that in London, at least, the level of literacy among even these groups was substantial. For the sophistication of marketing techniques (especially those aimed at the poorer market), see J. H. Plumb, 'The Commercialization of Leisure in Eighteenth-Century England' in *The Birth of a Consumer Society*, pp. 268–73. For the circulation of newspapers and political papers, see Brewer, *Party Ideology*, pp. 142–3. Perhaps the most successful item of printed matter for pulling in the plebeian sixpence was the political print (which, we must remember,

almost always included some commentary or dialogue). Advertisements for such prints were often aimed directly at the underclass reader; see, for example, the puff from the *Newcastle Journal* quoted by Brewer, *The Birth of a Consumer Society*, p. 255.

19. *Some Cool Thoughts on the present State of Affairs* (London, 1762); *A Letter to her R——l H———S THE P———S D-w-g-r of W———* On *the Approaching PEACE* (London, 1762). Quoted by Brewer, *Party Ideology*, p. 139.

20. Cf. Brewer, *The Birth of a Consumer Society*, pp. 253–4.

21. Smollett, *The Briton*, No. 6. The phrase 'patriot cit' is from *The North Briton: An Elegy* (London, 1764) in which we find one of this breed sitting in Lloyd's Coffee House lamenting Churchill's death. On the make-up of Wilkes's support, see Rudé, pp. 196–7, *et passim*.

22. Thompson, charting the schism of the lower and middle classes under the pressure of Jacobinism, industrialization, and counter-revolutionary repression, writes that 'the revolution which did not happen in England was fully as devastating, and in some features more divisive, than that which happened in France'. He goes on to endorse, with some qualifications, the view of the Hammonds that 'the French Revolution has divided the people of France less than the Industrial Revolution has divided the people of England'. See *The Making of the English Working Class*, pp. 196–7.

23. *Tirocinium*. It is difficult to refrain from speculating about Churchill's current reputation had he lived to participate in Wilkes's second coming. One can imagine a poem called *The King's Bench* or, given Churchill's penchant for one and two word titles, *The Election* (in four books?). One can imagine an increasingly dramatic self-presentation incorporating increasingly radical political positions. One can imagine, perhaps, a body of poetry significant enough to counterbalance the conservative point of view—Johnson's, Smollett's, Burke's—that dominates most classroom discussions of mid-century literature in its relationship to politics.

EPILOGUE

1. 25 Mar. 1765, in *Posthumous Letters . . . addressed to Francis Colman and George Colman the Elder* (London, 1820), p. 87.

2. 21 June 1765, Add. MS 30877, fos. 41–42. Because of its importance in defining the Colman–Thornton–Wilkes relationship in 1765, a substantial part of the letter bears transcription: 'I am infinitely obliged to you for your intentions concerning me, & could wish that my former coadjutor [Thornton] might escape your Severity. . . . You are no ordinary Satirist. Your words will leave deep scars behind them & I should be sorry to have you send his name down stinking to posterity, while at the same time you embalm me. I

have, as well as our friends, some occasions to complain of him—perhaps I might say *many*—but have I think a reverence due to former connections, and I must own that in my breast those sores rather heal than rankle by time. These I know are a good deal your sentiments, too, for at Paris I have heard you regret the difference between you & Hogarth. Resentment dies, the remembrance of old intercourse rekindles our good will, & we wish to have been able to have smothered the hasty sparks of passion. I do not say all this as Counsel for him, which by the flowerishness of the last period you might half-suspect—but as what naturally occurs. I leave him to your justice, but recommend him to your mercy. Spare him I beseech you Good Wilkes!' In the event, Wilkes wrote no satire on Thornton and the two seem to have been reconciled. In a note dated 15 May 1766, Thornton invited Wilkes (who had just returned from the Continent) to visit him: 'If Mr. Wilkes has not totally forgot that there was such a fellow formerly as Bonnell Thornton, perhaps he may believe, that nobody can long more to see him' (Add. MS 30869, fo. 34ʳ).

3. *Parables of Our Lord and Saviour Jesus Christ* (London, 1768), pp. v–vi.

4. Translated by Chalmers, XXV, p. xxxii; for the reaction to Thornton's death, see *SJC*, 10–12 May 1768.

5. The translations appear to have begun originally as complementary projects, for as early as the winter of 1762 Lloyd's *St. James's Magazine* carried an item announcing the expected publication of both works. See *The St. James's Magazine* I (Dec. 1762), p. 265. See also Thornton's letter to Colman about the translations, 22 Apr. 1765, in Houghton Library MS Am 1631 p. 401.

6. To William Unwin, *c*.1786, Cowper's *Correspondence*, III. 101.

7. *Poems* (Milford), p. 358.

8. To Lady Hesketh, 31 Jan. 1786, *Letters and Prose Writings*, II. 471.

APPENDIX: *THE CRAB*

1. None of Churchill's earlier editors or biographers mention *The Crab*, nor does the poem appear in *The New Foundling Hospital for Wit*, a miscellany that contains many of Churchill and Wilkes's fugitive pieces. Although the poem's 'moral,' Irish priest, and self-reflexivity are original, the central action (the simultaneous clutching of the female pubis and male nose) had long been part of oral tradition. An early version was recorded in the *Percy Folio Manuscript* (*c*.1650). This manuscript, discovered by Bishop Thomas Percy *c*.1756, circulated among various literati (including Samuel Johnson, William Shenstone, and Thomas Warton) before its partial publication as *Reliques of Ancient English Poetry* in 1765. See Albert B. Fried-

man, *The Ballad Revival: Studies in the Influence of Popular on Sophisticated Poetry* (Chicago, 1961), pp. 185-200. It is possible that Churchill became acquainted with the ballad at that time, although he may have simply known a version of the ballad from the oral tradition. For the ballad itself, see *Bishop Percy's Folio Manuscript: Loose and Humorous Songs*, ed. Frederick J. Furnivall (London, 1868), pp. 99-100. Guthrie T. Meade, Jr. discusses the various versions of the motif in 'The Sea Crab,' *Midwest Folklore*, VIII:2 (1958), pp. 91-100. See also G. Legman, *The Horn Book: Studies in Erotic Folklore and Bibliography* (New Hyde Park, New York, 1964), pp. 413-14. My thanks to Professor Roger de V. Renwick for these references.

2. *An Essay on Woman and other pieces . . .*, privately printed by J. C. Hutten (London, 1871), p. 13.

3. *An Essay on Woman*, pp. 5-6; Calhoun Winton, 'John Wilkes and "An Essay on Woman" ', in *A Provision of Human Nature*, ed. Donald Kay (University, Ala., 1977), p. 125.

4. Churchill's *Poetical Works*, p. 551.

5. Horace Walpole wrote of George Stone that he 'had with no pretensions in the world, but by being attached to the house of Dorset, and by being the brother of Mr. Stone, been hurried through two or three Irish Bishopricks up to the very Primacy of the kingdom, not only unwarrantably young, but without even the graver excuses of learning or sanctimony.' See *Memoirs of the Reign of George the Second*, ed. Lord Holland, 3 vols. (London, 1847), I. 280.

6. *Memoirs of the Reign of George the Third*, II. 27.

7. See, for example, Henry Fielding, *The Journal of a Voyage to Lisbon*, ed. Harold E. Pagliaro (New York, 1963), p. 38.

8. Text and translation are taken from Ovid, *Metamorphoses*, trans. Frank Justus Miller (Cambridge, Mass., 1946), II. 344-5.

9. *Ovid's Metamorphoses in Fifteen Books, Translated by the most Eminent Hands* (London, 1717), p. 500. This translation appeared in numerous editions throughout the eighteenth century.

10. *The Works of Edmund Spenser*, ed. Edwin Greenlaw, Charles Osgood, and Frederick Padelford, 8 vols. (Baltimore, 1932-49), III. 116.

11. *Rime couee*: 'A SESTET *stanza* made of two couplets of any length and two shorter lines. One of the short lines follows each couplet. The short lines rhyme with each other.' See Lewis Turco, *The Book of Forms: A Handbook of Poetics* (New York, 1968), p. 97.

12. *Virgil*, ed. and trans. H. Rushton Fairclough, rev. edn. (Cambridge, Mass., 1974), I. 82.

Index